STRANGE & UNEXPLAINED PHENOMENA

STRANGE & UNEXPLAINED PHENOMENA

Jerome Clark and Nancy Pear

Detroit   New York   Toronto   London

STRANGE AND UNEXPLAINED PHENOMENA

Jerome Clark and Nancy Pear, *Editors*

STAFF

Sonia Benson, *U•X•L Senior Editor*
Carol DeKane Nagel, *U•X•L Managing Editor*
Thomas L. Romig, *U•X•L Publisher*

Margaret A. Chamberlain, *Permissions Specialist*
Shanna P. Heilveil, *Production Associate*
Evi Seoud, *Assistant Production Manager*
Mary Beth Trimper, *Production Director*

Mary Claire Krzewinski, *Senior Art Director*
Cynthia Baldwin, *Product Design Manager*
Terry Colon, *Illustrator*

™ This book is printed on acid-free paper that meets the minimum requirements of American National Standard for Information Sciences—Permanence Paper for Printed Library Materials, ANSI Z39.48-1984.

ISBN 0-7876-2764-X

Printed in the United States of America

Visible Ink Press is an imprint of Gale Research Inc., an International Thomson Publishing Company.

10 9 8 7 6 5 4 3 2

CONTENTS

VII
Light Shows   101

VIII
Strange Showers:
Everything but
Cats and Dogs   119

IX
More Weird Weather   147

X
Cryptozoology   167

INTRODUCTION

Strange and Unexplained Phenomena is a book about *anomalies*, human experiences that go against common sense and break the rules that science uses to describe our world. In the words of folklorist Bill Ellis, "Weird stuff happens." *Strange and Unexplained Phenomena* takes a look at the "weird stuff" that abounds in the reports of ordinary people who have had extraordinary experiences. Accounts of flying saucers, reptile men, werewolves, and abominable snowmen grab our attention and send shivers down our spines. When similar strange accounts are repeated time and again by different witnesses in different times and places, they capture the attention of the scientific community as well.

The three hardest words for human beings to utter are *I don't know.* Because we like our mysteries quickly and neatly explained, in modern times we have come to ask scientists to find logical explanations for strange human experiences. Sometimes science can use its knowledge and tools to find the answers to puzzling incidents; at other times it offers explanations that don't seem to fit the anomalies and only add to the confusion about them. When experiences are especially unbelievable, scientists may simply decide that they never really happened and refuse to consider them altogether. Most of us believe that as science learns more, it will be able to explain more. Still, it is almost certain that science will never be able to account for all the "weird stuff" that human beings encounter.

When an anomaly is reported, it is natural not to believe it, to be skeptical. One usually wonders about the witness. Could the person be lying for some reason? Tricks and hoaxes do occur. There are people who go to great lengths to fool scientists and the public, who hope to find fame and fortune by false claims or simply to prove to themselves how clever they are. Photographs of extraordinary happenings are often fake; it is thought that nearly 95 percent of all UFO photos are false, and some of the best film footage of the Loch Ness monster is judged doubtful as well. As a matter of fact, most investigators of anomalies feel that a lot of photographs of an incident signals a fake, because: (1) most people don't walk around with cameras ready to snap strange sights; (2) people having weird or scary experiences are often in shock or terror, and taking pictures is the last thing on their minds; and (3) anomalies generally last for just a matter of seconds. Investigators also believe that the fuzzier the photo, the more likely it is to be real, because pictures taken by people with shaking hands rarely turn out clearly, while hoaxers know that poor photographs won't get the results they are looking for.

It is also natural to wonder about the mental health of a person who has witnessed an extraordinary happening. Common sense tells us that *all* weird accounts should be blamed on the poor memories, bad dreams, or wild imaginings of confused and unwell minds! Still, psychologists who have examined witnesses of anomalies find them, for the most part, to be the same as people who have had no odd experiences at all. Also, the sheer number of strange reports rattles our common sense a bit, as do cases of multiple witnesses, when large groups of people observe the same strange happenings together.

More interesting still are accounts that have been repeated for centuries; reports of lake monsters in the deep waters of Loch Ness, for example, began way back in A.D. 565! Interesting, too, are reports that are widespread. The Pacific Northwest region of North America has its Bigfoot sightings, western Mongolians tell stories about the Almas, and accounts of the yeti have been reported in the high reaches of the Himalayas. While the languages and cultures surrounding these legends may differ, it is clear that witnesses are describing a similar creature: a hairy, two-legged "apeman." When observers report sightings of sea serpents they may describe them as smooth and snakelike or maned like horses, with many humps or finned like fish. Even when details vary widely, it is difficult to ignore their basic sameness: all suggest the existence of large, as yet unknown, sea-going animals.

It is true that in many cases of strange happenings, people have been misled or mistaken. The Bermuda Triangle, an area of the Caribbean where ships and planes were reported to mysteriously disappear, for example, was considered a real threat for more than two decades. That is, until weather records and other documents were properly researched, proving that the location was as safe as any other body of water. In the same way, the strange cattle "mutilations" that worried farmers in Minnesota and Kansas in the 1970s—and stirred up all sorts of weird explanations—required the special skills of veterinary pathologists to find that the cause was a simple, but gruesome, infection. Sometimes strange accounts do seem to change and grow as they are reported over the decades and in print. Human beings do want the truth ... but they also like a good story!

Science, too, has made its mistakes over the years. When sailors gave accounts of large sea creatures with giant eyes and many tentacles they were told that they were seeing floating trees with large roots. We now know that their accounts described giant squids. Gorillas and meteors were also rejected by scientists not that long ago!

But then, of course, some anomalies are more believable than others. When an odd happening turns the way we think about the world upside down it is described as "high-strange"; less weird accounts are lower on the strangeness scale. It is not *completely* unthinkable that unknown creatures still exist in some remote regions of the globe as many cryptozoologists (people who study "hidden" animals) believe. Wildlife experts and marine biologists may, over time, find that creatures like Bigfoot and "Nessie" are real. In the same way, physicists and meteorologists may find the reasons for ball lightning, or for the mysterious ice chunks that fall from the sky. The discovery of intelligent beings from outer space, on the other hand, would really shake us up and force us to rethink our lives and our place in the universe. As high on the strange scale as this idea is, though, there is enough hard evidence—like odd radar trackings and soil samples from UFO landing sights—to make it worth considering.

Strange accounts, no matter how farfetched, deserve some careful thought. Although most readers set their own limits as to how high on the strange scale they can go, the kinds of questions raised by anomalies are worth pursuing, even if the event or object is beyond one's own limits of belief. True understanding of anomalies takes time, effort, and an open—but not a gullible—mind. *Strange and Unexplained Phenomena* doesn't deal with belief or disbelief. It only shows that human experiences come in more shapes and sizes than we could ever imagine!

PICTURE CREDITS

UFOs: The Twentieth-Century Mystery

- **UNIDENTIFIED FLYING OBJECTS**
- **UNIDENTIFIED AIRSHIPS**

UFOs: The Twentieth-Century Mystery

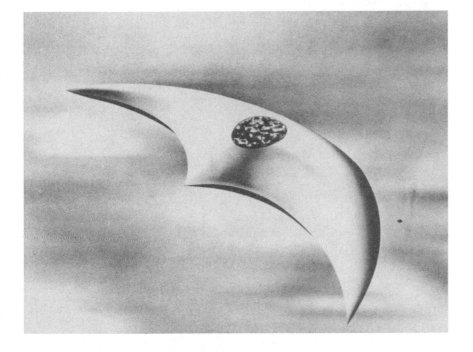

One of the nine "flying saucers" Kenneth Arnold sighted.

UNIDENTIFIED FLYING OBJECTS

One January evening in 1878, as he was hunting six miles south of Denison, Texas, John Martin saw a fast-moving object in the southern sky. When it passed overhead, he noted that it looked like a "large saucer." It would be a sight that many others would report in the years ahead, especially in the second half of the twentieth century.

"Flying saucers" were not really perceived or described as such until June 24, 1947, when a pilot named Kenneth Arnold spotted nine disc-shaped objects flying in formation at an estimated 1,200 mph over Mount Rainier, Washington. In a newspaper interview he compared their motion to that of stones skipping across water. Soon afterward, a newspaper in the area used the phrase "flying saucer" to describe what Arnold had seen—and the UFO age had begun. The more practical term "unidentified flying objects," or UFOs, first coined by a U.S. Air Force worker, would not come into common usage until the mid-1950s.

Yet, as demonstrated in the Martin account above, sightings of flying saucers and UFOs occurred well before 1947; they were probably just reported differently. From November 1896 until May 1897, for example, newspapers all across America were filled with stories about mysterious "airships"—cigar-shaped objects often said to flash bright searchlights and thought by some to be linked to visitors from Mars (also see entry: **Strange Clouds**). A few reports of what could be called UFOs can be found in scientific journals and newspapers of the earlier decades of the nineteenth century but are rare before that. For whatever reason, UFO sightings seem to be relatively recent phenomena.

Foo Fighters and Ghost Rockets

During World War II Allied pilots both in Europe and the Pacific observed many unidentified flying objects; they called them "foo fighters" and assumed they were enemy devices. When mysterious "ghost rockets" were sighted all over northern Europe during much of 1946, the Soviets were falsely blamed by observers who struggled to explain them.

Project Sign

The first U.S. Air Force effort to study UFO reports was conducted under the code name Project Sign and was established under the Air Materiel Command at Wright Field, Dayton, Ohio (later Wright-Patterson Air Force Base), on December 30, 1947. Routine sightings were usually handled at local air bases, but Sign investigated reported sightings considered important or unusual.

The first of these investigations was a January 7, 1948, case in which a Kentucky Air National Guard pilot, Captain Thomas F. Mantell, Jr., died in a plane crash while trying to check something that he described in one of his last radio messages as a "metallic object ... of tremendous size." The air force eventually identified the "object" as an air balloon connected with the navy's then-secret Skyhook Project.

A more puzzling report came later in 1948 from two Eastern Airlines pilots, Clarence S. Chiles and John B. Whitted. As their DC-3 flew over Alabama at 2:45 A.M. on July 24, Chiles and Whitted saw a wingless, torpedo-shaped object streak past them. It had two rows of square windows from which, Chiles reported, "a very bright light was glowing. Underneath the ship there was a blue glow of light." A flame extended 50 feet from the rear. Although the UFO was in view for no more than ten seconds, it was also seen by a passenger. Sign investigators also learned that an hour earlier, a ground-maintenance crewman at Robins Air Force Base in Georgia had seen an identical UFO. Weirder still, four days before that, a rocket-shaped object with two rows of windows had been seen over The Hague, Netherlands!

By the time of this sighting, Project Sign had split into several groups of investigators, each with a different view concerning UFOs. One group believed that the objects were spacecraft from other worlds, while another thought they were Soviet secret weapons, and still another felt they were common objects—the identity of which had somehow been confused. In the case of the Chiles-Whitted sighting, the first group of investigators won out: a top-secret report arguing that the UFO evidence pointed to otherworldly visitation was sent all the way to air force chief of staff General Hoyt S. Vandenberg. It was not the conclusion Vandenberg wanted to hear, and he ordered all copies of the report burned. The document remained secret until 1956, when a book by a retired air force UFO-project officer, Edward J. Ruppelt, reported the story behind it. Though other sources backed Ruppelt's account, the air force continued to deny that the report existed for many years.

> A top-secret report arguing that the UFO evidence pointed to otherworldly visitation was not what air force chief of staff General Hoyt S. Vandenberg wanted to hear. He ordered all copies of the report burned.

Project Grudge

Vandenberg's rejection of Project Sign's conclusion sent a clear message to the investigators; those who believed in the possibility of extraterrestrial visitors either left the air force or were reassigned to other duties. On February 11, 1949, Project Grudge replaced Project Sign, and most UFO investigations then consisted simply of "debunking"—demonstrating that sightings and reports revealed nothing unusual, that they were really distortions or mistakes. By the end of the year the project's administrators had put most of its files into storage,

A UFO photographed by George J. Stock at Passaic, New Jersey, in 1952—one of a series of five photographs.

and by the following summer it had dwindled to a single investigator.

Project Blue Book

High-ranking air force officials called for a reorganization of Project Grudge, though, after its poor investigation of a series of radar/visual sightings of fast-moving UFOs over Fort Monmouth, New Jersey, in September 1951. Project Blue Book replaced it in March 1952, headed by Lieutenant Ruppelt, an intelligence officer assigned to the Air Technical Intelligence Center (ATIC) at Wright-Patterson Air Force Base. Ruppelt insisted that his investigators hold no prior judgments about whether or not UFOs were real. By the time he left the project two years later, Ruppelt was largely convinced that space visitors did exist. His memoir of his experiences, *The Report on Unidentified Flying Objects* (1956), is considered one of ufology's (the study of UFOs) most important books.

After Ruppelt left, however, the project returned to its former pattern of debunking—not investigating. Such was the case when a spectacular series of UFO radar and eyewitness observations occurred over Washington, D.C., in July 1952. Government intelligence officials became concerned that the Soviet Union could somehow use the sightings to cause mass panic in the United States, and they set up a panel of five scientists to secretly examine Blue Book's data and devise a security strategy.

The Robertson Panel

Over the next four days, the five scientists studied a few sighting reports and two UFO films before declaring further official study a "great waste of effort." The Robertson panel (named after its head, physicist and CIA employee H. P. Robertson) also called for a public "debunking" campaign that "would result in the reduction of public interest in 'flying saucers.'" In addition, it urged that UFO groups made up of ordinary citizens "be watched because of their potentially great

influence on mass thinking," stipulating that the "possible use of such groups for subversive purposes should be kept in mind."

Though the Robertson panel and its recommendations remained secret for years, they would have a huge effect on the course of UFO history. The air force began almost immediately to reduce Project Blue Book's funds and importance, and the program became devoted to downplaying sightings. Even air force chief scientific adviser J. Allen Hynek, who had attended the project's meetings, complained, "The Robertson panel ... made the subject of UFOs scientifically unrespectable, and for nearly 20 years not enough attention was paid to the subject to acquire the kind of data needed even to decide the nature of the UFO phenomenon."

Air Force Ignores Its Own Think Tank

A similar official cover-up took place following the publication of *Project Blue Book Special Report 14* in 1955. The report contained the findings of a three-year study by the Battelle Memorial Institute, a

Close-up of UFO photographed by George J. Stock, New Jersey, 1952.

Josef Allen Hynek

(1910-1986)

Josef Allen Hynek called himself the "innocent bystander who got shot"—a respected astronomer who became, quite by accident, the world's leading expert on UFOs. Educated at the University of Chicago and a popular writer on astronomy, he was assigned to the post of chief scientific adviser to Project Sign, the air force's UFO investigation project. He received the assignment simply because he was the astronomer nearest to Wright Field in Dayton, Ohio, where the project was based.

Beginning his work as air force consultant in 1948, Hynek at first doubted that UFOs were real. But as time went on, he could not help feeling puzzled by some of the reports he was receiving. By 1952 he admitted that amid all the false reports there might be a "residue that is worthy of scientific attention." Eventually, Hynek became a firm believer in the existence of UFOs. With Chicago businessman Sherman J. Larsen, he created the Center for UFO Studies (CUFOS) as a formal organization through which scientific research could be conducted.

think tank (a group of specialists in different areas of study who come together to try to solve complex problems) that the air force had asked to analyze UFO reports. Called Project Stork, the study concluded that UFOs were extraordinary occurrences, but that they did, in fact, exist. This was not what the air force wanted to hear! The report's data were drastically changed so that Secretary of the Air Force Donald A. Quarles could declare, "On the basis of this study we believe that no objects such as those popularly described as flying saucers have overflown the United States."

Because the air force always seemed to refuse to even consider the possibility of UFOs and because it often fabricated explanations, many feared that such debunking was a cover-up of real concerns. Perhaps, critics such as retired marine corps major Donald E. Keyhoe argued, the air force was well aware of the reality of space visitors but feared a worldwide panic if it admitted as much.

Eventually, the unreliability of Project Blue Book earned ridicule from the press and criticism from members of Congress. Finally, testifying before the House Armed Services Committee in April 1966, Hynek urged that a panel of physical and social scientists—this time unconnected with the government—"examine the UFO problem critically for the express purpose of determining whether a major problem really exists."

The Condon Committee: Study or Cover-up?

At this point the air force was only too eager to get the problem of UFO sightings off its hands. It asked the University of Colorado to conduct an independent scientific study. Called the Condon Committee after its director, physicist Edward U. Condon, the study was, nonetheless, another setup. Condon was not open to the idea of UFOs, and he fired investigators who disagreed with him. Word eventually got out (through a book by one of those fired investigators and a *Look* magazine article) that the committee's efforts were every bit as poor and deceptive as had been those of the air force before it.

The Condon Committee published its report, *Scientific Study of Unidentified Flying Objects,* in 1969. Not surprisingly, it concluded that "further scientific study of UFOs probably cannot be justified in the expectation that science will be advanced thereby." Still, the report admitted that fully one-third of its cases were unexplainable, even after in-depth study. Just as with *Project Blue Book Special Report 14,* the report's conclusion did not follow from the data inside it. Still, the air force had what it wanted: an excuse to shut down Project Blue Book, which was officially terminated on December 17, 1969.

Hollywood director Steven Spielberg consulted Josef Allen Hynek and the Center for UFO Studies when filming his 1977 motion picture *Close Encounters of the Third Kind.*

Types of UFO Sightings

UFO sightings have been reported worldwide and vary little from one nation to another. The most commonly reported UFO shapes are discs and cigars; in recent years growing numbers of reports have

A man in Kansas in 1952 saw a large disc-shaped structure like the one pictured here hovering nearby— one of the many cases Project Blue Book could not explain.

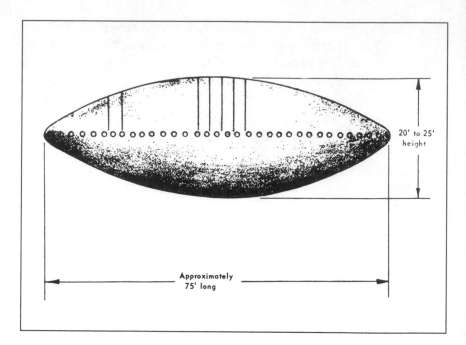

20' to 25' height

Approximately 75' long

included boomerangs and triangles. Quite a few sightings are simply points of light in the night sky. These cases have often been given common explanations—Venus, meteors, passing aircraft—but sometimes the behavior of the lights makes such explanations difficult to accept.

In his 1972 book *The UFO Experience,* Hynek divided reports into these general categories: lights seen at night; daylight discs; radar/visual cases; close encounters of the first kind (CE1s—a UFO seen at less than 500 feet from the witness); close encounters of the second kind (CE2s—a UFO that physically affects its surroundings); and close encounters of the third kind (CE3s—beings observed in connection with a UFO sighting).

The best evidence for the existence of UFOs comes from radar/visual cases and CE2s. An example of the first type occurred over several hours between August 13 and 14, 1956, at two English bases run jointly by the Royal Air Force and the U.S. Air Force. Unidentified objects traveling at high speed were tracked on air and ground radar and seen by observers on earth and pilots in flight. But the best-documented CE2 case, suggesting a UFO landing, took place late on the afternoon of January 8, 1981, in Trans-en-Provence, France. An old man working in his garden reported that he had seen the landing of a "ship ... in the form of two saucers upside down, one against the other." The object rested on the ground for a short time before flying away.

The site of the landing revealed traces, impressions, and other evidence that a large vehicle had been there. France's official UFO-investigating agency, Group d'Etude des Phenomenes Aerospatiaux Non-Identifies (GEPAN), began an intense study, taking soil, leaf, and plant samples to France's leading botanical laboratory. In 1983 GEPAN released a 66-page report on the case, which noted that the leaves had mysteriously lost 30 to 50 percent of their chlorophyll and had aged quickly in a manner that could not be repeated in the laboratory. The study concluded that a combination of "mass, mechanics, a heating effect, and perhaps certain transformations and deposits of trace minerals [phosphate and zinc]" had altered the site, leading scientists to believe "that something similar to what the eyewitness has described did take place there."

CE3s are usually the strangest UFO claims and the ones most likely to cause sensational publicity. And for many ufologists, they are also the most difficult to accept. In most cases the witnesses—both separately and in groups—seem believable, and psychological testing shows that they are not mentally ill. CE3s range from brief sightings of humanoids (beings humanlike in appearance; nearly all CE3s describe humanoids) to abductions, where observers are taken against their will into UFOs and aliens perform strange experiments on them.

Phony photographs, such as this "flying cup" taken during the 1950s, are the most common type of UFO hoax.

One of the most spectacular CE3 reports was logged at Boianai, Papua New Guinea, on the evenings of June 26 and 27, 1959. An Anglican missionary from Australia, the Reverend W. B. Gill, and three dozen other witnesses observed some well-lit human-like figures through the dome of a hovering UFO. Gill thought they were "busy at some unknown task." During the second sighting, he and the others waved at the figures, who waved back!

UFO Hoaxes and Contacts

Many people believe that UFO reports are tricks or hoaxes. In truth, the majority of UFO sightings are honest mistakes—misidentifications—and hoaxes are actually rare. Even the air force has found that only about 1 percent of the reports it receives involve trickery, with many of these centering on UFO photographs, which are very easy to fake. Still, hoaxes have been recorded.

For instance, just a few days after Kenneth Arnold's "flying saucer" sighting in 1947, two men in Tacoma, Washington, displayed some melted metal remains that they claimed had dropped from a "flying doughnut" hovering above nearby Maury Island. While investigating the claim, two army air force officers were killed in a plane crash, leading to rumors that they had been murdered for knowing too much. The men's story, however, ended up being nothing more than a practical joke that had gotten way out of hand.

From the early 1950s on, colorful figures, based mostly in southern California, claimed ongoing contact with kind visitors from Venus, Mars, Saturn, and other planets. Many of these "contactees" also told of space travel and meetings with extraterrestrials or "space brothers" in other worlds (also see entries: **Space Brothers** and **Ummo**). As proof they offered suspiciously clear close-up photographs of spaceships and conveniently blurred photographs of their space-brother friends.

The most famous contactee was George Adamski, whose adventures began on November 20, 1952, when he reportedly met Orthon, a visitor from Venus, in the California desert. Others would also claim contact and write books and lecture about their experiences, attracting followers who were interested in the most fantastic—or occult—features of UFO experiences. Although claims by contactees were often exposed as embarrassing lies, the belief of their fans remained unshakable.

In fact, most of the contactees were not tricksters; many believed that they were in psychic or spiritual—if not physical—contact with space people. Psychic contactees did not feel pressured to produce "evidence" of their meetings, though they did indicate their belief in strong, and even shocking, ways. Gloria Lee, for example, fasted to death after a friend from Jupiter told her to do so. And, through automatic writing (writing performed without thinking, seemingly directed by an outside force), Dorothy Martin of Oak Park, Illinois, received messages from the spaceman Sananda, who warned her of dire geological disasters to occur on December 20, 1954. She and her followers alerted the press, quit their jobs, and planned to escape by spaceship on the dreaded date. When the saucer failed to show, Martin and her group were ridiculed the world over.

Theories about UFOs

Until the mid-1960s, there were two primary explanations regarding UFOs. One was that UFOs were hoaxes or mistaken identifications. The other was that they were spacecraft from outside our world. Donald H. Menzel, a Harvard University astronomer, was a leading supporter of the first school of thought, and Donald E. Keyhoe, an aircraft writer, was a leading supporter of the second. Both wrote books and articles arguing their positions and, in turn, gained powerful supporters in science, government, and the military.

Near the end of the decade, some ufologists began considering new explanations for UFO accounts. They began to think that the key to the mystery lay in the strangest reports, which traditional ufologists—concerned with believability, documentation, and evidence—had often laughed at or ignored. Some ufologists began to think that UFO contact stories did not really involve flesh and blood visitors from other planets but that they were visions that sprang from a witness's imagination. Perhaps contact experiences were unusually vivid dreams; perhaps abduction by extraterrestrials was just a Space Age version of the "kidnapped by fairies" story that people told in earlier ages. This "psychosocial hypothesis" concerning UFO experiences became a major force in the study of UFOs, especially in Europe.

REEL LIFE

The Blob, 1958.

Sci-fi thriller about a small town's fight against a slimy Jell-o invader from space. Slightly rebellious Steve McQueen (in his first starring role) redeems himself when he saves the town with quick action. This low-budget horror/teen-fantasy became a camp classic. A hi-tech remake of the same name made in 1988 is an excellent tribute to this film.

E.T.: The Extra-Terrestrial, 1982.

The story of an alien creature stranded on earth and his special bonding relationship with a young boy. A modern fairy tale providing warmth, humor, and sheer wonder, this is one of the most popular films in history.

It Came from Outer Space, 1953.

Aliens take on the form of local humans to repair their spacecraft in a small Arizona town. A fine science-fiction film based on a story by sci-fi writer Ray Bradbury.

Crashes and Cover-ups

The psychosocial approach to UFO study did not take lasting hold in the United States, however. One reason for this was the release, by the late 1970s, of many formerly secret government UFO reports through the Freedom of Information Act. Many outstanding radar/visual cases and other sightings were uncovered, exciting traditional ufologists. These discoveries also renewed suspicions that the government was involved in UFO cover-ups.

Keyhoe and others who suspected a cover-up thought that the air force might be hiding other cases of radar trackings, films, and even testimonies of pilots who had managed contact with UFOs. Some thought that the air force might be hiding even stronger proof of visitors from space, such as the remains of crashed saucers and the bodies of their pilots. While no evidence existed to support these suspicions, the stories would not go away. In the 1970s ufologist Leonard H. Stringfield started collecting reports and interviewing people who claimed knowledge, sometimes first-hand, of such evidence.

Two other ufologists, Stanton T. Friedman and William L. Moore, focused on one particular occurrence, the supposed crash of a UFO in Lincoln County, New Mexico, in early July 1947 (also see entry: **Hangar 18**). They interviewed nearly three dozen people who were directly involved and also spoke with another 50 who had indirect involvement. A few years later a Chicago organization, the J. Allen Hynek Center for UFO Studies (CUFOS), conducted its own study, bringing the total of sources, ranging from area ranchers to air force generals, to over four hundred!

Called "the Roswell incident" (after Roswell Field, New Mexico, which the air force used as its first base of investigation), the case was well documented and truly puzzling. Yet as would be expected, Friedman and Moore sometimes met with people whose claims sounded too fantastic. Some related tales not only of spaceship crashes but of face-

Budd Hopkins

(1931-)

Budd Hopkins, whose specialty is UFO-abduction reports, first became interested in UFOs when he and two companions observed a disc in the sky in 1964. It was not until a friend told him about witnessing a UFO landing, complete with occupants, that Hopkins became active in the field.

With the help of psychiatrist Robert Naiman and psychologist Aphrodite Clamar, Hopkins tried to counter the memory loss that many UFO witnesses experienced after being abducted. Under hypnosis, some of these people told of frightening meetings with large-headed, gray-skinned humanoids who forced them into medical examinations. Hopkins published his first book of research, the popular *Missing Time,* in 1981.

In his second book, *Intruders* (1987), Hopkins updated his abduction research but presented findings that were more fantastic. A frequent lecturer on the subject, Hopkins created the Intruders Foundation in New York City in 1990 to fund research and to offer therapy to witnesses haunted by their disturbing memories.

to-face contact between aliens and U.S. government officials. One investigator close to the incident reported that some military and intelligence insiders promised him a "truckload of documents" to support their incredible stories, but they ultimately produced only a handful of papers. The most disturbing of these was a document that arrived one day in December 1984 in an envelope with no return address.

Inside the envelope was a roll of 35-mm film that, when developed, showed a portion of a presidential briefing document dated November 18, 1952. It appeared to have been written by Vice Admiral Roscoe H.

Hillenkoetter, telling then-President-elect Dwight D. Eisenhower of two UFO crashes: one in Roswell in 1947, the other along the Texas-Mexico border in 1950. It also spoke of "Operation Majestic-12," a scientific, military, and intelligence force set up to study the wreckage and bodies of the space beings (called "extraterrestrial biological entities" or EBEs).

When the document copy was released to the press, it caused a great uproar and massive publicity, including coverage in the *New York Times* and on television news show *Nightline.* The FBI launched an investigation, but it had as little luck as ufologists in getting to the bottom of the matter. Because the signature on the document appeared suspicious (as did its format), the copy was eventually judged a forgery. Why the unknown forger carried out his hoax remains a mystery.

The Future of Ufology

In recent years more social scientists and mental health professionals have become interested in UFO study. They are especially drawn to stories of UFO abductions reported by seemingly normal people. These professionals are eager to find out if such experiences spring from within an individual or really do come from outside the physical world.

Sources:

Clark, Jerome, *The Emergence of a Phenomenon: UFOs from the Beginning through 1959—The UFO Encyclopedia,* Volume 2, Detroit, Michigan: Omnigraphics, 1992.

Clark, Jerome, *UFOs in the 1980s: The UFO Encyclopedia,* Volume 1, Detroit, Michigan: Apogee Books, 1990.

Fawcett, Lawrence, and Barry J. Greenwood, *Clear Intent: The Government Coverup of the UFO Experience,* Englewood Cliffs, New Jersey: Prentice-Hall, 1984.

Hendry, Allan, *The UFO Handbook: A Guide to Investigating, Evaluating and Reporting UFO Sightings,* Garden City, New York: Doubleday and Company, 1979.

Hopkins, Budd, *Intruders: The Incredible Visitations at Copley Woods,* New York: Random House, 1987.

Hynek, J. Allen, *The UFO Experience: A Scientific Inquiry,* Chicago: Henry Regnery Company, 1972.

Jacobs, David Michael, *Secret Life: Firsthand Accounts of UFO Abductions,* New York: Simon and Schuster, 1992.

Randle, Kevin D., and Donald R. Schmitt, *UFO Crash at Roswell,* New York: Avon Books, 1991.

UNIDENTIFIED AIRSHIPS

Reports of unidentified airships began before the turn of the twentieth century, preceding and foreshadowing the phenomena of unidentified flying object reports that began to flourish in the 1940s. The first known printed account of a mysterious "airship" appeared in the March 29, 1880, issue of the *Santa Fe Weekly New Mexican*. The newspaper reported that late on the evening of March 26, observers in the village of Galisteo Junction watched a "large balloon" pass overhead and heard the merry shouts of its passengers. A couple of odd objects were dropped from the craft: a cup of "very peculiar workmanship" and a "magnificent flower, with a slip of exceedingly fine silk-like paper, on which were some characters resembling those on Japanese tea chests." The next evening a Chinese American visitor said that the paper carried a message from his girlfriend. According to the story she was a passenger on the airship, which was headed for New York City.

Like many other airship stories reported in the late nineteenth-century press, this one is almost certainly a tall tale. American papers back then tended to treat airship sightings as jokes—and were, in fact, behind many of the accounts themselves. In the years ahead, however, more believable reports would be made in the United States and other countries. And it is likely that these strange airships would have been viewed as UFOs (unidentified flying objects) had the sightings occurred decades later, in the second half of the twentieth century. In fact, sightings of airshiplike objects—cigar-shaped, with multicolored lights along the sides and flashing searchlights—continue to this day.

An outbreak of airship reports occurred along the border of Germany and Russian Poland in early 1892. As would be the case with later airship scares, the Germans were thought to have developed advanced aircraft that could fly against the wind (unlike balloons) and hover for long periods. No such aircraft existed at the time, nor had any been developed by 1896, when the great American airship scare hit California.

California Airship Scare

Beginning in mid-November 1896, many witnesses in both city and country areas of California reported seeing fast-moving or still lights at night and assumed that they were connected to airships. A daylight sighting reported in the *San Francisco Call* of November 22 described a "balloon" traveling on end, "with what appeared to be

American papers back then tended to treat airship sightings as jokes—and were, in fact, behind many of the accounts themselves.

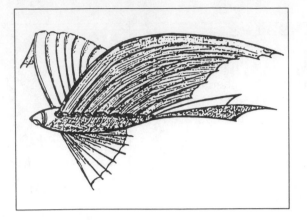

Dallas Morning News, 1897, sketch of an airship reported over Texas.

wings both before and behind the [bottom] light." A "great black cigar with a fishlike tail ... at least 100 feet long" and a surface that "looked as if it were made of aluminum" was described in another account in the December 1 issue of the *Oakland Tribune*. In other cases observers reported airships with propellers.

All during this time, the press was focusing its attention on George D. Collins, a San Francisco lawyer who claimed that he not only represented the inventor who created the airship, but had even seen the wonderful craft himself (both claims he later denied). The inventor was rumored to be E. H. Benjamin, a dentist from Maine who liked to tinker with machines. While Benjamin insisted that his "inventions [had] to do with dentistry," some refused to believe him and bothered the man so much that he had to go into hiding. Reporters even broke into his office in search of evidence—but found nothing but dental filings!

Then, according to an article in the *Oakland Tribune,* former California attorney general W. H. H. Hart claimed to represent the inventor of the mysterious airship. He said that Collins had been fired for talking too much. But Hart proved to be even more gabby, stating that there were actually two airships and that they would be used to bomb the Spanish fort in Havana, Cuba. When pressed for proof, Hart—like Collins before him—backed down, admitting that he had not personally seen the invention and had only met with someone who claimed to be the inventor.

The California airship scare soon faded away. But in February 1897, Nebraska newspapers began reporting night sightings in country districts of lights moving with "most remarkable speed." On February 4 witnesses at Inavale got a close look at the object to which the lights were attached: it was cone-shaped, 30 to 40 feet long, and had "two sets of wings on a side, with a large, fan-shaped rudder," according to the *Omaha Daily Bee* (February 6). Over the following weeks, a flurry of sightings were reported in Nebraska and then in neighboring Kansas. By early April airships were moving east, north, and south, and all that month newspapers were filled with sightings, rumors, and tall tales.

More Hoaxes

Many of these questionable stories focused, as they had in California, on secret inventors. Some accounts even reported that airships had landed and that their passengers, ordinary Americans, had identified themselves and spoken of their plans. These "conversations" with air travelers would appear word for word in newspaper stories. While they were treated like serious news, these accounts were almost certainly supplied by imaginative writers!

Other hoaxes focused on the idea that mysterious airships came from outer space. A rancher from Le Roy, Kansas, swore that he, his son, and his hired man had seen strange-looking beings in an airship lasso and steal a calf from a corral outside his house. Though the tale attracted wide attention (and was rediscovered and widely published in UFO literature of the 1960s), it turned out to be a prank played by the rancher and fellow members of a local liars' club.

One rancher swore that strange-looking beings in an airship roped and stole a calf from his corral.

Although there were no blimps in the United States in the late 1890s, there were many reported sightings of flying cigar-shaped structures.

Similarly, the *Dallas Morning News* of April 19, 1897, printed an Aurora, Texas, man's report of a local airship crash—and of the burial of its only passenger, a Martian, in the local cemetery. Invented as a joke, the story was rediscovered in the 1960s and 1970s and brought several shovel-carrying searchers to the tiny, fading village.

Amid all the hoaxes, though, there *were* real reports of cigar-shaped structures, with or without wings, and of night sightings of lights. Perhaps behind all the tall tales and the silliness, the first great modern UFO wave—with a full variety of UFO types—was taking place.

Twentieth-Century Sightings

While by late May 1897 the flurry of sightings had quieted, reports of airships continued into the next century. In the summer of 1900, for example, two young men from Reedsburg, Wisconsin, saw a huge blimp-shaped structure hovering in the night sky. As it passed over a grove of trees, the trees bent as if blown by a strong wind, though the night was still. The March 15, 1901, issue of New Mexico's *Silver City Enterprise* even reported that a local doctor had taken a clear photograph of an airship. But the picture was lost.

In 1901 a wave of airship sightings occurred in Great Britain, the United States, New Zealand, and Australia. In Britain the sightings began in March, and most described torpedo-shaped craft moving at a "tremendous pace" and flashing lights and searchlights; these renewed fears—first expressed 15 years earlier in eastern Europe and still unsupported—of high-flying German spies. In America, secret inventors were suspected in this new flurry of airship sightings.

New Zealand's wave began in July 1901 at the southern end of South Island and then moved northward. As with other airship scares, some witnesses there claimed to have seen humanlike figures in passing craft. In one case, said to have taken place on August 3, a Waipawa man reported that an airship passenger had shouted at him in an unknown language. In another account, a man in a boat thought he was being attacked when "missiles" were fired from an airship and hit the water. Australia also experienced a handful of sightings that August.

Another airship-sighting wave occurred in the fall of 1912, with reports all across Europe. Most of the objects were described as large and cigar-shaped, with very bright searchlights. Few, if any, of the accounts mentioned wings. And, as before, the airships could hover and move at great speeds, even against the wind. While this wave of sightings died down by the following April, airship reports continued from time to time in Europe and elsewhere.

On October 10, 1914, for example, a Manchester, England, man claimed that he saw an "absolutely black, spindle-shaped object" cross the face of the sun. A cigar-shaped object at least 100 feet long flew over Rich Field, Waco, Texas, one evening in early 1918. It left witnesses with—in the words of one— "the weirdest feeling of our lives." And in the summer of 1927, an airship was seen over Wolfe County, Kentucky. One observer compared it to a "perfectly shaped, huge fish, with big fins extended outward near the front and small, short ones near the rear."

After the 1920s, unidentified cigar-shaped objects were rarely called "airships." Still, they continued to be reported. On October 9, 1946, observers in San Diego, California, saw an airshiplike object that they compared to a "huge bat with wings." A similar object was seen over Havana, Cuba, the following February.

Driving to work at 5:50 A.M. on August 25, 1952, a Pittsburg, Kansas, radio musician said he came upon a 75-foot-long object with windows through which the head and shoulders of a human figure were visible. He told air force investigators that along the UFO's outer edges "were a series of propellers about six inches to eight inches in diameter, spaced closely together." And on the morning of February 6, 1967, Ruth Ford sighted two fast-moving "cigar-shaped craft"—each with two small propellers and a row of windows—as she drove between Deming and Las Cruces, New Mexico. She could see no one inside.

In the summer of 1927, an airship was seen over Wolfe County, Kentucky. One observer compared it to a "perfectly shaped, huge fish, with big fins extended outward near the front and small, short ones near the rear."

Sources:

UFOs from the Beginning through 1959—The UFO Encyclopedia, Volume 2, Detroit, Michigan: Omnigraphics, 1992.

Cohen, Daniel, *The Great Airship Mystery: A UFO of the 1890s,* New York: Dodd, Mead and Company, 1981.

Lore, Gordon I. R., Jr., and Harold H. Deneault, Jr., *Mysteries of the Skies: UFOs in Perspective,* Englewood Cliffs, New Jersey: Prentice-Hall, 1968.

Ancient ETs and Their Calling Cards

- ANCIENT ASTRONAUTS
- NAZCA LINES
- SIRIUS MYSTERY

Ancient ETs and
Their Calling Cards

ANCIENT ASTRONAUTS

In the 1970s, the idea that advanced space beings had visited the Earth early in man's history—and had played a part in the development of human intelligence and technology—became very popular. Sparked by the publication of Swiss writer Erich von Däniken's wildly popular book *Chariots of the Gods?: Unsolved Mysteries of the Past* in 1968, this "ancient astronaut" movement swept across Europe and then into Great Britain and the United States.

Von Däniken and other believers of the theory argued that space beings were behind the archaeological and engineering wonders of the ancient world, like the Egyptian pyramids and Peru's **Nazca lines.** They also believed that the gods of Judaism, Christianity, and other religions were actually extraterrestrials (beings from other planets) who, by mating with our primitive ancestors—or by changing their genes—created *Homo sapiens,* or modern men and women. According to von Däniken and his followers, God himself was an astronaut.

Von Däniken had no great interest in ufology, the study of unidentified flying objects, nor did he have scientific training. But at age 19 he did have a mystical vision that led him to "the firm belief that the earth had been visited by extraterrestrial astronauts." He began to read widely then, looking for evidence of ancient astronauts in historical and archaeological literature, even visiting archaeological sites in North Africa and the Americas. He also read the works of others who suggested that early space visits had occurred, including Jacques Bergier and Louis Pauwels's 1960 best-seller *The Morning of the Magicians* and Robert Charroux's 1963 book *One Hundred Thousand Years*

According to von Däniken and his followers, God himself was an astronaut.

Erich von Däniken.

of Man's Unknown History. Von Däniken would freely borrow ideas from both of these works.

Indeed, the theory of ancient astronauts was nothing new. It had been around for quite a long time, in fact. In the late nineteenth century, followers of the theosophy—teachings about God and the world based on mystical insight—of Helena Petrovna Blavatsky believed that space people played a part in human history. Many writers addressed the subject before von Däniken, including flying-saucer contactee George Hunt Williamson, who produced three books on ancient-astronaut themes in the 1950s. And M. K. Jessup (also see entry: **The Philadelphia Experiment**), a former astronomer, wrote *The Case for the UFO* (1955), *UFO and the Bible* (1956), and *The Expanding Case for the UFO* (1957), all detailing past and present alien influences. To Jessup, however, the "aliens" were earthlings: pygmy races who tens of thousands of years ago developed antigravity technology and escaped to the moon and beyond just as natural disasters wiped out other advanced civilizations. According to Jessup, this population nonetheless continues to observe Earth and may even be the "little people" so often described in folklore and UFO reports.

Clearly, von Däniken's ideas were not original, but he put them together in such a way and at the precise time that they would cause a sensation. While most scientists and journalists strongly questioned his theories and his "evidence"—based more on personal judgments than solid proof and careful reasoning—the public couldn't seem to get enough of the subject. When *Chariot of the Gods?* was made into a film in Germany, audiences flocked to the box office, and when an edited version was aired on television in the United States, 250,000 copies of the paperback were sold in the following 48 hours! Von Däniken wrote a number of successful sequels to his best-seller, triggering a flood of similar books by other authors.

An Ancient Astronaut Society was formed in 1973, headed by attorney Gene M. Phillips in the United States and von Däniken in his native Switzerland. Sponsoring archaeological expeditions to sites where "members may have an opportunity to examine the evidence firsthand," the organization was created—according to Phillips—to "*prove* that civilization, technology, and intelligence *originated* in outer space." Although by the early 1980s the ancient astronaut fad had run its course, the society remains active and publishes a bimonthly bulletin, *Ancient Skies.*

Sources:

Story, Ronald, *The Space-Gods Revealed: A Close Look at the Theories of Erich von Däniken,* New York: Harper and Row, 1976.
Von Däniken, Erich, *Chariots of the Gods?: Unsolved Mysteries of the Past,* New York: G. P. Putnam's Sons, 1969.

NAZCA LINES

At some time before 1000 B.C., the Nazca Valley, a desert region on Peru's southern coast, was inhabited by a people who developed advanced farming methods that allowed them to build an irrigation system, improve their crops, and expand the area of land they could farm. Over the next 1,500 years, they also developed outstanding skills in weaving, pottery, and architecture. Yet perhaps the most fascinating of their cultural achievements was the creation of a remarkable ground art—the exact purpose of which remains a mystery.

The so-called Nazca lines, of which there are thousands, consist, according to investigator William H. Isbell, of five kinds of markings: long straight lines; large geometric figures; drawings of plants and animals; rock piles; and figures decorating hillsides.

The lines may be as narrow as six inches or as wide as several hundred yards. Some run for many miles. The Nazca people created some of them by removing dark surface stones and placing them in the desired patterns. For others, according to William E. Shawcross, they removed the desert's "thin brown surface coating" by walking or sweeping across it, "[exposing] the creamy pink soil underneath." Because of the area's dry, stable climate, these light-colored Nazca lines have remained nearly unchanged for many centuries.

Nazca lines decorate hillside.

What makes the Nazca markings so very odd, though, is the fact that a great many of the forms are discernible only from the air! Archaeologists have developed several explanations for this: one is that the figures, probably of religious significance, were not meant to be seen as a whole by human eyes; a second is that the Nazca people built balloons that allowed them to view the figures when they flew over the sites. This suggestion, while not impossible, lacks supporting evidence.

Signals for the Gods?

The Nazca lines attracted public attention not long after the heyday of UFO sightings began. In the 1950s, as more and more books and magazine articles addressed UFOs, some writers looked back to ancient history and mythology for evidence of early space visitors. In

Ancient ETs and Their Calling Cards

Nazca lines viewed from the air—who or what could have viewed them from above?

an article in the October 1955 issue of *Fate,* James W. Moseley suggested that since the markings were largely invisible from the ground, the Nazca people must have "constructed their huge markings as signals to interplanetary visitors or to some advanced earth race ... that occasionally visited them."

In his 1959 book *Road in the Sky,* flying-saucer "contactee" George Hunt Williamson included a whole chapter on the mysterious Nazca lines. Like Moseley, Williamson believed that "sky gods" or space beings visited Earth in the distant past and that the Nazca lines were connected to them. Williamson also wondered if these space visitors were somehow related to the advanced civilizations, like Lemuria and Atlantis, described in ancient myths. He thought that perhaps the Nazca lines and other puzzling archaeological sites served as "magnetic centers," locations at which spaceships could refuel.

In the early 1960s a French best-seller by Louis Pauwels and Jacques Bergier, published in America as *The Morning of the Magicians,* included the Nazca lines in its theory of **ancient astronauts.** This idea, that advanced space beings visited the earth early in man's history and played a part in the development of human intelligence and technology, reached its greatest popularity with Swiss writer Erich von Däniken's book *Chariot of the Gods?,* first published in West Germany in 1968 and reprinted in translated editions around the world. According to von Däniken, the Nazca lines marked out an "airfield" on which spacecraft landed and took off.

Still, nothing in the nature of these lines points to such a purpose. In fact, a critic of von Däniken's ideas stated, "It hardly seems reasonable that advanced extraterrestrial spacecraft would require *landing strips,*" adding that Nazca's "soft, sandy soil" was hardly suitable for an airport. Regardless, this explanation of the Nazca lines was accepted for a time during the ancient astronaut craze of the 1970s.

Sources:

Pauwels, Louis, and Jacques Bergier, *The Dawn of Magic,* London: Anthony Gibbs and Phillips, 1963.

Story, Ronald, *The Space-Gods Revealed: A Close Look at the Theories of Erich von Däniken,* New York: Harper and Row, 1976.

Von Däniken, Erich, *Chariots of the Gods?: Unsolved Mysteries of the Past,* New York: G. P. Putnam's Sons, 1970.

SIRIUS MYSTERY

The **ancient astronaut** fad of the 1970s gave rise to a number of questionable books on the subject, works that were weak on evidence and careful reasoning. An exception to this was Robert K. G. Temple's *The Sirius Mystery* (1977), a thoughtful, well-researched look at the possible early influence of space beings on the Dogon, a tribe in West Africa.

The Dogon are believed to be of Egyptian descent. After living in Libya for a time, they settled in Mali, West Africa, bringing with them astronomy legends dating from before 3200 B.C. In the late 1940s four of their priests told two French anthropologists of a secret Dogon myth about the star Sirius (8.6 light-years from the earth). The priests said that Sirius had a companion star that was invisible to the human eye. They also stated that the star moved in a 50-year elliptical orbit around Sirius, that it was small and incredibly heavy, and that it rotated on its axis.

All of these things happen to be true. But what makes this so remarkable is that Sirius's companion star, called Sirius B, was first photographed in 1970. While people began to suspect its existence around 1844, it was not seen through a telescope until 1862—and even then its great density was not known or understood until the early decades of the twentieth century. The Dogon beliefs, on the other hand, were supposedly thousands of years old!

Even if these people had somehow seen Western astronomy textbooks, they could not have known about Sirius B. Also puzzling was their knowledge of the rotations and orbits of planets in our solar system and of the four major moons of Jupiter and the rings of Saturn. How did they learn all this? Dogon folklore says that this knowledge came from unearthly sources.

The Dogon tell the legend of the Nommos, awful-looking beings who arrived in a vessel along with fire and thunder. The Nommos, who could live on land but dwelled mostly in the sea, were part fish, like **merfolk** (mermaids and mermen). Similar creatures have been noted in other ancient civilizations—Babylonia's Oannes, Acadia's Ea, Sumer's Enki, and Egypt's goddess Isis. It was from the Nommos that the Dogon claimed their knowledge of the heavens.

The Dogon also claimed that a third star existed in the Sirius system. Larger and lighter than Sirius B, this star revolved around Sirius as well. And around it orbited a planet from which the Nommos came.

> Also puzzling was their knowledge of the rotations and orbits of planets in our solar system and of the four major moons of Jupiter and the rings of Saturn.

The Nommos, who were part fish, came to Earth in a strange vessel accompanied by fire and thunder.

Other Explanations

Although Temple's *The Sirius Mystery* was taken more seriously than many other ancient-astronaut writings when it was first published, it met with some bad luck; it was criticized by two important science figures, writer Ian Ridpath and celebrity-astronomer Carl Sagan. From that point on many felt that it did not get the kind of consideration that its well-laid-out case deserved.

Ridpath and Sagan had their own simple explanation for the Sirius mystery: the Dogon got their supposedly ancient knowledge of the heavens from modern informants. They asserted that Westerners had probably discussed astronomy with Dogon priests, who quickly added this new information to older folklore. French anthropologist Germaine Dieterlen, who had lived among the Dogon for most of her life and whose writings on their astronomy myths had caught Temple's attention in the first place, called this idea "absurd" when asked about it by a reporter for BBC-TV's *Horizon* program. Then she displayed for the show's audience a Dogon object crafted 400 years ago, which clearly indicated Sirius and its companion stars.

Despite the criticism, Temple continued to defend his position. He pointed out that some of the information, like that concerning the super-weight of Sirius B, was only a few years old when anthropologists first collected it from the Dogon in 1931. Temple wondered why Western astronomers would rush to far-off Mali to share their new astronomical knowledge with Dogon priests? And how, in two or three years' time, could this information then filter down through the entire Dogon and surrounding cultures of over two million people and show up in hundreds of thousands of objects, woven blankets, carved statues, and more?

These reasonable questions brought no response from Ridpath, Sagan, and other Temple critics. Whenever a writer of an article or book would report that the Dogon's Sirius beliefs came from modern informants, Temple would respond with a point-by-point account that argued otherwise. But his comments were simply ignored.

Now there are other factors that cast serious doubt on the Dogon's story. So far no third star has been detected in the Sirius system. And for scientists who search for evidence of intelligent life in the universe, Sirius has never been on their list of places to look.

Still, Temple raised serious questions about the Dogon's Sirius beliefs. Almost two decades after the publication of *The Sirius Mystery,* the book has been nearly forgotten. Yet the puzzle of the Dogon's remarkable astronomical knowledge remains.

Sources:

Ridpath, Ian, *Messages from the Stars,* New York: Harper and Row, 1978.
Sagan, Carl, *Broca's Brain: Reflections on the Romance of Science,* New York: Random House, 1979.
Story, Ronald, *Guardians of the Universe?,* New York: New English Library, 1980.
Temple, Robert K. G., *The Sirius Mystery,* New York: St. Martin's Press, 1977.

Unexpected Guests and Interplanetary Communications

- **FLYING HUMANOIDS**

- **HAIRY DWARFS**

- **FLATWOODS MONSTER**

- **SPACE BROTHERS**

- **MEN IN BLACK**

- **UMMO**

Unexpected Guests and Interplanetary Communications

FLYING HUMANOIDS

When a mysterious object passed over Mount Vernon, Illinois, on the evening of April 14, 1897, one hundred citizens, including Mayor B. C. Wells, saw something that "resembled the body of a huge man swimming through the air with an electric light on his back."

Batman and Birdman

Though rare, accounts like this one—of flying beings of human appearance—do occur from time to time. A "winged human form," for example, was observed over Brooklyn, New York, on September 18, 1877, according to W. H. Smith in the *New York Sun*. Three years later the *New York Times* of September 12, 1880, recorded reports from Coney Island of a "man with bat's wings and improved frog's legs ... at least a thousand feet in the air ... flying toward the New Jersey coast ... [with] a cruel and determined expression."

V. K. Arsenyev, a Russian writer, reported seeing a mysterious flying creature in the Sikhote Mountains near Vladivostok, Russia, on July 11, 1908. In a 1947 book he recalled the experience:

> The rain stopped, the temperature of the air remained low and the mist appeared over the water. It was then that I saw the mark on the path that was very similar to a man's footprint. My dog Alpha bristled up, snarled, and then something rushed about nearby trampling among the bushes. However, it didn't go away.

Arsenyev related that when he threw a stone "towards the unknown animal ... something happened that was quite unexpected": he "heard the beating of wings. Something large and dark emerged from the fog and flew over the river. A moment later it disappeared in the dense mist." When the writer told some local men about his experience, "they broke into a vivid story about a man who could fly in the air. Hunters often saw his tracks, tracks that appeared suddenly and vanished suddenly in a way that could only result if the 'man' alighted on the ground, then took off again into the air."

One night in 1952, U.S. Air Force Private Sinclair Taylor, on guard duty at Camp Okubo, Kyoto, Japan, said he heard a loud flapping noise. Looking up, he saw a huge "bird" in the moonlight. When it approached, he became frightened and put a round of ammunition into his gun. The "bird" now had stopped its flight and was hovering close by, staring at the soldier.

"The thing, which now had started to descend again, had the body of a man," Taylor recalled. "It was well over seven feet from head to feet, and its wingspread was almost equal to its height. I started to fire and emptied my carbine where the thing hit the ground. But when I looked ... to see if my bullets had found home there was nothing there." When the sergeant of the guard came to investigate the gunshots and heard the story, he told Taylor that he believed him—because a year earlier another guard had seen the same thing!

Another soldier's tale of a flying humanoid was reported by Earl Morrison, who served with the First Marine Division in Vietnam. While stationed near Da Nang in August 1969, he and two other guards saw an extraordinary sight just after one o'clock in the morning. They were sitting atop a bunker and talking when they noticed something approaching them in the sky. Morrison related:

> We saw what looked like wings, like a bat's, only it was gigantic compared to what a regular bat would be. After it got close enough so we could see what it was, it looked like a woman. A naked woman. She was black. Her skin was black, her body was black, the wings were black, everything was black. But it glowed. It glowed in the night—kind of a greenish cast to it.

The men watched the creature move about in the sky. At one point she was right above their heads, just six or seven feet up. She moved silently, without flapping her wings. Morrison said that she

"The thing, which now had started to descend again, had the body of a man," Taylor recalled. "It was well over seven feet from head to feet, and its wingspread was almost equal to its height.

blocked the moon once, but despite the increased darkness, they could still see her because she glowed brightly. It was only when the creature started to fly away that the men heard a flapping sound.

Morrison thought the covering on her skin was more like fur than feathers. "The skin on her wings looked like it was molded on to her hands," he said, and the movement of her arms suggested they had no bones in them.

In the 1950s, a Kansas boy said he saw a dark-skinned little man with pointed nose and ears.

Flying Humanoids and UFOs

In the second half of the twentieth century, most sightings of flying humanoids have been connected with UFOs.

Not all of the sightings have been of winged figures. Sometimes the humans or humanoids fly through the air with the aid of machines attached to their bodies. The first known account of this kind took place near Louisville, Kentucky, on July 29, 1880, according to the *Louisville Courier-Journal.* Another such case occurred in Chehalis, Washington, on January 6, 1948, when an elderly woman and a group of children reported seeing a man with long mechanical wings. Flying in an upright position, he moved the wings with instruments on his chest. Six and a half years later, the *Wichita Evening Eagle* reported that a 12-year-old Coldwater, Kansas, farm boy had observed a dark-skinned little man with pointed nose and ears float toward a UFO that was hovering nearby.

Three Houston, Texas, residents reported what may or may not have been a winged UFO in the early morning hours of June 18, 1953. As they sat on the front porch of their apartment building trying to escape the heat, a huge shadow fell across the lawn, then appeared to bounce into a pecan tree. They saw the "figure of a man ... dressed in gray or black [fitted] clothes," surrounded by a "dim gray light." Witnesses could not agree on whether he was wearing a cape or had wings. After 15 minutes the figure "just melted away," and soon after, a "loud swoosh" sounded across the street and a rocket-shaped object shot up and disappeared along the horizon.

Sources:

Bord, Janet, and Colin Bord, *Alien Animals,* Harrisburg, Pennsylvania: Stackpole Books, 1981.

Clark, Jerome, and Loren Coleman, *Creatures of the Outer Edge,* New York: Warner Books, 1978.

Keel, John A., *The Mothman Prophecies,* New York: E. P. Dutton and Company, 1975.

Keel, John A., *Strange Creatures from Time and Space,* Greenwich, Connecticut: Fawcett Gold Medal, 1970.

One witness saw six hairy dwarfs hauling rocks into a nearby spaceship.

HAIRY DWARFS

During the fall of 1954 a flurry of UFO sightings occurred worldwide. Many of the reports told of humanoid UFO occupants that resembled hairy dwarfs. On October 9, for example, three children roller-skating in the French countryside reported that a "round shiny machine came down very close to us. Out of it came a kind of man, four feet tall, dressed in a black sack.... His head was hairy, and he had big eyes. He said things to us that we couldn't understand and we ran away. When we stopped and looked back, the machine was going up into the sky very fast."

Five days later a French miner came upon a humanoid with a squat, furry body and oversized, slanted, bulging eyes. It was wearing a skullcap (a close-fitting cap without a brim) and had a flat nose and thick lips.

In Venezuela in early December of that year, there were several reports of night meetings with three-foot-tall, hairy—and hostile—dwarfs. In one case, said to have taken place on December 10, four such beings stepped out of a hovering UFO and tried to kidnap a young man. His companion, who happened to be armed because the two were hunting at the time, struck one of the beings on the head with the end of his gun. The gun butt splintered as if it had met with solid rock. The two men, bruised, cut, and terrified, told their story to the police soon afterward.

Nine days later, at Valencia, a jockey on a late-night training ride said he saw six hairy dwarfs hauling rocks into a nearby UFO. When they noticed him, one fired a beam of violet light and paralyzed him, even though he was trying to run away. Police found footprints at the scene, which they described as "neither human nor animal."

Accounts of meetings with UFO occupants, of course, continue to this day. But reports of sightings involving hairy dwarfs died out quickly by the end of 1954.

When they noticed him, one fired a beam of violet light and paralyzed him, even though he was trying to run away.

Sources:

Bowen, Charles, ed., *The Humanoids: A Survey of Worldwide Reports of Landings of Unconventional Aerial Objects and Their Alleged Occupants,* Chicago: Henry Regnery Company, 1969.

Lorenzen, Coral, and Jim Lorenzen, *Encounters with UFO Occupants,* New York: Berkley Publishing, 1976.

FLATWOODS MONSTER

On September 12, 1952, three boys in the tiny West Virginia town of Flatwoods (population 300) saw a slow-moving, reddish ball sail around a hill, hover briefly, and drop behind another. A bright glow seemed to come from the other side of that hill, as if the object had landed. On their way to investigate, the boys were joined by beautician Kathleen May, her two young sons, their friend Tommy Hyer, 17-year-old Eugene Lemon, and Lemon's dog.

The dog ran ahead of the group and was briefly out of sight. Suddenly it was heard barking fiercely and, moments later, seen fleeing with its tail tucked between its legs. A foul-smelling mist covered the ground and caused the searchers' eyes to water. Lemon and Neil Nunley, who were leading the group, reached the hilltop first and saw a "big ball of fire" 50 feet to their right when they looked down. One of the other witnesses reported that the ball was the size of a house.

An Armless, Legless Creature with an Odd-Shaped Head

To the group's left, on the hilltop and just under the branch of an oak tree, were two small lights. May suggested that Lemon turn his flashlight on them. To everyone's great amazement, the flashlight beam revealed an awful-looking creature with a head shaped—according to several of the observers—like the "ace of spades." Inside the head was a round "window," dark except for the two lights, from which pale blue beams shone straight ahead. In the short time that they observed the creature, the group members saw nothing that looked like arms or legs.

The creature, which appeared to be over six feet tall, moved toward the witnesses; it seemed to be gliding rather than walking. Seconds later it changed direction, turning toward the glowing ball down the hill. The witnesses reported that all of this took place in a matter of seconds. When Lemon fainted, the others dragged him away as they ran from the scene.

When interviewed half an hour later by A. Lee Stewart, Jr., a reporter for the *Braxton Democrat,* most members of the group were hardly able to speak. Some were given first aid. Stewart had no doubt that they had seen something that had frightened them terribly. Still, soon afterward he was able to get Lemon to take him to the hillside, where Stewart noticed an unusual odor in the grass that bothered his nose and throat. Returning to the site alone early the following morning, the reporter found "skid marks" leading down the hill toward an area of matted grass, suggesting that a large object had rested there.

Other Sightings

This strange meeting with what the press would soon call the "Flatwoods monster" took place during a flurry of sightings of unusual flying objects in the area. One man, Bailey Frame of nearby Birch River, told of seeing a bright orange ball circling over the place where the monster was reported. The object was visible for 15 minutes before it shot toward the airport at Sutton, where it was also observed.

The creature, which appeared to be over six feet tall, moved toward the witnesses; it seemed to be gliding rather than walking.

A representation of
what was reported
to be seen at
Flatwoods.

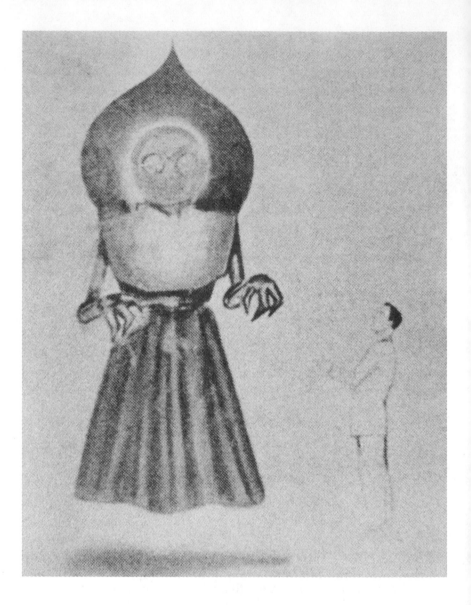

And according to another sighting, which took place a week before the Flatwoods event and 11 miles away, a Weston woman and her mother encountered a similar creature as they were driving to church. Both reported that it emitted a rank odor, and the younger woman was so frightened that she had to be hospitalized.

Of course, doubters of the Flatwoods event were plentiful; they suggested that May and her companions had seen a meteor and an owl, and only fright had caused them to think that they had seen anything else. Nonetheless, when interviewed separately shortly after the occurrence, the witnesses gave accounts that were nearly identical.

Many years later, a woman from Joliette, Quebec, would report seeing a similar creature as it gazed through a window of her home in the early morning hours of November 22, 1973. She woke her husband, who went outside to investigate. All he found was a dog that acted as if it were "scared to death." Local police believed that the woman was being truthful.

Sources:

Barker, Gray, "The Monster and the Saucer," *Fate* 6,1, January, 1953, pp. 12-17.
Sanderson, Ivan T., *Uninvited Guests: A Biologist Looks at UFOs,* New York: Cowles, 1967.

SPACE BROTHERS

On the afternoon of November 20, 1952, George Adamski—a lifelong student of the supernatural—reported meeting a being from Venus named Orthon in the southern California desert. This would be the first of many such contacts he would make with extraterrestrials: visitors from Venus, Mars, and Saturn. Adamski would also claim to travel into space, where he would attend a conference on Saturn.

Adamski related his space adventures in three books published between 1953 and 1961. The stories excited those interested in the more fantastic notions surrounding UFOs, and a movement based on these reported contacts spread from California to much of the rest of the world. Other "contactees" included Orfeo Angelucci, Truman Bethurum, Daniel Fry, Howard Menger, George Van Tassel, and George Hunt Williamson, who all published books in the 1950s and were popular lecturers in certain UFO circles.

According to these contactees, friendly, good-looking, humanlike space people come to the Earth on a peaceful mission for the Galactic Federation. For throughout the universe, the Earth is viewed as a backward place, its people primitive and violent; earthlings threaten to upset the "balance of the universe" with their nuclear weapons and warlike ways. Space people preach that if earthlings can act in a gentler manner, they will enter a New Age of peace and riches and claim their rightful place in the universe.

Early on, contactees and their followers used the affectionate nickname "space brothers" for these extraterrestrial messengers because of their kind nature and concern for the human race.

George Adamski.

Sometimes contactees would relay this message: the Earth is about to undergo huge geological changes that will destroy much of the planet's population; those who follow the space people's direction will be saved, either by relocating to safe places, or by entering space-ships that will pick them up at the exact time of the geophysical upheaval. Early on, contactees and their followers used the affection-ate nickname "space brothers" for these extraterrestrial messengers because of their kind nature and concern for the human race.

Hoaxes

In the early years of the UFO era, it was the "physical" con-tactees—those who reported meetings with extraterrestrials and space trips—who had the greatest influence on the UFO movement. They often produced questionable photographs and other "evidence" in an effort to prove their claims. One physical contactee, Eduard

(Billy) Meier of Switzerland, was caught in a particularly embarrassing lie: his photograph of a beautiful space traveler from a "Pleiades beamship" turned out to be a fashion model whose picture had been clipped from a popular European magazine! By the early 1960s, even some of Adamski's most devoted followers had begun to doubt him as his tales grew taller and taller.

Then "psychic" contactees, those who received messages from space beings mentally, in dreams, or through automatic writing (writing performed without thinking, seemingly directed by an outside force) dominated the UFO movement. These contactees, who did not feel pressured to produce evidence, strongly believed that their extraterrestrial communications were real.

Today's average space-brothers believer might appear in Laramie, Wyoming, in the summer to attend the yearly Rocky Mountain Conference on UFO Investigation run by psychologist and contactee R. Leo Sprinkle. Most who attend live in small western towns or on farms or ranches and believe that they have been chosen to receive the mental messages of kindly beings from outside our world.

REEL LIFE

Close Encounters of the Third Kind, 1977.

Middle-American strangers become involved in the attempts of benevolent aliens to contact earthlings. This Academy Award-winning film by director Steven Spielberg is a stirring achievement. The ending is an exhilarating experience of special effects and peace-on-earth feelings.

The Day the Earth Stood Still, 1951.

A gentle alien lands on Earth to deliver a message of peace and a warning against experimenting with nuclear power. He finds his views echoed by a majority of the population, but not the ones in control. One of the truly great science-fiction films of all times.

Starman, 1984.

An alien from an advanced civilization lands in Wisconsin. Hiding in the form of a grieving young widow's recently deceased husband, he persuades the widow to drive him across country to rendezvous with his spacecraft so he can return home. Karen Allen is earthy as the widow; Jeff Bridges is fun as the likeable starman.

Sources:

Adamski, George, *Inside the Space Ships,* New York: Abelard-Schuman, 1955.

Clark, Jerome, *The Emergence of a Phenomenon: UFOs from the Beginning through 1959—The UFO Encyclopedia,* Volume 2, Detroit, Michigan: Omnigraphics, 1992.

Clark, Jerome, *UFOs in the 1980s: The UFO Encyclopedia,* Volume 1, Detroit, Michigan: Apogee Books, 1990.

Evans, Hilary, *Gods, Spirits, Cosmic Guardians: A Comparative Study of the Encounter Experience,* Wellingborough, Northamptonshire, England: The Aquarian Press, 1987.

Albert K. Bender's sketch of one of the three "Men in Black" who visited his home in 1953 and gave him the solution to the UFO mystery.

MEN IN BLACK

In 1953 Albert K. Bender of Bridgeport, Connecticut, suddenly closed down his popular International Flying Saucer Bureau (IFSB). In the last issue of the bureau's magazine, *Space Review* (October), he included a puzzling statement. He said that he now knew the answer to the UFO mystery but could not publish it because of "orders from a higher source." He also urged "those engaged in saucer work to please be very cautious."

When further questioned by Gray Barker, who had been IFSB's chief investigator, Bender would only say that three men in black suits had visited him in September, told him what UFOs were, and threatened him with prison if he revealed this information. He told Barker that the strangers were "members of the United States government." So disturbing was the whole experience that Bender soon fell ill.

The exact nature of the men in black—or, as they would eventually be called in UFO circles, MIB—grew more unclear each time Bender reluctantly told his story. Soon some suspected that the MIB were not American intelligence agents but alien beings. Barker produced a frightening book about the event, *They Knew Too Much about Flying Saucers,* in 1956 and over the next few years wrote about the "Bender mystery" in a number of publications. In them, Bender's visitors were described as evil humans, aliens, or even demons.

In 1962 Bender wrote—and Barker published—*Flying Saucers and the Three Men.* It was a wild story that few readers accepted as true. In it Bender recalled being taken to the South Pole by monstrous aliens, who then followed his activities until 1960, when they returned to their home planet.

Men in Black Driving Cadillacs

Men-in-black stories appeared again in the 1960s. New York writer John A. Keel reported that UFO witnesses in New York, Ohio, West Virginia, and elsewhere had been accosted by MIB. Keel even claimed meetings of his own: "I kept rendezvous with black Cadillacs on Long Island and when I tried to pursue them, they would disappear impossibly on dead-end roads.... More than once I woke up in the middle of the night to find myself unable to move, with a dark apparition standing over me." According to Keel, the MIB were not government agents or even human beings but alien representatives. Often described as Oriental-looking, they behaved strangely, asking odd or even rude questions of those they visited. They usually traveled in large black cars.

Keel warned investigators: "Do not attempt to apprehend MIB yourself. Do not attack them physically. Approach them with great caution. They frequently employ hypnotic techniques." He also felt that the dangers of MIB visitation were so great for the weak-minded and the young that parents should "forbid their children from becoming involved [in UFO study]. Schoolteachers and other adults should not encourage teenagers to take an interest in the subject."

Meetings with MIB were not reported only by Keel's witnesses or just in the United States. In May 1975, two weeks after a dramatic UFO sighting from his plane (also recorded on radar screens at the Mexico City airport), a young pilot was on his way to a television interview when four black-suited men in a black limousine chased him down the freeway. After forcing him to the side of the road, they warned him not to discuss his sighting. A month later one of the strangers reappeared and threatened him again as he was on his way to a hotel to meet with J. Allen Hynek, the U.S. Air Force's top UFO adviser. That was the pilot's last encounter with the MIB, whom he remembered as tall and strangely white. He added: "I never saw them blink."

By the late 1980s, so many tales of MIB had been reported that the subject was included in the *Journal of American Folklore*. The author, Peter M. Rojcewicz, looked at the role of MIB in flying-saucer legends and related it to demon sightings reported in generations past. He also told of his own MIB experience. While doing research on UFOs in a library, he was approached by a dark-suited man who, speaking briefly in a slight accent about flying saucers, placed his hand on Rojcewicz's shoulder and said, "Go well in your purpose" and disappeared.

In May 1975, two weeks after a dramatic UFO sighting from his plane, a young pilot was chased down the freeway by four black-suited men in a black limousine.

Sources:

Barker, Gray, *They Knew Too Much about Flying Saucers,* New York: University Books, 1956.
Bender, Albert K., *Flying Saucers and the Three Men,* Clarksburg, West Virginia: Saucerian Books, 1962.
Keel, John A., *UFOs: Operation Trojan Horse,* New York: G. P. Putnam's Sons, 1970.

UMMO

The Ummo affair was one of the strangest, most complex UFO hoaxes ever recorded. It began in 1965, when Fernando Sesma—a "contactee" who directed the Society of Space Visitors—reported receiving a phone call from a man who spoke in Spanish. The caller said he represented an "extraterrestrial order." While refusing to meet with Sesma, he promised that he would contact him again.

Soon afterward Sesma and other society members began receiving documents in the mail. They were supposedly written by residents of Ummo, a planet said to revolve around the star Iumma, 14.6 light–years from the sun. Each document bore an unusual symbol that looked like this:)+(. While astronomers stated that neither Ummo or Iumma existed, a group of believers soon sprang up in Europe and North and South America.

On February 6, 1966, several soldiers and two other witnesses saw a large circular object touch down briefly in a Madrid, Spain, suburb. One observer who caught a glimpse of the UFO's underside saw an odd symbol. It was the secret Ummo sign.

An advertisement in the May 20, 1967, issue of the Spanish newspaper *Informaciones* announced that on June 1 an Ummo craft would land outside Madrid and carry some faithful believers to the home planet. On that date, in the Madrid suburb of San Jose de Valderas, a flying object bearing the Ummo symbol was seen by a number of witnesses. Afterward, two sets of photographs of this UFO surfaced, but they were soon exposed as fakes. The craft displayed in the photos was actually a model made from plastic plates, about eight inches across. The symbol was scrawled on the bottom of the model with a marker pencil.

Later that same evening, in the Madrid suburb of Santa Monica, witnesses reported seeing a UFO approach the ground, then take off and disappear. The next morning signs of a landing were found at the site. So were metal cylinders that, when opened, contained the Ummo symbol. When studied in a scientific laboratory, though, these otherworldly objects proved to be made of earthly materials. One investigator thought that the UFO seen in the two sightings might be a radio-controlled model, for he noted that both cases took place near an airport and the Aerotechnical School, "both of which would have been convenient places to build, control, and hide a disk-shaped model."

Meanwhile, growing numbers of Spanish ufologists were getting Ummo documents. By the end of the decade, at least 600 pages on Ummo science, philosophy, politics, and civilization had been collected. The documents arrived through the regular mail, and most had a Madrid postmark. But others were sent from Australia, New Zealand, England, Argentina, France, Czechoslovakia, Yugoslavia, and the United States.

These documents suggested that the author or authors were highly educated and conversant in physical and biological science. But to most who read them, they were clearly not the reflections of an advanced extraterrestrial race. As Jacques Vallee, a ufologist trained in astrophysics and computer sciences, attested, "The Ummo technology is without major surprises, and it matches the kind of clever extrapolations one finds in any good science-fiction novel."

One observer who caught a glimpse of the UFO's underside saw an odd symbol. It was the secret Ummo sign.

Ummites

The documents revealed that the Ummites, who look much like humans, arrived on Earth on April 24, 1950, when they landed in the French Alps. Since that time they have been observing Earth's affairs, though not interfering in them. They communicate with each other mentally—by telepathy—because at age 14 their vocal cords close up. Most of their documents were written in Spanish, but a few were in French.

The cult of Ummo believers is worldwide. Collections of Ummite documents have been published in Spanish and English, and letters from the Ummites continue to appear. According to Spanish ufologists Carlos Berche Cruz and Ignacio Cabria Garcia, Sesma and people within his organization (where the whole Ummo affair began) are quite likely perpetrators of a widespread hoax. Still, the charge can't be proven. They point out, though, that in the 1950s Sesma's writings about his space contacts included many concepts that suspiciously resembled those found in the Ummo documents.

A GOVERNMENT HOAX?

Some writers have suggested, though without evidence, that the Ummo affair is an experiment designed to explore human nature and society, run secretly by a government intelligence agency.

Sources:

Vallee, Jacques, *The Invisible College: What a Group of Scientists Has Discovered about UFO Influences on the Human Race,* New York: E. P. Dutton and Company, 1975.

Vallee, Jacques, *Revelations: Alien Contact and Human Deception,* New York: Ballantine Books, 1991.

Other Worlds

- HOLLOW EARTH

- FOURTH DIMENSION

- MOON ODDITIES

- VULCAN

Other Worlds

HOLLOW EARTH

The notion that the Earth has a hollow interior in which an underground civilization lives is an old one. Some would say that religious beliefs in hell and Hades are expressions of the concept. But the first American to try to prove the idea was the eccentric John Cleves Symmes (1779-1829). Symmes believed that the Earth was made up of a series of spheres, one inside the other, with 4,000-mile-wide holes at the North and South Poles. In spite of great ridicule, Symmes wrote, lectured, and worked hard to raise money for an expedition through the poles to the interior. There he planned to meet the inner-earth people and open "new sources of trade and commerce."

To the rest of the world, Symmes is remembered, if at all, as the inspiration for nineteenth-century American writer Edgar Allan Poe's early science-fiction tale of a hollow earth, *The Narrative of Arthur Gordon Pym* (1838). Yet Symmes was a pioneer of sorts, a man who paved the way for generations of freethinkers who imagined a new earthly geology and dreamed of another race secretly sharing the planet with us.

Tropical Splendor vs. Fiendish Race

By the late nineteenth century, there were many hollow-earth believers, especially after Symmes's son Americus published a collection of his father's lectures. While scientists dismissed the idea as absurd and physically impossible, that did not keep writers from detailing their own versions of the concept. Marshall B. Gardner, the author

In his 1974 book *Secret of the Ages,* Brinsley le Poer Trench reported that evil inner-earthers regularly kidnapped surface people and brainwashed them into becoming their agents.

Marshall B. Gardner's version of the hollow earth.

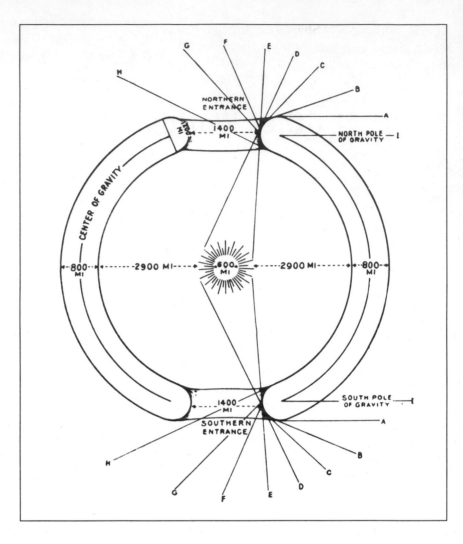

of the 1913 book *A Journey to the Earth's Interior,* for example, believed that there was a sun inside the Earth. Six hundred miles across, it gave the underworld a pleasant climate, allowing its inhabitants to live in tropical splendor! Guy Warren Ballard, who wrote *Unveiled Mysteries* (1934) under the name Godfre Ray King, told of the many out-of-body tours he had had beneath the Earth, led by an immortal "Master." There he found a beautiful world of scientific and spiritual marvels. And in time he even began meeting space people!

Nearly all nineteenth- and twentieth-century hollow-earth believers spoke of the inner world's inhabitants as members of an advanced, kindly race whose dealings with human beings could bring only good.

That is, until Richard Sharpe Shaver came along, describing his frightening experiences with a fiendish race beneath the earth in magazines like *Amazing Stories.* Called "deros," the evil creatures Shaver described (allegedly descendants of the people of Lemuria, whose continent was thought to have sunk into the Pacific Ocean thousands of years ago) had advanced technology that they used to torture kidnapped surface people. Deros also used their machines to cause accidents, madness, and other miseries in the world above.

The Nazis and the Hollow-Earth Theory

There is even a Nazi hollow-earth theory. According to Canadian Nazi sympathizer Ernst Zundel, who writes under the name Christof Friedrich, Nazi German dictator Adolf Hitler and his Last Battalion escaped to Argentina in a submarine as World War II ended. They then set up a base for advanced saucer-shaped aircraft inside the hole at the South Pole. To Zundel the Nazis were "outer earth representatives of the 'inner earth'"—which is one fantastic way of justifying Nazi claims of racial superiority.

Brinsley le Poer Trench wrote about the terror of this hidden world; in his 1974 book *Secret of the Ages,* Trench reported that evil inner-earthers regularly kidnapped surface people and brainwashed them into becoming their agents. Now, he said, the "ground work has ... been prepared for a takeover of this planet by those who live inside it."

But by far the most popular book on the subject was Walter Siegmeister's *The Hollow Earth* (1964), which he wrote under the pseudonym Raymond Bernard. It contributed little that was new to the inner-earth legend, quoting mostly from nineteenth-century texts on the matter. Still, it did introduce the author's belief that there existed a conspiracy to hide the truth about the hollow earth, flying saucers, and pole holes. The book sold well, going through numerous printings, and exposed many readers to the idea of a hollow earth for the first time.

REEL LIFE

At the Earth's Core, 1976.

A Victorian scientist invents a giant burrowing machine, which he and his crew use to dig deeply into the earth. To their surprise, they discover a lost world of subhuman creatures and prehistoric monsters.

Journey to the Center of the Earth, 1959.

A scientist and student undergo a hazardous journey to find the center of the earth. Along the way they find the lost city of Atlantis. Based upon the novel by Jules Verne.

Through the years, numerous expeditions have been planned to the North and South Poles to attempt to enter the inner earth. Many UFO enthusiasts, occultists, religious movement founders, and even quite a few contemporary pro-Nazis have advocated the hollow-earth theory as support for their views.

Sources:

Bernard, Raymond (pseudonym for Walter Siegmeister), *The Hollow Earth: The Greatest Geographical Discovery in History,* New York: Fieldcrest Publishing, 1964.

Friedrich, Christof (pseudonym for Ernst Zundel), *UFOs—Nazi Secret Weapons?,* Toronto: Samisdat, 1976.

Michell, John, *Eccentric Lives and Peculiar Notions,* San Diego, California: Harcourt, Brace, Jovanovich, 1984.

WHAT IS DIMENSION?

Dimension signifies a position in space. Space, as science has generally defined it, is three-dimensional; it is bound by width, height, and length. When a person looks at a picture of an apple, he or she is seeing only two dimensions, because the picture is flat. Its depth cannot be seen or felt. But when touching an actual apple, the observer can feel the three elements of its width, height, and length.

We can conceive of the three dimensions, but what about a fourth—or even a fifth—dimension? These can only be imagined. Other dimensions either do not exist, as many scientists believe, or most human beings are not equipped to experience them.

FOURTH DIMENSION

In February 1945, N. Meade Layne, a San Diego man interested in the supernatural, founded Borderland Sciences Research Associates (later the Borderland Sciences Research Foundation). The organization was devoted to Layne's belief in "ethereans," beings like us who live in another dimension. Layne explains that "just as there is a spectrum of sound and color (ending in sounds we cannot hear and colors we cannot see)," there is also a spectrum of matter—of places and people—of which we ordinarily have no awareness. This matter is, in fact, too dense to be touched; that is, according to Layne, until ethereans lower their atomic vibratory rates—and we can see or feel them.

Ethereans and UFOs

Layne believed that it is ethereans who pilot flying saucers. More advanced than us, the ethereans nonetheless live in a world much like our own— almost a mirror reflection. The stars and planets of our universe have their etheric doubles. As the theory goes, ethereans are really just fourth-dimension human beings.

While Layne did not invent the idea of an etheric world, he was the first to link it with flying saucers. By working with a psychic medium who supposedly received communications from ethereans, Layne claimed to learn the secrets of that parallel world's science and philosophy.

Layne's "etherean ships" appealed only to those interested in the most fantastic ideas surrounding **UFOs.** Still, the thought of unidentified flying objects coming from another dimension did gather interest. Next to the "beings from outer space" idea, the fourth dimension (4-D) theory became ufologists' favorite UFO explanation; though seldom credited, Layne's ideas had a marked impact on how ufologists perceived UFOs.

Other writers offered their own versions of the connection between UFOs and a dimension outside our own. In his 1970 book *UFOs: Operation Trojan Horse,* for instance, John A. Keel declared that shape-changing "ultraterrestrials" from other levels of reality "can make us see what they want us to see and remember only what they want us to remember." Similar to Layne's ethereans, these ultraterrestrials could appear in our world by "manipulations of electromagnetic energy," entering "a solid state" that would even allow them to "leave impressions on the ground." But unlike Layne's harmless ethereans, Keel's ultraterrestrials were up to no good. Secret rulers of the earth for many centuries, they still have us under their control: "We are biochemical robots helplessly controlled by forces that can scramble our brains, destroy our memories and use us in any way they see fit," wrote Keel. "They have been doing it to us forever."

The idea of a fourth dimension intrigued writers because it suggested an order or control system beyond our own. Maybe strange events that were unexplainable in our world did originate from another place, where they made perfect sense. Some writers combined two terms, *paranormal* (outside the normal) and *physical,* to create a new word, "paraphysical." This concept encompasses occurrences once called "etheric"—events that have both natural (like leaving tracks) and unnatural (like disappearing instantly) features.

> Next to the "beings from outer space" idea, the fourth dimension (4-D) theory became ufologists' favorite UFO explanation.

REEL LIFE

The 4D Man, 1959.

A physicist's special project gets out of control, leaving him able to pass through matter and see around corners. He also finds that his touch brings instant death.

Sources:

Keel, John A., *Strange Creatures from Time and Space,* Greenwich, Connecticut: Fawcett, 1970.

Keel, John A., *UFOs: Operation Trojan Horse,* New York: G. P. Putnam's Sons, 1970.

Layne, N. Meade, *The Ether Ship and Its Solution,* Vista, California: Borderland Sciences Research Associates, 1950.

MOON ODDITIES

Transient lunar phenomena," or TLP, are short-lived oddities that appear on the moon's surface, observed by professional or amateur astronomers through telescopes or, more rarely, with the naked eye. TLP include dark spots, lights, and moving objects. Dark spots are sometimes explained as optical effects, shadows of moon features like mountains or valleys, for example. Some of the lights may be no more than reflections from the sun. And objects observed moving across the moon's surface may actually be earthbound things, like birds or seeds, that enter a witness's field of vision and mistakenly *appear* to be located in outer space. Meteors passing between the earth and the moon may also account for some TLP sightings.

Between 1540 and 1970, over 900 reports of TLP were recorded. These include sightings of reddish patches, clouds, and flashes on the moon. And while astronomers have been able to supply reasons for many of these lunar oddities, even they admit not all TLP can be easily explained.

Extraterrestrials on the Moon

Most scientists feel that sightings of TLP do not mean that intelligent activity—carried out by alien beings—is taking place on the moon. Still, quite a few books have been written about the subject, and their popularity has demonstrated that the public is receptive to the idea.

Perhaps the most famous person to believe in intelligent life on the moon was the great British astronomer Sir William Herschel (1738-1822). Though best remembered as the discoverer of Uranus, Herschel noted in a paper read to the Royal Society in 1780, "the great probability, not to say almost absolute certainty, of [the moon] being inhabited." His observations of both TLP and the moon's ordinary surface features led him to believe that he had seen cities, towns, roads, canals, forests, and even circuses there! Herschel's reputation perhaps survived these outlandish notions because he never went so far as to publish them; he recorded them only in his private journal, which has been discovered just recently.

In stories published between August 25 and 31, 1835, the *New York Sun* reported that Sir John Herschel, Sir William's son, observed two species of "bat-men" on the moon. The simpler creatures averaged "four feet in height" and were "covered, except on the face, with short and glossy copper-colored hair" and had "wings composed of a thin

> The *New York Sun* reported that Sir John Herschel, Sir William's son, observed two species of "bat-men" on the moon.

Sir William Herschel, astronomer, discovering Uranus, assisted by his sister.

membrane, without hair, lying snugly upon their backs, from the top of the shoulders to the calves of the legs." Their faces resembled those of orangutans. The higher species of lunar bat-men were "of infinitely greater personal beauty ... scarcely less lovely than ... angels."

Later, *Sun* reporter Richard Adams Locke admitted he had made up the story. His trick, referred to as the Moon Hoax, had fooled thousands of readers, even those who were well educated and should have

Herschell recorded observing cities, forests, and even circuses on the moon.

known better. Writer Edgar Allan Poe noted with astonishment that "not one person in ten discredited it." Was Locke a true hoaxer, playing his trick to gain attention? Michael J. Crowe, a historian of science, did not believe this perception of Locke, but thought Locke only intended to poke fun at the popular belief that life existed in other worlds. He thought that his readers would laugh at his account. Imagine his surprise when they accepted it as true!

TLP, Extraterrestrials, and UFOs

Charles Fort, one of the first to research and catalog reports of strange events, believed that intelligent beings from other worlds did exist. From scientific journals he collected many accounts of strange lights and oddities on or near the moon, and sometimes he would connect these with unusual events that took place on the earth, arguing that beings from outer space were responsible for both. Fort believed that otherworldly beings were always watching us. After his death in 1932, Fort's followers continued to collect reports supporting the idea of "space visitors," and science-fiction magazines like *Amazing Stories* also ran articles on the subject.

In July 1951 *Fate,* a magazine about incredible "true mysteries," published the account of George Adamski of Palomar Gardens, California, describing his success photographing spaceships through his six-inch telescope. Adamski wrote:

> I have taken all my pictures at night by the light of the moon because often I had noticed that a good number of the ships I saw moving through space appeared headed for the moon. Some of them seemed to land on the moon, close to the rim; while others passed over the rim and disappeared behind it....
> I figure it is logical to believe that space ships might be using our moon for a base in their interplanetary travels.

On November 20, 1952, Adamski reported that he actually met a spaceship pilot, from Venus, in the desert of southern California. He would later claim many more meetings with beings from Venus, Mars, and Saturn. One such contact occurred in August 1954, when Adamski insisted that a Venusian scout craft flew him around the moon, where he saw extraterrestrial cities and spaceship hangars as well as forests, lakes, and rivers (also see entry: **Space Brothers**).

Adamski published a book about this moon adventure, *Inside the Space Ships,* in 1955. Most people, including a great many ufologists, concluded that Adamski's otherworldly experiences existed only in his head. Still, some did believe the author and tried to provide "proof" for his claims. Fred Steckling, head of the George Adamski Foundation, wrote the book *We Discovered Alien Bases on the Moon* (1981), which lent support to Adamski's ideas. In it Steckling insists that the U.S. government is involved in a huge cover-up—hiding the fact that both space people and an atmosphere exist on the moon.

Like Adamski, others claimed contact with space visitors during the 1950s and 1960s and told of bases and beings on the moon. One of them, Howard Menger, even claimed to have taken a photograph there. His 1959 book *From Outer Space to You* contains a picture that claims to show a "spacecraft landing near dome-shaped building." Ozark farmer Buck Nelson also claimed that he landed on the moon one April day in 1955, in the company of his dog Teddy, a Venus resident named Little Bucky, and Little Bucky's dog Big Bo. Buck observed children playing with several dogs while on the moon. Then the group took off for Venus!

Even those who studied UFOs seriously—and rejected the outlandish stories of "contactees"—were intrigued by the idea of extraterrestrials on the moon. Donald E. Keyhoe, a retired marine corps major, aircraft writer, and ufologist, for example, reacted with great excitement when two amateur astronomers observed, in 1953, what they thought was a natural bridge that suddenly appeared near the moon's Mare Crisium crater. Keyhoe wrote that the bridge's sudden appearance ruled out a natural explanation and that "evidence of some intelligent race on the moon seemed undeniable." (Astronomers have since decided that the "bridge" is an optical illusion.)

ATLANTIS

Atlantis is a large island in Greek legend located in the Atlantic Ocean west of Gibraltar. The Greek philosopher Plato admired the Atlanteans' educated and cultured way of life, which was snuffed out when an earthquake caused the island to be swallowed up by the sea. Some still believe in the legend today, and societies for the rediscovery of Atlantis actively look for remains of the civilization.

Another writer of the period, M. K. Jessup, had an even more fantastic idea concerning beings on the moon. In his book *The Expanding Case for the UFO* (1957) he wrote that tens of thousands of years ago pygmy races—much older than other human races—developed antigravity spaceships and escaped to the moon just as natural disasters wiped out other advanced civilizations, like the mythical Atlantis. The pygmies continue to observe us from their present home, thus explaining both UFOs and the "little men" often seen with them (also see entries: **Ancient Astronauts** and **Philadelphia Experiment**).

Clear photographs of the moon's surface became available to the public following the U.S. lunar explorations that took place between 1969 and 1972. Some who saw the pictures believed that they showed evidence of extraterrestrial activity; George H. Leonard, who wrote *Somebody Else Is on the Moon* (1976), and Don Wilson, author of *Our Mysterious Spaceship Moon* (1975), were the best known of these individuals. They accused NASA (the National Aeronautics and Space Administration) of trying to hide this fantastic discovery. Furthermore, Wilson believed not only that spaceships were on the moon, but that the moon itself *was* a spaceship—a huge hollow harbor built thousands of years ago by an alien race.

Responding to the growing number of writings about extraterrestrial activity on the moon, Francis Graham of the Pennsylvania Selenological Society (a branch of astronomy that deals with the moon) took a look at all the claims. While open-minded on the subject of UFOs, he concluded that "there is not a single piece of unambiguous [clear] evidence for the existence of alien bases on the moon." The astronomer felt that people who claimed to see evidence in NASA lunar pho-

Astronauts walk
on the moon.

tographs reached false conclusions because they were unfamiliar with
the moon's natural features and geological oddities, and the photographs they used were often unclear.

The Apollo Aliens

Shortly after the first moon landing, on July 16, 1969, the *National
Bulletin,* a supermarket tabloid, published a tall tale that captured the
public's imagination. According to the story, the Apollo 11 astronauts
saw spaceships when they arrived on the moon, and NASA managed to
censor their radio report so that the news media, and therefore the rest
of the world, would not learn of the shocking discovery. Yet somehow
someone had slipped a tape of the astronauts' message—reporting the
appearance of two UFOs along a crater rim—to the *Bulletin.*

Four years later, Stuart Nixon of the National Investigations Committee on Aerial Phenomena looked into the story and found, not to his

surprise, that it contained no shred of truth. The printed record of the supposed conversation between the astronauts—Neil Armstrong, Edwin "Buzz" Aldrin, and Michael Collins—and Mission Control contained so many errors in fact and terminology that it had to be false. And no such conversation could have been censored at the time it was sent, for even a short break in communication would have been noticed immediately. The *Bulletin* could not produce the original tape of the message, nor could it even produce the reporter, Sam Pepper, who wrote the account.

Though it appeared that the story was simply made up in the *Bulletin* office, it would be retold again and again—in one form or another—and become a part of Space Age folklore. Maurice Chatelain wrote about it in his 1978 book *Our Ancestors Came from Outer Space;* he claimed to get his information from sources within NASA. Charles Berlitz and William L. Moore discussed it in 1980 in their book *The Roswell Incident.* According to their sources, which they did not make altogether clear, "NASA was forced to change the originally intended landing site for the Eagle lander module because it was discovered that the first site was 'crawling'—presumably with somebody else's space hardware." Berlitz and Moore were later sued by astronaut Aldrin for writing a false story about him.

Sources:

Adamski, George, *Inside the Space Ships,* New York: Abelard-Schuman, 1955.
Crowe, Michael J., *The Extraterrestrial Life Debate 1750-1900: The Idea of a Plurality of Worlds from Kant to Lowell,* New York: Cambridge University Press, 1986.
Graham, Francis G., *There Are No Alien Bases on the Moon,* Burbank, California: William L. Moore Publications and Research, 1984.

VULCAN

In 1846 Urbain Leverrier of the Paris Observatory was one of two astronomers to suggest that an eighth planet existed in the outer reaches of our solar system. Disturbances in the orbit of Uranus led Leverrier to believe that another large heavenly body was causing the irregularities; from these he was able to calculate almost exactly where the new planet could be found. Others duplicated his calculations and discovered that an eighth planet did, indeed, exist.

Leverrier, who had a very high opinion of himself, wanted the new planet named after him, but it was soon called Neptune. He also fought to exclude British astronomer John Adams from any recognition for the discovery, even though Adams had made similar calculations concerning an eighth planet. Many, in fact, thought that the two scientists should have been named Neptune's co-discoverers.

Perhaps Leverrier's hunger for honor and fame explains his odd behavior a few years later. The French astronomer had begun to focus his attention on the opposite end of the solar system, toward Mercury, which, like Uranus, had its own orbit irregularities. Though the theory of relativity would later provide an explanation for these, in Leverrier's time the only cause he could imagine was an intra-Mercurial planet—in other words, a world in orbit between Mercury and the sun.

Urbain Leverrier, French astronomer.

The New Planet

On December 22, 1859, Leverrier received a letter from a country doctor and astronomy hobbyist named Lescarbault. The man made an extraordinary claim: that on March 26, 1859, he had seen a round black spot—a planet—move across the upper part of the sun's face. Leverrier immediately went to the village of Orgeres, where Lescarbault lived. Without identifying himself, the astronomer badgered the physician with questions and even made fun of him, but Lescarbault stood by every detail of his story. Finally, Leverrier revealed who he was, warmly congratulated the physician, and on his return to Paris saw to it that Lescarbault would be decorated with the Legion of Honor.

Within days the new discovery had the world of astronomy buzzing. Leverrier, perhaps more careful after the unpleasant competition surrounding the detection of Neptune, suggested that the planet be named Vulcan. By January, excited discussions about the discovery were appearing in astronomy journals. Leverrier calculated the new planet's size (about 1/17th that of Mercury, he thought) and guessed

The solar
system.

that it crossed the sun's face in early April and early October. He also
cited 20 earlier sightings, which he now felt sure identified Vulcan.

From the beginning, however, there were doubters. One was a
Brazilian astronomer who reported observing the sun's face at the
same time as Lescarbault. The Brazilian had seen nothing out of the

ordinary, and his telescope was much more powerful than the good doctor's! Over the next few decades, astronomers watched for Vulcan during the periods Leverrier predicted it would appear. Results were disappointing, with most sightings really observations of sunspots. By the end of the century, there was scarcely a Vulcan believer left. In 1899 Asaph Hall, the discoverer of the moons of Mars, remarked that the planet was no longer a part of "rational astronomy."

Still, some of the sightings that pointed to the existence of Vulcan were, and remain, puzzling. Perhaps the mysterious objects that astronomers observed near the sun were really much closer to them than they thought (UFOs?) and that was why observers at other locations could not duplicate their findings. Such would seem the case with two U.S. astronomers (one in Wyoming and one in Colorado) who observed two shining objects some distance from the sun during a total solar eclipse on July 29, 1878. No one else reported the phenomenon, and their reports caused heated discussions among other astronomers, who accused the two of making the simplest of errors: mistaking two well-known stars for two unknown objects. Nevertheless, the two observers rejected the accusations. "I have never made a more valid observation," one of them, Lewis Swift, wrote in *Nature,* "nor one more free from doubt."

SUNSPOTS

Sunspots are dark, usually irregularly shaped patches that appear in groups on the sun's surface and are actually magnetic storms. Periods of great sunspot activity usually occur in cycles of 11 years. During these times, various corresponding disturbances take place on earth, such as magnetic storms, faulty radio reception, and malfunctioning magnetic compasses.

Sources:

Corliss, William R., ed., *Mysterious Universe: A Handbook of Astronomical Anomalies,* Glen Arm, Maryland: The Sourcebook Project, 1979.
Fort, Charles, *The Books of Charles Fort,* New York: Henry Holt and Company, 1941.
Grossinger, Richard, *The Night Sky,* Los Angeles: Jeremy P. Tarcher, 1981.

Government Cover-ups

- **HANGAR 18**

- **PHILADELPHIA EXPERIMENT**

- **AREA 51**

Government Cover-ups

HANGAR 18

In the 1960s Arizona senator and U.S. Air Force Reserve brigadier general Barry Goldwater asked a friend, General Curtis LeMay, for a favor. Senator Goldwater wanted to see a room at Wright-Patterson Air Force Base in Dayton, Ohio, where UFO wreckage and deceased UFO pilots were rumored to be secretly stored. As the senator recalled years later in a *New Yorker* article, General LeMay "just gave me holy hell. He said, 'Not only can't you get into it but don't you ever mention it to me again.'"

In the summer of 1947, not long after pilot Kenneth Arnold sighted flying saucers over Mount Rainier, Washington (also see entry: **Unidentified Flying Objects**), the world press reported that army air force workers had recovered the remains of a "flying disc" that had crashed in remote Lincoln County, New Mexico. Within hours a "correction" went out over the wires, with army officials assuring reporters that the story had been a mistake, that the wreckage of a weather balloon had been misidentified as something extraordinary.

The explanation—now known to be false—was widely accepted at the time, and the story died a quick death. The event was rarely mentioned again, that is, until ufologists (researchers of unidentified flying object sightings) began a reinvestigation of the case in the late 1970s. By 1992 four books had been written about "the Roswell incident" (so named because the recovery operation took place at the army air force base in Roswell, New Mexico), and the investigation continues to this day.

Newspapers took their cue from authorities' claims that material initially reported to be recovered from a "flying disc" was actually from a downed balloon.

Army Finds Air Saucer On Ranch in New Mexico

Disk Goes To High Officers

Picked Up Last Week

ROSWELL, N.M. — (AP) — The Army Air Force here today announced a flying disk had been found on a ranch near Roswell and is in Army possession.

Lt. Warren Haught, public information officer of the Roswell Army Air Field, announced the find had been made "sometime last week," and had been turned over to the airfield through the operation of the sheriff's office.

It was transferred at the Roswell Army Air Field and subsequently turned "by Maj. Jesse A. Marcel" of the 509th bomb group intelligence office at Roswell "to higher headquarters."

The Army gave no other details.

'Flying disc' turns up as just hot air

Fort Worth, Tex., July 9 (AP).—An examination by the Army revealed last night a mysterious object found on a lonely New Mexico ranch was a harmless high-altitude weather balloon — not a grounded flying disc.

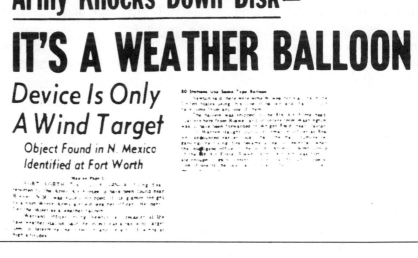

Army Knocks Down Disk—
IT'S A WEATHER BALLOON

Device Is Only A Wind Target

Object Found in N. Mexico Identified at Fort Worth

Was on Page 1

FORT WORTH, Tex. — (AP) — A "flying disk" reported to the Army Air Forces to have been found near Roswell, N.M. was today ripped to a gamer-tongue's at a Fort Worth Army air base as a mere object by an officer who identified the object as a weather balloon.

Warrant officer Irving Newton, a forecaster at the base weather station, said he made an examination of the target item. In layman's language, the device was nothing more than a target used to determine the direction and velocity of winds at high altitudes.

80 Stations Use Same Type Balloon

Newton said there were some 80 weather stations in the United States using this type of balloon and that he had come from any one of them.

The balloon was shipped to the 8th Air Force headquarters here from Roswell, and to officers from Washington was on its way here forwarded to Wright Field near Dayton.

Warrant Haught, public information officer at the base, announced earlier in the day the discovery of the balloon during this became a matter of record. The intelligence officer at the Roswell base said that the 8th Air Force headquarters had ordered an investigation into the discovery of one of the so-called flying discs.

According to some informants, searchers found the bodies of four gray-skinned humanoids at a location two miles from the main crash site. They reported that officials swore all who knew of the event, military or otherwise, to secrecy. Decades later investigators would find witnesses and participants who still would not discuss what they knew. Regardless, by the early 1990s, ufologists like William Moore, Stanton Friedman,

Kevin Randle, and Don Schmitt had collected the testimonies of several hundred people—from local ranchers to air force generals—and from these reconstructed what they believed had occurred. The Roswell incident has become perhaps the best-documented case in UFO history.

Unearthly Rumors

Before this wide-scale investigation, ufologists had heard rumors about "little men in pickle jars"—preserved remains of alien crash victims—but could not find any real proof. They were concerned that such rumors were merely hoaxes, like the one con artists Silas Newton and Leo A. GeBauer used to scam unlucky author Frank Scully. Claiming to know of spaceship crashes in the Southwest in order to sell phony oil-detection devices based on "extraterrestrial" technology, the two related their bogus experiences to Scully, who recorded them in the popular book *Behind the Flying Saucers* (1950). Later exposed for the shady characters they were, Scully's informants made him look like a trusting fool.

So that hoax, along with a lack of evidence of other claimed crashes and recoveries, made most ufologists doubt that UFO wrecks and corpses existed. As Ed J. Sullivan stated in the September 1952 issue of *Civilian Saucer Investigation Quarterly Bulletin,* crash stories "are damned for the simple reason, that after years of circulation, not one soul has come forward with a single concrete fact to support the assertions. If there were one single iota of fact, certainly someone, somewhere, would be willing to bring it into the open."

Still, rumors continued, many focusing on the crash landings of one or more spacecraft in the Southwest. Military workers reportedly transferred the wreckage and bodies to Wright-Patterson Air Force Base in Dayton, Ohio, where the air force had set up its first UFO investigation unit. In some cases, individuals said that they had actually seen the evidence, either at the recovery site or—accidentally—in a secret room at Wright-Patterson. At some point this room came to be known as "Hangar 18" or "Blue Room." A 1980 science-fiction film, *Hangar 18,* dramatized the story. Of course, the air force has long denied that any such room exists.

In the 1970s well-known ufologist Leonard H. Stringfield decided that, unlike his doubting colleagues, he would actively seek out crash testimony, including Hangar 18 stories. He published his findings in a series of reports, with the most interesting accounts coming from eyewitnesses, some of which are excerpted here.

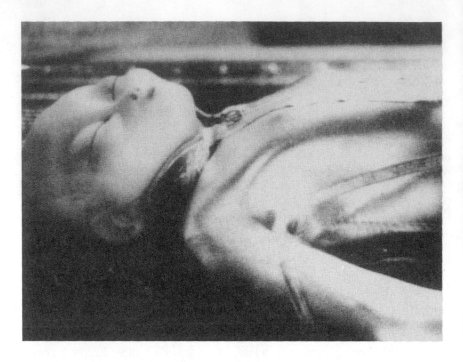

To many UFO buffs, this widely circulated photograph represents a picture of an extraterrestrial in a secret U.S. government vault. In fact, it is a wax dummy displayed in Canada in the early 1980s.

Humanoid Corpses Seen in 1953

A former army pilot said he had been inside a Wright-Patterson hangar one day in 1953 when a DC-7 arrived with five crates. The informant saw three of them opened; inside each lay the body of a small humanoid on fabric stretched over a bed of dry ice. Four feet tall, the beings had large, hairless heads and small mouths; the bodies were thin and looked brown under the hangar lights. They were dressed in tight-fitting uniforms, and one, with two bumps on the chest, appeared to be female. The pilot said crew members from the DC-7 later told him that a flying saucer had crashed in the Arizona desert and that one of the humanoids was still alive when a recovery team arrived, which tried without success to save it.

Heavily Guarded Bodies Seen in 1966

A retired army intelligence officer stationed at Wright-Patterson in 1966 reportedly saw nine alien bodies in a heavily guarded section of the base. They were four feet tall and gray-skinned. He was told that a total of 30 such bodies were stored there, along with the wreckage of spacecraft. The officer also revealed that "since 1948 secret information concerning UFO activity involving the U.S. military has been contained in a computer center at Wright-Patterson AFB," with backup files stored at other military locations.

Another source, a retired air force pilot, told ufologist Stringfield that in 1952, while attending a "high-level secret meeting" at Wright-Patterson, he saw an alien body deep-frozen in an underground chamber. Four feet tall and hairless, it had a big head and long arms. He said he learned that some of the Wright-Patterson UFO material was eventually taken to the air force's underground complex at Colorado Springs, Colorado.

The most remarkable of Stringfield's witnesses was a medical doctor associated with a major hospital. The physician claimed that he had performed an autopsy on an alien body while serving in the military in the early 1950s. In a 1979 statement he prepared for Stringfield from his medical files he stated:

> The specimen observed was four feet three inches in length.... The head was pear-shaped in appearance and oversized by human standards for the body.... The ends of the eyes furthest from the nasal cavity slanted upward.... The eyes were recessed into the head. There seemed to be no visible eyelids, only what seemed like a fold. The nose consisted of a small fold-like protrusion.... The mouth seemed to be a wrinkle-like fold. There were no human type lips as such—just a slit that opened into an oral cavity about two inches deep.... The tongue seemed to be atrophied [wasted away] into almost a membrane. No teeth were observed.... The outer "ear lobes" didn't exist.... The head contained no hair follicles. The skin seemed grayish in color.

Perhaps what is most striking about these accounts is that they describe beings that look very much like those reported by UFO abductees—people who have claimed (or reveal under hypnosis) to have been kidnapped by aliens. Humanoids of this type are rare in early UFO accounts, which report spaceship occupants resembling humans or human dwarfs (also see entries: **Flying Humanoids** and **Hairy Dwarfs**), or in rare cases, monsters.

Stringfield had other medical sources who gave similar descriptions of alien corpses. But because the ufologist—as respected in the field as he was—insisted on keeping the names of his sources secret, the stunning testimonies he collected could be viewed only as stories; they could not be independently verified, a vital step if they were to become actual evidence.

More Than Rumors?

In other cases, however, names have been revealed, and these people tell tales similar to those related above.

Norma Gardner worked at Wright-Patterson for a number of years. Her high-level security clearance allowed her to view secret materials, including—as she once told Charles Wilhelm, a young friend interested in UFOs—items recovered from crashed spacecraft. She was responsible for cataloging, photographing, and tagging them. Once, she said, she saw two humanoid bodies being carted from one room to another. They were generally human in appearance, though they did have large heads and slanted eyes. She told Wilhelm that she was passing on the information only because she was dying of cancer and "Uncle Sam can't do anything to me once I'm in my grave."

One evening in July 1952, Pan American pilot William Nash and copilot William Fortenberry sighted a UFO while flying over Virginia. The next morning, as they waited for investigators from the air force's Project Blue Book to interview them, they agreed to ask if the rumors about crashed spacecraft at Wright-Patterson were true. Fortenberry got a yes answer from one of his interviewers. But when Nash asked a group of investigators whose commanding officer was present, he got a resounding "NO!" from the ranking official. It seemed to Nash that the response was meant less for him than to "shut up" the investigators who had already "opened their mouths to answer the question."

There have been other people who—while not claiming to have personally seen wreckage or bodies at Wright-Patterson—did acknowledge that such things existed. One was physicist Robert Sarbacher, who, in the late 1940s and early 1950s, was a consultant for the Defense Department's Research and Development Board (RDB). On September 15, 1950, during a meeting in his office with a group of Canadian government scientists and engineers, Sarbacher was asked if there was any truth to the constant rumors that the U.S. government was holding UFO remains. He answered yes, adding, "We have not been able to duplicate their performance.... All we know is, we didn't make them, and it's pretty certain they didn't originate on earth." The subject, he said, "is classified two points higher even than the H-bomb." He would say little more, except that a top-secret project had been formed to study the materials.

Ufologist Arthur Bray found evidence of this remarkable conversation three decades later in the personal papers of Wilbert B. Smith, a deceased Canadian radio engineer and UFO buff who had been at that September meeting with Sarbacher and had asked the key questions. As one would imagine, the discovery of these papers sent several investigators in search of Sarbacher, to see if what Smith had recorded was true. The physicist was located in Florida and admitted

Science fiction or
reality? A huge,
hi-tech UFO project
hidden in Middle
America, in this scene
from Steven
Spielberg's *Close
Encounters of the
Third Kind.*

that he had knowledge of spaceship crash recoveries from the official reports that had crossed his RDB desk. He recalled that "certain materials reported to have come from flying saucer crashes were extremely light and very tough," which is how witnesses described the material reportedly recovered in the Roswell incident. Sarbacher added that "there were reports that instruments or people operating these machines were also of very light weight, sufficient to withstand the tremendous deceleration and acceleration associated with their machinery." Even more remarkable, the doctor related that once he had been invited to a high-level meeting at Wright-Patterson, where air force investigators planned to discuss what they had learned from their work on wreckage and bodies stored there.

Perhaps more important still was the testimony of air force officer Arthur Exon. Exon stated in July 1947, when he was a lieutenant colonel at Wright Field (which became Wright-Patterson AFB), that the remains of a flying saucer and its occupants recovered in New Mexico were flown in from Eighth Army Headquarters to undergo study at the base's laboratories. Like other witnesses, he told investigators Randle and Schmitt that some of the material from the craft was "very thin but awfully strong and couldn't be dented with heavy hammers." He reported that all present at the time agreed that "the pieces were from space."

He noted that the bodies "were in fairly good condition." A top-secret committee took over the investigation of this and other UFO cases.

In 1964 Exon, by now a general, became base commander at Wright-Patterson. Even so, the area where secret UFO studies took place was off-limits to him, so he knew very little about them. He related that from time to time a "team of uniformed officers would arrive on a commercial [not military] flight" to talk with UFO project workers at the base before going out to investigate an important case. Then groups of them would board military aircraft Exon would make available to them and be gone for several days before returning. Exon was never told of their whereabouts. "We were never informed about any reports. They all went to Washington," he recalled.

Clearly, stories of this sort—and there are many more of them—seem to point to the existence of space visitors and of top secret government projects. Although the accounts do not prove anything by themselves, when gathered together they paint a convincing picture. Investigations into spaceship crashes, the Roswell incident, and Hangar 18 continue.

Sources:

Berlitz, Charles, and William M. Moore, *The Roswell Incident,* New York: Grosset and Dunlap, 1980.
Bernstein, Burton, "Profiles: AuH20," *New Yorker,* April 25, 1988, pp. 43-73.
Friedman, Stanton T., and Don Berliner, *Crash at Corona,* New York: Paragon Books, 1992.
Randle, Kevin D., and Donald R. Schmitt, *UFO Crash at Roswell,* New York: Avon Books, 1991.
Stringfield, Leonard H., *Situation Red, the UFO Siege!,* Garden City, New York: Doubleday and Company, 1977.

PHILADELPHIA EXPERIMENT

In October 1955 Morris Ketchum Jessup, author of a recently published book entitled *The Case for the UFO,* received a strange letter from a man named Carlos Miguel Allende. The poorly written, rambling letter told of a World War II experiment with physicist Albert Einstein's Unified Field Theory that made a ship—a destroyer and all of its crew members—completely invisible while at sea. This allegedly occurred in October 1943.

According to Allende, the experimental ship had also been transported from a dock in Philadelphia, Pennsylvania, to one in the Norfolk/Newport News/Portsmouth area of Virginia and back in a matter of minutes. Apparently, the temporary vanishing had caused most of the crew to go insane; at one point, while still invisible, they ransacked a tavern near the navy dock. "The expieriment [sic] Was a Complete Success," Allende wrote. "The Men Were Complete Failures."

Jessup paid little attention to this odd letter or to a second Allende sent in January 1956; that is, until he was invited to the Office of Naval Research (ONR) in Washington, D. C., where he found that ONR officers had received a copy of Jessup's book from an unknown sender. Puzzling comments about UFO intelligence and technology had been written in the margins of the book by three individuals in three different-colored inks. Jessup told the officers that the writings reminded him of Allende's, especially references to the Philadelphia experiment. For some reason, the officers became convinced that Allende's letters and the book notes were important and held possible "clues to the nature of gravity." They made a small number of copies of Jessup's book, this time including the notes and letters.

Suicide or Murder?

Meanwhile, personal difficulties unrelated to the Allende affair plagued Jessup. The three sequels he wrote to *The Case for the UFO* were poorly received. And he had money and marriage problems and was badly injured in a car accident. When he visited writer Ivan T. Sanderson in October 1958, he was deeply depressed. In April 1959 Jessup died of carbon-monoxide poisoning in his car in Dade County Park, Florida, after writing what appeared to be a suicide note to a friend. Authorities ruled that Jessup took his own life.

Few UFO buffs knew of the Jessup/Allende case until 1962, when Borderland Sciences Research Associates made the reprinted material widely available. Vincent Gaddis devoted a chapter in his 1965 book *Invisible Horizons* to the episode, and other writers soon did the same. In 1979 the case inspired a book of its own, William L. Moore's *The Philadelphia Experiment* (on which the 1984 science-fiction film of the same name was based). Anna Lykins Genzlinger provided more fuel for the growing modern legend with her book *The Jessup Dimension* (1981). She even speculated that government agents had murdered Jessup because he knew too much about the Philadelphia experiment.

It didn't seem to matter that no evidence could be found to support Allende's story. In fact, the Philadelphia experiment grew more fantastic with each retelling. Eventually the unlucky crew members were

> Apparently, the temporary vanishing had caused most of the crew to go insane; at one point, while still invisible, they ransacked a tavern near the navy dock.

Morris K. Jessup

(1900-1959)

Morris Ketchum Jessup was born March 2, 1900, in Rockville, Indiana. He attended the University of Michigan in Ann Arbor as both undergraduate and graduate student in astronomy. There he participated in some groundbreaking astronomy projects.

From the 1930s through the 1950s Jessup spent much time in Mexico and Central and South America, where he observed archaeological sites with great interest. By the 1950s he was living in Washington, D.C., running an export business and writing about modern and ancient mysteries.

Jessup's first book, *The Case for the UFO* (1955), sought to link flying saucers with other strange or unexplained events and claims, including disappearances and falls from the sky. Two later works, *UFO and the Bible* (1956) and *The Expanding Case for the UFO* (1957), speculated about early human history, anticipating the themes of the ancient astronaut movement that would be popular twenty years later. Jessup believed that the pygmy races are millions of years older than scientists believe; long ago they developed an advanced technology which took them to the moon and beyond. These "little people," who figure in folklore and in UFO sightings, continue to observe us (also see entry: Moon Oddities).

Depressed by personal problems, Jessup dropped out of sight in 1958 and committed suicide a year later. Because of his involvement in the Allende hoax, tales began to arise that government agents killed Jessup because he knew too much.

said to have fallen into another dimension, where they interacted with aliens!

The Mysterious Carlos Allende

And who was the mysterious Carlos Miguel Allende? Some thought he might be an extraterrestrial himself. In actuality, he was an eccentric drifter, born Carl Meredith Allen in Pennsylvania in 1925. His wide reading in fantastic literature led him to develop his own strange ideas. Family members described him as a "master leg-puller" and recalled letters in which he all but admitted inventing the Philadelphia experiment. He also told them that he alone had written the notes in the Jessup book sent to the ONR.

Despite this damning information, the tale of the Philadelphia experiment lives on. Alfred Bielek, for example, lectures to New Age groups on his experiences during and after the event; he claims that he and his brother were aboard the ship—the U.S.S. *Eldridge*—when the experiment went awry. Bielek says that he and his brother jumped overboard, trying to escape, but found themselves hurled through "what seemed like a tunnel" into 1983. He also claims that later they met up with one of the mathematicians who designed the experiment. According to Bielek, he sent them back to 1943 just long enough for them to "destroy the equipment on board because it had created a time warp around the ship that could possibly engulf the planet."

REEL LIFE

The Philadelphia Experiment, 1984.

A World War II sailor falls through a hole in time and lands in the mid-1980s, whereupon he woos an attractive woman.

Philadelphia Experiment 2, 1993.

Melodramatic sci-fi thriller has Germany winning World War II by dropping a bomb on Washington. Southern California becomes one big labor camp with an evil mad scientist and a beleaguered hero who must time-travel back to 1943 to prevent the Germans from dropping that bomb.

Sources:

Genzlinger, Anna Lykins, *The Jessup Dimension,* Clarksburg, West Virginia: Saucerian Press, 1981.

Jessup, M. K., *The Case for the UFO,* New York: The Citadel Press, 1955.

Moore, William L., with Charles Berlitz, *The Philadelphia Experiment: Project Invisibility— An Account of a Search for a Secret Navy Wartime Project That May Have Succeeded— Too Well,* New York: Grosset and Dunlap, 1979.

Vallee, Jacques, *Revelations: Alien Contact and Human Deception,* New York: Ballantine Books, 1991.

AREA 51

Area 51 is located in a corner of the U.S. Nevada Test Site, where top-secret national security projects have been developed for several decades. These have included spy planes like the U-2 and the SR-71, the Stealth bomber, and the technology behind "Star Wars," or the Strategic Defense Initiative.

In recent years many observers have reported seeing odd lights moving in a manner that ordinary aircraft do not and cannot: flying at great speeds, stopping suddenly, and hovering for periods of time. Early sightings were almost all at night, but in a few cases witnesses saw the objects reflected in the moonlight and were able to tell that they resembled huge triangles. In May 1990 observers reported seeing such a craft in the daytime as well!

The Strategic Defense Initiative, commonly known as "Star Wars," is a space-based defense system that utilizes a layered weapon shield to track and destroy nuclear missiles heading for the United States—launched either from submarines or across continents—in any stage of flight. In March 1983 President Ronald Reagan called for a $30 billion, five-year program to research and develop the system, which combines several advanced technologies.

Writing in the October 1, 1990, issue of *Aviation Week & Space Technology,* John D. Morrocco reported that such triangles had been spotted not only in central Nevada but in parts of California. It appeared to him that a "quantum leap in aviation" had taken place, under conditions of great secrecy.

There had been similar sightings—as well as films and radar trackings—of giant triangles over Belgium and other European countries. These were usually considered UFO sightings. Yet to some, the Nevada/California reports and European accounts shared a link: the belief that the technology responsible for the remarkable new aircraft was from an unearthly source.

Outer Space Technology

Several close observers of the phenomenon thought that the breakthrough had come from studies of crashed extraterrestrial spacecraft stored at Area 51 of the Nevada test site. Rumors of this became so strong that hardly a magazine or newspaper account of the site failed to mention the notion. After investigating the stories, aircraft writer James C. Goodall reported, "Rumor has it that some of these systems involve force field technology, gravity drive systems, and 'flying saucer' designs. Rumor further has it that these designs are not necessarily of

Earth human origin, but of who might have designed them or helped us do it, there is less talk."

Other writers and researchers interviewed people who described secret projects based on extraterrestrial technology, but none of these informants were able to supply any proof. The one who attracted the most attention was Robert Scott Lazar, who, in November 1989, revealed startling information on a Las Vegas television news show. Lazar claimed that while working at Area 51 he learned that the advanced propulsion systems under development there involved almost unimaginable technology, powered by what he described as an "anti-gravity reactor." He also said that he had seen the crashed UFOs from which these technological secrets had come. According to Lazar, not even Congress knew about the project, and it was unlikely that the American public was meant to either.

Lazar's report caused a stir, but an investigation into his background—it was suggested that he was a liar and a lawbreaker—cast heavy doubt on his reliability. Still, the rumors surrounding Area 51 continued. And wild tales sprang up about government-extraterrestrial contact; one involved a treaty in which aliens supplied the American government with their technology in exchange for permission to kidnap its citizens!

One wild tale sprang up about a treaty in which aliens supplied the American government with their technology in exchange for permission to kidnap its citizens!

Sources:

Cooper, Milton William, *The Secret Government: The Origin, Identity, and Purpose of MJ-12,* Fullerton, California: The Author, May 23, 1989.
Good, Timothy, *Alien Liaison: The Ultimate Secret,* London: Random Century, 1991.
"Multiple Sightings of Secret Aircraft Hint at New Propulsion, Airframe Designs," *Aviation Week & Space Technology,* October 1, 1990, pp. 22-23.

Vanishing Acts

- **THE BERMUDA TRIANGLE AND FLIGHT 19**
- **DEVIL'S SEA**
- **VILE VORTICES**

Vanishing Acts

THE BERMUDA TRIANGLE AND FLIGHT 19

The term "Bermuda Triangle" was coined in 1964 by researcher Vincent Gaddis to describe an area in the Atlantic Ocean roughly bounded by Puerto Rico, the Bahamas, and the tip of Florida. Since the 1940s, several dozen ships and planes have disappeared in this area. Gaddis and many other writers have suggested that the Bermuda Triangle spelled doom for many who ventured into its domain, and many have speculated about "time warps," UFO kidnappings, and other paranormal reasons for the disappearances.

Of all the "mysterious disappearances" connected to the Bermuda Triangle, none is more famous than Flight 19. As with many of the stories behind the Triangle legend, however, research has demonstrated a serious gap between what has been claimed and what actually occurred in the ill-fated flight.

The Flight 19 Tragedy

At 2:10 on the afternoon of December 5, 1945, five Avenger torpedo bombers left the Naval Air Station at Fort Lauderdale, Florida, and headed east. Flight 19 was comprised of 14 men, all students in the last stages of training except for flight leader Charles Taylor. Taylor knew the Florida Keys well, but he did not know the Bahamas.

They were to conduct a practice bombing at Hens and Chicken Shoals, 56 miles away. Once that was done, the Avengers were to con-

But fuel was a problem now; Taylor told his companions that as soon as one of them ran out of fuel they would all go down together.

tinue eastward for another 67 miles, then head north 73 miles. After that they would turn west-southwest and take the remaining 120 miles straight home. In short, they were flying a triangular flight path through what would later be called the Bermuda Triangle.

At 3:40 P.M. pilot and flight instructor Lieutenant Robert Cox, who was about to land at Fort Lauderdale, overheard a radio transmission among the Avenger bombers indicating that they were lost. A few minutes later he was able to contact Taylor, who told Cox that his compasses were not working. Because Taylor said he was sure he was over the Florida Keys, Cox urged him to fly north toward Miami.

Taylor was not, however, in the Keys. He was in the Bahamas. By flying north he would only go further out to sea. Cox and others (like the Port Everglades Boat Facility, an Air Sea Rescue Unit based near Forth Lauderdale) tried to pinpoint the location of Flight 19 but could not because of poor radio communications. Taylor was urged to turn over control of the flight to one of his students, which he did not do; overheard were arguments between him and other Flight 19 pilots, who thought that the group should fly west. Had they done so, they would have been saved.

By 4:45 P.M. observers on the ground were seriously concerned. It was clear from further messages from Taylor that, far from being temporarily lost, which happens to many pilots, he had no idea where he was. As dusk approached, radio transmissions grew fainter. Finally, at 5:15 Taylor radioed to Port Everglades that they were at last heading west. But fuel was a problem now; Taylor told his companions that as soon as one of them ran out of fuel they would all go down together.

The sun set at 5:29 P.M. With bad weather moving in from the north, the situation was growing ever more critical. Still, no one on the ground knew where Flight 19 was. At one point, Taylor was urged to switch to an emergency radio frequency, but he refused to do so for fear that he and the other planes would lose contact with one another.

By 5:50 P.M. the ComGulf Sea Frontier Evaluation Center thought it had determined the flight's position: east of New Smyrna Beach, Florida, and far to the north of the Bahamas. Soon after, however, Taylor was overheard ordering his other pilots to "turn around and go east again," explaining, "I think we would have a better chance of being picked up." Mistakenly, he still believed his group was over the Gulf of Mexico.

Because Flight 19's position had been so uncertain, no rescue aircraft had yet gone out. But at last a Dumbo flying boat (seaplane) left

A group of Avenger torpedo bombers like Flight 19, which vanished December 5, 1945.

Miami at 6:20 P.M., heading northeast in an effort to reestablish contact with the lost flight. The Dumbo itself soon fell out of contact with shore, however, and for a while it was feared that it, too, was lost. The problem turned out to be ice on the radio antenna, and the seaplane continued on what would prove to be an unproductive search.

Within the hour, other aircraft, including two Martin Mariners, joined in the Dumbo's search. Mariner Trainer 32 had taken off around 7 P.M. east of New Smyrna Beach. Trainer 49 left the Banana River Naval Air Station some 20 minutes later and was to join up with the first Mariner. Lieutenant Gerald Bammerlin, 32's pilot, later told naval investigators, "When we arrived in the area of Flight 19's 5:50 position fix, about 8:15, ... the air was very turbulent and the sea very rough. We flew manually on instruments throughout the night."

In the meantime, Mariner 49 had failed to make its scheduled meeting. At 7:50 P.M. the crew of the S.S. *Gaines Mill* observed an enormous sheet of fire caused by the explosion of an airplane. A few minutes later the ship passed through a big pool of oil and looked without success for survivors or bodies. Though they saw some debris, crew members did not retrieve any of it because of the rough ocean. Weather conditions were worsening quickly.

By now it was certain that the Flight 19 aircraft had run out of fuel and were down. Taylor's last radio transmission was heard at 7:04 P.M. The search for the planes continued through the night, though with difficulty because of the high winds and raging sea. The next day hundreds of planes and ships looked, without success, for the missing Avengers and Mariner. No trace of them has ever turned up.

THE HOLLYWOOD RETURN OF FLIGHT 19

At the conclusion of Steven Spielberg's 1977 science-fiction film *Close Encounters of the Third Kind,* a UFO returns the Flight 19 crew to earth!

The Investigation

On April 3, 1946, at the end of an intense investigation of this much-discussed air disaster, the navy placed the blame on Taylor. According to investigators, the "flight leader's false assurance of identifying as the Florida Keys, islands he sighted, plagued his future decisions and confused his reasoning.... [He] was directing his flight to fly east ... even though he was undoubtedly east of Florida." When Taylor's mother and aunt refused to accept this verdict, the navy set up a panel to review the report. In August this panel announced it could only agree with the first conclusion. Furious, the two women hired a lawyer for a hearing the following October. On November 19 the Board for Correction of Naval Records retracted the original verdict and officially blamed the disaster on "causes or reasons unknown."

The fate of Mariner 49, however, seemed clear. The Mariners were called "flying gas bombs" because of the dangerous fumes they were known to emit. Something as small as a lighted cigarette or an electrical spark could ignite them. As for the Avengers, the 50-foot-high waves tearing across the ocean surface had probably chewed them up and sent what remained to the bottom in a matter of seconds.

Although Flight 19—along with everything else connected with the Bermuda Triangle—became a sensation from the 1950s through the 1970s, later writers examined the event carefully, some digging even

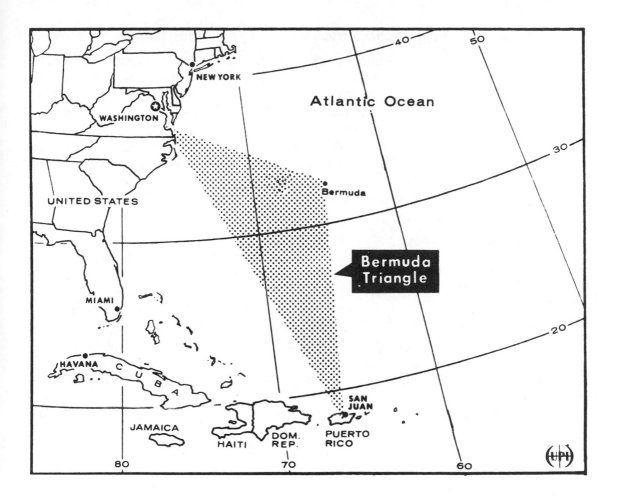

deeper than the navy's original investigation. In 1980 Larry Kusche, whose meticulous research debunked the Bermuda Triangle and "devil's sea" phenomena, published *The Disappearance of Flight 19.* Kusche felt that the navy correction board should not have excused Taylor. Though the "decision was a kindness to Mrs. Taylor [Charles's mother] ... it was incorrect. The conclusion of the original Board of Investigation, that Charles Taylor was at fault, was correct."

Reflecting on the mission of Flight 19 in 1985, Willard Stoll, who had taken off with Flight 18 half an hour before Taylor's mission, remarked: "What the hell happened to Charlie? Well, they didn't call those planes 'Iron Birds' for nothing. They weighed 14,000 pounds empty. So when they ditched, they went down pretty fast. But they found the *Titanic,* and maybe one day they'll find him and the others. Wherever they are, they're together."

The Bermuda Triangle.

Mystery and Myth

In September 1950 Associated Press reporter E. V. W. Jones sent a story out over the wires. In it he wrote that the same triangular area connecting Florida, Bermuda, and Puerto Rico in which Flight 19 disappeared was a "limbo of the lost" where planes and ships often "vanished in the thin air." Especially baffling, he noted, was the disappearance of Flight 19 and the Martin Mariner that had gone in search of it. An October 1952 article in *Fate,* a popular magazine devoted to "true mysteries," was largely based on the Associated Press piece; it discussed the case of Flight 19, as well as other disappearances.

In the 1955 book *The Flying Saucer Conspiracy*, Donald E. Keyhoe, a retired marine corps major and believer in extraterrestrial visitors, suggested that a "giant mother ship" from space had snatched the planes of Flight 19. Like many other writers who would follow, Keyhoe claimed that the sea had been calm that day. More influential, however, was an *American Legion* magazine article written by Allan W. Eckert. He concocted dialogue that other Triangle writers would reprint again and again. According to Eckert, Taylor had radioed Fort Lauderdale that "everything is wrong ... strange ... the ocean doesn't look as it should."

A later writer, Art Ford, reported that he had interviewed a radio operator who had heard Taylor say, "They look like they're from outer space—don't come after me." Nothing in the records of Taylor's conversations during the flight supported that claim.

In a February 1964 *Argosy* piece, and the next year in the book *Invisible Horizons,* Vincent Gaddis called Flight 19's case the "most incredible mystery in the history of aviation." Other authors would report equally fantastic and misleading versions of the episode. Rejecting all possible ordinary explanations for the tragedy, they seized on aliens, the fourth dimension, space-time travel, and mysterious magnetic forces.

Others Vanish in the Triangle

In February 1963 the *Sulphur Queen*, a tanker carrying 15,260 tons of molten sulphur, mysteriously disappeared as it neared the Straits of Florida. After an extensive air and sea search, no bodies, lifeboats, or

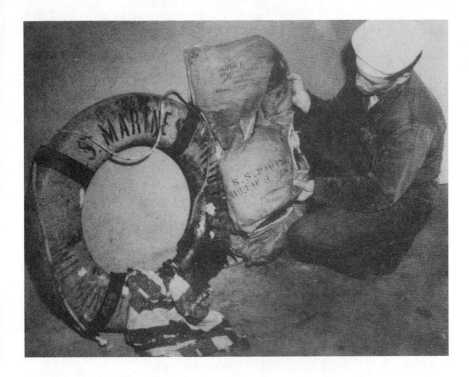

A life preserver and life jacket stenciled with the words S.S. *Sulphur Queen* were discovered after the disappearance of the tanker.

oil slicks were found. Many people believed that the ship was forever lost in the Bermuda Triangle.

Eventually, however, some wreckage did surface, including a piece of an oar, a name board with the letters "ARINE SULPH," and a life preserver and life jacket that bore the ship's name. Investigators speculated that the ship (which was structurally weak) could have encountered bad weather and either blown up due to its flammable cargo or simply sank into the deep water.

Still another Triangle mystery occurred in December 1967, when a 23-foot cabin cruiser called *Witchcraft* disappeared with its two-man crew just off Miami Beach. The men reported a damaged propeller to the Coast Guard and asked to be towed back to port. They also reported that the boat's hull was intact and that the built-in flotation chambers rendered the craft virtually unsinkable. Yet when the Coast Guard reached the location—after only nineteen minutes had passed—there was no trace of the boat, the men, or their life preservers.

Bermuda Triangle Writings Abound

In his 1955 book *The Case for the UFO,* M. K. Jessup suggested that aliens were responsible for the Bermuda Triangle disappearances, a view shared by authors Donald E. Keyhoe (*The Flying Saucer Conspiracy,* 1955) and Frank Edwards (*Stranger Than Science,* 1959). In "The Deadly Bermuda Triangle," an *Argosy* article published in February 1964, Vincent H. Gaddis introduced the catch-all phrase "Bermuda Triangle," which was forever associated with the phenomenon. Soon nearly every book on "true mysteries" discussed the Bermuda Triangle or, as some called it, the "devil's triangle" or "hoodoo sea." Ivan T. Sanderson, author of *Invisible Residents* (1970), felt that an intelligent, technologically advanced underwater civilization was behind the Triangle disappearances, as well as other mysterious occurrences like UFOs.

The first book devoted solely to the Triangle, John Wallace Spencer's 1969 *Limbo of the Lost,* enjoyed a huge readership when it was published as a paperback in 1973. In 1970 a feature-film documentary, *The Devil's Triangle,* brought the subject to a new, larger audience. Public interest peaked in 1974 with the publication of *The Bermuda Triangle,* written by Charles Berlitz with J. Manson Valentine; it sold five million copies worldwide. That same year two paperbacks, Richard Winer's *The Devil's Triangle* and John Wallace Spencer's *No Earthly Explanation,* also sold extremely well.

But readers began to notice that Triangle authors seemed to be rewriting each other's work, their articles and books indicating little evidence of original research. In 1975 Larry Kusche, a librarian at Arizona State University, published *The Bermuda Triangle Mystery—Solved,* a book based on detailed information other authors had failed to unearth. Weather records, reports of official investigative agencies, newspaper accounts, and other documents showed that Triangle writers had played fast and loose with the evidence. For example, calm seas in their writings turned out to be raging storms in reality; mysterious disappearances were sinkings and crashes with ordinary causes; the remains of ships "never heard from again" had really been found long before.

In an April 4, 1975, letter to *Fate* magazine editor Mary Margaret Fuller, a spokesman for Lloyd's of London, an international insurance corporation known for its underwriting of shipping, wrote: "According to Lloyd's Records, 428 vessels have been reported missing throughout the world since 1955, and it may interest you to know that our intelligence service can find no evidence to support the claim that the 'Bermuda Triangle' has more losses than elsewhere. This finding is upheld by the United States Coastguard [sic] whose computer-based records of casualties in the Atlantic go back to 1958."

Triangle believers could not defend their position in light of these findings. The Bermuda Triangle had turned out to be—in Kusche's words—a "manufactured mystery." While articles on the subject still appear in sensational publications from time to time, it is viewed by most as a fad that once had a stronghold in the collective imagination.

Sources:

Berlitz, Charles, with J. Manson Valentine, *The Bermuda Triangle,* Garden City, New York: Doubleday and Company, 1974.

Berlitz, Charles, with J. Manson Valentine, *Without a Trace,* Garden City, New York: Doubleday and Company, 1977.

Cazeau, Charles J., and Stuart D. Scott, Jr., *Exploring the Unknown: Great Mysteries Reexamined,* New York: Plenum Press, 1979.

Clary, Mike, "Mystery of 'Lost Patrol' May Be Solved," *Los Angeles Times,* May 18, 1991.

Gaddis, Vincent, *Invisible Horizons: True Mysteries of the Sea,* Philadelphia, Pennsylvania: Chilton Books, 1965.

Kusche, Larry, *The Disappearance of Flight 19,* New York: Harper and Row, 1980.

Kusche, Lawrence David, *The Bermuda Triangle Mystery—Solved,* New York: Harper and Row, 1975.

Winer, Richard, *The Devil's Triangle,* New York: Bantam Books, 1974.

DEVIL'S SEA

During the **Bermuda Triangle** fad of the 1970s, several writers maintained the existence of another mysterious area of lost ships and planes, this one off the eastern or southeastern coast of Japan. Called the "devil's sea," it was a place where disappearances were so sudden that affected craft usually had no time to send out distress signals before vanishing.

As with the Bermuda Triangle, it was theorized that unknown space-time, magnetic, or gravitational forces (or kidnappers from outer space) were behind the disappearances. It was also claimed that the Japanese government was extremely alarmed by the phenomenon.

The devil's sea was called a "true mystery" in articles and books on such subject matter until Larry Kusche, an Arizona State University librarian whose detailed research debunked the Bermuda Triangle, took a closer look at it. Kusche traced the origins of the devil's sea legend to *New York Times* stories published on September 27 and 30, 1952. They told of an unusual ocean disaster, the sinking of two Japanese ships by a tidal wave stemming from an underwater volcano. A January

15, 1955, *Times* report of another ship disaster in the area used the term "devil's sea" and called it the "mystery graveyard of nine ships in the last five years."

In the early 1970s Kusche corresponded at length with officials from Japan and nearby islands. None had ever heard of the "devil's sea," and all insisted that sinkings in the area were not mysterious or inexplicable. Indeed, the absence of radio messages in some cases from the early 1950s was easily explained: poor owners of smaller fishing vessels could not afford radios.

Writing about the devil's sea in 1975, Kusche concluded, "The story is based on nothing more than the loss of a few fishing boats 20 years ago in a 750-mile stretch of ocean over a period of five years. The tale has been reported so many times that it has come to be accepted as fact."

Sources:

Kusche, Larry, *The Bermuda Triangle Mystery—Solved,* Buffalo, New York: Prometheus Books, 1986.

Nichols, Elizabeth, *The Devil's Sea,* New York: Award Books, 1975.

Sanderson, Ivan T., *Invisible Residents: A Disquisition upon Certain Matters Maritime, and the Possibility of Intelligent Life Under the Waters of This Earth,* New York: World Publishing Company, 1970.

> Called the "devil's sea," it was a place where disappearances were so sudden that affected craft usually had no time to send out distress signals before vanishing.

VILE VORTICES

Ivan T. Sanderson was a zoologist who made a career of studying all kinds of strange physical events. Sanderson believed that an intelligent civilization lived in the oceans of the earth. He suspected that its members, whom he called "Other Intelligences" or OINTS, came from "elsewhere" and had settled in the ocean to avoid detection. At least some UFOs (also see entry: **Unidentified Flying Objects**), Sanderson felt, were this civilization's aircraft, which doubled as submarines.

Noting that planes and ships seemed to be disappearing mysteriously, Sanderson suggested that these ocean OINTS might be responsible. According to Sanderson, the **Bermuda Triangle** was one of ten diamond-shaped areas stretching in parallel bands above and below the equator in which the OINTS operated. Sanderson used the term "vile vortices" for these areas. (A vortex is a body of water or other fluid that runs in a whirling, circular motion, like a whirlpool, forming a vacuum that draws all things to its center.) The two polar regions were also included in Sanderson's list of vile vortices.

Sanderson pointed out that, aside from mysterious plane, ship, and submarine disappearances, an unusual number of UFO sightings had been reported in these areas. So had strange weather occurrences—like sudden high winds, storms, and rough water. He suspected that OINTS were forced to take dramatic action at times to keep their presence a secret. This might even require seizing a "whole ship and everything in and on it."

Sanderson's evidence of the existence of vile vortices was feeble at best; in some cases it hinged on shadowy rumors of unexplained events in the areas in question. Even in the case of the most famous and best-studied "vortice" (vortex)—the Bermuda Triangle—detailed research by Larry Kusche and others exposed the disappearances as a "manufactured mystery." Weather records, official investigations, newspaper accounts, and other documents revealed that ordinary causes were behind the sinkings and crashes that occurred there.

Sanderson believed that an intelligent civilization lived in the oceans of the earth.

Sources:

Kusche, Larry, *The Bermuda Triangle Mystery—Solved,* Buffalo, New York: Prometheus Books, 1986.

Sanderson, Ivan T., *A Disquisition upon Certain Matters Maritime, and the Possibility of Intelligent Life Under the Waters of the Earth,* New York: World Publishing Company, 1970.

Sanderson, Ivan T., *More "Things,"* New York: Pyramid Books, 1969.

Light Shows

- **GHOST LIGHTS**
- **GREEN FIREBALLS**
- **BROWN MOUNTAIN LIGHTS**
- **MARFA LIGHTS**

Light Shows

GHOST LIGHTS

Ghost lights are usually luminous, glowing points or spheres of light the appearance, behavior, or location of which puts them in a different category from **ball lightning** or **unidentified flying objects.** Ghost lights have often been considered supernatural, with their appearances signaling coming death or earthly visits from those who have already departed. Where ghost lights have appeared regularly in one place over a period of time—as with the famous **Brown Mountain lights** or the **Marfa lights**—legends have sprung up around them.

Lights in Folk Tradition

Over three hundred years ago, in the book *The English Empire in America* (1685), Nathaniel Crouch reported how he once witnessed the mysterious flame of which the Indians spoke, which would appear at night before the wigwams of those who were soon to die.

Three decades earlier, in 1656, John Davis, the vicar of Geneu'r Glyn, Cardiganshire, Wales, had also reported how he and others had observed colored lights that seemed to predict death. The lights could appear anywhere: in the open air, on their way through a door, or inside a house. A small light signaled the death of a child, a bigger light that of an adult. Several lights together meant as many deaths. A relative, Davis related, had once seen five lights in a room, and that very night five servants suffocated to death in a freak accident there.

In 1897 R. C. Maclagan published a long survey of ghost-light traditions, stories, and reports from Scotland's West Highlands.

Many of them told how lights appeared on the rocky shores there, predicting exactly where shipwrecks and boating accidents—and the resulting drownings—would occur. Accounts of these "corpse candles," as the lights were sometimes called, continued into the twentieth century.

One Welsh witness offered folk scholar W. Y. Evans-Wentz these observations:

> The death-candle appears like a patch of bright light; and no matter how dark the room or place is, everything in it is as clear as day. The candle is not a flame, but a luminous mass, lightish blue in color, which dances as though borne by an invisible agency [agent], and sometimes it rolls over and over. If you go up to the light, it is nothing, for it is a spirit.

What was believed to be a "corpse candle" was sighted in the mountains of Stockton, Pennsylvania, in February 1909. It caused great excitement among local residents and was the subject of several newspapers accounts. One described the "appearance at night of an arrow of flame, which hovers over the spot on the mountain where the dismembered body of a woman was found in a barrel two years ago.... The light appears every night at about 9 o'clock and hovers over the spot until midnight, but it disappears when anyone approaches the spot to investigate." The account added that some superstitious villagers believed that the light was the spirit of the slain woman, trying to keep the memory of the crime alive so that her murderers would someday be caught.

Lights have also been associated in folk tradition with appearances of **fairies.** A young Irishman who attended Oxford University with Evans-Wentz told the folk scholar about his strange experience in the winter of 1910. He and a companion were on their way home from Limerick on horseback when they noted a light in the distance "moving up and down, to and fro, diminishing to a spark, then expanding into a yellow luminous flame." Later the travelers noticed two lights similar to the first they had seen, these expanding into flames "about six feet high by four feet broad. In the midst of each flame we saw a radiant being having human form." The lights moved toward one another and when they made contact the two men could see the beings walking side by side, their bodies "formed of a pure dazzling radiance, white like the radiance of the sun, and much brighter than the yellow light or aura surrounding them." So dazzling were the haloes that surrounded the beings' heads, in fact, that the observers were unable to make out their faces.

Religious Lights

In early December 1904, a 38-year-old Welsh housewife and folk preacher, Mary Jones of Egryn, Merionethshire, reported seeing a vision of Jesus. Jones quickly became the leading figure in a Christian revival that, in the weeks and months ahead, attracted international attention. While the evangelist's message about Christian ideals was not unusual, the strange lights that were often seen when she preached were! Odder still, the lights were visible to some people—including many doubting journalists—but not to others.

A *London Daily Mirror* reporter related a sighting he witnessed while in the company of the newspaper's photographer; they were stationed in Egryn one evening, hoping to see the lights. After a three-and-a-half-hour wait, a light resembling an "unusually brilliant carriage lamp" appeared not far from the chapel where Jones led her ministry. As the reporter walked nearer, "it took the form of a bar of light quite four feet wide," he wrote, and "a kind of quivering radiance flashed with lightning speed from one end of the bar to the other" before it disappeared. While two women near the reporter also marveled over the light, he was astonished to find that a nearby group of some 15 or 20 people had seen nothing at all!

Beriah G. Evans of the *Barmouth Advertiser* also wrote of his strange experience with the lights. While walking with the preacher Jones and three others early in the evening of January 31, 1905, he saw "three brilliant rays of light strike across the road from mountain to sea.... There was not a living soul there, nor house, from which it could have come." Half a mile later, a "blood-red light" appeared immediately before them, a foot above the ground, in the middle of a village street. Only the reporter and Jones witnessed these phenomena. Evans wrote of another London journalist who experienced a similar event soon afterward: the man and his companion saw a broad band of white light on the road and walls near the chapel, but a group of a half dozen other people there detected nothing at all.

Sightings of these lights were plentiful, with many separate and multiple witnesses. Once, as Jones was holding a revival meeting in a chapel in Bryncrug, a ball of fire cast rays downward, lighting up the church. On another occasion, Jones and three companions were traveling in a carriage in broad daylight when a bright light with no visible source suddenly shined on them. The riders of two trailing carriages, including a pair of skeptical journalists, witnessed the sight, as did Barmouth residents awaiting the preacher's arrival. Some accounts of the lights included supernatural or spiritual elements.

> Odder still, the lights were visible to some people—including many doubting journalists—but not to others.

On February 23 the *Advertiser* noted that two men—one an important farmer—reported a "gigantic human form rising over a hedgerow. Then a ball of fire appeared above and a long ray of light pierced the figure, which vanished."

During all this, Jones and some of her followers were also visited by Christ and angels, through dreams or visions. And one dark night, as she walked along a country road, Jones said she met a shadowy figure who turned into a **black dog,** which charged her and was driven off only after she began to sing a hymn. She believed the attacker was Satan. While such religious experiences are highly subjective, open to all sorts of questions and explanations and thus regularly discounted, these lights, at least, have been the source of serious research for nearly a century. The appearance of the lights may or may not have been related to the religious revival led by Mary Jones, for history shows that most accounts of strange lights do not have religious connections.

Local Lights

Vincent H. Gaddis, who writes about mysterious events, felt that in hundreds, possibly even thousands, of places around the world, "strange lights haunt the earth." Unlike UFOs or ball lightning, "they are usually small in size and appear close to the ground," he described, with "their outstanding characteristic [being] that they are localized to one area or place." Legends often grow up around these frequent lights; a common one describes them as lanterns carried by ghosts who are searching for something they lost in life, including—in the scariest cases—their heads!

Few accounts of strange lights are actually investigated by scientists or serious researchers, and when they are the results are usually disappointing. Many lights, for example, turn out to be from headlights of cars on distant highways or from stars and planets the light from which has been refracted, or bent, through layers of air of different temperatures. Still, there are some cases that have scientists and trained observers baffled. Two such examples are the lights at the Yakima Indian Reservation of south-central Washington and those frequenting the Hessdalen Valley of Norway.

Yakima

The Yakima reservation is a thinly populated area 3,500 miles square and divided between rugged wilderness in the west and flat-

> Legends often grow up around these frequent lights; a common one describes them as lanterns carried by ghosts who are searching for something they lost in life, including—in the scariest cases—their heads.

lands in the east. Beginning in the late 1960s (though a few sightings had occurred before then), forest rangers, fire-control workers, and others began reporting the movement of bright white lights low in the sky. When chief fire-control officer W. J. (Bill) Vogel heard these reports, he judged them unimportant and even foolish—that is, until he experienced some strange sightings of his own!

Late one night when he was on patrol, he saw a luminous object that had a teardrop shape, with the small end pointing up. It was "brilliantly white in the center," surrounded by a fluorescent tan or light orange halo. Vogel reported that the object's "most awe-inspiring feature was a mouselike tail or antenna protruding from the small end and pointing upward. The antenna, as long as the object itself, was segmented into colors of red, blue, green, and white which were constantly changing brilliancy and hue."

Over the next 90 minutes Vogel took a series of photographs of the object, which eventually vanished over the mountains. It would be the first of many sightings he would report. Soon the fire-control chief was busy collecting and investigating reports made by others, most of them from his own highly trained and reliable fire lookouts. And many local people also had stories to tell.

Investigators came to Yakima, including astronomer and former air force UFO adviser J. Allen Hynek. He persuaded the Indian Tribal Council to allow an observer to set up equipment on the reservation to note the lights' activity. The observer, David Akers of the Aerial Phenomena Research Organization (APRO), brought with him cameras and other recording devices. On August 19, 1972, his first night on the reservation, Akers, along with Vogel, saw two round, glowing, reddish-orange lights circling, changing places, and flashing on and off. He took four photographs. Other sightings and more photographs followed until Akers left the reservation at the end of the month.

While equipment difficulties kept Akers from obtaining some of the data he was seeking, he left the reservation convinced that "something very strange and unusual is taking place." He returned over the next few days to interview witnesses and to view and photograph more strange lights. The detailed records that he and Vogel kept showed that the lights appeared at ground level, above ground level, and at high altitudes. Observer Greg Long would later join the investigation and write a book about his findings.

Some of the oddest experiences reported at Yakima by fire lookouts involved a sort of mental communication with the lights. While most sightings involved distant lights, lookouts sometimes were able to view them from several hundred yards. Still, they could not get any closer: lookouts reported "hearing" a voice inside their heads warning, "Stay back, or you'll get hurt," and feeling restrained.

One lookout saw a shaft of bright purple light shining down around her cabin. When she tried to go outside to investigate, she felt as if "two magnets [were] repelling each other" and blocking her exit. Puzzled but determined, she ran at the doorway several times but could not get through. Weirder still, some observers of the lights reported feeling as if they were seeing something that they were not meant to see and removed themselves altogether from the objects they had originally set out to investigate.

It should also be noted that a handful of the Yakima reports included sightings of spacecraft and alien beings. So, while the lights there seemed to behave like true ghost lights, they may, in fact, have had some connection to UFOs. In any case, the number of sightings at the Yakima Indian Reservation fell off to a large degree after 1986.

Hessdalen

The Hessdalen lights also subsided in 1986, but for a period of several years they were the target of an all-out investigation by ufologists, scientists, and local residents. The Hessdalen Valley, stretching across 12 kilometers (about 7 1/2 miles) of central Norway near the Swedish border and having no more than 150 inhabitants, began to experience odd light shows in November 1981.

The lights sometimes appeared as often as four times a day, often along mountain-tops, near the ground, or on the roofs of houses. Usually white or yellow-white, they typically were shaped like cigars, spheres, or an "upside-down Christmas tree."

In one case of an upside down Christmas tree shape, the light, according to miner Bjarne Lillevold, was "bigger than the cottage beside it. It was about four meters above the hill and had a red blinking light on it.... The object moved up and down like a yo-yo for about 20 minutes. When it was close to the ground, the light faded, but at the height of the maneuver it was so bright that I could not look at it for long. When the light was near the ground, I could see through it as though it was made of glass."

Project Hessdalen

Once in a while, according to other witnesses, a red light held a position in front. The lights hovered, sometimes for an hour, then shot off at extraordinary speed. Most of the time they traveled from north to south. Investigators from UFO-Norway brought valley residents together to discuss their sightings on March 26, 1982. Of the 130 who attended, 35 said they had seen the lights.

In the summer of 1983 Scandinavian ufologists established Project Hessdalen, an investigative force that included scientists from the Universities of Oslo and Bergen. A variety of equipment was set up on three mountains. The month-long winter watch, from January 21 to February 26, 1984, produced some sightings, radar trackings, and photographs that proved interesting but settled nothing. Most exciting, perhaps, was the fact that the lights seemed to respond when laser beams were aimed at them. Once, on February 12, for example, the lights changed their single flashes to a double-flash pattern—in a way that seemed almost knowing—whenever investigators used the laser.

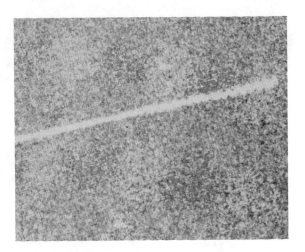

This 10-second time exposure was taken by Roar Wister on the evening of February 21, 1984, in Norway's Hessdalen Valley.

Ultimately, investigators disagreed on what the lights could be, with some convinced they were a reflection of some—as yet unknown—geophysical event (occurring beneath the earth's surface), others feeling that they showed a guiding intelligence. The strange "coincidences" that took place throughout the investigation also seemed to point to an intelligence behind the lights.

Investigator Leif Havik wrote: "On four separate occasions, it happened that we came to the top of Varuskjolen, stopped the car, went outside, and there 'it' came immediately and passed by us. The same thing happened once on Aspaskjolen. All these instances happened at different times of the day and most of the time it was an impulse which made us take video equipment which recorded the radar screen. One evening the pen of the magnetograph failed to work. At the same time the video tape had come to an end, and the phenomenon appeared less than one minute later. The next evening we made certain that the pen had sufficient ink and turned on the video recorder ten minutes later than the night before. We thought then ... everything was ready for the usual 10:47 'message.' [One light appeared regularly at 10:47 P.M.] The video tape ran out at 10:57 P.M. and we thought that tonight 'it' had failed us. But at 10:58 the usual phenomenon appeared."

Nonetheless, in terms of reliable scientific data, Project Hessdalen was a disappointment. Investigators logged 188 sightings. Some of

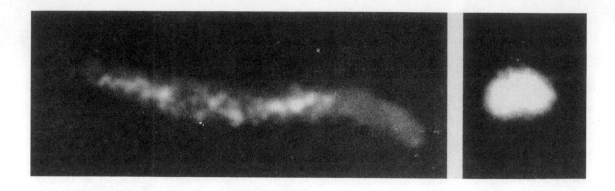

These two Hessdalen photographs were snapped just a few seconds apart, showing the light's abrupt change in shape.

these were passing aircraft, and most photographs proved too unclear to study. Looking back on the investigation, University of Oslo physicist Elvand Thrane, a member of the project, remarked, "I'm sure that the lights were real. It's a pity we cannot explain them."

Explaining Ghost Lights

Unexplained lights in the sky are probably caused by a number of things, from the ridiculously common to the truly mysterious. Two interesting ideas, Paul Devereux's "earthlights" and Michael Persinger's "tectonic stress theory," suggest that sightings of strange lights are caused by geophysical activity. While rejected by most scientists, both theories hold that ghost lights are produced by subterranean (underground) processes that not only create luminous energy on the earth's surface, but may cause hallucinations in its observers as well!

Sources:

Devereux, Paul, *Earth Lights Revelation: UFOs and Mystery Lightform Phenomena: The Earth's Secret Energy Force,* London: Blandford, 1989.

Gaddis, Vincent H., *Mysterious Fires and Lights,* New York: David McKay Company, 1967.

Long, Greg, *Examining the Earthlight Theory: The Yakima UFO Microcosm,* Chicago: J. Allen Hynek Center for UFO Studies, 1990.

McClenon, James, *Deviant Science: The Case of Parapsychology,* Philadelphia: University of Pennsylvania Press, 1984.

GREEN FIREBALLS

For a three-year period, between late 1948 and 1951, a flurry of sightings of "green fireballs" occurred in the southwestern United States. At one point military and other government agencies feared that enemy agents were somehow connected with the fireballs, which were spotted near some of America's most secret national-security bases.

Early Sightings

The first sightings to attract official attention took place on the evening of December 5, 1948, when two pilots flying over New Mexico reported two separate observations, 22 minutes apart, of a pale green light that was visible for no more than a few seconds. The witnesses insisted that it was not a meteor that they had seen, but some kind of strange flare. The next day a similar "greenish flare" was spotted for three seconds over the supersecret nuclear installation Sandia Base, part of the Kirtland Air Force Base complex in New Mexico.

Also on December 6, the Seventh District Air Force Office of Special Investigations (AFOSI) at Kirtland launched a study. And two pilot investigators observed one of the strange objects about 2,000 feet above their aircraft the following evening. They noted that it seemed to move parallel to the earth's surface and that it resembled the flares commonly used by the air force. "However, the light was much more intense and the object appeared to be considerably larger than a normal flare," they reported. "[It] was definitely larger and more brilliant than a shooting star, meteor, or flare." After only a couple of seconds, "the object seemed to burn out [and] ... a trail of glowing fragments reddish orange in color was observed falling toward the ground."

The next day one of the officers contacted Lincoln La Paz, director of the University of New Mexico's Institute of Meteoritics (meteor studies) and an air force consultant on top-secret matters. La Paz acknowledged that the green flares were different from any meteors he had ever heard of. Not long afterward, the scientist saw one of the lights himself. From his own observations and those of two other witnesses, from the Atomic Energy Security Service or AESS, La Paz decided that the object had flown too slowly and too silently to be a meteor. In a letter to the investigation's commanding officer, he noted that "none of the green fireballs has a train of sparks or a dust cloud.... This contrasts sharply with the behavior noted in cases of meteoritic fireballs—particularly those that penetrate to the very low levels where the green fireball of December 12 was observed."

After only a couple of seconds, "the object seemed to burn out [and] ... a trail of glowing fragments reddish orange in color was observed falling toward the ground."

At La Paz's suggestion, the AESS organized patrols to try to photograph the fireballs. And scientists and engineers at New Mexico's Los Alamos Scientific Laboratory set up a group to study sighting reports. As the number of accounts continued to grow, the army and the air force became more and more concerned; they were especially disturbed when La Paz concluded, by early 1949, that the fireballs were not a natural occurrence, but had been put there by somebody or something.

METEOR

A meteor is one of the small pieces of matter in the solar system that can be seen only when it falls into the earth's atmosphere, where friction may cause it to burn or glow. When this happens it is sometimes called a "falling" or "shooting" star.

Military Scare?

On February 16 a Conference on Aerial Phenomena brought military officers and scientists to Los Alamos, where they were assured that the fireballs were not the result of any secret U.S. military operation. La Paz was eager to ask if any of the conference members knew of meteors that acted like the green fireballs—moving in long horizontal paths at a steady speed, eight to ten miles off the ground.

In late April Pentagon and air force officials sent physicist Joseph Kaplan to Kirtland. He, La Paz, and others discussed establishing a network of instruments and observers at several locations in New Mexico. Meanwhile, since early March, tiny white lights or "flares" had been spotted regularly near Killeen Base, a nuclear-weapons storage site inside Camp Hood in central Texas. This caused great alarm. Colonel Reid Lumsden, commander of AFOSI at Kelly Air Force Base in San Antonio, Texas, stated that the "unknown phenomena in the Camp Hood area could not be attributed to natural causes."

Still, despite the testimony of local experts and witnesses, officials in Washington decided that the fireballs and lights were natural occurrences, even if they did have features that—in Kaplan's words—were "difficult to explain." The sightings continued.

In the summer of 1949, samples of the New Mexico atmosphere were examined; they revealed an unusually large and unexplained amount of copper particles, suggesting a connection with the fireball sightings. La Paz viewed this as further evidence that the fireballs were not meteors: "I know of no case in which even the tiniest particle of copper has been reported in a dust collection supposedly of meteoritic origin," he maintained.

Project Twinkle

After meeting with high-ranking air force officials, Kaplan urged that a photographic and spectrographic patrol be set up to collect data on the fireballs and the lights. (A spectrograph is an instrument that photographs and measures the display of light or other radiation of an object or substance by breaking it into a spectrum.) Thus Project Twinkle began, which consisted of two observers stationed at an operations post at Holloman AFB in New Mexico. La Paz thought the matter deserved a far more "intensive, systematic investigation" than this basic program and was very disappointed.

Despite some interesting sightings, Project Twinkle shut down in December 1951 because of problems with funding, instruments, workers, and officials. Many felt that the failure of the project was the loss of an opportunity to collect solid information on at least one kind of unidentified flying object. Many of the scientists who were involved in the investigation remained convinced that the fireballs were not natural, but artificially created. When Captain Edward J. Ruppelt, head of the air force's UFO investigation unit, discussed the subject with Los

The spectacular "green fireballs" observed in the southwestern United States in the 1940s and 1950s remain great puzzles to UFO buffs.

Alamos scientists in 1953, for example, they told him that they believed the objects were fired from extraterrestrial spacecraft.

Sources:

Clark, Jerome, *The Emergence of a Phenomenon: UFOs from the Beginning through 1959—The UFO Encyclopedia,* Volume 2, Detroit: Omnigraphics, 1992.
Ruppelt, Edward J., *The Report on Unidentified Flying Objects,* Garden City, New York: Doubleday and Company, 1956.

BROWN MOUNTAIN LIGHTS

Brown Mountain (altitude 2,600 feet) is located in the Blue Ridge Mountains of western North Carolina near Morganton. Many stories, and even songs—including Scotty Wiseman's popular bluegrass tune "The Brown Mountain Light"—have sprung up around the mysterious lights that have long appeared there.

Sightings

Writing in a 1925 issue of *Literary Digest,* Robert Sparks Walker reported that sightings of the lights varied greatly. One person described the light he observed as "pale white ... with a faint, irregular halo." This witness said that the light moved in a circle several times, disappeared, then returned and continued its circular motion. Another observer saw "a steady glowing ball of light" that was yellow in color. "Like a star from a bursting skyrocket," the witness reported, it lasted for about half a minute, then quickly disappeared. "To some people it appears stationary; to others, it moves sometimes upward, downward, or horizontally," Walker noted. "A minister says that it appeared like a ball of incandescent light in which he could observe a seething motion."

The first printed account of the lights appeared in the *Charlotte Daily Observer* on September 13, 1913. A group of fishermen had reported seeing a "very red" mystery light "just above the horizon almost every night." Not long afterwards, D. B. Sterrett of the U.S. Geological Survey investigated and concluded that train headlights were the cause. But members of a 1916 expedition to the area swore that they had seen the lights act in a very "unheadlightlike" way: floating in and out of gullies and ravines, for example.

Members of a 1916 expedition to the area swore that they had seen the lights act in a very "unheadlight-like" way: floating in and out of gullies and ravines, for example.

Fireflies?

More sightings—and arguments about their source—brought
another Geological Survey scientist, George Rogers Mansfield, to the
area in March and April 1922. He examined the mountains, interviewed
local residents, and observed the lights for seven nights. He concluded
that 44 percent of the light sightings were related to automobiles, 33
percent to trains, 10 percent to other, stationary lights, and 10 percent
to brushfires—leaving just 3 percent of the accounts unexplained. He
also thought that the 1916 report might have involved fireflies.

In the years since then, witnesses have reported more mystery
lights, which have resembled "toy balloons," "misty spheres," "flood-

lights," and "sky rockets." A few times, when observers have gotten close to the lights, they have reported hearing a sizzling noise. A 1977 experiment beamed a powerful arc of light from a town 22 miles away to a location west of the mountain where observers waited. According to them, the blue-white beam looked like an "orange-red orb apparently hovering several degrees above Brown Mountain's crest."

This pretty much convinced investigators that the sightings were caused by the refraction (bending through layers of air) of distant lights. Still, the folklore of the Blue Ridge Mountains is rich with stories of people who witnessed the lights long before the age of trains and cars and electric lights!

Sources:

Devereux, Paul, *Earth Lights Revelation: UFOs and Mystery Lightform Phenomena: The Earth's Secret Energy Force,* London: Blandford Press, 1989.

Walker, Robert Sparks, "The Queer Lights of Brown Mountain," *Literary Digest,* November 7, 1925, pp. 48-49.

MARFA LIGHTS

They observed three lights this time; one seemed to be aware of their presence, almost daring them to chase it!

Marfa, a ranching town of about 2,400 people at the west end of southern Texas, seems like an ordinary place except for one thing: it is the regular site of ghost lights. While they do not show up every night, they do appear often and are visible to anyone who looks southwest toward the Chinati Mountains 50 miles away.

Sometimes the lights, which resemble train or automobile headlights, do little more then flicker. Sometimes they jump across the desert floor or split into new lights. At other times they rise lazily into the air. Many photographs have been taken of these remarkable lights.

Geologists Pat Kenney and Elwood Wright reported two extraordinary sightings of the lights on March 19 and 20, 1973. They had been working in the area and, when hearing about the lights, went to view them at a popular site to the east of Marfa, near the town of Alpine. The first night they saw lights rocking and looping as if "playing," they thought. The next night they drove without headlights in the same direction of the lights, hoping to sneak up on them. They observed three lights this time; one seemed to be aware of their presence, almost daring them to chase it! It moved low to the ground, darting

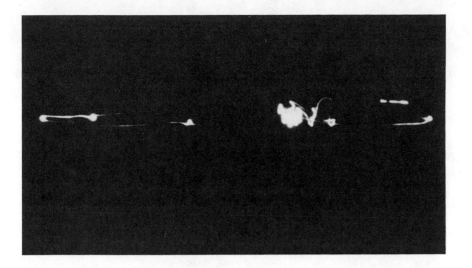

around bushes, or hovered in the middle of the road, coming to within 200 feet of them. It resembled an ordinary household light bulb but was larger, about half the size of a basketball. After a short time the light moved to the east to join the others, and they all disappeared.

Some have explained Marfa's lights as reflections of stars and planets bent through layers of air of different temperatures or of headlights from cars passing along nearby Highway 67. While these explanations may account for some sightings, reports like the one above seem to challenge any reasoning. And there is no doubt that the Marfa lights have been around for quite a while: folklorists have collected stories that go back to the early white settlers and to the Apaches before them.

Sources:

Devereux, Paul, *Earth Lights Revelation: UFOs and Mystery Lightform Phenomena: The Earth's Secret Energy Force*, London: Blandford Press, 1989.

Stacy, Dennis, *The Marfa Lights: A Viewer's Guide*, San Antonio, Texas: Seale and Stacy, 1989.

Strange Showers: Everything but Cats and Dogs

- **FALLS FROM THE SKY**
- **STRANGE RAIN**
- **ICE FALLS**
- **STAR JELLY**

Strange Showers: Everything but Cats and Dogs

FALLS FROM THE SKY

For as long as human beings have been keeping records, things—both inorganic (composed of matter other than plant or animal) and organic (coming from living plant or animal matter)—have been falling out of the sky. While such falls usually take place in the middle of fierce storms, some do occur out of a clear sky.

Theories

For many centuries those who doubted that matter could fall from the sky believed the reports were mistakes, made by witnesses who failed to understand the natural process of *spontaneous generation*. Once widely believed, the concept of spontaneous generation held that living things could spring from nonliving material; thus, when rain hit the ground it could give rise—out of the mud, slime, and dust—to all sorts of living matter. This view eventually gave way to more realistic notions concerning the appearance of animals, vegetation, man-made objects, and other nonliving materials; doubters believed that these things were on the ground all along, unseen until rain drove or washed them into view.

Still, even more sophisticated theories failed to explain the many reliable accounts (some by scientists) of things falling from the sky. Thus other explanations arose, one suggesting that waterspouts (funnel- or tube-shaped columns of rotating, cloud-filled wind, usually with spray torn up from the surface of an ocean or lake), tornados, and whirlwinds (small rotating windstorms) pick up materials and drop

Waterspouts, from *L'Atmosphère* by Camille Flammarion, Paris, 1888.

them off somewhere else. While it is true that strong winds do rip objects from the ground and leave them elsewhere, this does not explain the odd *selectivity* seen in strange falls from the sky. Violent storms drop everything they pick up, but most falls drop only *one* thing or *one type* of thing. Often, too, the amount of material that descends is so great that its disappearance from another place would surely be noticed! Some falls go on for hours, with the given material falling in a steady stream over a very large area. While most falls of matter from the sky consist of dust or ash and can be easily explained, the cases that follow have scientists baffled.

Fire in the Sky

On October 18, 1867, residents of Thames Ditton, Surrey, England, were startled by a "shower of fire" in the evening sky. The light it cast was "brilliant" for the ten minutes that it burned. As reported in *Symons's Monthly Meteorological Magazine,* villagers found an explanation the next morning when "the waterbutts and puddles in the upper part of the village were thickly covered with a deposit of sulphur."

The fall of "a combustible substance of a yellowish color" also thought to be sulphur or a sulphur compound was reported in the village of Kourianof, Russia, some years earlier, in 1832. According to the *American Journal of Science,* villagers there first mistook the cottony material, which covered nearly seven hundred square feet of fields in a two-inch layer, for odd-colored snow. Samples, however, were quick to burst into flame and gave off a strange smell. This convinced witnesses that here was no ordinary snowfall! Because sulphur deposits are very rarely found on the earth's surface, scientists are doubtful that winds could pick up much and leave it somewhere else. Still, they can think of no other explanation for these strange fires from the sky.

Stones

In a March 1912 issue of the well-respected British scientific journal *Nature,* reporter G. E. Bullen described a strange happening that took place at Colney Heath, near St. Albans, Hertfordshire, England. During the stormy afternoon of March 4, witness H. L. G. Andrews watched a large stone hit the ground near him with such impact that it sunk down three feet, and a huge clap of thunder filled the air. The irregularly shaped rock weighed nearly six pounds and measured about 7 x 6 inches, and its surface was deeply pitted. Magnification showed that the rock was crystal and studded with rounded granules of nickel-containing iron. When Dr. George T. Prior of the British Museum of Natural History studied the stone, he concluded that it was "not of meteoritic origin."

There are many more accounts of nonmeteoritic (not from meteorites) rocks and stones falling from the sky. Huge numbers of small black stones, for example, fell on Birmingham, England, in August 1858 and again at Wolverhampton, England, in June 1860. Both incidents took place during violent storms.

In late 1921 and early 1922, stones and rocks fell repeatedly on buildings and people in Chico, California. Events there began in November, when J. W. Charge, the owner of a grain warehouse along the Southern Pacific railroad tracks in Chico, complained to city marshal J. A. Peck that an unseen person was throwing rocks at his building daily. At first thinking the rock-throwing was a harmless prank, the marshal finally took action on March 8, when stones and rocks ranging in size from peas to baseballs battered the warehouse all day. He and his men searched the surrounding area but failed to locate a guilty party.

Whether somehow related to the falling stones or not, more than four decades earlier *fish* had fallen out of a clear sky in great numbers and landed on a roof and surrounding streets there!

Other rock falls have been recorded around the country. In 1943 Oakland, California, was the site of a stone-fall case very much like the one that took place in Chico. And showers of stones, described as warm to the touch, rained down on the pavement outside the office of the *Charleston News and Courier,* a South Carolina newspaper, at three separate times—2:30 and 7:30 A.M. and 1:30 P.M.—on September 4, 1886. According to witnesses, the stones fell straight down from the sky and only in a 75-square-foot area. Another stone-falling incident, which took place in a housing development outside Tucson, Arizona, lasted for four months, between September and December 1983. It was the subject of careful study by both police and D. Scott Rogo, an expert in the supernatural.

Pennies from Heaven

On the morning of May 28, 1982, a young girl walking through the yard of St. Elisabeth's Church in Redding, a small town near Manchester, England, saw a 50-pence coin fall "from nowhere." As the day went on other children found a number of coins at the same spot. Finally, the owner of a local candy store became concerned that the children were stealing from the church's poor box and told the Reverend Graham Marshall about the sudden rush to buy sweets. No money was missing, and the children all swore—when questioned by the clergyman—that the coins seemed to come out of the sky; they would hear a tinkling sound on the sidewalk and, looking down, find a coin.

Money has also fallen from the sky in other locations. One December day in 1968, shoppers in the English town of Ramsgate, Kent, heard pennies bouncing off the pavement. "Between 40 and 50 of them came down in short scattered bursts for about 15 minutes," one witness, Jean Clements, told the *London Daily Mirror.* "You could not see them falling—all you heard was the sound of them hitting the ground." The coins hit the ground hard enough to be dented. There were "no tall buildings nearby," Clements added, "and no one heard a plane go overhead."

Other money falls were reported in Meshehera, Russia, in the summer of 1940 (during a storm); in Bristol, England, in September 1956; in Bourges, France, April 15, 1957 (the "thousands" of 1,000-franc notes that fell were never claimed); and Limburg, West Germany, in January 1976 (2,000 marks, seen falling by two clergymen).

The coins seemed to come out of the sky; they would hear a tinkling sound on the sidewalk and, looking down, find a coin.

In 1969 a wheel sailed out of the sky and onto a California woman's car, leaving a one-foot dent.

Thunderstones

Some of the most fantastic claims are those concerning falls of human-made objects. Thunderstones (shaped stones such as axe heads), for example, were once the subject of worldwide folklore. Thunderstones came down right after a spectacular roar of thunder and bolt of lightning. In the modern world thunderstones have been replaced by other objects, like coins, that have been reported to drop out of the atmosphere.

Most of these human-made objects don't fall in clusters but by themselves. On April 17, 1969, the *New York Times* reported the bizarre experience of a California woman, Ruth Stevens, who was driving in Palm Springs when a wheel sailed out of the sky and onto her car's hood, where it left a one-foot dent. No local airport received a report of a missing wheel from any pilot.

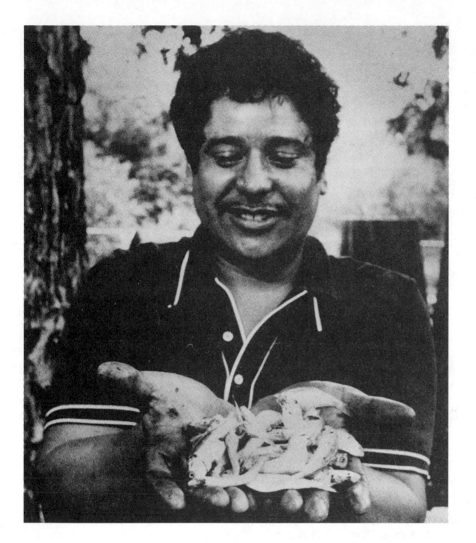

Louis Castoreno with some of the fish that fell in his yard at Fort Worth, Texas, in 1985.

Fish Stories

Late on the morning of February 9, 1859, residents of Mountain Ash, Glamorganshire, Wales, witnessed a strange event. As a heavy rain fell and a strong wind blew, a sea of fish fell out of the sky.

One observer, John Lewis, described his experience for the *Annual Register*: while getting ready to saw a piece of lumber, he "was startled by something falling all over me—down my neck, on my head, on my back. On putting my hand down my neck I was surprised to find they were little fish. By this time I saw the whole ground covered with them. I took off my hat, the brim of which was full of them. They were jumping all about." Covering a nearby shed and surrounding plants, the fish filled an area measuring "about 80 yards by 12." Witnesses gathered a bucketful of the fish, releasing them into a rain pool, where they happily swam about.

Between 7 and 8 A.M. on October 23, 1947, wildlife expert A. D. Bajkov and residents of Marksville, Louisiana, witnessed the fall of many thousands of fish, which landed—cold, and even frozen in some cases—on a strip of ground 75 feet wide and 1,000 feet long. Weather conditions were foggy but calm, which makes this case unusual, for most falls take place during storms.

While the Marksville fish were, according to biologist Bajkov, identical to those found in local waters, Science writer J. Hedgepath witnessed a brief fish fall in Guam in 1936 where one of the specimens was identified as a tench, common only to the fresh waters of Europe!

At Nokulhatty Factory, India, on February 19, 1830, a great number of fish dropped from the sky. Writing in the American Journal of Science, M. Prinsep reported: "The fish were all dead; most of them were large; some were fresh, others rotted and mutilated. They were seen at first in the sky like a flock of birds descending rapidly to the ground. There was rain drizzling at the time, but no storm." Some of the fish had no heads.

Toads

On September 23, 1973, *tens of thousands* of toads fell on Brignoles, France, during what was described as a "freak storm." They were all young toads. In September 1922 young toads fell for two days on another French village, Chalon-sur-Saone.

Especially fascinated by accounts of living material falling from the sky, investigator of odd physical events Charles Fort collected some 294 of them before his death in 1932. Many more have been reported since. The following demonstrates just *some* of the living creatures involved in falls. Still, with the exception of the turtle incident, falls of these items have occurred not once, but again and again!

Alligators

December 1877: At a Silvertown Township, South Carolina, turpentine farm—set on high, sandy ground about six miles north of the Savannah River—Dr. J. L. Smith noticed something fall and begin to crawl toward the tent in which he sat. "On examining the object he found it to be an alligator," reported the *New York Times* (December 26). "In the course of a few moments, a second one made its appearance. This so excited the curiosity of the Doctor that he looked around

On September 23, 1973, tens of thousands of toads fell on Brignoles, France, during what was described as a "freak storm."

Charles H. Fort

(1874-1932)

Charles Hoy Fort is recognized for his study of odd physical events. Until Fort's undertaking, beginning in the late nineteenth century, no one had collected and organized the numerous reports of physical anomalies.

A struggling journalist, Fort spent much of his time in libraries, where he read widely and took notes mostly on oddities of nature or sightings of objects that pointed to the presence of otherworldly intelligences. He wrote four books on anomalies: *Book of the Damned* (1919), *New Lands* (1923), *Lo!* (1931), and *Wild Talents* (1932). In all of them, Fort offered wacky "theories" to explain strange events, trying to show that his ideas were really no weirder than those scientists used to try to "explain away" happenings they did not understand.

So important were Fort's books, in fact, that the odd events he described came to be known as "Fortean phenomena." A Fortean Society, formed in 1931 in the United States to collect and record "quite extraordinary occurrences," was later replaced by the International Fortean Organization.

to see if he could discover any more, and found six others within a space of 200 yards. The animals were all quite lively, and about 12 inches in length."

Blood and flesh

July 1869: As mourners prepared for a funeral at a farm near Los Angeles, blood and meat rained out of a clear sky for three

BY CHARLES FORT

An early cover of *Lo!* magazine showing a fall of frogs.

minutes. It covered two acres of a cornfield. When examined, the blood was found to be mixed with what looked like hairs from animal fur. The flesh ranged in size from small particles to six- and eight-inch strips and included what observers believed were pieces of kidney, liver, and heart. One witness brought samples to the *Los Angeles News,* the editor of which later wrote in the August 3 issue, "That the meat fell, we cannot doubt. Even the parsons in the neighborhood are willing to vouch for that." (Also see entry: **Strange Rain**.)

Grain

March 24, 1840: During a thunderstorm, a shower of grain covered Rajket, India, and a large area of the surrounding countryside. According to the *American Journal of Science,* a British captain named Aston collected samples and sent them to England. The man related that Indian witnesses were upset not only by the frightening sight of grain falling from the sky, but by the fact that the grain was not even grown in their country—it was of a type entirely unknown to them!

Green slime

September 5 and 6, 1978: An "unexplained green slime," according to the *Journal of Meteorology,* splattered an area of Washington, D.C., injuring animals and plants and soiling automobiles. The roof of a 12-story building was coated with the substance, suggesting it had fallen from great height. Officials did not even try to explain it.

Hazelnuts

May 9, 1867: Hazelnuts "fell in great quantities and with great force" over a small area of Dublin, Ireland. They came down so hard, in fact, "that even the police, protected by unusually strong head covering, were obliged to take shelter," wrote a reporter in *Symons's Monthly Meteorological Magazine.*

Leaves

April 7 and 11, 1894: On two clear, still days, leaves fell for half an hour on two French villages, first at Clairvaux, then at Pontcarre. Though it was spring and trees were just starting to bud, the fully grown leaves were dried and dead—autumn leaves.

Lizards

December 1857: During a rain shower, lizards fell on streets and sidewalks in Montreal, Quebec.

Mussels

August 9, 1892: A rapidly moving yellow cloud suddenly released crushing rains, as well as hundreds of mussels onto the streets of Paderborn, Germany.

Salamanders

June 1911: Arlene Meyer recalled that once, when she was a girl, she was walking along the banks of the Sandy River near Boring, Oregon, when she got caught in a sudden rainstorm. Feeling large objects hit her on the head and shoulders, she looked around her and was shocked to see hundreds of salamanders "falling from the sky, literally covering the ground and wriggling and crawling all over."

Seeds

Summer 1897: Shortly before sunset a large number of small, dark-red clouds filled the sky over Macerata, Italy, and an hour later a powerful storm erupted. Immediately, "the air became filled with myriads of small seeds," R. Hedger Wallace reported in *Notes and Queries,* which "fell over town and country, covering the ground to a depth of about half an inch." The following day scientists at Macerata began looking for explanations. Prof. Cardinali, a respected Italian naturalist, identified the seeds as those of a plant commonly called the Judas Tree, found only in central Africa or the Antilles (in the West Indies, bordering the Caribbean Sea)! Even more incredible, a great number of the seeds had already begun growing!

Straw

August 1963: Straw in huge amounts began falling from clouds over Dartford, Kent, England, and continued for an hour. "I looked up," one witness said, "and the sky was full of it." The fall stopped as suddenly as it had begun. "We are mystified," a government weather expert told the Associated Press. A police officer commented on the straw, insisting, "There was far too much of it for it to have been dropped from an airplane."

Turtle

May 11, 1894: A gopher turtle, six by eight inches, fell during a hailstorm at Bovina, Mississippi.

Worms

July 25, 1872: The magazine *Nature* reported that at 9:15 on a hot evening with a clear sky, "a small cloud appeared on the horizon, and a quarter of an hour afterwards rain began to fall, when, to the horror of everybody, it was found to consist of black worms the size of an ordinary fly. All the streets were strewn with these curious animals."

More Theories

If waterspouts and whirlwinds are not responsible for the fall of plants and animals from the sky—or if specimens are not actually earthbound objects mistaken by witnesses—what other theories could explain such a relatively widespread oddity? Few have tried to supply answers to so puzzling a question, and those without much success.

Fort, for example, had his own favorite theory, which he cheerfully admitted was ridiculous and unscientific. He suggested that giant land masses floated above the earth, and tornadoes, hurricanes, and cyclones carried all sorts of items upward and dumped them on these lands. He also described a "Super-Sargasso Sea," an ocean in the atmosphere that contained castoffs from other times and even other worlds—a crazy mix of spaceship wrecks, dinosaurs and fossils, "horses and barns and elephants and flies"—just about anything one could imagine. And just as fierce earth storms could dump things onto these heavenly land masses or into its sea, they could also force the fall of all sorts of organic and inorganic matter back to earth.

Other explanations include John Philip Bessor's theory involving space animals. Because of the "many falls of flesh and blood from the sky," Bessor believed that UFOs were really meat-eating atmospheric life forms, or space animals. According to him, this idea also explained the mysterious disappearances of people! Morris K. Jessup, a UFO writer, felt that the fall of living things from the sky occurred when space beings—who collected and raised earth creatures in special hydroponic tanks in outer space—needed to empty the tanks for cleaning or to rid them of extra specimens.

Other writers have tried to make sense of falls from the sky by using the idea of teleportation—the instant movement of an object from one place to another. But as teleportation is unproven, trying to explain one mysterious occurrence with another is rarely convincing! And just like other theories, teleportation doesn't explain the baffling selectivity seen in falls or the huge amounts of things that fall in many cases.

Damon Knight, a biographer of Charles Fort, added scientific research to Fort's playful theory about falls and came up with an interesting idea of his own. He matched weather records with the reports of falls and unusual space and sky happenings in Fort's books and found strong connections: the years 1877 through 1892, for example, had both an unusually high number of odd reports and some extraordinary weather. He also studied physics and astronomy and the effect of solar system activities on everything from weather patterns to human behavior. He came to the conclusion that "under certain conditions of gravidic [gravity] and electromagnetic strain in the solar system, channels open through which material objects can reach the Earth from parts unknown, or can be transferred from one part of the Earth's surface to another." Referring to the puzzling selectivity seen in most falls, Knight added, "All living things have electric charges, and it is possible to imagine that an electromagnetic field would discriminate between them."

Sources:

Fort, Charles, *The Books of Charles Fort,* New York: Henry Holt and Company, 1941.
Knight, Damon, *Charles Fort: Prophet of the Unexplained,* Garden City, New York: Doubleday and Company, 1970.
Michell, John, and Robert J. M. Rickard, *Phenomena: A Book of Wonders,* New York: Pantheon Books, 1977.
Rogo, D. Scott, *On the Track of the Poltergeist,* Englewood Cliffs, New Jersey: Prentice-Hall, 1986.

STRANGE RAIN

It is hard to imagine that something as commonplace as rain can be full of mystery. Yet some rainfalls have been so odd that they have frightened witnesses and puzzled scientists.

One kind of strange report, though rare, involves the falling of water from clear skies. In October 1886 in Charlotte, North Carolina, the local newspaper ran a story about a patch of land between two trees that had received a rain shower every afternoon, for three weeks, whether the sky was cloudy or clear.

A worker for the U.S. Signal Corps arrived to check out the account and was amazed to find the report true. Writing in the October issue of *Monthly Weather Review,* he noted—on the first day—"rain drops at 4:47 P.M. and 4:55 P.M. while the sun was shining brightly." The second afternoon he returned. Between 4:05 and 4:25, "a light shower of rain fell from a cloudless sky." Sometimes the rain fell "over an area of half an acre," but it always seemed "to center at these two trees, and when lightest [fell] there only." Not long after the signal corps visit, the odd rain stopped as mysteriously as it had begun. But a similar happening occurred that October in Aiken, South Carolina. Rain fell from morning till late at night on two graves in the town cemetery—and nowhere else—with not a cloud in the sky. Witnesses there numbered in the hundreds.

Science usually explains such rain from clear skies as water blown from another, cloudier, place. This doesn't explain why the rain falls on the exact same spot again and again, however! An even more common type of strange rainfall involves colored rain. There are accounts of blood-red rains that have completely baffled scientists!

Blood-Red Rains

In July 1841, for example, slaves in a field in Wilson County, Tennessee, reported a small red cloud in an otherwise clear sky. From the cloud fell a shower of blood droplets and small pieces of muscle and fat. The local doctor, W. P. Sayle, took samples from the site and sent them to a professor of chemistry at the University of Nashville for study. Physician G. W. Bassett of Virginia reported a similar event in the spring of 1850. On Good Friday, a small cloud passed over a friend of the doctor's, who was with several servants. Pieces of flesh and liver rained to the ground. The next morning Bassett collected

Rain fell from morning till late at night on two graves in the town cemetery—and nowhere else—with not a cloud in the sky.

15 to 20 pieces and sent some to a fellow doctor in an effort to find out what kind of flesh it was. The rest he preserved in alcohol for future examination.

Other accounts of bloody rain appeared in the nineteenth century. On February 15, 1849, in Simpson County, North Carolina, fresh pieces of flesh, liver, brains, and blood fell out of a red cloud and splattered over an area 30 feet wide and 250 to 300 yards long. The *San Francisco Herald* of July 24, 1851, reported a two- to three-minute shower of blood and flesh, with pieces ranging in size from a pigeon's egg to a small orange, that fell on an army station at Benicia, California. And a bloody rain containing hairs and portions of organs fell on two acres of a cornfield outside Los Angeles in July 1869; it was witnessed by a funeral party, which included several members of the clergy.

On March 8, 1876, "flakes of meat" fell from the sky and landed on a Bath County, Kentucky, field, and one brave witness tasted a "perfectly fresh" sample. It reminded him, he told *Scientific American,* of "mutton or venison." The case sparked much attention—and two weak explanations. One stated that the matter befouling the field was a form of algae, which had been on the ground all along but sprouted when the rain soaked it; in fact, the sky was clear during the fall. The second rationale was that the material was buzzard vomit, even though it fell in flakes of one to four inches square and covered ground, trees, and fences on a strip of land 100 yards long and 50 yards wide.

Locales outside the United States have experienced blood-red rains as well. On October 16 and 17, 1846, French witnesses were terrified by a blood shower. After red rain fell in Messignadi, Calabria, Italy, weather experts identified it as bird blood. And in 1888 two red rains fell on the Mediterranean region, 12 days apart. Samples that were burned emitted the strong "odor of animal matter," according to the French scientific journal *L'Astronomie.* In the only twentieth-century account on record, meat and blood showered two small towns between São Paulo and Rio de Janeiro, Brazil, on August 30, 1968. Said a police officer who witnessed the scene, "The sky at the time was quite clear. No aircraft had been seen just prior to, during, or after the event, nor were there any birds in the sky."

It is not known whether bloody rains happen less often in our time or whether witnesses are too reluctant now, in our more scientific age, to report such unbelievable sights.

Sources:

Constance, Arthur, *The Inexplicable Sky,* New York: The Citadel Press, 1957.

Corliss, William R., ed., *Handbook of Unusual Natural Phenomena,* Glen Arm, Maryland: The Sourcebook Project, 1977.

Corliss, William R., ed., *Tornados, Dark Days, Anomalous Precipitation, and Related Weather Phenomena: A Catalog of Geophysical Anomalies,* Glen Arm, Maryland: The Sourcebook Project, 1983.

ICE FALLS

On the evening of September 2, 1958, in his home in Madison Township, New Jersey, Dominick Bacigalupo stood up from a kitchen chair and took a step or two just before his roof caved in. Unhurt but shaken, the man looked about him and realized what had happened: a 70-pound chunk of ice had crashed through the top of his house and had fallen in three big pieces in the cooking area.

It was not storming that night. Bacigalupo's 14-year-old son, Richard, had noticed two airliners flying by just before the bizarre fall, but airport officials denied that the planes were carrying ice. Weather experts at nearby Rutgers University said conditions in the atmosphere could not have created ice chunks of such size and weight. So where did the ice come from?

Ice chunks dropping from the sky is one of meteorology's most frequent and puzzling mysteries. Usually weather experts explain such falls as the result of ice buildup on planes. But this explanation fails to satisfy for many reasons. One is that the electrical heating systems on most modern aircraft prevent ice buildup on wings or other surfaces. Also, according to the Federal Aviation Agency, even older planes—without such heating systems—rarely build up large amounts of ice because of the way they are constructed and because of their swift flying speed. More important, some reported ice chunks have been so huge and heavy that any aircraft carrying them, even for a short time, would be in serious danger of crashing!

Early Reports of Ice Falls

In fact, large blocks of ice have been falling from the sky since long before the invention of the airplane. Late in the eighteenth century, for example, a chunk "as big as an elephant" reportedly fell on Seringapatam, India, and took three days to melt. As unbelievable as this may sound, accounts of enormous falling ice blocks have been recorded frequently.

An 1849 issue of the *Edinburgh New Philosophical Journal* noted that on one August evening that year, a large mass of ice fell on the Balvullich farm, on the estate of Orda in Scotland, measuring nearly 20 feet around and 20 feet thick! A resident farmer named Moffat reported a huge clap of thunder as the irregularly shaped chunk fell near his house. Examination of the block demonstrated that it "had a beautiful crystalline appearance being nearly all quite transparent ... except [for] a small portion of it which consisted of hailstones of uncommon size,

> Late in the eighteenth century, for example, a chunk "as big as an elephant" reportedly fell on Seringapatam, India, and took three days to melt.

Beryl Voyle displays a small portion of a gigantic block of ice that fell in a nearby field in Wales, 1986.

fixed together. It was principally composed of small squares, diamond-shaped, of from 1 to 3 inches in size, all firmly congealed together." While observers could not figure out how to weigh the huge mass of ice, all agreed that Moffat and his household had been very lucky, narrowly avoiding being crushed to death! Oddly enough, no hail or snow was reported anywhere else in the district that day.

On December 26, 1950, another Scottish man, driving near Dumbarton, watched as a mass of ice fell from the sky—nearly hitting him—and crashed to the road. When police arrived at the scene and gathered the pieces, they weighed 112 pounds. This was just one of many ice falls that took place in Great Britain over a two-month period between November 1950 and January 1951. In Kempten, West Germany, also in 1951, tragedy struck when a block of ice six feet long and six inches around fell on a carpenter working on a roof and killed him. In February 1965 a 50-pound mass of ice smashed through the Phillips Petroleum Plant roof in Woods Cross, Utah.

It is interesting to note that the largest recorded hailstones are slightly over five inches around and weigh a little more than two pounds. Hailstones fall, of course, during storms, where winds and

Hailstones.

updrafts keep them aloft before they hit the ground. Ice falls, on the other hand, most often come out of clear skies.

Scientists Investigate

One of the best-studied cases of falling ice was reported by British meteorologist R. F. Griffiths in 1973. On April 2 of that year, while waiting at a street crossing in Manchester, England, the scientist saw a large object strike the road near him and shatter into pieces. He picked up the largest chunk, weighing three and a half pounds, and rushed home to store it in his freezer. He later wrote that the sample proved puzzling, because "whilst it is clearly composed of cloud water, there is no conclusive evidence enabling one to decide precisely how it grew.... In some respects it is very much like a hailstone, in others it is not." A look at flight records for the area showed that no planes had passed overhead at the time.

While not sure of a connection, Griffiths reported that the fall took place nine minutes after another strange happening in the sky: a "single flash of lightning." Many others noticed it as well "because of its severity, and because there were no further flashes." The scientist also noted "unusual meteorological conditions" in England that day, including gales and heavy rains. Manchester itself had had snow in the morning, but skies were clear at the time the ice fell; sleet followed later that day. In a 1975 issue of *Meteorological Magazine*, Griffiths stated his determination that the lightning was triggered by a plane flying into a storm further to the east. About the ice sample, however, he could draw no conclusion.

Another well-studied ice fall that proved even more puzzling took place on a farm in Bernville, Pennsylvania, in 1957. Early on the evening of July 30, farmer Edwin Groff heard a "whooshing noise" and looked up to see a large, white, round object sailing out of the southern sky. After it crashed and shattered a few yards from him, a second, similar, object struck a flower bed close to where he and his wife stood. The first of these was a 50-pound ice cake; the second was half the size and weight of the first.

Witnesses immediately called Matthew Peacock, a meteorologist who lived in nearby Reading. The scientist asked a colleague, Malcolm J. Reider, to examine the fallen ice. It was cloudy and white, as if it had been frozen rapidly, and was filled with "sediment"—dust, fibers, algae. Put together like a "popcorn ball," the ice chunk appeared to be made up of many one-inch hailstones frozen together in a single mass. Yet hailstones do not contain such sediment.

Chemical analysis also showed that the ice mass lacked iron and nitrate, two elements always present when ordinary groundwater is rapidly frozen. Indeed, the specimen seemed to be related neither to ordinary precipitation nor to water swept up from the ground. Another scientist who examined the ice chunk, Paul Sutton, chief of the U.S. Weather Bureau station at Harrisburg, declared that the ice was "not formed by any natural process known to meteorology."

Theories

Charles Fort, one of the first persons to collect and study reports of such anomalies, made clear—with his many scientific journal accounts—that ice falls were a fairly common meteorological oddity. His own theory, made half-jokingly, was that "floating in the sky of this earth, there are fields of ice as extensive as those on the Arctic Ocean"; violent thunderstorms sometimes loosen pieces and they fall below (also see entry: **Falls from the Sky**).

William R. Corliss is a physicist who has written a number of books on rocketry and space travel. He is best known, however, for the Sourcebook Project, an enormous collection of articles and reports about physical and natural mysteries. More oriented to conventional science than the unorthodox Charles Fort—the first great investigator of physical anomalies, who died in 1932 (also see entry: Falls from the Sky)—Corliss researched mainly from scientific publications. Over the years he has collected thousands of accounts of unusual happenings, concentrating mostly on subjects like unusual weather and geophysical (earth-related) oddities—occurrences that, while important, are less likely to outrage scientists than the UFOs and monstrous creatures that delighted Fort.

Beginning with the publication of *Strange Phenomena* in 1974, Corliss began reprinting some of the articles he had uncovered. Nearly a decade later, he had published 16 volumes and well over 7,000 pages of source material on scientific anomalies. And this was only a small part of his collection! In 1982 Corliss stated: "The cataloging task is just beginning, for the anomalies in the world's scientific and semiscientific literature seem nearly infinite in number." Corliss also publishes a newsletter on current anomalies, *Science Frontiers*.

Other, more recent, theories center on UFOs; ufologist M. K. Jessup, for instance, offered this explanation of ice falls: "It seems most natural that a space contrivance [vehicle], if made of metal, and coming from cold space, would soon become coated with ice. That the ice should fall off, or be pushed off by de-icing mechanisms, or even melt off when the space ships are heated by friction with the air or become stationary in the sunshine, seems equally natural." But, in actuality, few ice fall reports include UFO sightings.

Scientists generally rely on two theories concerning ice falls. One suggests that the ice originates somewhere within the earth's atmosphere; strange-weather expert William R. Corliss, for example, feels that "some unappreciated mechanism in hailstorms permits the sudden aggregation [clustering] of many hailstones." The second theory—once ridiculed but now taken more seriously—suggests that ice chunks are true meteorites, coming from outer space. The only problem with this idea, according to critic Ronald J. Willis, is that "there is little indication of high speed entry into the atmosphere that we would expect from any meteorite, whatever its origin." Because fallen ice chunks vary so much in appearance and composition, perhaps more than one such theory is needed to explain them.

Sources:

Corliss, William R., ed., *Handbook of Unusual Natural Phenomena,* Glen Arm, Maryland: The Sourcebook Project, 1977.
Fort, Charles, *The Books of Charles Fort,* New York: Henry Holt and Company, 1941.
Hitching, Francis, *The Mysterious World: An Atlas of the Unexplained,* New York: Holt, Rinehart and Winston, 1978.
Lorenzen, Coral E., *The Shadow of the Unknown,* New York: Signet, 1970.

STAR JELLY

Pwdre ser, or star jelly, is a strange phenomenon that has been around for centuries. The Welsh phrase *pwdre ser* means "rot from the stars," and it describes the glowing, jellylike material that witnesses observe on the ground after seeing strange lights or meteorlike objects move across the sky. In 1541 the poet Sir John Suckling wrote a poem about the oddity, as did writer John Dryden in 1679. While unable to explain pwdre ser, men of science—back then, at least—had no doubt that the oddity was real. Scientists today, however, are not so sure because of what they know about meteors and meteorites; they believe that no such matter could survive the fiery trip through the earth's atmosphere.

Still, consider this story, recorded in the *Transactions of the Swedish Academy of Sciences* in 1808: on May 16 of that year, on a warm, cloudless afternoon, the sun dimmed for an unknown reason. Slowly, from the west, a great number of dark brown balls, about the size of the top of a hat, rose and approached the sun. They became darker and for a brief time stopped moving and hung in the air; when they resumed motion, they picked up speed and traveled in a straight line until they disappeared in the east. During that time, some vanished and others fell down. The strange parade continued in the same manner for nearly two hours. There was no noise—banging, whistling, or buzzing—in the air. Tails nearly 20 feet in length trailed some of the faster balls; but these slowly faded away.

Some of the balls fell to earth not far from K. G. Wettermark, an official of the Swedish Academy. The man noted that as the objects fell they lost their dark color, disappeared briefly, then became visible again but in changing colors—like "those air-bubbles which children ... produce from soapsuds." Wettermark added, "When the spot, where such a ball had fallen, was immediately after examined, nothing was to be seen, but a ... film ... as thin and fine as a cobweb, which was still changing colors, but soon entirely dried up and vanished."

Another case of pwdre ser was reported in the *American Journal of Science* in 1819 by a Prof. Rufus Graves. Earlier that year, between 8 and 9 P.M. on August 13, a fireball "of a brilliant white light resembling burnished silver" fell slowly from the sky and onto the front yard of an Amherst, Massachusetts, man named Erastus Dewey. Two neighbor women

> ### METEORS
>
> A *meteor* is one of the small pieces of matter in the solar system that can be seen only when it falls into the earth's atmosphere, where friction may give it a temporary glow (incandescence). It is sometimes called a "falling" or "shooting" star. A *meteorite* is a meteor that reaches the surface of the earth without being completely destroyed by the heat of friction.

also noticed the light. In the morning Dewey found a strange material 20 feet from his door (which Graves soon examined). Circular in form, eight inches across and one inch high, the tan blob had a fuzzy coating that, when removed, revealed a soft center that gave off an awful smell—so awful, in fact, that it made witnesses dizzy and sick to their stomachs! After awhile the blob turned a blood-red color and began to absorb moisture from the air. Some of the material was collected in a glass, where it began to change into a paste, taking on the color, look, and feel of regular household starch. Within two or three days, the material had disappeared from the glass altogether. All that remained was a dark-colored film that, when rubbed between the fingers, turned into a fine, odorless ash.

Reports of the British Association also printed an account of pwdre ser that occurred late on the evening of October 8, 1844, near Coblentz, Germany. Two men walking in a plowed field were startled to witness the fall of a glowing object that crashed to earth not 20 yards from them. Because it was too dark to investigate that night, they marked the spot and returned to it early the next morning.

One night a bright light fell over the neighborhood. The next morning Mrs. Christian found three purple blobs on the front lawn.

Expecting to find the remains of a meteorite, the two, instead, found a gray, jellylike mass that shook when they poked it with a stick. They did not try to preserve it.

Science Looks for Other Explanations

By the 1860s, as scientists came to learn more about meteors and meteorites, they began to doubt pwdre ser's connection with the stars and looked, instead, for more earthly explanations. Some scientists thought the material might be bird vomit; plant specialists believed it might be *nostoc,* a blue-green algae. Edward Hitchcock, an Amherst College chemistry professor, was sure, in fact, that the material in the Amherst case was a "species of gelatinous fungus, which I had sometimes met with on rotten wood in damp places." The professor believed it was an "entire mistake" that had caused observers to connect it with the falling object. Still, not too long ago scientists doubted that meteorites were real. They thought it an "entire mistake" for observers to connect stones and rocks with the glowing "falling stars" that they had seen go down at the exact same spots. Now, of course, no one doubts meteorite witnesses.

Reports of pwdre ser in our time are rare. The most famous recent case took place in 1979 in Frisco, Texas, outside Dallas. On the night of August 10, a bright light fell over the neighborhood where Martin and Sybil Christian lived. The next morning Mrs. Christian found three purple blobs on her front lawn. One of the blobs dissolved; the other two were frozen and sent away to be studied. They were identified as waste from a nearby battery factory, but the factory strongly disagreed with this finding and refused to accept blame. Chemical reports, in fact, demonstrated that the purple blobs were very different from the factory's waste, and the two materials did not even appear similar.

Sources:

Burke, John G., *Cosmic Debris: Meteorites in History,* Berkeley, California: University of California Press, 1986.

Corliss, William R., ed., *Handbook of Unusual Natural Phenomena,* Glen Arm, Maryland: The Sourcebook Project, 1977.

More Weird Weather

- **STRANGE CLOUDS**

- **BALL LIGHTNING**

- **SKYQUAKES**

- **TUNGUSKA EVENT**

More Weird Weather

STRANGE CLOUDS

One pleasant summer morning in 1975, science teacher Tom D'Ercole of Oyster Bay, New York, was in his driveway and about to enter his car when he glanced up at the sky. There, hovering above the roof of his house, he saw a small dark cloud different from the other few clouds that were floating by much higher in the sky. D'Ercole reported that the "cloud" seemed to move and grow as he watched it. At first the size and shape of a basketball, it floated back and forth across the peak of the roof, then became egg-shaped, then became "multicurved, dark, [and] vaporous." D'Ercole observed that "it finally measured about six feet in height and one and one-half feet in width."

Stunned and unable to think of an explanation, he continued to watch in disbelief as things got even stranger. The cloud seemed to inhale, pucker its "lips," and direct a stream of water toward him and the car, soaking both! After a minute the spray stopped, and the cloud disappeared instantly. After changing his clothes, D'Ercole took his wet shirt to the junior high school where he taught to run chemical tests on it. The wet substance was indeed merely water.

This event seems like nature's idea of a practical joke. Yet clouds *are* capable of strange appearances and behaviors, which science can sometimes explain—and sometimes cannot. In his study *Tornados, Dark Days, Anomalous Precipitation, and Related Weather Phenomena* (1983), physicist William R. Corliss looked at scientific reports of cloud arches, glowing clouds, rumbling clouds, clouds with holes in them, and more. Though the reports are puzzling, meteorologists have ideas about the causes behind most cloud phenomena. But other reports have revealed clouds so odd that no explanations seem possible!

> The cloud seemed to inhale, pucker its "lips," and direct a stream of water toward him and the car, soaking both!

Nature's idea of a practical joke?

Runaway Clouds

One interesting case reported in several scientific journals involved a small, slow-moving, perfectly round white cloud that suddenly appeared in an otherwise clear sky northwest of Agen, France, in the late morning of September 5, 1814. After a few minutes, it stopped and remained still for a time before suddenly speeding southward, all the while spinning and making ear-shattering rumbling noises. It then exploded and rained down a variety of stones, some quite large! The cloud stopped its movement then and slowly faded away. Incredibly, similar events have been recorded in Sienna, Italy, in 1794; Chassigny, France, in 1815; Noblesville, Indiana, in 1823; and elsewhere.

Cigars in Clouds

Just before the wave of UFO sightings that took place in France in the autumn of 1954, several witnesses—including a businessman, two

More Weird Weather

police officers, and an army engineer—observed an extraordinary sight over the town of Vernon. Watching from his driveway at 1 A.M. on August 23, businessman Bernard Miserey saw a huge vertical cigar, 300 feet long, hovering above the north bank of the Seine River 1,000 feet away. According to his testimony, "a horizontal disc" suddenly dropped from the bottom of the cigar, swaying and diving in the air. As it approached him it became "very luminous" before vanishing in the southwest. Over the next 45 minutes other, similar discs dropped out of the cigar. By this time the mother craft had lost its glow and disappeared into the darkness.

Clouds—or more specifically, "cloud cigars"—were described in a number of UFO sightings that occurred from the late 1940s into the 1960s. Usually these objects were seen with smaller, disc-shaped structures; thus the cloud cigars came to be viewed as the "motherships."

Although no clouds were mentioned in that sighting, it set the scene for an even more spectacular event. This one, with hundreds of witnesses, took place three weeks later on September 14, in the southwest of France along the Atlantic coast. At 5 P.M., while working with his men in a field, a wealthy farmer who lived near Saint-Prouant saw a "regular shape something like a cigar or a carrot" drop quickly out of a thick layer of clouds. The object was horizontal, luminous, and rigid, and it did not move with the clouds above it. It looked, farmer Georges Fortin said, like a "gigantic machine surrounded by mists." When the object completed its descent, it moved into a vertical position and became still.

By now citizens of half a dozen local villages, as well as farmers living in the region, were watching the sky in awe. White smoke or vapor began to pour out of the bottom of the object, shooting straight down before slowing and rising to circle the cigar in spirals. When the wind had blown all the smoke away, its source was revealed: a small metal disc that shone like a mirror and reflected light from the larger object. The disc darted about the area, sometimes moving with great speed, sometimes stopping suddenly, before finally streaking toward the cigar and disappearing into its lower part.

Fortin reported that about a minute later, the "carrot" leaned back into "its original position, point forward." It sped ahead "and disappeared into the clouds in the distance." The whole event had lasted "about half an hour." Other witnesses up and down the valley repeated this account. Weather experts reported that no tornado or other unusual meteorological activity had taken place at the time of the sighting.

A 300-foot-long, dull-gray, cigar-shaped machine came out of a cloud during a rainstorm over Cressy, Tasmania, Australia, on October 4, 1960. Among those who saw it was Lionel Browning, an Anglican

Spectacular cloud formation over Mount Shasta, California.

minister. As he and his wife watched the object, which they guessed was 300 feet above the ground, five or six domed discs measuring about 30 feet across shot out of the clouds just above and behind the cigar. They headed toward it "like flat stones skipping along water"— exactly how pilot Kenneth Arnold described the motion of the discs he saw over Mount Rainier, Washington, on June 24, 1947, in a sighting that would launch the UFO age (also see entry: **Unidentified Flying Objects**). According to Browning, the ship seemed to sail on "for some seconds unaware that it had shed its protection. Possibly when this was discovered, the saucers were called to the mother ship. The objects then moved back into the cover of the rain storm."

UFO-like Clouds

The sighting of a very odd cloud was recorded in the log of the ship *Lady of the Lake* on March 22, 1870, as it was sailing off the coast of West Africa, south of Cape Verde. Called by his men to the rear of the ship to witness the strange sight, Captain F. W. Banner observed a round cloud with five rays or arms extending from its center. Light gray in color, it had a tail similar to that of a comet. Moving along much lower than the other clouds in the sky, it was visible for nearly a half hour before darkness fell.

In another strange sighting nearly a century later, a pair of clouds resembling "puffy-like daubs of cotton" passed over Sunset, Utah, late on the afternoon of October 14, 1961. The clouds were linked by a cord of long, stringy material. Behind them were two smooth, metallic, disc-shaped structures. All four objects disappeared over the horizon. Ronald Miskin, an investigator for the Aerial Phenomena Research Organization, interviewed witnesses the next day. One was Sunset's mayor, who was pointing skyward and describing the objects' path when a "puffy" white object again flew overhead and was quickly joined by another. They streaked across the sky in the same direction taken by the objects seen the day before.

Aliens in the Clouds

Late one afternoon in the spring of 1965, a tourist looking out the window of a clifftop house along the seashore in Sydney, Australia, noticed a beautiful pink cloud that did not move. An hour later, when she looked again, the cloud was moving in her direction. It was soon below her eye level, which allowed her to look down on it, and to her amazement she saw a round, white object inside. Vents along the object's side gave off gray steam, which, as it covered all but the top, turned pink. The object appeared to be making its own cloud!

As if this were not fantastic enough, an engine sound came from the still-lowering object. A glowing ladder dropped from its underside, and a humanlike figure climbed down to a lower rung. There it sat and directed a searchlight toward the sea below. Some distance out on the water, a pink flare shot into the air. The ladder pulled in at once, and the object shot off in the direction of the flare. The witness then noticed a long (though not clearly visible) shape in the water from where the flare had come. Both the UFO and the underwater shape vanished in a "vivid pink flash."

On the afternoon of January 7, 1970, two Finnish skiers came upon a mysterious glowing red "cloud." When it got within 50 feet of them, the cloud seemed to dissipate somewhat, and they saw that a smoke-blowing domed disc was at its center. The object hovered near them and in the light it cast, they could see a three-foot-tall humanoid with a pale, waxy face, no eyes, and a hooklike nose standing on the ground just beneath it. After about 20 seconds, the red fog suddenly reappeared, and by the time it cleared, both the object and the being were gone.

"Saucer Clouds" seen over Marseilles, France, in 1955.

Although there have been other cases in which "clouds" or "fogs" have played a role in meetings with alien beings, they are not common in such reports.

Mysterious Planes and Vanishing Clouds

A drought that began in 1973 and continued for well over a decade was the starting point for a number of strange "sightings" that were reported by Spanish farmers in three southern provinces in the early 1980s. With their thirsty farmland all but useless, they began charging that the lack of rainfall was not an unfortunate condition of nature but an evil conspiracy planned by the big tomato growers. The small farmers were certain that these growers did not want rain to fall on their humble crops—and that to make certain of this, the tomato growers had hired pilots to destroy rain clouds.

Despite the fact that no technology exists to break up rain clouds, the farmers stood by their story. Assurances by scientists, legal officers, and flying experts (who swore that small planes could not fly into storm clouds without serious risk of crashing) meant nothing. The farmers insisted that on many occasions they had seen the appearance of a thundercloud on the western horizon, followed within minutes by the approach of an unmarked aircraft. The aircraft would fly into the cloud, leave off chemicals, and reduce it to wisps.

A drought in southwestern France in 1986 brought similar complaints. This time the villain was said to be a corporation developing anti-hail technology. It did no good for experts to report that nothing could be done to stop hail. Fortunately, heavy rains that summer put an end to the affair!

To social scientists, these cases demonstrate how stressful conditions can stir people's fears and imaginations. What is odd, though, is that even individuals not directly affected by the drought said they had seen the planes in action. One of them, agriculture ministry engineer Francisco Moreno Sastre, insisted, "It's not just the collective imagination." He told *Wall Street Journal* reporters that witnesses numbered in the "thousands." A priest, Father Manuel Prados Munoz of the mountain village of Maria, claimed repeated sightings, sometimes as many as a dozen a month. He said the planes would show up whenever his desktop barometer—and his eyes—registered that a storm was coming. (A barometer is an instrument for measuring atmospheric pressure, usually indicated by the movement of a column of mercury in a sealed glass tube. A storm is expected when the barometer is falling quickly; when it is rising, fair weather is predicted.) When local people began to report their sightings of planes to Munoz, he learned of hundreds of similar cases.

With these sightings, no explanation really makes sense. There was absolutely no evidence that a supersecret military or other weather-control operation was the cause. And happily for all concerned, when rain ended the droughts, the mystery planes—real or imagined—passed out of sight and soon out of mind.

Sources:

Corliss, William R., ed., *Handbook of Unusual Natural Phenomena,* Glen Arm, Maryland: The Sourcebook Project, 1977.

Corliss, William R., ed., *Tornados, Dark Days, Anomalous Precipitation, and Related Weather Phenomena: A Catalog of Geophysical Anomalies,* Glen Arm, Maryland: The Sourcebook Project, 1983.

Michell, John, and Robert J. M. Rickard, *Phenomena: A Book of Wonders,* New York: Pantheon Books, 1977.

BALL LIGHTNING

At 6:30 P.M. on October 8, 1919, at a busy downtown street crossing in Salina, Kansas, a "ball of fire as large as a washtub floating low in the air" struck the side of a building, ripped out bricks, and destroyed a second-story window.

Just moments after hearing what sounded like thunder, a Parisian man reported an extraordinary sight: a fireball the size of a human head emerged from the fireplace of his fourth-story apartment and darted toward him "like a cat." The man quickly raised his feet, and the ball moved to the center of the room. Though bright, it gave off no noticeable heat. It rose slightly, headed back to the fireplace, and retreated up the chimney, exploding just before it escaped into the open air. The chimney top received a fair amount of damage.

This 1852 account describes ball lightning, a strange—and so far unexplained—natural occurrence. While some scientists believe that ball lightning is real, others question it, because reliable data is rare, with most evidence consisting of hearsay reports and questionable photographs. More bothersome still is the fact that no known scientific principle can account for it!

Some doubters of ball lightning feel that witnesses are reporting optical illusions, visual afterimages caused by watching something very bright, like a flash of lightning. Others believe that observers are experiencing a natural phenomenon like St. Elmo's fire, the "halo" of electricity sometimes discharged from an object projecting above ground during an electrical storm.

While the second explanation seems a reasonable one, James Dale Barry, a leading scientific expert on the subject, pointed out that St. Elmo's fire cannot move about like ball lightning, explaining, "It may move along a conductor, sometimes pulsating as it moves, but it does not free itself from the conductor. Thus, it does not exhibit the descending, hovering, or flying motions that are common to ball lightning."

The first investigator to describe ball lightning in scientific literature was the Russian G. W. Richman. Tragically, his study led to his death. In 1754, during a thunderstorm, Richman was trying to measure the energy of a lightning strike. As he stood behind his equipment, a small, blue, fist-sized ball came out of the electrodes and floated toward his face. A moment later it exploded, killing him and knocking his assistant unconscious.

Fortunately, deaths related to ball lightning are rare, but many observers have witnessed its destructive power. During an electrical storm in Paris in July 1849, a red ball hung about 20 feet above a tree. The tree suddenly caught fire, burned, and burst open, jagged streaks of lightning shooting out in all directions. One hit a nearby house and blew a cannon-size hole in it. What remained of the lightning ball started to spin and spark and then exploded with great force, knocking down three people nearby.

At 6:30 P.M. on October 8, 1919, at a busy downtown street crossing in Salina, Kansas, a "ball of fire as large as a washtub floating low in the air" struck the side of a building, ripped out bricks, and destroyed a second-story window. It then exploded with a "bang that resembled the noise made by the discharge of a large pistol, filling the air with balls of fire as large as baseballs, which floated away in all directions," reported that month's issue of *Monthly Weather Review*. "Some of these balls followed trolley and electric-light wires in a snaky sort of manner and some simply floated off through the air independently of any objects

In 1852 a Parisian man reported that a fireball emerged from his fireplace and darted toward him "like a cat."

Fireball seen during a storm in Salagnac, France, 1845, possibly ball lightning. From Camille Flammarion, *L'Atmosphère,* 1888.

near by. An electric switch box across the street was ripped open and a transformer destroyed, leaving the east side of the town in darkness."

In the summer of 1960, as Louise Matthews of south Philadelphia lay on her living room couch, she looked up to see a huge red ball coming through a window and its blinds, both closed and neither disturbed by the entry. When the globe, which made a sizzling sound, passed by her, Mrs. Matthews felt a tingling on the back of her neck. She put her hand to the spot but felt nothing. The ball went through the living room and into the dining room, leaving—again without damage—through another closed window. She called her husband, who came home from work to find the back of her hand burned. And the hair at the back of her head had fallen out, leaving the skin there as smooth as that on her face.

During a violent early-evening thunderstorm on August 12, 1970, a "red ball of fire" appeared above Sidmouth, England, crackled for a few seconds, then exploded with a deafening roar. Jagged flashes of lightning shot from it toward the ground. At that moment, 2,500 area television sets were cut off.

Despite the nature of these accounts, ball lightning is not always harmful, nor does it always explode at the end of its run. In a November 1930 issue of *Nature,* British scientist Alexander Russell recalled a sighting where two balls of lightning acted very differently. "One of them struck a building and burst with a loud report, causing inhabitants to open the windows and look out to see what had happened," he related, while "the other drifted slowly away." The scientist added that when ball lightning drifts about it makes a slight noise—like "the purring of a cat."

More Theories

Much of the problem behind explaining ball lightning is the result of the varying descriptions witnesses have given. The ball either explodes loudly or disappears silently; it is white, orange, red, blue, or purple; it is small or large; it lasts for a few seconds or several minutes. Science writer Gordon Stein remarked that while these differences may seem minor, "they cause theorists no end of difficulties. Explanations that will work for a ball of one second's duration, for example, cannot account for a 10-second ball," for a ball that lasts one minute or more "requires an energy content so high that there is no known way for it to be formed."

Also making an explanation tricky is ball lightning's ability to penetrate the metal walls of in-flight aircraft. On March 19, 1963, R. C. Jennison, a professor of electrical energy, saw a globe of lightning first outside, then inside, an airliner he was taking from New York to Washington. An electrical storm was in progress. According to Stein, the incident casts doubt on several theories about ball lightning because "microwave, electric, radio or heat energy ... could not have gotten through the metal fuselage [body of the plane]." He also felt that it disproved the ideas of E. T. F. Ashby and C. Whitehead, who suggested that ball lightning consisted of antimatter. "When antimatter—matter composed of the counterparts of ordinary matter—comes in contact with normal matter, both are annihilated," Stein wrote. "Antimatter would have a difficult time getting through the body or window of an airplane without colliding with some regular matter, thus destroying itself."

Sources:

Barry, James Dale, *Ball Lightning and Bead Lightning: Extreme Forms of Atmospheric Electricity,* New York: Plenum Press, 1980.

Constance, Arthur, *The Inexplicable Sky,* New York: The Citadel Press, 1957.

Evans, Hilary, ed., *The Frontiers of Reality: Where Science Meets the Paranormal,* Wellingborough, Northamptonshire, England: The Aquarian Press, 1989.

SKYQUAKES

While exploring the Rocky Mountains on July 4, 1808, members of the Lewis and Clark expedition heard strange noises coming from some distant mountains. They were heard at different times of the day and night, ringing out one at a time or in five or six loud bursts. Weather didn't seem to affect the sounds, for they were often heard when the sky was cloudless and the wind was still. As unlikely as it seemed in this wild country, the noises resembled heavy cannon fire!

An 1829 exploration party along the Darling River, near what is now Bourke, New South Wales, Australia, was also puzzled one afternoon by the sound of heavy gunfire in the unsettled territory. The expedition leader recorded this in his diary on February 7:

> the day had been remarkably fine, not a cloud was there in the heavens, nor a breath of air to be felt. On a sudden we heard what seemed to be the report of a gun fired at the distance of between five and six miles. It was not the hollow sound of an earthly explosion, or the sharp cracking noise of falling timber, but in every way resembled a discharge of a heavy piece of ordnance [cannon]. On this all were agreed, but no one was certain where the sound proceeded.... I sent one of the men immediately up a tree, but he could observe nothing unusual.

It is likely that the faraway gunfire that both expeditions heard (but could not locate) was the oddity known as skyquakes. Described as muffled thunder or cannon fire, skyquakes have been heard all over the world. One instance of skyquakes takes place in India and is known as the Barisal Guns; another example in Connecticut is called the Moodus Noises.

Theories

In past centuries witnesses to the strange sounds have attempted to record and explain them in their folklore and legends; in our time, imaginative writers have even linked them to UFOs or parallel universes. Scientists, however, offer a more sensible explanation: skyquakes are not really sounds from the sky but come, instead, from under the ground. Earthquakes and other earthly vibrations—sometimes so small that only an instrument can measure them—create these odd noises; it is because the sounds come from so deep underground that confusion follows—they *do* seem to be made in the sky.

As unlikely as it seemed in this wild country, the noises resembled heavy cannon fire!

While scientists don't know why skyquakes are heard in some places and not others, they are working hard to find out. Since 1981 the Weston Observatory of Boston College has been studying earthquake activity in New England and its connection to the Moodus Noises. Perhaps sometime soon they will discover exactly what causes skyquakes.

Did the Lewis and Clark expedition experience skyquakes in the Rocky Mountains?

Sources:

Corliss, William R., *Handbook of Unusual Natural Phenomena,* Glen Arm, Maryland: The Sourcebook Project, 1977.
Fort, Charles, *The Books of Charles Fort,* New York: Henry Holt and Company, 1941.

TUNGUSKA EVENT

In 1908 a strange explosion took place in a remote swampy area of Siberia, Russia. Today, nearly a century later, the event is still the source of wonder, argument, and a number of explanatory theories.

At 7:15 on the morning of June 30, a blazing white light was seen falling over the forests northwest of Lake Baykal near the Stony Tunguska River. It was so bright that it cast shadows on the earth beneath it. As it fell, it flattened trees and smashed houses, finally exploding with such force that seismic shocks (earth vibrations) were recorded around the world. A giant "pillar of fire" rose straight up and was seen hundreds of miles away. As huge thunderclaps sounded, a blistering current of hot air tore through the area, setting off fires in forests and towns. At least three shock waves followed the thermal (heat) wave. The destruction was massive, extending for 375 miles. Thick, dark clouds rose above the site of the explosion, and a black rain of dirt and particles fell on central Russia. That night the sky remained eerily bright all through northern Europe.

Perhaps an explanation for this gigantic explosion would have been easy to find had scientists been able to go to the site immediately. But because Russia was suffering from grave political upheaval—which would soon erupt into war and revolution—scientists focused on other concerns. The first expedition to the area, led by Leonid Kulik of the Russian Meteorological Institute, did not take place until 13 years later.

Expedition members expected to come upon a huge meteorite crater but were surprised to find nothing of the sort. Instead, they discovered that trees there had been damaged from above. Moreover, those closest to the impact site were still standing, though missing bark and branches. Trees farther away were flattened and pointing out from the site. Kulik and his companions searched carefully but could find no meteorite fragments.

Nonetheless, Kulik, whose work continued until the outbreak of World War II (in which he was killed), remained certain that a meteorite was the cause of the explosion. A colleague, Vasili Sytin, disagreed, because there was no evidence that indicated a source outside the earth's atmosphere. Instead, he suggested an earthly explanation: an unusually violent windstorm.

> That night the sky remained eerily bright all through northern Europe.

METEOROIDS

A *meteoroid* is any piece of matter—ranging in mass from a speck of dust to thousands of tons—that travels through space; it is composed largely of stone or iron or a mixture of the two. When a meteoroid enters the earth's atmosphere it becomes visible and is called a *meteor*. A *meteorite* is a meteor that survives the fall to earth.

Extraterrestrial Explanations

After learning of the destruction left by atomic bomb attacks on the Japanese cities of Hiroshima and Nagasaki at the end of World War II, Soviet science-fiction writer A. Kasantsev published a story about Tunguska in the January 1946 issue of *Vokrug Sveta*. In his story a Martian spaceship—vaporized in a nuclear explosion—causes the destruction of Tunguska.

Though the story was only a fantasy, Kasantsev was attacked by Soviet scientists for presenting what they believed was a ridiculous explanation. Nonetheless, the idea that a spaceship had exploded over Tunguska caught on, capturing the public's imagination—first in the Soviet Union, then around the world. Two Soviet scientists, Felix Zigel and Aleksey Zolotov, were strong supporters of the theory in later decades, with Zolotov even claiming to have detected "abnormal radioactivity" at the Tunguska site. Testing by other scientists, however, provided no solid proof. A popular 1976 book, *The Fire Came By*, defended the spaceship idea, but most Western—and Russian—scientists continued to reject the theory.

1929 photograph of trees devastated by the Tunguska catastrophe of 1908.

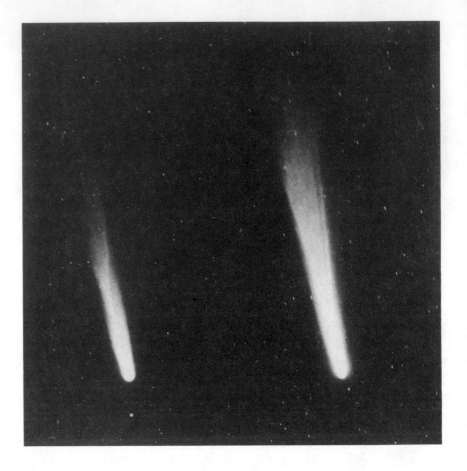

A 1910 photo of Halley's Comet.

COMETS

A comet is a small heavenly body consisting mostly of gases, the movement of which depends on the sun's gravity. As a comet approaches the sun, particles and gases are driven off, often to form a tail, which can extend up to 100 million miles.

Today explanations for the Tunguska event have refocused on meteorites, comets, and asteroids. Almost all scientists agree that the object, possibly as large as 200 yards around, never struck the earth but exploded in midair because of the air pressure that built up beneath it as it fell.

"Had the Tunguska object been a comet," wrote Stephen P. Maran in *Natural History,* "the failure to find fragments of rock or iron from the explosion would be understandable. Any cometary ice that reached the ground probably would have melted before the first scientific expedition reached the site.... [If] the Tunguska object was an asteroid or meteoroid and thus made of stone and iron ... either there are fragments, which have been overlooked by repeated Soviet scientific expeditions, or ... the incoming object ... shattered totally into dust in the explosion."

Sources:

Baxter, John, and Thomas Atkins, *The Fire Came By: The Riddle of the Great Siberian Explosion,* Garden City, New York: Doubleday and Company, 1976.

Ganapathy, Ramachandran, "The Tunguska Explosion of 1908: Discovery of Meteoritic Debris Near the Explosion Site and at the South Pole," *Science* 220,4602, June 10, 1983, pp. 1158-61.

Maran, Stephen P., "What Struck Tunguska?," *Natural History* 93,2, February 1984, pp. 36-37.

Cryptozoology

- THE SCIENCE OF "UNEXPECTED" ANIMALS

Cryptozoology

THE SCIENCE OF "UNEXPECTED" ANIMALS

The two best-known areas of investigation in unusual phenomena are ufology (the study of UFOs) and cryptozoology. The term *cryptozoology* comes from the Greek words *kryptos* (hidden), *zoon* (animal), and *logos* (discussion)—in short, it means the study of hidden animals. Bernard Heuvelmans, the man who named the field, favored the word "hidden" instead of "unknown" to describe these mystery animals. This is because he felt that such animals were usually known to the local people who lived near them, who often supplied the eyewitness accounts and information about appearance and behavior that would make its way into the larger world and capture the interest of scientists. Heuvelmans thought it would be better to call them animals "undescribed by science." Two of cryptozoology's most famous subjects are **Bigfoot** and the **Loch Ness monster.**

In 1982, at the Smithsonian Institution in Washington, D.C., the International Society of Cryptozoology (ISC) was created so that biologists interested in unknown, hidden, or doubted animals would have a formal organization through which research could be done. There the definition of cryptozoology was made even more clear. It was agreed that cryptozoology should include the possible existence of *known* animals in areas where they were not supposed to be, as well as the possible existence of animals thought to be extinct. "What makes an animal of interest to cryptozoology," the *ISC Newsletter* decided, "is that it is unexpected."

PTERODACTYLS.   LONG-NECKED SEA-LIZARD.   CUTTLE-FISH.

PLATE VI.   *Plesiosaurus dolichodeirus.* Length 22 feet.

Some cryptozoolo-
gists have found
evidence of the
modern-day existence
of animals thought to
have been extinct for
millions of years, like
the pterosaur and sea
lizard (dinosaur)
pictured here.

The Prehistory of Cryptozoology

In the eighteenth century Swede Carolus Linnaeus was the first to put plants and animals into modern, scientific classifications. He believed that God created the forms and functions of these plants and animals and that they never changed. (Charles Darwin would present another theory called evolution—based on gradual transformation of a species—more than a century later.) Animals that did not fit into the classifications put forth by Linnaeus, like unicorns or **sea serpents**, were no longer considered worthy of scientific study.

By the nineteenth century, scientists felt that they had found and classified nearly all the creatures on earth. In 1812 Baron Georges Cuvier, the great French naturalist remembered today as the father of paleontology (the study of the past through fossils), declared that all species of large quadrupeds—animals that walked on four feet—had been discovered. It was a belief shared by most other scientists. Nonetheless, thousands of new species of animals, including large quadrupeds, have been discovered since Cuvier's time.

The fierce-looking, humanlike *pongo,* known to us as the gorilla, was officially recognized in 1847. The **giant squid** (called the Kraken in folklore) and the giant panda were also discovered around that time. Because odd new creatures continued to appear, some scientists began to give the strange animals of legends and folklore a second look. The question of sea serpents, for example, captured the attention of scientists and writers who thought that the witnesses were too reliable and the sightings too detailed to be ignored. These creatures became a popular topic of discussion in European and American scientific journals in the nineteenth century.

Zoologist editor Edward Newman, for one, hoped for a shift in scientific thinking—a greater open-mindedness. Of the sea serpent question, he wrote in 1847, "A natural phenomenon of some kind has been witnessed; let us seek a satisfactory solution rather than terminate enquiry by the shafts of ridicule." Defenders of the sea serpent's existence included some important natural scientists. In 1892 Dutch zoologist Antoon Cornelis Oudemans collected all available reports and carefully examined them in a widely read book, *The Great Sea-Serpent.* Heuvelmans considered the volume the "true starting point of the new discipline" of cryptozoology.

But at the same time, powerful scientists—whose doubts would win out in the end—attacked sea serpent reports as lies and mistaken identifications (as many of them were) and poked fun at witnesses. And scientists who dared to disagree sometimes had to pay a high price. The highly regarded French-American zoologist Constantin Samuel Rafinesque, for example, found his reputation and career in ruins following his writings on the sea serpent issue.

In the twentieth century, there is a growing feeling that the discovery of large, still unknown animals is *very* unlikely. Yet such animals are still being found. The three major discoveries of our time—though far from the *only* discoveries—were of the okapi (1900), the mountain gorilla (1903), and the coelacanth (1938). The okapi, a short-necked African animal related to the giraffe but resembling more of a donkey-zebra mix, would eventually become the symbol of cryptozoology, appearing on the ISC's logo. The coelacanth, found in the net of a South African fishing boat, was believed to have become extinct some 60 million years ago. (Thought to be 400 million years old, the species was around long before the dinosaurs!) The discovery of the coelacanth is considered one of the twentieth century's most important zoological finds.

That discovery made some scientists and writers wonder: if the prehistoric coelacanth could be found, what other strange animals had

The coelacanth, found in the net of a South African fishing boat, was believed to have become extinct some 60 million years ago.

escaped extinction? A few, who had heard reports from Africa of a strange sauropod-like animal (like the brontosaurus) called the **mokele-mbembe,** suggested that perhaps dinosaurs were not extinct after all. Other reports from the continent sounded like sightings of another prehistoric reptile, the flying **pterosaur**. In the January 3, 1948, issue of the popular magazine the *Saturday Evening Post,* biologist Ivan T. Sanderson brought these questions before the public in his article "There Could Be Dinosaurs." Willy Ley, educated in paleontology and zoology, also wrote about unknown animals in magazine articles and books for the general public. But worldwide interest in strange animals had already been stirred in 1933, when the first photo of the Loch Ness monster appeared. Hundreds of magazine and newspaper articles and books were written about the creature, either making the case for or against its existence.

Heuvelmans and Modern Times

The most important cryptozoological book of all time, *On the Track of Unknown Animals,* appeared in French in 1955 and in English in 1958. Its author, Franco-Belgian zoologist Bernard Heuvelmans, had spent years collecting reports of strange animals from a wide variety of popular and scientific literature. *Unknown Animals,* a thick book that addressed only land-based creatures, did not use the word "cryptozoology." In fact, Heuvelmans did not coin the phrase until after his vol-

Bernard Heuvelmans

(1916-)

Two books sparked French cryptozoologist Bernard Heuvelmans's interest in strange animals during his youth: Jules Verne's *Twenty Thousand Leagues Under the Sea,* with its momentous giant squid battle scene, and Sir Arthur Conan Doyle's *The Lost World,* with its living dinosaurs. Later, as a successful science writer and zoologist, Heuvelmans read Ivan T. Sanderson's (also see entry: Hairy Bipeds in North America) 1948 article "There Could Be Dinosaurs" and decided then and there to focus his studies on the mysterious animals that so fascinated him.

His first book, *On the Track of Unknown Animals* (1955), brought together all the printed sources on unexpected land animals that Heuvelmans could find. The book, though scientific in its approach, was written to captivate the largest possible audience. It sold about one million copies worldwide. In 1968 Heuvelmans published *In the Wake of the Sea-Serpents,* an in-depth examination of giant ocean creature sightings. His numerous other books have been published only in French.

Heuvelmans coined the term *cryptozoology* and he is considered the most influential writer in this field. He established the Center for Cryptozoology in southern France in 1975. In 1982 he participated in the founding of the International Society of Cryptozoology (ISC) and serves as its president from his home in France.

ume was published. But he began using it when writing letters, and in 1959 a friend dedicated a book to Heuvelmans, the "master of cryptozoology." Thus the word appeared in print for the first time.

Translated into many languages, *Unknown Animals* sold a million copies worldwide and almost single-handedly turned the study of such beasts into a science all its own. Other events led to interest in the subject as well. In the 1950s, magazines with huge readerships like *Life* and *National Geographic* ran stories on the **Yeti** (a Himalayan Bigfoot also known as the "abominable snowman"). And later in the decade, sightings and tracks of Bigfoot in America's Pacific Northwest attracted much attention.

The 1960s unleashed a flood of cryptozoological writings that continues to this day. And the manner in which writers approached these zoological mysteries varied widely—from careful and detailed scientific studies to the most breathlessly outlandish tales and theories. Sometimes this antiscientific point of view was described as Fortean, after **Charles Fort** (also see entry: **Falls from the Sky**), a pioneer in the field of anomalistics, or unusual events, who sometimes poked fun at science's weak attempts to explain away strange events—and who offered wacky theories of his own.

But for the most part, the new era focused on field research and evidence. Professionals and amateurs alike prowled forests, jungles, beaches, rivers, and lakes looking for specimens or other clues—mostly with poor results. The newly founded International Society of Cryptozoology played an important role in such field investigations. When anthropologist Roy Wagner reported that residents of New Guinea were seeing creatures they described as half-human and half-fish, for instance, the ISC sent investigators to accompany Wagner. Eventually they determined that the dugong—a plant-eating water mammal also known as the sea cow—was the creature the natives were actually seeing (also see entry: **Ri**). Over the next ten years ISC members also traveled to the Congo in search of mokele-mbembe and to China looking for "wild men," that country's version of Bigfoot. Other field research was done at Lake Champlain, the supposed home of water monster **Champ**, and in the Oregon/Washington wilderness where Bigfoot reportedly roamed.

The ISC also looked at less spectacular but still interesting "cryptids" (as puzzling animals are called), like the **thylacine**, an Australian flesh-eating marsupial said to be extinct but still reported in sightings, and the Eastern cougar. ISC secretary J. Richard Greenwell even obtained, from the mountains of western Mexico, a slain specimen of a large cat identified as the **onza**, which was mentioned in legends but the existence of which had long been doubted. Greenwell's fantastic cryptozoological find, however, became a disappointment when cursory laboratory studies produced no evidence that the creature was genetically different from other big cats native to the area.

As the ISC became more active, cryptozoology gained the support of some important scientists—and drew the attacks of others. Most of its critics believed, like Cuvier back in 1812, that no significant large animals were left to be discovered. In the late 1980s, while speaking at a zoological meeting, Greenwell found himself openly mocked! But that was unusual, for most scientists are aware of the field of cryptozoology and seem willing to hear it out. *Cryptozoology,* the ISC's yearly journal, publishes the work of well-respected biologists. Even contributors who are doubtful that cryptozoology's efforts will bring any real results admit that—despite the long odds—the search is still worthwhile. Of course the discovery of a specimen, living or dead, of a spectacular "unexpected animal" would make cryptozoology acceptable at once.

Paracryptozoology

Paracryptozoology addresses cases of unexpected animals the existence of which, even to the most open-minded, seems *totally* impossible ("paracryptozoology" means "beyond cryptozoology"). Nearly all the cryptids considered by Heuvelmans, the ISC, and other cryptozoologists trained in the biological sciences are thought to live in remote or thinly populated regions or in deep bodies of water. In places like these the existence of large unknown animals is at least a slim possibility.

But of course, these are not the only places where such creatures are sighted. Bigfoot and other similar-looking **hairy bipeds** (animals that walk on two feet) have been reported all over the United States and Canada, not just in the Pacific Northwest wilderness. And "monsters" of other sorts—from **werewolves** to **reptile men**—have been frequently reported in newspapers and other writings. Though witnesses who see these very strange creatures seem as solid and as normal as those who report more ordinary "cryptids," cryptozoologists have stayed clear of them and their claims. Most science-based cryptozoologists ignore paracryptozoology because it asks them to stretch reality a little *too* far.

Sources:

Bauer, Henry H., *The Enigma of Loch Ness: Making Sense of a Mystery,* Urbana, Illinois: University of Illinois Press, 1986.

Bord, Janet, and Colin Bord, *Alien Animals,* Harrisburg, Pennsylvania: Stackpole Books, 1981.

Clark, Jerome, and Loren Coleman, *Creatures of the Outer Edge,* New York: Warner Books, 1978.

Heuvelmans, Bernard, *In the Wake of Sea-Serpents,* New York: Hill and Wang, 1968.

Heuvelmans, Bernard, *On the Track of Unknown Animals,* New York: Hill and Wang, 1958.

Holiday, F. W., *The Dragon and the Disc: An Investigation into the Totally Fantastic,* New York: W. W. Norton and Company, 1973.

Keel, John A., *Strange Creatures from Time and Space,* Greenwich, Connecticut: Fawcett Publications, 1970.

Misplaced Animals

- WANDERING KANGAROOS

- BLACK PANTHERS AND OTHER STRANGE CATS

- BEAST OF EXMOOR

- BEAST OF GEVAUDAN

- ALLIGATORS IN SEWERS

- ENTOMBED ANIMALS

- NORTH AMERICAN APES

Misplaced Animals

WANDERING KANGAROOS

Kangaroos live only in the southern part of the world—in Australia, New Guinea, Tasmania, and surrounding islands. Yet oddly enough, the animals have been sighted living wild in the United States for nearly a century! While no one knows exactly how they got here, the number of sightings—and the witnesses reporting them (many being police officers)—make it almost certain that a few kangaroos have made America their home.

The reports began in 1899, when a Richmond, Wisconsin, woman saw a kangaroo run through her neighbor's yard. Because a circus was in town, she assumed that the animal had escaped. But, in fact, the circus had no kangaroo! The following year, in Mays Landing, New Jersey, a farm family heard a scream coming from near their barn. From what they could tell, the thing doing the screaming was a 150-pound kangaroo! From then on the family often saw the animal's tracks, eight to ten feet apart, leading to a large cedar swamp at the rear of their property.

In 1934 a "killer kangaroo" terrified Tennessee countryfolk, attacking and killing dogs, geese, and ducks. Because kangaroos are rarely violent—and never eat meat—the accounts were reported in newspapers around the country poking fun at area residents. Still, the witnesses stood by their stories and the local newspaper (the *Chattanooga Daily Times*) defended them, stating, "There is absolutely no doubt about these facts, a kangaroolike beast visited the community and killed dogs right and left, and that's all there is to it." However, because no other "killer" kangaroos have since been reported, this Tennessee case is still in question.

Two men saw and photographed this huge kangaroo in April 1978 as it lurked in the bushes along a Wisconsin highway.

There have been other kangaroo sightings. The headlights of a Greyhound bus driven by Louis Staub shone on a kangaroolike animal as it leaped across a highway near Grove City, Ohio, in 1949. Residents of Coon Rapids, outside Minneapolis, reported numerous sightings of kangaroos, sometimes traveling in pairs, from 1957 through 1967. And in 1958, kangaroos were sighted around several Nebraska towns, some 100 miles apart. One witness, beer brewer Charles Wetzel, took advantage of the accounts, naming one of his products "Wetzel Kangaroo Beer."

Arresting a Kangaroo

Residents of cities surrounding and including Chicago experienced a number of kangaroo incidents in the autumn of 1974. They began on October 18 when a Chicago man called police at 3:30 A.M. about a kangaroo on his porch.

The two unbelieving officers were amazed to find the report true; not sure of what to do, officer Michael Byrne tried to handcuff the animal, which—according to the policeman—"started to scream and got vicious." A scuffle followed, with the five-foot-tall kangaroo kicking officer Leonard Ciagi hard and often! The policemen called for backup, but by then the kangaroo was escaping down the street at about 20

A scuffle followed, with the five-foot-tall kangaroo kicking officer Leonard Ciagi hard and often!

miles per hour. Over the next two or three weeks, more sightings were reported in cities in Illinois and Indiana, some at the very same time; a kangaroo also made a second appearance in Chicago. Finally, on November 25, farmer Donald Johnson of Sheridan, Indiana, made the last reported sighting of the year. Johnson spotted a kangaroo running down the middle of a deserted country road; when the animal spotted him, it jumped over a barbed-wire fence and disappeared into a field.

Kangaroos continue to be seen around the United States and in parts of Canada. Because none of the animals have ever been caught or killed, the experience of two Menomonee Falls, Wisconsin, men takes on special importance. On April 24, 1978, the pair snapped two Polaroid photographs of a huge kangaroo in the bush along a local highway. Loren Coleman, the leading expert on North American kangaroo sightings, felt the animal looked very much like a "Bennett's wallaby or brush Kangaroo, a native of Tasmania."

Sources:

Coleman, Loren, *Mysterious America,* Boston: Faber and Faber, 1983.
Shoemaker, Michael, "Killer Kangaroo," *Fate* 38,9, September 1985, pp. 60-61.

BLACK PANTHERS AND OTHER STRANGE CATS

Early one November morning in 1945, Wanda Dillard was driving along Highway 90 in southern Louisiana (then a narrow two-lane road) when she noticed a set of glowing red eyes at the edge of the woods ahead. Fearing that the animal might sprint into the middle of the road, she slowed down. She recalled what happened next:

> As I braked, this huge black cat left the woods, and streaked across in front of the headlights and down the embankment on the left. It was such a beautiful thing that as soon as I could maneuver a turn, I went back to see if I could get another look at him, although I expected him to be at least over in the next parish [county] by then. But lo and behold, there he was, red eyes and all, crouched at the edge of the woods just as if he were waiting to play tag with the next motorist.

A black panther.

Dillard related that as the cat got used to the headlights of her car, it "simply sat down like any common old house cat and began to groom himself." She watched the animal for some ten minutes before traffic forced her to move on. She described the animal as "jet black, very sleek looking and well muscled, with a long black tail that he wrapped around himself as he sat there." She added that while "a bit smaller," it resembled a "mountain lion in both looks and movement."

Bill Chambers, a farmer in Champaign County, Illinois, came upon a similar sight nearly two decades later. While driving along just before sunset, he spotted a large cat in a nearby field. Moving to within 190 yards of it, Chambers watched through his binoculars, hoping to kill it with a clear shot. He would have no luck, however, because the cat was almost hidden by tall clover. Still, Chambers could clearly see its tail and noted that it appeared "jet black except for two tawny streaks under the jaws." The next day the farmer returned to the site and from the size and height of the clover patch guessed that the cat was about 14 inches tall at the shoulder and roughly four and a half feet long. Chambers also found tracks in the soft, wet ground. Nearly three inches across, "they had no claw marks like a dog would make."

The above sightings are extraordinary for several reasons. For one thing, during the last half of the nineteenth century, *Felis concolor*—a family of large cats commonly known as panthers, mountain lions, cougar, or puma—was hunted to extinction everywhere (except for a small population in Florida's Everglades) east of the Rocky Mountains. Secondly, these animals are almost *never* black!

Plenty of Panthers

Constant sightings—as well as some claimed (but unproven) killings—have led a number of wildlife specialists to conclude that a small population of *Felis concolor* has survived in the eastern United States and Canada. If nothing else, the argument about whether people are seeing big cats or mistaking large dogs or wild house cats for them has largely been concluded; few doubt that big cats are out there. But the question remains: Where did they come from? One theory suggests that pet owners bought panthers as kittens and secretly released them into the wild, where they grew up and out of control.

Of course, some investigators reject black panther reports. Robert L. Downing, who undertook a study of the subject for the U.S. Fish and Wildlife Service, trumpeted the traditional view: "Some black animals, such as Labrador retrievers, are reported to be black panthers because that's the color that panthers are supposed to be, according to folklore." His caution makes some sense—tracks reportedly belonging to black panthers *have* actually been proven to be prints of dogs.

But biologist Bruce S. Wright, director of the Northeastern Wildlife Station at the University of New Brunswick, Canada, became convinced that some of these black panther sightings deserved a closer look. Over the course of his research, he collected 20 reports that he felt were reliable. All occurred in daylight and at close range.

One of these cases is especially fantastic. It took place in Queens County, New Brunswick, on November 22, 1951. A man walking near his home around 6 P.M. "heard five loud yells off in the woods." After walking further he heard more yells and, turning around, saw a large animal come leaping at him. Unable to outrun the beast, the witness "had to stop and face it." He reported, "When I stopped, it stopped and stood up on its rear legs with mouth open and 'sizzling' and with forepaws waving." The witness swung the axe he was carrying at the animal but missed and began to run again. Meanwhile, the creature apparently returned to the woods. The witness described the animal as "black or dark grey in color. The tail was at least two and one-half feet long, and the animal was at least six feet long."

> "When I stopped, it stopped and stood up on its rear legs with mouth open and 'sizzling' and with forepaws waving."

Few doubt that big cats are out there. But the question remains: Where did they come from?

This account is remarkable for three reasons. One, the panther was black; two, it stood upright; and three, it was not afraid to attack a human being. "Real" panthers have learned through bitter experience to keep as far away as possible from their mortal enemy—humans—who nearly destroyed their species. They have been rendered fearful of people.

As unbelievable as the New Brunswick story might seem, a report half a continent away and nearly two decades later also included these three amazing details. It took place a mile south of Olive Branch, Illinois, on a dark, mostly deserted road that runs along the edge of the vast Shawnee National Forest. Mike Busby of Cairo, Illinois, was on his way to pick up his wife when his car stalled. As he was releasing the hood latch, he heard something off to his left. When he turned to look, he was startled to see two quarter-sized, almond-shaped, greenish, glowing eyes staring at him.

Suddenly the strange form—six feet tall, black, and upright—hit him in the face with two padded front paws. Busby fell, the animal on top of him, and as the two rolled around, it ripped his shirt to pieces and used its dull, two-inch claws to cut his left arm, chest, and stomach. He managed to keep its open mouth, with its long, yellow teeth, away from his throat. Though he never got a good look at the creature, Busby later said that he felt what seemed like whiskers around the mouth. Its deep, soft growls were like nothing he had ever heard before. In the lights of a passing diesel truck, the creature appeared to be a slick, shiny black and, for the first time, Busby saw the "shadow of a tail." The light seemed to frighten the animal, which loped across the road with "heavy footfalls" and disappeared into the woods.

Confused and in pain, the young man crawled back to his car. To his immense relief, it started without trouble. Busby drove to Olive Branch, where he met truck driver John Hartsworth, who said that he had seen Busby struggling with what looked like a *big* cat" but was unable to brake his vehicle and help. Later that evening Busby went to St. Mary's Hospital in Cairo to get a tetanus shot and relief for his pain. For days afterward he suffered dizzy spells and had trouble walking.

But black panther sightings number in the hundreds, perhaps even in the thousands. And they have occurred in places where neither *Felis concolor* nor any other big cat has *ever* existed. In areas where *Felis concolor* is known to exist—northern California or the southeastern United States—a large number of reported sightings were of black panthers. As a matter of fact, of the 615 big cat sightings collected between 1983 and 1990 by Eastern Puma Network News, some 37 percent of them were of black panthers. J. Richard Greenwell of the International Society of Cryptozoology found the situation "mind-boggling"; for despite all the reports, no one had ever come forward with a clear photo of a black panther, or a single skin.

Big Cats Sighted in Great Britain

There is one wildcat native to the British Isles—*Felis silvestris grampia*. A small cat that once roamed much of Great Britain, it now

Drawing of a creature spotted at Van Etten Swamp, New York, in the mid-1970s.

lives only in Scotland and possibly in some isolated regions of northern England. Still, Britain has had its share of big cat sightings, and it is very unlikely that *Felis silvestris* is responsible. Arguments and theories about the presence of big cats in Britain became particularly heated in the early 1960s, when the "Surrey puma" began to prowl the country lanes of southern England.

In the late summer of 1962, something described as "a young lion cub—definitely not a fox or a dog" was seen near a reservoir in a Hampshire park. Other sightings occurred but garnered no more than local attention. But that changed early on the morning of July 18, 1963, when a truck driver passing through Oxleas Wood, Shooters Hill, London, was startled to see a "leopard" leap across the road and into trees on the other side. Later that day four police officers had an even closer look: a "large golden animal" jumped over the hood of their squad car before disappearing into the woods. The only evidence turned up by a huge search involving dozens of officers, soldiers, and dogs were large footprints of a catlike animal.

Other reports from southeastern England followed. The cats were described as large panthers or pumas, either "fawn gold" or "black" in color. Deer, sheep, and cattle in the area were found slaughtered, with huge claw marks on their sides. One woman even claimed that a "puma" had struck her in the face with its two front paws as she was walking through a wooded area in Hampshire.

To wildlife biologists, all of this seemed impossible. Weighing early reports, Maurice Burton indicated the many reasons that made the whole episode so unbelievable. He noted that "from September 1964 to August 1966, the official records show 362 sightings," with perhaps just as many "claimed but not officially reported. In other words this animal [*Felis concolor*], declared by American experts to be 'rarely seen by man,' was showing itself on average once a day for a period of two years." Burton also noted that "in two years it was reported from places as far apart as Cornwall and Norfolk, over an area of southern England of approximately 10,000 square miles. It has even been in two places many miles apart at the same time on the same day." Another wildlife expert, Victor Head, remarked that a single panther would need to eat 250 British roe deer a year to survive; yet England's deer population showed no signs of such a loss.

Still, in the years to come, big cats—along with footprints and slain farm animals—would continue to be reported all over Britain. These accounts would try the patience of those who viewed the sightings as mistaken identifications, wild imagination, or trickery. These doubters would focus on the few recorded cases that *did* have logical explanations. For example, in August 1983 a Buckinghamshire woman saw a large pumalike black cat "wearing a studded collar"—suggesting, of course, that someone had once owned it before releasing it into the wild. In August 1975, in fact, a Manchester man had captured a leopard cub with a collar. And in Inverness, Scotland, a female puma was trapped in 1980. After a short time examiners concluded that it had been a pet for most of its life.

Yet it is hard to believe that Britain is crawling with big cats that are escaped pets. To be sure, experience shows that such creatures are

> Later that day four police officers had an even closer look: a "large golden animal" jumped over the hood of their squad car before disappearing into the woods.

A "Surrey puma," photographed at Worplesdon, Surrey, from a distance of 35 yards in August 1966. The two ex-police photographers were sure it was not a wild tomcat.

poorly suited to the wild and usually starve to death or are recaptured or killed shortly after their release or escape. And if escaped pets and circus cats are out there in the numbers that sightings suggest, it is truly remarkable that so few have been recovered.

Di Francis, author of *Cat Country* (1983), has a different idea about big cats in Britain. He believes that a large, pantherlike cat has survived on the British Isles since Pleistocene times—more than 10,000 years ago! But where is the evidence, asks critic Lena G. Bottriell: "[Not] one skin in a period of some 1,000 years or more? No reports when the population of the same island [England] reduced a smaller cat [*Felis silvestris grampia*] to the point of virtually killing it out?" And like other doubters, she also pointed out the feeding needs of such cats and the serious effect that they would have on the stag and deer population—and on farm animals.

These holes have led others to suggest even stranger theories. One of them is teleportation. Here we are asked to believe that these big cats are real animals that are instantly transported from their native homes to distant places—where they stay for a few days to a few months—before returning in the same way. Other "paranormal," or outside the normal, explanations suggest that the creatures are materialized mental images from the human mind or that they are intruders from a parallel world outside our own (also see entry: **Fourth Dimension**). But what these theories fail to account for is that sightings of big cats almost *never* include supernatural features. The only strange thing about such sightings is that these big cats are in places where they have no right to be.

Big Cats Down Under

Black panthers are still sighted in Australia. Most reports come from the southern coast of New South Wales, but Paul Cropper, who has been investigating the matter for two decades, has collected others from all over the continent.

As with such sightings elsewhere in the world, some have occurred in daylight and at close range. And the animals have been

Misplaced Animals

linked to the slaying of livestock—between 1956 and 1957, one Uralla, New South Wales, farmer lost 340 sheep to a large black cat that hunters could not destroy. Prints found at the scenes of sightings usually contained claw marks, but none of the cats have ever been caught or killed. Cropper investigated one report of a killing on the Cambewarra Range in November 1977. When shown the animal's skin, though, he found it to be that of a wild house cat.

While it is tempting to explain all sightings this way—as cases of mistaken identification—the theory does not fit all reports. Consider this sighting, said to have taken place in mid-1975 in the Southern Highlands of New South Wales. Cropper wrote:

> [A farmer] and his son had been out feeding their pigs around 5 o'clock when he ... looked up and [saw] a large black animal unhurriedly ambling along a fence, past their sawmill for a couple of hundred yards. They both had watched this creature at a distance of 300 yards for at least 4 or 5 minutes. He estimated the animal weighed between 4 or 5 hundred pounds and stood 2 foot 6 inches high at the shoulder and looked exactly like a black panther. As they watched, the animal sprang 9 ft. to clear a creek, and then disappeared into the bush, leaving a perfect set of pawprints in the soft soil of the creek bank.

The farmer told a neighbor, who had seen the animal earlier, as had his granddaughter in a separate sighting. The two farmers, with several others, went to the creek bank and took a cast of the best preserved of the creature's tracks. They were huge: four inches by five inches.

Far better known is the case of the Queensland tiger. First reported by a number of witnesses around Queensland's Cardwell Bay district, the mysterious animal would be seen in other parts of Australia as well. One early account of the

REEL LIFE

Cat People, 1942.

A young dress designer is the victim of a curse that changes her into a deadly panther who must kill to survive. A classic among the horror genre with unrelenting terror from the beginning to end. Remade in 1982.

creature came from police magistrate Brinsley G. Sheridan, whose 13-year-old son had run across the beast during a walk along the shore of Rockingham Bay. The boy's small terrier had picked up the animal's scent and followed it for roughly half a mile. Then the boy observed: "It was lying camped in the long grass and was as big as a native Dog [dingo; a wild dog found in Australia]; its face was round like that of a cat, it had a long tail, and its body was striped from the ribs under the belly with yellow and black." The animal threw the terrier when it came too close and retreated up a leaning tree. Then it savagely rushed toward the two—and the boy and his dog took off running.

Later witnesses of the Queensland tiger included naturalist George Sharp, who, in the early part of the century, saw a similar creature at twilight along the Tully River. It was, he said, "larger and darker than the Tasmanian Tiger, with the stripes showing very distinctly." Not long afterward a farmer killed such a beast after it had attacked his goats. Sharp followed its tracks through the bush until he came upon its lifeless form. By then wild pigs had eaten most of the head and body, but just enough remained to show that it was about five feet long. Sharp had nothing with which to preserve what was left, though, so it soon rotted away.

Ion L. Idriess, a longtime York Peninsula resident, reported once seeing a "tiger" rip out the insides of a fully grown kangaroo. Another time he found the body of such a creature along the Alice River, where it had died in a fight with his hunting dog, which also lay dead nearby. Idriess described the "tiger-cat" as the size of a "hefty, medium-sized dog. His body is lithe and sleek and beautifully striped in black and grey. His pads are armed with lance-like claws of great tearing strength. His ears are sharp and pricked, and his head is shaped like that of a tiger."

And A. S. Le Souef and H. Burrell wrote of a similar creature in their 1926 book *The Wild Animals of Australasia.* They referred to a "large striped animal which has been aptly described as 'a cat just growing into a tiger.' The animal ... lives in country that man seldom penetrates.... Its stronghold appears to be the rough, rocky country on top of the ranges ... usually covered with heavy forest."

Sightings of this animal, though rare, continue to the present day. If reports of dead specimens are true, then the creature may, in fact, be *real.* While most Australian zoologists find black panther sightings highly questionable, they do not feel the same about reports of the Queensland tiger. As one writer put it, the animal is a "near-candidate for scientific recognition"—not as a big cat, but as the marsupial or pouched "lion" known as *thylacoleo,* which was thought to have died out some 10,000 years ago, having left many fossil remains. It does seem to be the animal that eyewitness accounts describe, even down to the creature's protruding fangs. If this is so, it is perhaps only a matter of time before a living or dead specimen falls into the hands of a zoologist and its existence is proven at last—unless, of course, the species has died out in recent years.

Sources:

Bord, Janet, and Colin Bord, *Alien Animals,* Harrisburg, Pennsylvania: Stackpole Books, 1981.

Clark, Jerome, and Loren Coleman, *Creatures of the Outer Edge,* New York: Warner Books, 1978.

Coleman, Loren, *Mysterious America,* Boston: Faber and Faber, 1983.

Heuvelmans, Bernard, *On the Track of Unknown Animals,* New York: Hill and Wang, 1958.

Shuker, Karl P. N., *Mystery Cats of the World: From Blue Tigers to Exmoor Beasts,* London: Robert Hale, 1989.

BEAST OF EXMOOR

In the spring of 1983 the name "Beast of Exmoor" was given to a mysterious roaming animal that killed a ewe belonging to farmer Eric Ley of South Molton, Devonshire, England. In the next two and a half months, Ley would lose 100 more sheep. The killer beast did not attack its victims at the hindquarters, as a dog or a fox would. Instead, it ripped out their throats.

Most who have seen the Beast of Exmoor describe it as a huge, jet-black cat, eight feet long from nose to tail, though a few witnesses have reported that it is tan-colored. In some cases, two giant cats—one black and one tan—have been seen traveling together! And a small number of witnesses have reported seeing large animals that look like unusual dogs.

First Sightings

Sightings of the "Beast" go back at least to the early 1970s. But it was not until the Ley sheep killings that Britain's Royal Marines were called into the area and London's *Daily Express* offered a one-thousand-pound reward for the beast's death or capture. Marine sharpshooters hid in the hills, and some even said they saw a "black and powerful animal" but were unable to get a clear shot at it. The beast or beasts seemed to quiet their activities while the soldiers were around, but as soon as they left the attacks began again.

One witness, local naturalist Trevor Beer, reported that he saw the beast in the summer of 1984 while watching birds in an area where slaughtered deer had been found. "I saw the head and shoulders of a

The killer beast did not attack its victims at the hindquarters, as a dog or a fox would. Instead, it ripped out their throats.

Black Beast of Exmoor, Somerset, England, photographed by Trevor Beer in 1987.

large animal appear out of the bushes," he wrote. "It looked black and rather otter-like, a first impression I shall always remember for the head was broad and sleek with small ears. The animal's eyes were clear greeny-yellow.... As it stared back at me I could clearly make out the thickish neck, the powerful forelegs and deep chest, and then without a sound it turned and moved swiftly away through the trees. That it was jet black I was sure, and long in the body and tail. I guessed at four and a half feet in body length, and about two feet at the shoulders." Beer chased the animal to the edge of the woods; the way it ran made him think of a "beautiful, very large black panther."

In 1988 an area farmer reported seeing a "fantastic cat going at a hell of a speed. Every time it moved you could see the lights shine back across its ribs." Another time the same man saw a huge cat "jump a hedge, 15 feet from standing, with a fair-sized lamb in its mouth." Late one night in December 1991, a family watched a large pantherlike animal for some minutes as it prowled around their country home. Several weeks earlier the son, 13, had seen it or a similar animal climbing a tree.

An article in London's *Daily Telegraph* reported that by early 1992, a large number of people living in the wild countryside of southwestern England had seen the beast or beasts. There were a variety of theories to explain the sightings: witnesses had mistaken large dogs for the creature, or—more likely—overjudged the size of the animals, which were really house cats gone wild. Other theorists suggested that a small breeding population of pumas, let loose by people who once kept them as pets, roamed England's wild West Country. A more far-fetched idea, held by author Di Francis but rejected by most zoologists, proposed that large cats had secretly lived in Britain since prehistoric times.

Complicating Britain's big cat puzzle is the fact that the creatures have been sighted *all over* the country. Officially, Britain's only native wildcat is *Felis silvestris grampia,* a small feline that lives in the rugged regions of northern England and Scotland (also see entry: **Black Panthers and Other Strange Cats**).

Sources:

Beer, Trevor, *The Beast of Exmoor: Fact or Legend?* Barnstaple, Devonshire, England: Countryside Productions, 1985.

Francis, Di, *Cat Country: The Quest for the British Big Cat,* North Pomfret, Vermont: David and Charles, 1983.

Martin, Andrew, "In the Grip of the Beast," *London Daily Telegraph,* January 4, 1992.

BEAST OF GEVAUDAN

One June day in 1764 in a forest in southeastern France, a young woman tending cows looked up to see a hideous beast bearing down on her. It was the size of a cow or donkey, but it resembled an enormous wolf. The woman's dogs fled, but the cattle drove the animal away with their horns. This cowherd was much more fortunate than most later witnesses of what would come to be known as the "Beast of Gevaudan."

Before long the maimed bodies of shepherd men, women, and especially children became common to the area. The first suspected victim was a little girl who was found in July with her heart ripped from her body. The killings resumed in late August or early September, and soon the creature was fearlessly attacking groups of men. The terrified countryfolk were certain that a *loup-garou* (**werewolf**) was running wild. These rumors gained authority when those who had shot or stabbed the creature reported that it seemed unaffected by their attempts to kill it. On October 8, after two hunters pumped several rifle balls into it from close range, the creature limped off. When word of the incident spread, it was believed, briefly, that the beast had gone off to die. But within a day or two it was killing again!

Terror in the French Countryside

Late in 1764 the Paris Gazette put together a general description of the beast from eyewitness accounts: it was "much higher than a wolf ... and his feet are armed with talons. His hair is reddish, his head large, and the muzzle of it is shaped like that of a greyhound; his ears are small and straight; his breast is wide and gray; his back streaked with black; his large mouth is provided with sharp teeth." On June 6, 1765, the English St. James's Chronicle remarked of the creature, "It appears that he is neither Wolf, Tiger, nor Hyena, but probably a Mongrel, generated between the two last, and forming, as it were, a new Species."

After a frightening public attack on two children, who were bitten and torn even as older youths slashed at the creature with pitchforks and knives, an appeal for help was sent to the Royal Court at Versailles. King Louis XV responded with a troop of horsemen, under the direction of Captain Duhamel. Duhamel ordered several of his men to dress as women on the theory that the creature was especially attracted to females. The soldiers spotted the beast a number of times and shot at it, but it always managed to escape. Finally, after the killings seemed to have stopped, Duhamel assumed that the beast had died of its wounds. After he and his men left, however, the bloodshed resumed.

A large reward for the slaying of the beast brought professional hunters and soldiers to the area. More than 100 wolves were killed, but the creature's rampage continued. Some hunters, including a professional wolf-tracker who had been sent personally by the king, reported that they had badly wounded the beast. But nothing seemed to stop it. During the summer of 1765 the massacre of children was especially fierce.

As the months dragged on, whole villages were abandoned after residents claimed they had seen the beast staring through their windows. Those who ventured out into the streets were attacked. Many peasants were too petrified to fire on the creature even when they had an open shot.

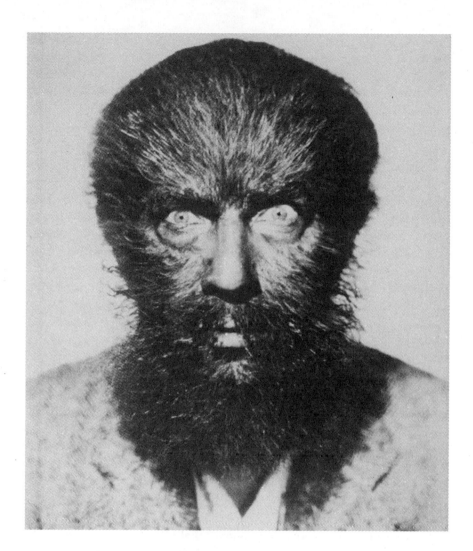

Close-up of wolf-man from 1932 film *Island of Lost Souls*. Many of the country-folk terrorized by the Beast of Gevaudan believed it to be a form of the legendary werewolf.

Death by a Silver Bullet

The crisis was finally resolved in June 1767. The Marquis d'Apcher, who lived in the western part of Gevaudan, marshaled several hundred hunters and trackers who fanned out in smaller bands over the countryside. On the evening of the 19th, the beast charged members of one group. Jean Chastel, who had loaded his weapon with *silver* bullets because the creature was so widely rumored to be a werewolf, fired on it twice. The second shot hit it squarely in the heart and killed it. The collarbone of a young girl was found in the animal's stomach when it was cut open. By the time of its death, the beast had killed some 60 people.

By the time of its death, the beast had killed some 60 people.

After the monstrous carcass was paraded throughout the region for two weeks, it was packed up to be sent to Versailles. By that time, though, it had begun to rot. Before it reached the king's court, it had to be buried somewhere in the French countryside.

Modern wildlife experts doubt reports of wolves attacking people, maintaining that the animals try to stay clear of humans. Yet there are widespread and seemingly believable reports of man-eating wolves, especially in the days before guns. Folklorists W. M. S. and Claire Russell point out that "modern wolves have had many generations' experience of fire-arms, and are likely to be more cautious than their ancestors." The story of the Beast of Gevaudan demonstrates extraordinary animal behavior. And the sheer size of the creature makes one wonder if it really was a wolf. Perhaps it was a fierce and unknown wolflike creature.

Sources:

Caras, Roger A., *Dangerous to Man: The Definitive Story of Wildlife's Reputed Dangers,* New York: Holt, Rinehart and Winston, 1975.

Russell, W. M. S., and Claire Russell, "The Social Biology of Werewolves," *Animals in Folklore,* edited by J. R. Porter and W. M. S. Russell, Totowa, New Jersey: Rowman and Littlefield, 1978.

ALLIGATORS IN SEWERS

There is a persistent American legend that alligators live under New York City, in its sewer system. Supposedly, tiny pet alligators were flushed down toilets when their owners grew tired of them—and they survived, growing so large that they became a threat to sewer workers! New York City officials today deny that any such creatures exist.

Though the rumor was most widespread in the 1960s, it was actually based on real and puzzling events that took place in the 1930s. The first of these occurred on June 28, 1932, when "swarms" of alligators were seen in the Bronx River. A three-foot-long specimen was found dead along its banks. In March 1935 and June 1937 both live and dead alligators were discovered.

Perhaps the most remarkable event was the one reported in the *New York Times* of February 10, 1935. Several teenage boys were shov-

Alligators and crocodiles have a history of showing up in the most unexpected places!

eling snow into an open manhole near the Harlem River when they spotted something moving in the icy water ten feet below. It turned out to be an alligator trying to free itself. The boys got a rope, twisted it into a lasso, and pulled the animal to the surface. When one of them tried to take the rope off the alligator's neck, however, it snapped at him. Feeling threatened, the young men beat it to death with their shovels.

The boys dragged the dead creature to a nearby auto repair shop, where the animal was weighed and measured. It was 125 pounds and seven and a half feet long! The police were informed, and a city sanitation worker took the body of the alligator off to be burned.

Around that time, Teddy May, New York City's superintendent of sewers, was receiving complaints from his workers about alligators. At first he thought the reports were just the imaginings of those who were secretly drinking alcohol on the job, and he even hired investigators to observe the habits of his employees. When these investigators came

It was 125 pounds and seven and a half feet long!

back with nothing to report, however, May himself went into the sewers with a flashlight—which soon enough revealed the presence of alligators! Shaken, May had the animals destroyed by poison or gunshot.

It was not clear how the animals got there, though it was generally thought that they were unwanted or escaped pets.

According to animal expert Loren Coleman, who specializes in these strange appearances, between 1843 and 1983 some 84 such animals were either sighted or recovered dead or alive across the United States and Canada. Coleman believed that the "pet escapee explanations cannot deal adequately with these accounts of alligators in northern waters—when it is caimans [animals similar to alligators from Central or South America] that are sold as pets." For caimans live in tropical waters and could not survive long in harsh northern climates. But alligators and crocodiles do have a history of showing up in the most unexpected places, and the mystery of these displaced animals has never been satisfactorily resolved.

Sources:

"Alligator Found in Uptown Sewer," *New York Times,* February 10, 1935.

Coleman, Loren, "Alligators-in-the-Sewers: A Journalistic Origin," *Journal of American Folklore,* July/September 1979, pp. 335-338.

Coleman, Loren, *Mysterious America,* Boston: Faber and Faber, 1983.

Michell, John, and Robert J. M. Rickard, *Living Wonders: Mysteries and Curiosities of the Animal World,* London: Thames and Hudson, 1982.

ENTOMBED ANIMALS

In 1890 a writer for *Scientific American* noted that "many well authenticated stories of the finding of live toads and frogs in solid rock are on record." Twenty years later a *Nature* editor forcefully disagreed, stating, "The thing is absolutely impossible, and ... our believing it would involve the conclusion that the whole science of geology (not [to] speak of biology also) is a mass of nonsense." Because of their outrageousness, accounts of entombed toads, frogs, and other animals are seldom discussed in the scientific literature of our time. But they were reported frequently in respected journals of the nineteenth and earlier centuries.

Loads of Toads, Frogs, and Lizards

One such account was related by Ambroise Pare, chief surgeon to Henry III of France, during the sixteenth century. It was reprinted in the 1761 edition of the *Annual Register.* While watching a quarryman "break some very large and hard stones, in the middle of one we found a huge toad, full of life and without any visible aperture [opening] by which it could get there," Pare stated. "The laborer told me it was not the first time he had met with a toad and the like creatures within huge blocks of stone."

On April 7, 1865, laborers at Hartlepool, England, made a discovery that caused quite a stir. While breaking up a block of magnesium limestone 25 feet underground, they split open a cavity in which, to their astonishment, was a living toad. "The cavity was no larger than its body, and presented the appearance of being a cast of it," the *Hartlepool Free Press* reported on April 15. "The toad's eyes shone with unusual brilliancy, and it was full of vivacity on its liberation."

At first the toad seemed to have some difficulty breathing, and a "barking" sound came out of its nostrils. This soon stopped, however, though the creature still gave a startled bark whenever it was touched. When discovered, the toad was of a pale color that matched its stony prison. But in a short time it grew darker until it became olive-brown. "The claws of its fore feet are turned inwards," the newspaper noted, "and its hind ones are of extraordinary length and unlike the present English toad."

Lumbermen also reported finding living toads embedded in or tumbling out of the solid trunks of trees that they were sawing. In 1719 the *Memoires* of the French Academy of Sciences related that a medium-sized live toad was found "in the foot of an elm, ... three or four feet above the root and exactly in the center, ... filling up the whole vacant space." In the fall of 1876, South African timbermen cutting a 16-foot trunk into lumber had just removed the bark and the first plank when a hole the size of a wine glass was uncovered. Inside this space were 68 small toads, each about the size of the tip of a human finger! According to the *Uitenhage Times* (December 10), "They were ... of a light brown, almost yellow color, and perfectly healthy, hopping about and away as if nothing had happened. All about them was solid yellow wood, with nothing to indicate how they could have got there, how long they had been there, or how they could have lived without food, drink, or air."

Next to toads, frogs are the most frequently entombed animals. Celebrated twentieth-century biologist-philosopher Sir Julian Huxley

While breaking up a block of magnesium limestone 25 feet underground, they split open a cavity in which, to their astonishment, was a living toad.

"The toad's eyes shone with unusual brilliancy, and it was full of vivacity on its liberation."

related this story, told to him in a letter from Eric G. Mackley, a gas fitter from Barnstaple, Devonshire, England. Mackley explained that in the midst of a road expansion, he and a fellow worker had to move gas meters located inside the front gates of a row of bungalows. The meter-houses had concrete floors, which had to be broken up for pipe extensions. "My mate was at work with a sledge hammer when he dropped it suddenly and said, 'That looks like a frog's leg,'" Mackley recalled. "We both bent down and there was the frog.... [The] sledge was set aside and I cut the rest of the block carefully. We released 23 perfectly formed but minute frogs which all hopped away to the flower garden."

Tilloch's Philosophical Magazine offered a lizard-in-stone tale in 1821. A Scottish mason, David Virtue, was fashioning "a barley mill-stone from a large block" when "he found a lizard imbedded in the stone. It was about an inch and a quarter long, of a brownish yellow color, and had a round head, with bright sparkling projecting eyes. It was apparently dead, but after being about five minutes exposed to the air it showed signs of life.... It soon after ran about with much celerity." Virtue noted that when the lizard was first discovered, "it was coiled up in a round cavity of its own form, being an exact impression of the animal," and that the stone and creature were of the same color. The block from which the animal sprang had come from 21 or 22 feet below the earth's surface! The mason remarked that "the stone had no fissure [and] was quite hard."

Explanations

Like all mysteries, entombed animal stories have stirred both excitement and disbelief. The *Nature* writer quoted earlier offered this explanation for the phenomenon: "The true interpretation of these alleged occurrences appears to be simply this—a frog or toad is hopping about while a stone is being broken, and the non-scientific observer immediately rushes to the conclusion that he has seen the creature dropping out of the stone itself."

But this explanation is not consistent with such reports; it does not take into account the presence of a "smooth" or "polished" cavity—only slightly larger than the creature's body—inside the rock, concrete, or tree. And often the animal is spotted within that cavity before freeing itself or being freed from it. Also, the beast in question frequently boasts an unusual appearance that suggests it has been confined for some length of time.

In a modern case reported in August 1975, construction workers in Forth Worth, Texas, were startled to find a living green turtle in concrete they were breaking up; the surface had been laid more than a year before. The smooth, body-shaped cavity in which the turtle rested during its imprisonment was clearly visible. The animal's good fortune, however, was short-lived; it died within 96 hours of its rescue.

It has been suggested that animals trapped inside rocks have been able to survive by drinking water seeping through cracks. But many witnesses have claimed that no such openings could be observed. What is more, this does not explain how the animals got there in the first place.

Sources:

Michell, John, and Robert J. M. Rickard, *Mysteries and Curiosities of the Animal World,* New York: Thames and Hudson, 1982.

Michell, John, and Robert J. M. Rickard, *Phenomena: A Book of Wonders,* New York: Pantheon Books, 1972.

"Toads in Rocks," *Scientific American* 63, 1890, p. 180.

NORTH AMERICAN APES

Loren Coleman, an expert in strange animal sightings, believes that a population of apes has existed for some time in the dense forests of the Mississippi Valley and surrounding areas. He calls these animals North American apes, or NAPEs.

He bases his idea on a number of reports from mostly southeastern states of "ape-like, hairy, and tailless" creatures. Some are referred to in folklore: for example, early settlers spoke of a tribe of "monkeys" that lived in the surrounding woods of Monkey Cave Hollow near Scottsville, Kentucky. Other evidence includes twentieth-century reports of contacts with "gorillas" and "chimpanzees" in the North American wild.

Though these animals are often viewed as escapees from circuses or zoos, in fact such escapes are rare. In the 1970s officials admitted that small populations of wild primates did exist in Florida and Texas. But Coleman believes that NAPEs are something else; he thinks that they are descendants of *Dryopithecus,* a widespread great ape about the size of a chimpanzee. The dryopithecines were supposed to have died out during Pleistocene times, more than 10,000 years ago. According to Coleman, the animals remain in North America and, moreover, have learned how to swim. He feels that "their range up and down the Mississippi" and its branches demonstrates that they travel by water as well as through the "forests bordering the river systems."

Though sightings of NAPEs have brought doubts and varying explanations, Coleman's best evidence consists of footprints that seem

Coleman's best evidence consists of footprints that seem to show the opposed left toe of a chimpanzee or, possibly, a lowland gorilla.

to show the opposed left toe of a chimpanzee or, possibly, a lowland gorilla. Coleman's interest in the subject began, in fact, with his own discovery of such a print along a dry creek bed near Decatur, Illinois, in the spring of 1962. Similar prints have been found in Florida, Alabama, and Oklahoma.

Most anthropologists and primatologists have paid no attention to Coleman's rather wild theory. Roderick Sprague of the University of Idaho, however, has praised Coleman's efforts, although he admitted that Coleman's idea of a modern *Dryopithecus*—without any fossil evidence—"is a weak point in an otherwise well developed argument" for the existence of apes in North America.

Sources:

Coleman, Loren, *Mysterious America,* Boston: Faber and Faber, 1983.
Sanderson, Ivan T., *Abominable Snowmen: Legend Come to Life,* Philadelphia: Chilton Books, 1961.

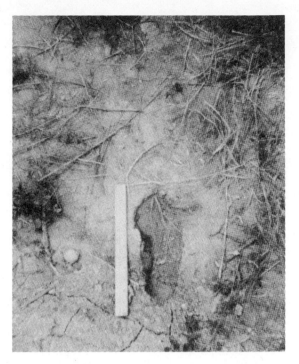

Loren Coleman found this apelike print in a creek bed in Decatur, Illinois, in 1962.

Shaggy, Two-footed Creatures in North America

- HAIRY BIPEDS

- BIGFOOT

- MOMO

- LAKE WORTH MONSTER

- JACKO

- MINNESOTA ICEMAN

Shaggy, Two-footed Creatures in North America

HAIRY BIPEDS

One night in January 1992, two men driving on a dark country road were startled when their headlights made out two figures. The larger figure stood seven to eight feet tall and appeared to weigh over 500 pounds; the shorter one looked roughly five feet and 300 pounds. The creatures were moving toward the car. Frightened, the driver backed up until he found a place to turn around. Looking over their shoulders as they sped away, the witnesses saw that the bigger creature was still heading in their direction.

This story sounds like it should originate in the Pacific Northwest, the reported home of **Bigfoot** (also known as Sasquatch), the giant apelike human or humanlike ape that many think exists but has managed to escape scientific detection. But the above report comes from Tuscola County in eastern Michigan. According to local monster expert Wayne King, it is the county's 38th hairy biped (an animal that walks on two feet) report since 1977. In fact, similar sightings have been recorded in nearly every state and province in the United States and Canada.

While they seem similar, there is a difference between Bigfoot reports and accounts involving hairy bipeds (HBs). Bigfoot sightings and the physical evidence that goes with them (mostly footprints) do not shake our ideas about reality; they actually adhere to the laws of zoology. In

> ### PRIMATOLOGY AND ANTHROPOLOGY
>
> **T**he order of Primates includes man, apes, monkeys, and related forms. Scientists who study primates are called *primatologists*. *Anthropologists* study human beings. They focus on the physical, social, and cultural development and behavior of men and women.

In the 1945 film *White Pongo,* this mythic white gorilla is believed to be the "missing link."

fact, several well-respected anthropologists and primatologists, especially Grover Krantz and John Napier, have written about the creature's possible place in the families of ape and man (also see entry: **Bigfoot**). But sightings of HBs can be out of this world, as we shall see.

Nineteenth- and Twentieth-Century Hairy Biped Reports

The mystery of Bigfoot grabbed worldwide attention in the late 1950s. Therefore, it might seem that Bigfoot's popularity inspired those with active imaginations to encounter their own HBs. But Americans were reporting HBs long before they had ever heard of Bigfoot. For example, in the early 1970s, while teaching at Newfoundland's Memorial University, American folklore expert David J. Hufford found a late-nineteenth-century book that recorded sightings of the "Traverspine gorilla," a beast that derived its name from the settlement around which it was often seen.

Ivan Terence Sanderson was a natural scientist known for several popular books—*Animal Treasures*, *Animals Nobody Knows*, and *Living Mammals of the World.* During his career he appeared often on television, presenting exotic animals to audiences.

Ivan T. Sanderson

(1911-1973)

Born in Edinburgh, Scotland, he spent part of his childhood on his father's game preserve in Kenya. Sanderson later earned master's degrees in zoology, botany, and geology. After launching a number of scientific expeditions in remote locales around the world in the 1930s, he began a full-time career as a writer and lecturer on the natural sciences.

Sanderson's focus on unexplained natural events brought cryptozoology to the attention of the public. In 1948 he wrote a popular article about still-living dinosaurs in Africa. In 1961 he published *Abominable Snowmen: Legend Come to Life,* the first book of its kind to explore worldwide reports of apeman-like creatures. Sanderson also wrote about everything from UFOs to sky-born falling rocks to the Bermuda Triangle. In 1965 he formed the Society for the Investigation of the Unexplained (SITU).

In the late 1960s Sanderson wrote two books with unusual theories about UFOs. *Uninvited Visitors* (1967) argued that UFOs were atmospheric life forms (also see entry: Star Jelly). *Invisible Residents* argued that some UFOs were piloted by an advanced underwater civilization that has always lived side by side with us (also see entry: Vile Vortices). Sanderson died of cancer in 1973.

As she frantically tried to restart the car, the creature— seven feet tall and emitting a rank odor—reached through the open window and grabbed the top of her head.

Sightings in the early twentieth century include a *Washington Post* report of a "huge gorilla" wandering in the woods near Elizabeth, Illinois, on July 25, 1929. In *Wild Talents* (1932) strange-animal expert Charles Fort wrote about a hunt for an "apelike animal—hairy creature, about four feet tall" that went on for three weeks in June and July 1931. Local circus and zoo spokesmen insisted that none of their apes were missing. The police were called in, a "gorilla" was spotted several times, and tracks were found that "seemed to be solely of those of the hind feet." And the following January, in a country area north of Downington, Pennsylvania, John McCandless heard a moaning sound in a bush. Its source, he told a reporter, was a "hideous form, half-man, half-beast, on all fours and covered with dirt or hair." Soon afterward other people told of coming upon the creature, which managed to dodge search parties.

Between the 1920s and the 1950s, other reports of HBs were recorded in New Jersey, Maryland, Missouri, Indiana, Michigan, Alabama, and other states. Later, during the Bigfoot era (from the late 1950s to the present), a number of people came forward to describe sightings from earlier in the century. A woman told biologist Ivan T. Sanderson—the first writer to bring Bigfoot to wide public attention— about a 1911 event that took place when she was living in far northern Minnesota; there, she said, two hunters saw a "human giant which had long arms and short, light hair" and left strange prints. A man remembered that in 1942, while he was cutting trees in a New Hampshire forest, a "gorilla-looking" creature followed him for some 20 minutes. And in 1914, according to an account given in 1975, a boy saw a gorilla-like creature sitting on a log in his backyard in Churchville, Maryland.

Later HB Sightings

From the 1950s to the present, HB reports have been recorded in startling numbers. Here are a few examples:

Monroe, Michigan, August 11, 1965

As they rounded a curve in a wooded area, Christine Van Acker, 17, and her mother were astonished as a hairy giant stepped out onto the road. In her panic, Christine hit the brakes instead of the gas. As she frantically tried to restart the car, the creature—seven feet tall and emitting a rank odor—reached through the open window and grabbed the top of her head.

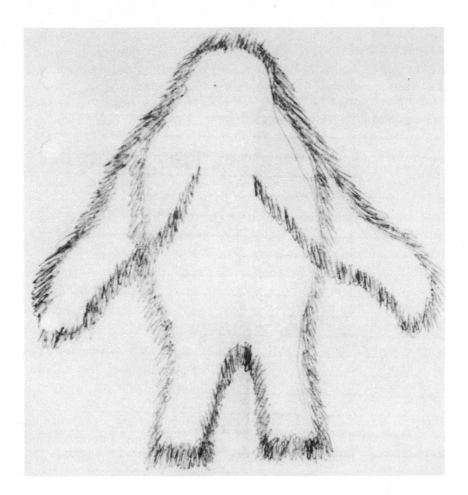

The screams of Christine and her mother and the honking car horn caused the HB to retreat to the woods. Nearby workmen arrived at the scene moments later, finding the two women dazed with fear. Somehow in the course of the attack, Christine had received a black eye. The story received national attention, with a photograph of Christine's bruised face appearing in hundreds of newspapers around the country.

Rising Sun, Indiana, May 19, 1969

At 7:30 P.M., as George Kaiser was crossing the farmyard on the way to his tractor, he spotted a strange figure standing 25 feet away. He was able to watch it for about two minutes before it spotted him. Kaiser described the creature as "upright," "about five-eight or so," and "very muscular." He added, "The head sat directly on the shoulders, and the face was black.... It had eyes set close together, and with a very short forehead. It was covered with hair except for the back of the hands and the face. The hands looked like normal hands, not claws." Seeing Kaiser, the creature made a grunting sound, turned around, leaped over a ditch, and dashed off at great speed down the road. Plaster casts of the tracks it left showed three small toes plus a big toe.

Putnam County, Indiana, August 1972

Randy and Lou Rogers, a young couple living outside tiny Roach-dale (population 950), 40 miles west of Indianapolis, experienced regular late-night visits from a shadowy creature. Brief glimpses revealed a large, hairy "gorilla." It traveled on two feet most of the time, but when it ran, it did so on all fours. Mrs. Rogers reported the odd observation that "we could never find tracks, even when it ran over mud. It would run and jump, but it was like somehow it wasn't touching anything. When it ran through weeds, you couldn't hear anything. And sometimes when you looked at it, it seemed you could see through it."

Regardless, local farmer Carter Burdine claimed to have lost 30 of his 200 chickens to the creature, which tore them apart. Burdine, his father, and his uncle saw the HB in the chicken house and chased it into the barn. The uncle opened fire on it as it fled to a nearby field. "I shot four times with a pump shotgun," Bill Burdine said. "The thing was only about 100 feet away when I started shooting. I must have hit it. I've killed a lot of rabbits at that distance." Still, the HB appeared unharmed! At least 40 other persons claimed to have seen the creature before sightings suddenly stopped later in the month.

Vaughn, Montana, December 26, 1975

In the late afternoon, two teenaged girls went to check on their horses, which seemed upset. Two hundred yards from them and 25 yards from a thicket, they observed a huge figure, seven and a half feet tall and twice as wide as a man. Intending to frighten it off, one of the girls fired a .22 rifle into the air. When nothing happened, she fired again, and this time the creature dropped to all fours, walked a short distance, then stood up again. The girls took off running. As one looked over her shoulder, she saw three or four similar creatures with the first beast, all heading toward the thicket. Law officers asked the girls to take a lie-detector test, which they passed. Other sightings, hearings, and tracks of HBs were recorded in Montana in the mid-1970s.

Salisbury, New Hampshire, October 1987

Two or three days after a hunter had told him of seeing two strange beasts walking across a field next to Mill Brook, Walter Bowers, Sr., sensed that he was being watched while hunting in the area. Then, standing between two groups of trees, he saw a "thing ... at least nine feet" tall, "maybe less, maybe more"—a creature covered with grayish-colored hair. Because the sun was in his eyes, Bowers could not make out the beast's face, but he noted that the "hands were like yours or mine, only three times bigger.... It was just like ... a gorilla, but this here wasn't a gorilla." The HB ran into a swamp, and Bowers ran to his car and sped away. A reporter described the witness as a "man of sound mind and sober spirit." Nonetheless, a game warden suggested that the man had merely spotted a moose.

Furry Objects and Flying Objects

The HB sightings in Roachdale (Putnam County), Indiana, were linked to another strange occurrence. Late one August evening in 1972, a witness in Roachdale saw a glowing object hover briefly over a cornfield before it seemed to "blow up." Lou Rogers, who lived on the other side of the field, observed an HB soon afterward.

While the witness may have just seen an exploding meteor, unconnected to the sighting, a handful of cases do link HBs and **UFOs** (unidentified flying objects). Some investigators, especially Stan Gordon and Don Worley, have suggested that HBs are a kind of UFO visitor. Though most of their cases are poorly documented—usually no more than a UFO sighting in the same general area as an HB report—there have been a few incidents that have proven startling. For example:

Uniontown, Pennsylvania, October 25, 1973

Having observed a red light hovering above a field just outside town, a 22-year-old man and two 10-year-old boys rushed to the site in a pickup truck. There they saw a white dome-shaped UFO resting on the ground, "making a sound like a lawn mower." "Screaming sounds" could be heard nearby. Two large apelike creatures with glowing green eyes were walking along a fence. The taller, eight-foot HB was running its left hand along the fence, while the other hand nearly touched the ground; behind it, a shorter, seven-foot creature was trying to keep up. The whining sound they both made seemed to be their way of communicating. The eldest witness, who had a rifle, fired three times

directly into the larger HB, which whined and reached out for its companion. At that moment the UFO vanished and the two creatures disappeared into the trees. A state police officer called to the scene soon afterward noticed a 150-foot glowing area where the UFO had sat. He also heard loud crashing sounds in the woods, made by someone or something big and heavy. At this point, the 22-year-old witness experienced a nervous collapse.

More Strangeness

On March 28, 1987, at 11:45 P.M., Dan Masias of Green Mountain Falls, Colorado, happened to look out his window to see "these creatures ... running down the road right in front of my house, which at one point is 30 feet from my front window. The whole road there was covered with about a quarter of an inch of fresh, cold snow that had fallen. They ran down the road in a manner with their arms hanging down, swinging in a pendulum motion. The first impression I got was that they were covered with hair. It was the most incredible thing I've ever seen."

After Masias's sighting was reported in the newspapers, other residents of the area, near Pike National Forest, came forward with their own accounts (which they had kept quiet for fear they'd be mocked). Sightings and hearings—of unearthly howls and growls—continued, and some people who followed HB tracks in snow swore that they vanished in midstep.

Just as the idea that apelike creatures could secretly live in states like Indiana and New Hampshire seems biologically impossible, the very nature of HBs seem biologically impossible as well. Sometimes they don't leave tracks when it seems that they should; and when they do leave tracks, they may be two-, three-, four-, five-, or even six-toed! In a handful of accounts, we are told that HBs have been shot and killed, but more often witnesses insist that the bullets barely bother the creatures. Sometimes HBs seems to disappear instantly like ghosts, but they leave things—like strands of hair caught in fences—behind.

Even more incredible, some witnesses, in locations as far apart as southern California and South Dakota, have reported *invisible* HBs! During a flurry of sightings at a Native American reservation in South Dakota in 1977, a creature was seen throughout the afternoon and evening hours on November 3. By then local residents and law officers had the area staked out. One of them, rancher Lyle Maxon, reported this weird event:

> We were out there walking in the dark, and I could hear very plainly something out of breath from running.... I put my flashlight right where I could plainly hear it, only where it

REEL LIFE

King Kong, 1933.

The original beauty and the beast film classic tells the story of Kong, a giant ape captured in Africa and brought to New York as a sideshow attraction. Kong falls for Fay Wray, escapes from his captors, and rampages through the city. Remade numerous times.

The Planet of the Apes, 1968.

Astronauts crash land on a planet where apes are masters and humans are merely brute animals. Charlton Heston delivers a believable performance and superb ape makeup creates realistic pseudo-simians of Roddy MacDowall and other stars. Followed by four sequels and two television series.

Return of the Ape Man 1944.

Campy fun with John Carradine and Bela Lugosi. A mad scientist transplants Carradine's brain into the body of the "missing link."

Scene from 1933 horror classic *King Kong.*

should have been, there was nothing in sight. Now what I'm wondering is, can this thing make itself invisible when things get too close for comfort?

In *Bigfoot,* a 1976 book on HB sightings in southern California, B. Ann Slate and Alan Berry tell of similar events.

It is certain that at least some HB reports are hoaxes—stories told by liars or by people who were truly fooled by pranksters wearing costumes. Other HBs (for example, a figure observed by a number of Lawton, Oklahoma, residents in February 1971) turn out to be dirty, bearded, mentally ill humans like the "wild men" of so many nineteenth-century accounts. And in some cases HBs are probably bears. Still, these explanations can't possibly account for all the HB sightings—and there are now many—that have been reported. So far no general theory has been suggested to explain these puzzling reports.

Sources:

Bord, Janet, and Colin Bord, *Alien Animals,* Harrisburg, Pennsylvania: Stackpole Books, 1981.

Brandon, Craig, "Bigfoot!!! Apeman Stalks Woods Near Us, Book Claims,"*Albany* [New York] *Times Union,* February 16, 1992.

Drier, Mary, "Bigfoot Returns, Area Men Maintain, *Bay City* [Michigan] *Times,* March 24, 1992.

Sanderson, Ivan T., *Things,* New York: Pyramid Books, 1967.

Slate, B. Ann, and Alan Berry, *Bigfoot,* New York: Bantam Books, 1976.

BIGFOOT

Bigfoot is, without a doubt, North America's most prominent cryptozoological (the science of hidden animals) mystery. If its existence is ever proven (and nothing short of an actual specimen would satisfy most scientists) it would provide an amazing new look into human evolution. For if Bigfoot is out there, it may be a relative of ours. In fact, Bigfoot believers think that it is either an ape or a kind of early human being.

Bigfoot, or Sasquatch, as it is known in Canada, is the giant manlike ape or apelike man reported in the northwestern United States (northern California, Oregon, Washington, and Idaho) and far western Canada (British Columbia and Alberta). This region of mountains and forests is so vast that the idea that such a beast could survive—undetected by all but a few startled eyewitnesses—is at least possible, if still incredible.

According to John Green, a leading Canadian Bigfoot investigator and writer, the creatures average seven and a half feet in height. (Bigfoot eyewitness accounts number in the many hundreds.) They seem to prefer being alone and are seldom seen in the company of others. Hair covers almost all of their bodies, and the length of their limbs is more human than apelike. Nonetheless, their broad shoulders, lack of a neck, flat faces and noses, sloped foreheads, pronounced eyebrow ridges, and cone-shaped heads are more animal-like than human. They eat both animals and plants, are largely nocturnal (active at night), and are mostly inactive during cold weather.

John Napier, a primatologist (one who studies primates, an order of mammals made up of humans and apes), notes that in a number of the most reliable reports, the Sasquatch is "covered in reddish-brown or auburn hair." Still, black, beige, white, and silvery-white hair have also been noted. Napier added that footprints range in size from 12 to 22

The word "Sasquatch" comes from a term used by the Coast Salish Indians.

Noted Sasquatch investigator John Green (left) with two companions and Bigfoot casts.

inches, with the average sample measuring 16 inches in length and 7 inches across.

Background

Reports of a creature resembling Bigfoot began with early American Indian legends of giant woodland bipeds (animals that walk on two feet). The closest creature to Bigfoot in this folklore is the Witiko (or Wendigo), known to the Algonkian Indians of the northern forests. But Witikos were cannibalistic giants with supernatural powers; they could possess people and turn them into other Witikos, for instance.

Published reports of Bigfoot references started to appear in the early twentieth century. The Victoria, British Columbia, newspaper the *Colonist,* in 1901 related the experience of Mike King, a lumberman working on Vancouver Island near Campbell River. King was alone because his packers refused to go with him, fearing the "monkey men" they said lived in the forest. Late in the afternoon the lumberman saw a "man beast" washing roots in the water. When the creature became aware of him, it cried out and scooted up a hill, stopping at one point to look over its shoulder at him. King described the beast as "covered with reddish brown hair, and his arms were peculiarly long and were used freely in climbing and in brush running; the trail showed a distinct human foot, but with phenomenally long and spreading toes."

Three years later, on December 14, 1904, the *Colonist* reported that four reliable witnesses had also seen a Bigfoot-like creature on Vancouver Island. And three years after that, it told of an American Indian village that was abandoned, its inhabitants frightened into moving by a "monkey-like wild man who appears on the beach at night [and] ... howls in an unearthly fashion."

Residents of western Canada were well aware of the hairy giants called Sasquatches. This was because of the writings of J. W. Burns, a schoolteacher at the Chehalis Indian Reserve near Harrison Hot Springs, British Columbia. From the Chehalis Indians, Burns learned that Sasquatch was not so much an apeman as a fabulous superman, an intelligent "giant Indian" with supernatural powers.

Other people who claimed that they had really seen the hairy giants included a British Columbia man named Albert Ostman, who came forward in 1957 to report an incident he claimed took place in 1924. While on a prospecting trip at the head of Toba Inlet, opposite Vancouver Island, he was scooped up one night inside his sleeping bag and carried many miles. When he was finally dumped out he discovered that he was the prisoner of a family—adult male and female, young male and female—of giant apelike creatures! Though the beasts were friendly, they clearly did not want him to escape, and Ostman managed to do so only after the larger male choked on his chewing tobacco. He was gone for six days. Those who interviewed the man, including strange-animal experts John Green and Ivan T. Sanderson, did not doubt his honesty or his mental health. Even primatologist Napier found the account "convincing."

Another fascinating story tells of an attack by Bigfoot creatures on a group of miners in the Mount St. Helens/Lewis River area of southwestern Washington. The event began one evening in July 1924, when two of the miners—already jumpy from listening to a week's worth of strange whistling and thumping sounds coming from nearby ridges—spotted a seven-foot-tall apelike creature and fired on it. They fled to their cabin and, along with two other men, endured a night-long attack by a number of the creatures, who threw rocks and repeatedly tried to smash the door

While on a prospecting trip at the head of Toba Inlet, opposite Vancouver Island, a man was scooped up one night inside his sleeping bag and carried many miles. When he was finally dumped out he discovered that he was the prisoner of a family of giant apelike creatures!

in. *Portland Oregonian* reporters who came to the scene later found giant footprints. The spot where the episode occurred was thenceforth called Ape Canyon.

In 1967 one of the men involved in the incident, Fred Beck, published a booklet with his son Ronald recalling the event; it was titled *I Fought the Apemen of Mt. St. Helens.* Later, however, in a 1982 interview with a Vancouver newspaper, Rant Mullens, 86, confessed that he and his uncle were responsible for the long-ago episode. On their way home from a fishing trip, they "rolled some rocks down" near the cabin as a joke. Ronald Beck rejected the idea that the complicated story of the attack was "a common hoax."

Sasquatch sightings continued and were reported from time to time, mostly in Canadian newspapers. At some point in the 1920s the name "Bigfoot" came into use, as northwestern residents marveled at the size of the tracks they were encountering in remote areas. In 1958 the mystery of Bigfoot grabbed American attention when heavy-equipment operators near Willow Creek in northwestern California discovered a large number of tracks left by a huge biped, which had seemingly examined a land-clearing bulldozer left at the site overnight. After the tracks appeared several more times, casts were made, bringing wide press coverage. A few weeks later, in late October, two men driving down a wilderness road saw a huge hairy biped cross in front of them and disappear into the trees, leaving prints behind.

The Patterson Film

By the 1960s Bigfoot, sometimes called "America's abominable snowman," held a firm place in the public's imagination. Though scientists refused to believe that witnesses were actually seeing what they claimed (reports were blamed either on hoaxes or bear sightings), several investigators, such as John Green, Rene Dahinden, and Jim McClarin, looked for witnesses, went into the bush in search of sightings themselves, studied the data, and wrote articles and books about their findings. Ivan T. Sanderson's 1961 *Abominable Snowmen: Legend Come to Life*—the first book to fully discuss the Bigfoot/Sasquatch phenomenon—linked the North American reports with worldwide accounts of "wild men," including the **Almas** of Mongolia and the **yeti,** or "abominable snowman," of the Himalayas.

Among those who went looking for Bigfoot in the wild was Roger Patterson, a onetime rodeo rider and sometime inventor and promoter. After a 1959 *True* magazine article about Bigfoot sparked his interest, he roamed the Pacific Northwest woods when time permitted, hoping to catch a glimpse of the creature. Eventually he decided to make a documentary film about the mystery and began taking a motion-picture camera with him on his expeditions. He shot footage that he thought might prove useful in his future movie.

At a little after 1:15 on the afternoon of October 20, 1967, Patterson and a companion, Bob Gimlin, were riding north up the partly dry, 100-yard-wide bed of Bluff Creek in the Six Rivers National Forest of northern California. (This area had seen so much Bigfoot activity—both sightings and tracks—that it had become something of a tourist attraction.) At one point a high pile of logs in the center of the stream blocked their way, and they had to direct their horses around it. As they passed the logs and took up their original course, they saw—or would claim to have seen—something that has become the source of heated argument for decades.

Bob Gimlin with prints from the Patterson film site.

They saw a female Bigfoot stand up from the creek water in which she was squatting and walk briskly away into the surrounding trees, swinging her arms all the while. This caused the horses that Patterson and Gimlin were riding (as well as their packhorse) to panic. Patterson's animal reared up and fell over sideways on its rider's right leg. As his horse staggered to its feet, Patterson felt around for the 16-mm camera in the saddlebag, then jumped off to follow the retreating creature on foot. Only 28 feet of film remained in the camera, and Patterson used it to record the Bigfoot from three different positions.

Patterson died in 1972, swearing to the end that both the sighting and the film were real. Gimlin, still alive, also sticks by the story. The first investigator on the site, Bob Titmus, found tracks in locations that exactly matched the Bigfoot's route in the film; he made casts of ten of them. The prints also indicated that the creature had gone up a hillside and sat down for a while, apparently to watch Patterson and Gimlin, who had stopped their tracking efforts in order to recover two of their horses.

Of course Patterson's film did not solve the mystery of whether an "abominable snowman" of America existed or not. As a matter of fact, debate over the Patterson film goes on and will probably continue to

Photograph by Roger Patterson taken northeast of Eureka, California: evidence of Bigfoot or a "man in a suit"?

until the "man in the suit" confesses or someone produces a physical specimen of Bigfoot to compare with the figure in the film. Everyone agrees, at least, that the Patterson footage is worth discussing, unlike many other Bigfoot films that are clearly fake.

More Recent Sightings

The next big stir in the Bigfoot mystery took place in 1982. Though it first looked like a promising development, it would ultimately prove a disappointment.

The event began with a story told by Paul Freeman, a sometimes employee of the U.S. Forest Service. On the morning of June 10, he was driving through the Blue Mountains in the Umatilla National Forest, which stretches across southeastern Washington and northeastern Oregon. Spotting some elk, he stopped his truck, jumped out, and followed the animals on foot. He wanted to find out if there were any calves among them.

As he rounded a bend, he noticed a "stench" and at the other side of the turn saw something coming down a bank though some thick plant growth. When the figure stepped into the clearing, Freeman froze and stared in disbelief at an "enormous creature"—an eight-and-a-half-foot Bigfoot—which stared back at him. For a few seconds the two studied each other from a distance of 150 to 200 feet, then fled in opposite directions.

Very upset, Freeman notified his bosses in Walla Walla, Washington, at once, and two hours later a group of Forest Service workers arrived at the site, which was located in Oregon near the Washington border. They found 21 footprints measuring 14 inches long and seven inches wide. They took three casts and some photographs of the prints.

On June 14 the Walla Walla station made a public statement recounting Freeman's sighting and remarking that "no determination can be made" about the identity of the creature he had claimed to see. The Forest Service also reported that it had no further plans to investigate. Still, four days later it revealed that on the 16th, Freeman and patrolman Bill Epoch had discovered about 40 new tracks in the Mill Creek Watershed on the Washington side of the border. On the 17th, Joel Hardin, a U.S. Border Patrol tracking expert and a Bigfoot doubter, examined the prints and judged them hoaxes. He said that among other suspicious features, they exhibited dermal ridges (lines in the skin), which animals do not have. He failed to mention, however, that higher primates—monkeys, apes, and human beings—do have such ridges on their toes and fingers (thus, fingerprints).

Search for Body Reveals Big Footprints

The day after Freeman's sighting, Oregon's Umatilla County Sheriff's Department sent a five-person team of volunteers to the same Tiger Creek area. The searchers were not looking for a Bigfoot, however, but for the body of a boy who had disappeared the autumn before. They went to the site because of Freeman's mention of a terrible smell, which they thought might be that of a decaying corpse. Though the team found neither the odor nor a body, it did make another discovery.

According to Art Snow, a local businessman who headed the team, the search party was able to follow the tracks beyond the 21 found by the Forest Service. In fact, Snow said, the tracks could be seen for three-quarters of a mile. The team made a cast of one of the better prints. Snow related that all evidence found by his group supported Freeman's story.

Soon afterward Washington State University anthropologist Grover Krantz, one of Bigfoot's leading scientific supporters, studied casts from both the Tiger Creek and Mill Creek Watershed areas. He also obtained a cast from Snow. After weeks of study, Krantz concluded that the prints were from "two individuals." For it seemed that one creature had a big toe larger than that of the average Bigfoot track. And the second had a "splayed-out second toe."

Aside from these differences, the prints were generally alike and typical of those connected with Bigfoot reports. The feet were about 15 inches long, and the toes were more equal in size than those of a human being. The arches were nearly flat, and there was a "double ball" at the base of the big toe.

What made the Bigfoot prints more credible was the fact that there were no human tracks around them. And the distance between the prints suggested that whatever made them had a *long* stride. In addition, Krantz noted, the tracks were so deeply pressed into the ground that most investigators felt it would take more than six hundred pounds of force to make them; no evidence of any mechanical device capable of faking this effect was found.

Other investigators, however, had serious questions about the tracks. For one thing, the prints were just too perfect. The stride did not vary, and there was no evidence of slipping up and down hillsides. When the prints were found in mud, they were not nearly as deep as they should have been if the animal weighed the 800 to 1,000 pounds that investigators estimated. (In fact, the Bigfoot prints were shallower than the tracks left by searchers' boots!) In addition, according to wildlife biologist Rodney L. Johnson, "it appeared that the foot may have been rocked from side to side to make the track." Johnson also noted that at one place where tracks were seen, "it appeared that fine forest litter

---

REEL LIFE

Harry and the Hendersons, 1987.

An ordinary American family vacationing in the Northwest has a collision with Bigfoot. Thinking that the big guy is dead, they throw him on top of the car and head home. Lo and behold, he revives and eventually endears himself to the family.

Legend of Boggy Creek, 1975.

A dramatized version of various Arkansas Bigfoot sightings.

([pine] needles, etc.) had been brushed sideways from the track area in an unnatural manner."

There were also doubts about Freeman's honesty. Longtime Bigfoot tracker Bob Titmus expressed suspicions that Freeman had manufactured evidence. And—in a television interview—Freeman once admitted that he had faked Bigfoot prints!

Though the Freeman tracks may not be real, there are many other Bigfoot prints that resist explanation. John Napier wrote that in order to judge all tracks fake, we would have to believe in a conspiracy taking place "in practically every major township from San Francisco to Vancouver." If such animals *do* live in the Northwest, it seems unlikely that they can remain hidden forever!

Sources:

Beck, Fred, and R. A. Beck, *I Fought the Apemen of Mt. St. Helens,* Kelso, Washington: The Authors, 1967.

Bord, Janet, and Colin Bord, *The Bigfoot Casebook,* Harrisburg, Pennsylvania: Stackpole Books, 1982.

Green, John, *On the Track of Sasquatch,* New York: Ballantine Books, 1973.

Napier, John, *Bigfoot: The Yeti and Sasquatch in Myth and Reality,* New York: E. P. Dutton and Company, 1973.

Sanderson, Ivan T., *Abominable Snowmen: Legend Come to Life,* Philadelphia: Chilton Book Company, 1961.

Shoemaker, Michael T., "Searching for the Historical Bigfoot," *Strange Magazine,* vol. 5, 1990.

Sprague, Roderick, and Grover S. Krantz, eds., *The Scientist Looks at the Sasquatch,* Moscow, Idaho: University Press of Idaho, 1979.

MOMO

For a few days in the summer of 1972, the story of Momo, an apeman-like creature seen in and around the small Missouri town of Louisiana (population 4,600) appeared in newspapers around the country. Momo got its name from the abbreviation of Missouri—Mo.—and the first two letters of the word *monster.*

First Sighting

The Momo scare actually began in 1971. In July of that year two picnickers in a wooded area outside town reported seeing a "half-ape

and half-man" that emitted an awful smell. Stepping out of a thicket, it walked toward them while making a "little gurgling sound." They fled and locked themselves inside their car. The creature ate a peanut butter sandwich that they had left behind and strolled back into the woods. The women reported the incident to the Missouri State Police but did not come forward publicly until a year later—after many others had reported similar sightings.

Two Weeks of Terror

Momo earned its name after a series of sightings that began on July 11, 1972. That afternoon three children saw a creature "six or seven feet tall, black and hairy," standing next to a tree. It was flecked with blood, probably from the dead dog it carried under its arm. The same day a neighbor heard strange growling sounds, and a farmer found that his new dog had disappeared.

Three evenings later, the children's father, Edgar Harrison, stood talking with friends outside his home. Suddenly, they saw a "fireball" come over a nearby hill and appear to land behind an unused school-house across the street. Five minutes later a second fireball did the same thing. Not long afterward, they heard a loud growling from the hilltop, though they could not see what was making the sound. The police investigated but found nothing.

An hour or two later, as they poked around the hilltop in the darkness, Harrison and his companions came across an old building. It was befouled by the strong, rank odor linked with Momo's appearances. Later, other Louisiana witnesses reported seeing small, glowing lights, which exploded and left the same smell behind.

The scare continued for two more weeks, during which time others reported seeing a hairy biped with both ape and human features. Some even claimed that they heard voices drifting through the air. One voice said, "You boys stay out of these woods," and another asked for a cup of coffee! Footprints supposedly made by the creature were found several times, but the only one to undergo scientific examination was judged a hoax by Lawrence Curtis, director of the Oklahoma City Zoo. And a number of Louisiana residents reported seeing fireballs and other unusual objects in the air. One, described as a UFO with lighted windows, reportedly landed for five hours on a hilltop. Another was a "perfect gold cross on the moon." The family that claimed to witness this sight said it "lit up" the road "as bright as day."

That afternoon three children saw a creature "six or seven feet tall, black and hairy," standing next to a tree. It was flecked with blood, probably from the dead dog it carried under its arm.

Sources:

Clark, Jerome, and Loren Coleman, "Anthropoids, Monsters, and UFOs," *Flying Saucer Review* 19,1, January/February 1973, pp. 18-24.
Coleman, Loren, *Mysterious America,* Boston: Faber and Faber, 1983.
Crowe, Richard, "Missouri Monster," *Fate* 25,12, December 1972, pp. 58-66.

LAKE WORTH MONSTER

In the summer of 1969, residents of Forth Worth, Texas, were terrified by repeated sightings of a hairy bipedal (two-legged) monster near local Lake Worth. Though the case is not well known, it *is* one of the best documented of the many and varied **hairy biped** accounts on record. And it produced one of the very few photographs ever taken of such reported beasts.

Early on the morning of July 10, John Reichart, his wife, and two other couples showed up at a Forth Worth police station. They were so terribly frightened that—as incredible as their story sounded—the officers had no trouble believing that the six had seen something extraordinary. According to the witnesses, they had been parked along Lake Worth around midnight when a huge creature leaped out of a tree and landed on the Reicharts's car. It was, they said, covered with both scales and fur and looked like a cross between a man and a goat.

Four police cars rushed to the scene but found nothing. They were impressed, however, by the 18-inch scratch running along the side of the witnesses' car. Swearing that it had not been there before, the Reicharts were sure it was a mark left by the monster's claws.

Over the previous two months, other reports of a monster had come to police attention, but officers had dismissed the sightings as pranks. And while they believed that the Reicharts and their friends were probably victims of a prank as well, the frightening, violent nature of the event made them take the matter more seriously than they had other such encounters.

Almost 24 hours after the Reichart attack, Jack Harris was driving along on the only road going into the Lake Worth Nature Center. There he saw the creature cross in front of him. It ran up and down a bluff and was soon being observed by 30 to 40 people who had come to the area hoping to see it—lured by the *Fort Worth Star Telegram*'s headline "Fishy Man-Goat Terrifies Couples Parked at Lake Worth." Within a short time, officers from the sheriff's department were also on the scene, watching the incredible sight. But when it appeared that some of the onlookers were going to approach the creature, it threw a spare tire, rim and all, at them. Witnesses jumped back into their cars, and the beast escaped into the underbrush.

Witnesses guessed that the creature was about seven feet tall and weighed 300 pounds. It walked on two feet and had whitish-gray hair. The beast had a "pitiful cry—like something was hurting him," Harris told a reporter. "But it sure didn't sound human."

> They were impressed, however, by the 18-inch scratch running along the side of the witnesses' car. Swearing that it had not been there before, the Reicharts were sure it was a mark left by the monster's claws.

Investigations

In the weeks ahead, groups of searchers, many carrying guns, made nightly trips into the woods and fields along the lake. Most who viewed the creature thought it resembled a "big white ape." It left tracks (they were not preserved) that reportedly measured 16 inches long and eight inches wide at the toes. One time searchers fired on the beast and followed a trail of blood and tracks to the edge of the water.

When it appeared that some of the onlookers were going to approach the creature, it threw a spare tire, rim and all, at them.

Another time three men claimed that it leaped on their car and got off only after the vehicle collided with a tree.

A second trio of searchers spent a week tracking the creature without ever seeing it, though they did hear its cry and smelled the awful odor associated with it. They also came upon dead sheep with broken necks—victims, they believed, of the beast. Allen Plaster, owner of a dress shop, took a fuzzy black and white photograph said to show the creature at close range.

Sightings would continue on and off for years. But the last report of the 1969 scare was made by Charles Buchanan on November 7. The man said he had been dozing inside his sleeping bag in the back of his pickup truck when something suddenly lifted him up. It was the monster! Buchanan grabbed a bag with chicken in it; the creature stuffed it into its mouth, then plunged into the lake and swam toward Greer Island.

Ultimately, Helmuth Naumer, a spokesman for the Forth Worth Museum of Science and History, and Park Ranger Harroll Rogers came to the hard-to-believe conclusion that the creature was a bobcat. Another explanation, though never confirmed, was the claim that police had caught pranksters with a costume. Now if a trickster *was* the monster, he would certainly have to have been remarkably brave or stupid, considering how many searchers were carrying guns and were ready to fire on sight.

Sources:

Coleman, Loren, *Mysterious America,* Boston: Faber and Faber, 1983.
Green, John, *Sasquatch: The Apes Among Us,* Seattle, Washington: Hancock House, 1978.

JACKO

On June 30, 1884, a strange creature was captured near the village of Yale in south-central British Columbia. It was spotted from a passing British Columbia Express train by engineer Ned Austin, who thought it was a man lying dangerously close to the tracks. He quickly brought the train to a stop. Suddenly, the "man" stood up and made a barking sound, then scrambled up one of the bluffs along the Fraser River. The train crew chased the "Indian"—which is what they thought the figure was—until they finally trapped it on a rocky ledge. Conductor R. J. Craig climbed up above the ledge and dropped a rock on the creature's head, knocking it out. The crew members then tied the beast up and brought it to town, where they put it in the jail.

According to the *Daily British Colonist* of July 4, the creature—quickly named Jacko—turned out to be "something of the gorilla type standing about 4 feet, 7 inches in height and weighing 127 pounds. He has long, black, strong hair and resembles a human being with one exception, his entire body, excepting his hands (or paws) and feet are covered with glossy hair about one inch long. His forearm is much longer than a man's forearm, and he possesses extraordinary strength." Noting that some of the local residents had reported seeing an odd creature over the past two years, the *Colonist* asked, "Who can unravel the mystery that now surrounds Jacko? Does he belong to a species hitherto unknown in this part of the country?"

In the 1950s, after **Bigfoot** reports in the Pacific Northwest captured widespread attention, newspaperman Brian McKelvie began searching for earlier press accounts of such beasts and found the Jacko story. He pointed it out to John Green and Rene Dahinden, who were just beginning what would turn out to be lifelong careers as Sasquatch hunters. He told them that this was the only surviving record of the event; other area newspapers, which might also have carried the story, had been lost in a fire. In 1958 Green interviewed an elderly Yale man, August Castle, who said that he remembered when Jacko came to town, though his parents had never taken him to the jail to view the creature.

The first book in which the Jacko story appeared was Ivan T. Sanderson's 1961 *Abominable Snowmen: Legend Come to Life*. The author found the account very convincing: "excellent ... factual ... hardly being at all speculative." From that point on, nearly every book on Sasquatch mentioned Jacko. In 1973 Dahinden and coauthor Don Hunter wrote that, according to the grandson of a man who had been a judge in Yale in 1884, Jacko "was shipped east by rail in a cage, on the way to an English sideshow." No more was heard of him, and local residents assumed that he had died along the way.

From the *Colonist*'s description, primatologist John Napier thought that Jacko sounded like "an adult chimpanzee or even a juvenile male or adult female gorilla." "But unless it was an escapee from a circus it is difficult to imagine what an African ape was doing swanning about in the middle of British Columbia," he remarked. "At that time chimpanzees were still fairly rare creatures in captivity."

The creature—quickly named Jacko—turned out to be "something of the gorilla type standing about 4 feet, 7 inches in height and weighing 127 pounds."

If Jacko was a gorilla, like the one pictured here, what was he doing in British Columbia?

During all this time, Green was still trying to get to the bottom of the mystery. He learned that microfilm of early British Columbia newspapers did exist. They were not in the British Columbia Archives, where McKelvie had looked, but they were at the University of British Columbia. And there, in a July 1884 issue of New Westminster's Mainland Guardian, he came upon these comments about Jacko from a reporter who was passing through Yale: "How the story originated, and by whom, is hard for one to conjecture. Absurdity is written on the face of it. The fact of the matter is, that no such animal was caught, and how the Colonist was duped in such a manner, and by such a story, is strange." Another newspaper, the British Columbian, reported that the story had sent some 200 people scurrying to the jail. There, it related, the "only wild man visible was [jailer] Mr. Murphy, ... who completely exhausted his patience" answering questions about the nonexistent beast.

It was these newspaper findings that finally convinced Green that Jacko had not been real. Still, there were those who were unwilling to put the story to rest. In *Pursuit* magazine, for instance, Russ Kinne argued that competing newspapers were simply trying to make the *Colonist* look bad by attacking the Jacko report as untrue.

Sources:

Bord, Janet, and Colin Bord, *The Bigfoot Casebook,* Harrisburg, Pennsylvania: Stackpole Books, 1982.

Green, John, *On the Track of the Sasquatch,* Agassiz, British Columbia: Cheam Publishing, 1968.

Halpin, Marjorie, and Michael M. Ames, eds., *Manlike Monsters on Trial: Early Records and Modern Evidence,* Vancouver, British Columbia: University of British Columbia Press, 1980.

Hunter, Don, and Rene Dahinden, *Sasquatch,* Toronto: McClelland and Stewart, 1973.

Napier, John, *Bigfoot: The Yeti and Sasquatch in Myth and Reality,* New York: E. P. Dutton and Company, 1973.

Sanderson, Ivan T., *Abominable Snowmen: Legend Come to Life,* Philadelphia: Chilton Book Company, 1961.

MINNESOTA ICEMAN

One day in the fall of 1968, a University of Minnesota zoology student named Terry Cullen phoned natural science investigator and writer Ivan T. Sanderson with an amazing story: it appeared that a **Bigfoot** body frozen in a block of ice was being displayed around the country as a carnival exhibit. Sanderson, a biologist long interested in unknown animals, was understandably excited. So was his houseguest, the famous Bernard Heuvelmans, a Belgian scientist known as the founder of the study of unexpected animals, or cryptozoology.

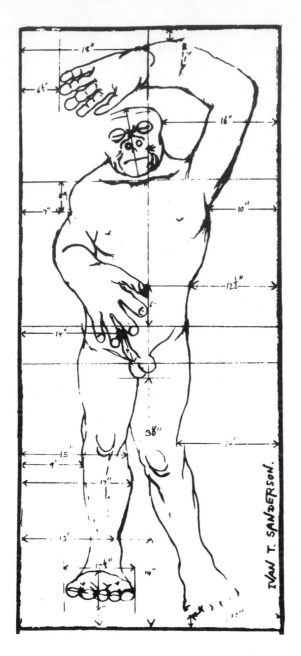

Ivan T. Sanderson's outline drawing of the Minnesota Iceman.

The two scientists lost no time in getting to tiny Rollingstone, Minnesota. There they met Frank Hansen, on whose farm the body was kept over the winter months when the carnival was not running. Hansen led them to a tiny trailer where the "Iceman"—as it was called—rested in a refrigerated coffin. Sanderson and Heuvelmans spent the next two days studying, sketching, and photographing the figure. Heuvelmans noted that it resembled an adult male human being, except that it was "entirely covered with dark brown hair three to four inches long." He also observed that the specimen showed major injuries. The left arm was twisted strangely "due to an open fracture midway between the wrist and the elbow where one can distinguish the broken ulna in a gaping wound," he reported. The creature also appeared to have been shot in the right eye. The force seemingly knocked the left eye out of its socket and blew out the back of the head.

Sanderson and Heuvelmans became convinced that the figure was what it seemed: a real body and not a model. The two scientists even examined what they thought were gas bubbles and odors escaping from the creature's slowly decaying remains.

Hansen claimed that the creature had been found floating in a 6,000-pound block of natural ice in the Russian Sea of Okhotsk. The men who discovered it were Russian seal hunters. (Though in a later version he would say they were Japanese whalers.) Eventually, according to Hansen, the body turned up in Hong Kong, where an agent of a California millionaire bought it. In time the owner rented it to Hansen, who began touring the country with it in May 1967.

Early in February 1969 Sanderson called on an old friend, John Napier, a primate expert at the Smithsonian Institution in Washington, D.C. Sharing his Iceman report and diagrams with the primatologist, Sanderson was hoping to interest the Smithsonian in joining the investigation.

As Napier would later write in his 1973 book *Bigfoot,* when he first looked at Sanderson's Iceman information, he was filled with doubt, for to him the creature seemed a crazy mixture, combining the worst traits of apes and human beings; it had "none of the best features which make these two groups extremely successful primates in their respective environments," he explained. Zoologically speaking, the Iceman did not make sense.

Still, the Smithsonian tried to obtain the specimen from Hansen. But the man said he could not provide it because its owner had, all of a sudden, reclaimed it. Hansen related that when he went back on tour it would be with a model that would "in many respects resemble" the original. After further investigation, the Smithsonian concluded that the story and the figure were a hoax.

Over the years Hansen continued to tour the United States with his Iceman exhibit, neither insisting nor denying that the figure was real. In the material he used to promote his show, however, he quoted the views of "scientists" (probably Heuvelmans and Sanderson), declaring that the Iceman was genuine.

> The creature seemed a crazy mixture, combining the worst traits of apes and human beings.

The Model Mystery

In August 1981, C. Eugene Emery, a science reporter for Rhode Island's *Providence Journal-Bulletin,* wrote an article about Hansen's exhibit, which was on display at a local shopping mall. Soon after the story appeared, Emery learned of a man named Howard Ball, then dead, who had built models for Disneyland. His specialty had been prehistoric beasts. "He made [the Iceman] here in his studio in Torrance [California]," Ball's widow, Helen, told Emery. "The man who commissioned it said he was going to encase it in ice and pass it off, I think, as a prehistoric man."

Ball's son Kenneth helped his father build the figure. He said its "skin" was half-inch-thick rubber. "We modeled it after an artist's conception of Cro-Magnon

THE CRO-MAGNON RACE

The Cro-Magnon race lived 35,000 years ago and is of the same species as modern human beings (*Homo sapiens*). Cro-Magnons stood straight and were six or more feet tall; their foreheads were high and their brains large. Discoveries of skillfully made tools, jewelry, and cave wall paintings suggest that the Cro-Magnon race had an advanced culture.

man and gave it a broken arm and a bashed-in skull with one eye popped out," he related. "As I understand it, [the man who commissioned the job] took the creature to Mexico to have the hair implanted." The Balls were pretty amused when they saw Sanderson's article in the May 1969 issue of *Argosy* and recognized their creation in the photographs published along with it.

When Emery questioned Hansen, the carnival exhibitor admitted that Ball *had* made a figure for him, but he insisted that it "was discarded." Hansen also told Emery that Ball's widow and son were mistaken about the identity of the creature shown in the *Argosy* photographs.

Had there really been a true Iceman specimen exhibited for some time before a model replaced it? Sanderson died in 1973, still convinced that the creature he and Heuvelmans had seen was not the one later shown around the country—the one they had studied had been a real animal. Similarly, Heuvelmans wrote a book defending the original Iceman (published in French and never translated into English) and even today insists that it was some kind of humanlike creature.

Sources:

Emery, C. Eugene, Jr., "News and Comment: Sasquatch-sickle: The Monster, the Model, and the Myth," *Skeptical Inquirer,* Winter 1981/1982, pp. 2-4.

Hansen, Frank, "I Killed the Ape-Man Creature of Whiteface," *Saga,* July 1970, pp. 8-11, 55-60.

Sanderson, Ivan T., "The Missing Link," *Argosy,* May 1969, pp. 23-31.

Sanderson, Ivan T., "Preliminary Description of the External Morphology of What Appeared to Be the Fresh Corpse of a Hitherto Unknown Form of Living Hominid," *Genus* 25, 1969, pp. 249-278.

Shaggy, Two-footed Creatures Abroad

- YETI
- MONO GRANDE
- ORANG-PENDEK
- ALMAS
- YEREN
- YOWIE

Shaggy, Two-footed Creatures Abroad

YETI

Southern Asia's Himalayan Mountains extend in a 1,500-mile arch across northern India, Nepal, Sikkim, Bhutan, and the southern end of Tibet. In these mountains, according to many reports, lives the legendary yeti. The first English printed reference to a strange bipedal (two-legged) creature that roamed the Himalayas may have been in the *Journal of the Asiatic Society of Bengal* in 1832. There B. H. Hodgson, British Resident of the Court of Nepal, recalled an experience he had while collecting specimens in a northern Nepal province. His native guides came upon an erect, tailless creature with long, dark hair all over its body. Thinking it was a demon, they fled in terror. Hodgson, however, thought it might be an orangutan.

In 1889 Major L. A. Waddell became the first Westerner (non-Asian) to discover a mysterious humanlike footprint in the Himalayan snows. His Sherpa (Tibetan) guides told him that the track, found at 17,000 feet, was made by a hairy wild man that lived in the area. While noting in *Among the Himalayas* (1899) that "the belief in these creatures is universal among Tibetans," Waddell complained that those who told him the tales could never present any evidence or an eyewitness. The major himself believed that such wild men were really "great yellow snowbears."

Lieutenant Colonel C. K. Howard-Bury, who led a fact-finding expedition up Mount Everest in September 1921, came upon a large number of such mysterious prints. Three times the size of human tracks, the footprints were found at 20,000 feet on the side of the mountain that faces northern Tibet. In his official report, Howard-Bury wrote down

the Sherpa word for the creature, which meant "manlike thing that is
not a man." But he transcribed it incorrectly, and a *Calcutta Statesman*
writer mistranslated the word as "abominable snowman." The "abominable snowman" captured the English-speaking public's imagination
due to widespread newspaper coverage of C. K. Howard-Bury's expedition report. Howard-Bury, however, believed the tracks "were probably caused by a large 'loping' grey wolf, which in the soft snow formed
double tracks rather like those of a barefooted man."

Four years later N. A. Tombazi, a British photographer and member
of the Royal Geographical Society, saw a strange creature in the

Himalaya range. The sighting took place near the Zemu Glacier, at 15,000 feet. He reported: "The intense glare and brightness of the snow prevented me from seeing anything for the first few seconds; but I soon spotted the 'object' referred to, about two to three hundred yards away down the valley to the east of our camp. Unquestionably, the figure in outline was exactly like a human being, walking upright and stopping occasionally to uproot or pull at some dwarf rhododendron bushes. It showed up dark against the snow and, as far as I could make out, wore no clothes. Within the next minute or so it had moved into some thick scrub and was lost to view."

Two hours later, as Tombazi's group returned to its camp, he went to check the area where he had seen the creature. There he found 16 footprints "similar in shape to those of a man," though smaller in size. Still, the photographer had no doubt that they belonged to a creature that walked on two legs.

From these accounts—plus more detailed ones from native witnesses—the yeti (from the Sherpa word *yeh-teh,* meaning "that thing") stirred worldwide interest. Since then it has been the subject of countless expeditions, arguments, and theories. Evidence has been sketchy, and it does not appear that an answer to the yeti mystery will be found anytime soon.

Ivan T. Sanderson's 1970 drawing of the yeti.

Probably the most interesting sighting by a Westerner took place on Mount Annapurna in 1970. The witness, well-known British mountaineer Don Whillans, was looking for a campsite one evening when he heard odd cries. His Sherpa companion said that they were a yeti's call, and Whillans caught a glimpse of a dark figure on a distant ridge. The next day he found humanlike tracks sunk 18 inches into the snow. That night, sensing the creature's presence, he looked out of his tent and saw in the moonlight an ape-shaped animal as it plucked at tree branches. He watched it for 20 minutes through binoculars before it wandered away.

Two Types of Yetis

The Sherpas (Tibetans) have described two types of yetis: the *dzu-teh* ("big thing"), seven to eight feet tall, and the *meh-teh,* which ranges between five and six feet. Sightings of the meh-teh are reported far more often than those of the larger creature, and most people think of the meh-teh as the "abominable snowman."

Zoologist Edward W. Cronin, Jr., gave this general description of the meh-teh: "Its body is stocky, apelike in shape, with a distinctly human quality to it.... It ... is covered with short, coarse hair, reddish-brown to black in color, sometimes with white patches on the chest. The hair is longest on the shoulders. The ... teeth are quite large ... and the mouth is wide. The shape of the head is conical, with a pointed crown. The arms are long, reaching almost to the knees. The shoulders are heavy and hunched. There is no tail."

Physical Evidence?

Most scientific and serious examinations of the yeti question focus on the footprints. For no matter how poor a sighting is or how questionable a witness may be, the tracks—without a doubt—exist. Some researchers explain them away as the prints of known animals like snow leopards, foxes, or bears, which have become distorted into "yeti" shapes through melting. This has become a popular theory. Yet primate scientist John Napier, no great yeti supporter himself, wrote that "there is no real experimental basis for the belief that single footprints can become enlarged and still retain their shapes, or that discrete prints can run (or melt) together to form single large tracks." In any case some fresh tracks were found by Cronin and physician Howard Emery during a 1972 expedition in far-eastern Nepal. The tracks were found before the sun, wind, and weather had a chance to alter them.

Still, other types of yeti evidence have proved disappointing. Members of a 1954 *London Daily Mail* expedition, for instance, examined a "yeti scalp" said to be 350 years old, preserved as a kind of sacred object in a Tibetan lamasery (a house of Lamaist monks). Four years later the members of an expedition led by Texas oilman Tom Slick also looked at it and another specimen. And in 1960, in a much-followed expedition sponsored by the publishers of the *World Book Encyclopedia,* Sir Edmund Hillary (the first to scale the Himalayan peak Mt. Everest, the world's tallest mountain, and a famous yeti nonbeliever) was able to obtain a third specimen. After a complete examination, most scientists agreed that it was the skin of a goat antelope.

The next day he found humanlike tracks sunk 18 inches into the snow. That night, sensing the creature's presence, he looked out of his tent and saw in the moonlight an ape-shaped animal as it plucked at tree branches.

Tom Slick, a wealthy Texas oilman, led expeditions that collected yeti evidence, including what may be parts of the hand of an unknown biped.

Sir Edmund Hillary (the first to scale the Himalayan peak Mt. Everest, the world's tallest mountain) cast doubt on the existence of yetis.

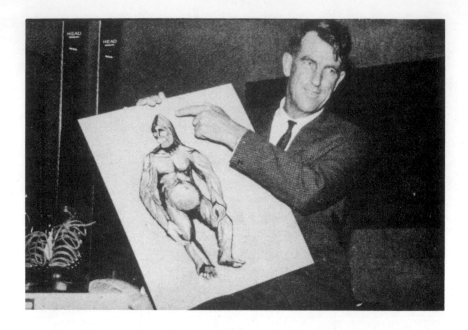

The 1958 Slick expedition also resulted in two specimens of what were supposed to be yeti hands. One proved to be the paw and forearm of a snow leopard. But the other specimen appeared to be something else again. It may be the single best piece of evidence for the yeti's existence.

In early 1959 expedition member Peter Byrne was allowed into a lamasery at Pangboche, Nepal, where he had learned that the bones of a hand supposedly belonging to a yeti were kept. The monks insisted that the hand not leave the building, but Byrne had other ideas. In a carefully thought-out plan, Byrne got the lamas to let him examine the specimen by himself. He had with him parts of a human hand; he secretly switched its thumb and part of the index finger with those of the Pangboche specimen. When Byrne left the monastery, the lamas had no reason to suspect that the yeti hand had been partially dismantled and rebuilt.

The stolen samples, which also included a piece of skin, had to be smuggled out of the country. Crossing the Nepal border was managed easily but getting the contraband out of India, where customs officials were far stricter, looked difficult. But as luck would have it, two close friends of expedition cosponsor Kirk Johnson were staying at a Calcutta hotel. Hollywood film actor Jimmy Stewart and his wife, Gloria, wrapped the samples in underwear, buried them deep in their luggage, and took them to London undetected. There they delivered them to Johnson.

British primatologist W. C. Osman Hill, who had supplied Byrne with the human hand parts, received the specimen on February 20. His first impression was that it was "human" and he was disappointed. Later, however, he thought that the thumb and phalanx (finger bone) appeared less than fully human—that, as unlikely as it seemed, they might even be the remains of a Neanderthal man. Two other scientists who examined the samples also admitted that they were puzzled. Zoologist Charles A. Leone regretted that he could not "make a positive identification." And anthropologist George Agogino told writer Gardner Soule, "Many people who have examined this hand feel that it is a human hand with very primitive characteristics.... I do not feel that this hand is a normal human hand at all.... It is highly characteristic, however, of all the giant anthropoids [large, tailless, semi-upright apes]." Blood tests of the skin sample showed it was from no known primate or human.

Because of the unscrupulous way in which the samples were collected, they received no news coverage or publicity. Thus when Hillary made his expedition in 1960, he was not aware that the Pangboche hand had been tampered with. In his opinion, the yeti was something of a joke, and he declared with much amusement that the Pangboche hand was "essentially a human hand, strung together with wire, with the possible inclusion of several animal bones." This, of course, is exactly what it was after Bryne got through with it. Had Hillary looked more closely at the "animal" bones—instead of the added human ones—he might have been as puzzled by them as Hill and the other scientists.

The negative results of Hillary's expedition quieted scientific and public interest in the "abominable snowman," though a few books, magazine articles, and trips into the Himalayas (such as Cronin's in 1972-74) would revive the subject from time to time. In a comical case in 1986, an English traveler took what he truly believed was a photograph of a yeti—but later investigation showed that the "yeti" was a mountain rock. In February and March of the same year, the New World Explorers Society collected reports of recent sightings by Himalayan residents and returned with samples of what was supposed to be yeti hair: "long, black, and coarse." The samples were turned over to the International Society of Cryptozoology for study, but the results have yet to be released.

Fecal droppings supposedly left by yetis are another kind of evidence in the abominable snowman mystery. Samples collected by Slick's expedition contained eggs of an unknown worm parasite.

An English traveler took what he believed was a photograph of a yeti—but later investigation showed that the "yeti" was a mountain rock.

Famous cryptozoologist Bernard Heuvelmans remarked, "Since each species of mammal has its own parasites, this indicated that the host animal is also equally an unknown animal."

Those who study the yeti believe that the dzu-teh, the larger version of the beast, is probably a blue bear. If there truly is a yeti, it is almost certainly the meh-teh. And those who believe the yeti is real agree that it does not live in the high mountain snows, but in the mountain forests below the snowfields.

With this in mind, Nicholas Warren thinks that yeti sightings can be credibly explained: the animal seen is really "a vegetarian ape, occasionally straying from the forests into the high snowfields." Yet yeti experts seem to favor a more extraordinary explanation: they believe that it (as well as other reported but unrecognized apeman creatures like Bigfoot and the Chinese wild man) is a surviving *Gigantopithecus*. This was a large prehistoric ape the fossil remains of which have been uncovered in, among other places, the Himalayan foothills.

Slick reported that when he showed native witnesses photographs of different animals and asked which one the yeti most resembled, the choices were always the same. The natives first chose "a gorilla standing up." The next selection was "an artist's drawing of a prehistoric apeman, *Australopithecus*." And their third pick was "an orangutan standing up, which they liked particularly for the long hair."

Sources:

Coleman, Loren, *Tom Slick and the Search for the yeti,* Boston: Faber and Faber, 1989.

Cronin, Edward W., Jr., "The yeti," *Atlantic Monthly,* November 1975, pp. 47-53.

Heuvelmans, Bernard, *On the Track of Unknown Animals,* New York: Hill and Wang, 1958.

Hillary, Sir Edmund, "Epitaph to the Elusive Abominable Snowman," *Life,* January 13, 1961, pp. 72-74.

Napier, John, *Bigfoot: The yeti and Sasquatch in Myth and Reality,* New York: E. P. Dutton and Company, 1973.

Sanderson, Ivan T., *Abominable Snowmen: Legend Come to Life,* Philadelphia: Chilton Books, 1961.

Soule, Gardner, *Trail of the Abominable Snowman,* New York: G. P. Putnam's Sons, 1966.

MONO GRANDE

The mystery of the *mono grande*—Spanish for "big monkey"—has puzzled zoologists for years. The only known primates in North and South America are small, long-tailed monkeys. Yet sightings of larger, tailless, anthropoid (manlike) apes have been reported from time to time in the remote regions of the northern climates of South America. In fact, a photograph of such a creature is at the heart of the argument that scientists have waged over the subject.

The Fateful Expedition

Between 1917 and 1920 an expedition led by Swiss oil geologist Francois de Loys explored the swamps, rivers, and mountains west and southwest of Lake Maracaibo near the Colombia-Venezuela border. The explorers suffered great hardship, and a number of them died from disease or were murdered by hostile natives. In the last year, what remained of the expedition was camped on the banks of a branch of the Tarra River. Suddenly, two creatures, apparently male and female, stepped out of the jungle. De Loys at first thought they were bears, but

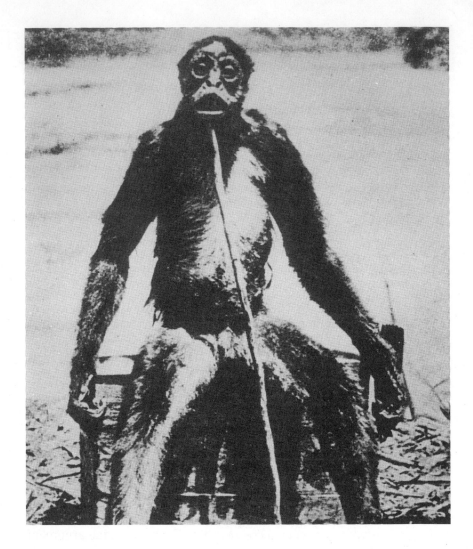

Unknown ape photographed by Francois de Loys in Venezuela/Colombia area of South America.

as they neared the camp, he could see that they were apes of some sort, about five feet in height. His account does not, however, include the important detail of whether each walked on two or four feet.

The creatures, which appeared to be very angry, broke off branches from nearby trees and swung them as weapons, meanwhile crying out and moving wildly. Finally, they emptied their bowels into their hands and hurled the results at the party, who by now had their rifles to their shoulders. In the gunfire that followed, the female was killed, and the wounded male escaped back into the underbrush.

Though no one in the expedition was a zoologist, everyone somehow understood that the animal was extraordinary. Even the native guides swore they had never seen anything like it. Propping it up with a stick, members sat the creature on a gasoline crate and took a picture of it from ten feet away. According to de Loys, "Its skin was afterward removed, and its skull and jaw were cleaned and preserved." Though de Loys did not state it explicitly, it is believed that he and his starving companions ate the animal's flesh! Later, the creature's remains were reportedly lost. Of the 20 members who began the expedition, only four survived.

Photo Draws Scientist's Attention

The photograph, however, was discovered by a friend of de Loys—anthropologist George Montandon—when he was looking through the geologist's records and other expedition materials. Montandon considered the picture so important that he immediately started planning a trip to "the area in question to find the great ape of America." De Loys, he noted, showed no interest in publishing the photograph or talking publicly about it. Only when Montandon insisted was it brought to the world's attention, when he reported it in three French scientific journals in 1929. In his articles Montandon honored de Loys by offering the formal name *Ameranthropoides loysi* for what he believed was a new animal. That same year de Loys told his story publicly for the first time in the popular magazine *Illustrated London News* (June 15).

The Doubter's View

Hardly any time had passed before doubters attacked de Loys's photograph and Montandon's judgment in bringing it before the public. Leading the pack was renowned British anthropologist Sir Arthur Keith, who felt that de Loys had taken a picture of a smaller, tailless animal, the spider monkey—which did live in South America—and tried to pass it off as something more interesting. Keith wrote: "A photograph of the animal from behind would have clinched matters, but the only photograph taken was one of the front—the animal being placed in a sitting position on a box of unknown size and with no standard object in or near the body of the animal to give a clue to the dimensions of its parts."

But if the gasoline crate on which the ape sat was a common one (and there is no reason to think that it was not), then the size of the creature could be guessed. Such crates measure a standard 20 inches—making the figure atop it about 5'2" or 5'3" tall! That would be a

highly irregular spider monkey, for the largest known specimen measured 3'7".

Keith also sneered at de Loys's claim that the animals had thrown their feces at the party, as if the idea were ridiculous. But spider monkeys and some apes do such things when faced with enemies. Keith also found it suspicious that de Loys had lost all evidence but the photograph. Yet considering the expedition's problems, it is hardly surprising that hanging on to the creature's remains was not of paramount importance; de Loys and his men were more concerned with staying alive.

Indeed, nothing about the case suggested that de Loys was trying to pull off a hoax; it was only Montandon's interest that kept the photo and its story from being buried forever. Still, the arguments of Keith, however refutable, remained the last word on the subject. In 1951, for example, *Natural History* reported that Keith had "easily demolished the 'new anthropoid.'"

The Nature of the Beast

Michael T. Shoemaker, a researcher of strange events, examined de Loys's photograph at length and published his observations in *Strange Magazine* in 1991. He wrote that the creature in the picture had features of both spider monkeys and anthropoid apes. Its flat nose, ridged eye sockets, long hair, and very long fingers and toes were monkeylike, but its body resembled a gibbon's, and its limbs and small thumbs looked like those of an orangutan. Most important to Shoemaker was the shape of the animal's head: its jaws were much heavier and more powerful than a spider monkey's, and its forehead was far more developed than that of any monkey type he knew.

De Loys may have taken the only photograph of a possibly unknown species of anthropoid ape, but he was not the only one to report seeing such an animal. The first printed report appears in the 1553 records of Pedro de Cieza de Leon, who mentions native sightings and refers to a Spaniard who said "he had seen one of these monsters dead in the woods." In *An Essay on the Natural History of Guiana* (1769), Edward Bancroft relates Indian reports of creatures "near five feet in height, maintaining an erect position, and having a human form, thinly covered with short, black hair." In 1860's *The Romance of Natural History,* Philip Gosse wrote that he felt fairly sure that a "large anthropoid ape, not yet recognized by zoologists," did exist in South America.

In 1876 Charles Barrington Brown, explorer of what was then British Guiana (now Guyana), wrote about a creature that natives called the *Didi,* a "powerful wild man, whose body is covered with hair, and who lives in the forest." He heard it spoken of many times and even saw its footprints once, or so they were identified to him. Sighting reports of anthropoid apes have continued into the twentieth century.

In 1968 explorer Pino Turolla, while traveling in the jungle-covered mountains of eastern Venezuela, was told of the mono grande. His guide said that three of the creatures, using branches for clubs, had attacked him and killed his son several years earlier. On his return to the United States, Turolla researched the matter and came upon the de Loys photograph; on his next expedition that year he showed the picture to his guide, who said that, yes, this was what the mono grande looked like. Turolla had the guide take him to the canyon where the awful attack had taken place—and there, after hearing eerie howling sounds, the explorer saw a pair of apelike creatures about five feet tall running upright on two legs. Turolla claimed a second, briefer sighting two years later while on an expedition in the Andes Mountains of Ecuador.

Turolla had the guide take him to the canyon where the awful attack had taken place—and there, after hearing eerie howling sounds, the explorer saw a pair of apelike creatures about five feet tall running upright on two legs.

The most recent published sighting is from Guyana in 1987. The witness, plant scientist Gary Samuels, was gathering fungi from the forest floor when he heard footsteps. Expecting to see a Guyanese forest worker, he was startled to look up and find a five-foot-tall, upright ape "bellowing an occasional 'hoo' sound."

Sources:

Camera, I., and G. H. H. Tate, "Letters: The 'Ape' That Wasn't an Ape," *Natural History* 60,6, June 1951, p. 289.

Picasso, Fabio, "More on the Mono Grande Mystery," *Strange Magazine* 9, spring/summer 1992, pp. 41, 53.

Shoemaker, Michael T., "The Mystery of the Mono Grande," *Strange Magazine* 7, April 1991, pp. 2-5, 56-60.

Turolla, Pino, *Beyond the Andes,* New York: Harper and Row, 1980.

ORANG-PENDEK

"Its eyebrows were frankly moving; they were of the darkest color, very lively, and like human eyes."

Sumatra is a large Indonesian island graced by millions of acres of rain forest. It is the home of the gibbon (a small, tailless ape), the orangutan, and the sun bear (the last of a species of bear that stands on its hind feet, though it does not run on them). And many islanders also speak of another extraordinary animal in these forests: the *orang-pendek,* or "little man." (Some call it the *sedapa.*)

Orang-pendeks are said to stand between two and a half and five feet tall and to be covered with short dark hair, with a thick, bushy mane that goes halfway or farther down the back. Their arms are shorter than an ape's, and—unlike Sumatra's other apes—they more often walk on the ground than climb in trees. An orang-pendek's footprint is like that of a small human being, only wider. It eats fruits and small animals.

Early Sightings

Witnesses often mention how much orang-pendeks look like human beings. A Dutch settler named Van Herwaarden said he came upon one in October 1923; and though he had his rifle and was an

Witnesses of orang-pendeks denied that they might be orangutans, which are native to Sumatra.

experienced hunter, he reported, "I did not pull the trigger. I suddenly felt that I was going to commit murder." He observed that "the creature's brown face was almost hairless, whilst its forehead seemed to be high rather than low. Its eyebrows were frankly moving; they were of the darkest color, very lively, and like human eyes. The nose was broad with fairly large nostrils, but in no way clumsy.... Its lips were quite ordinary, but the width of its mouth was strikingly wide when open. Its canines [pointed teeth] showed clearly from time to time.... They seemed fairly large to me, ... more developed than a man's.... I was able to see its right ear which was exactly like a little human ear. Its hands were slightly hairy on the back." Van Herwaarden believed that the creature he had come upon was a female and that she was about five feet tall.

Because primatologists (scientists who study primates) have never been shown a living or dead specimen, most have rejected such eyewitness reports as tricks or mistaken identifications of orangutans or gibbons. Some footprints thought to be those of orang-pendeks were later identified as belonging to sun bears, for example.

New Investigations

In the summer of 1989, British travel writer Deborah Martyr visited the rain forests of southwestern Sumatra. There her guide told her about orang-pendeks and where they could be found. When Martyr expressed her doubts about such a creature, the guide related his own two sightings.

Fascinated, Martyr began to interview residents in the area and collected many sighting reports. "All reports included the information that the animal has a large and prominent belly—something not mentioned in previous literature on the subject," she wrote. Some reported that the mane was dark yellow or tan, others that it was black or dark gray. When Martyr suggested to witnesses that the creatures they saw might really be orangutans, gibbons, or sun bears, they strongly denied it.

Martyr herself traveled to the south edge of the Mount Kerinci region, where she was told the creatures were often seen. Though she did not have a sighting of her own, she did find tracks. Of one set she noted, "Each print was clearly delineated, the big toe and four smaller toes easily visible. The big toe was placed as it would be in a human foot." Each measured about six inches in length and four inches wide at the ball of the foot. Martyr added that "if we had been reasonably close to a village, I might have momentarily thought the prints to be those of a healthy seven-year-old child. The ball of the foot was, however, too broad even for a people who habitually wear no shoes."

Because of falling rain and poor lighting, the photographs Martyr took of the tracks did not turn out well. But she did manage to make a plaster cast of a footprint, which she took to the headquarters of the Kerinci Seblat National Park in Sungeipenuh. The park's director had ignored earlier orang-pendek reports because, as he told Martyr, the local people were "simple." But when he and his workers saw the cast, they agreed that it was of an animal they did not know.

Unfortunately, the cast—a promising piece of evidence—was sent to the Indonesian National Parks Department, where it was never seen or heard about again. Martyr repeatedly tried to get a judgment on it or at least have it returned to her, but she had no luck at all.

Martyr hopes to continue her investigations. She is 80 percent sure that the orang-pendek exists in the high rain forests of southwestern Sumatra. "If it is ground-dwelling and elusive," she says, "this could explain how it has escaped zoological notice, and is known only to the native people."

Sources:

Heuvelmans, Bernard, *On the Track of Unknown Animals,* New York: Hill and Wang, 1958.
Martyr, Deborah, "An Investigation of the *Orang-Pendek,* the 'Short Man' of Sumatra," *Crypto-zoology* 9, 1990, pp. 57-65.

ALMAS

In the Mongolian language, *Almas* means "wild man." These strange creatures, half human, half ape, reportedly live in the Altai Mountains in western Mongolia and in the Tien Shan of nearby Sinkiang in the People's Republic of China.

History

The earliest known printed account of Almases appeared in a journal written by Bavarian nobleman Hans Schiltberger. In the 1420s Schiltberger traveled through the Tien Shan range as a prisoner of the Mongols. "In the mountains themselves live wild people, who have nothing in common with other human beings," he recorded. "A pelt covers the entire body of these creatures. Only the hands and face are free of hair. They run around in the hills like animals and eat foliage [leaves] and grass and whatever else they can find." Schiltberger saw two of them for himself, a male and a female that a local warlord had caught and given as gifts to the Bavarian's captors.

A late-eighteenth-century Mongolian manuscript on natural history contains a drawing of an Almas. The figure is identified as a "man-animal." All of the other illustrations in the book are of real animals, demonstrating that Almases were not considered legendary beings; they were viewed as ordinary creatures of flesh and blood.

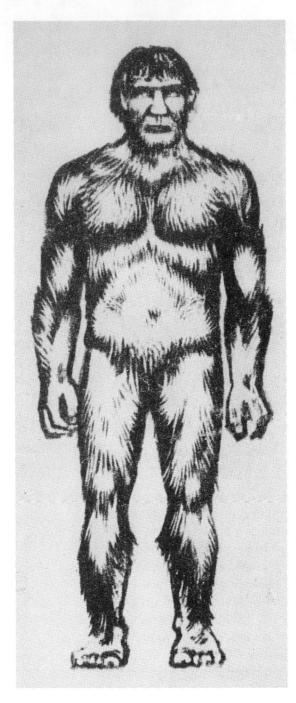

"Wild man" (Almas) seen in Buinaksk, Dagestan, in the former U.S.S.R. in 1941

Professor Tsyben Zhamtsarano conducted the first real scientific study of Almases, collecting reports from nomads and others in the remote areas where the creatures—adults and children—were said to live. He plotted the sightings on maps and brought an artist with him on his field trips to interview witnesses. But while living in Leningrad, Russia, in the 1930s under Soviet dictator Joseph Stalin, Zhamtsarano was imprisoned for his interest in Mongolian folklore, and he died captive in 1940. The records of his Almas research have been lost.

Still, one of Zhamtsarano's associates, Dordji Meiren, said that their research showed fewer Almas sightings in the later decades of the nineteenth century. The Almases had largely disappeared from Inner Mongolia and southern Outer Mongolia; it appeared that they were migrating westward to escape ever-growing civilization. Another early researcher, anatomy expert V. A. Khakhlov, shared his Almas findings with the Russian Imperial Academy of Sciences in 1913. These studies, too, no longer exist.

In the 1920s writer M. K. Rosenfeld heard about Almases during a trip across Mongolia. He later used the creatures in the plot of his adventure novel, *The Ravine of the Almases,* published in 1936. By that time another Mongolian scholar, Y. Rinchen, was conducting his own Almas research, and in the 1950s—with renewed interest in the Himalayan **yeti** or "abominable snowman"—the Soviet Academy of Sciences set up a Commission for the Study of the Snowman Question. The commission's leader, Boris Porschnev, encouraged Rinchen to publish some of his findings. Like researchers before him, Rinchen concluded that the Almas population was shrink-

ing and retreating. Since then other Russian and Mongolian scholars have published Almas studies.

Zhamtsarano associate Meiren claimed to have seen an Almas skin being used as a ceremonial carpet in a Buddhist monastery in the southern Gobi region of Mongolia. The creature had been skinned by a straight cut down the spine, so its features were preserved. The body had red, curly hair, and there was long hair on the head, but the face was hairless except for eyebrows. The nails at the ends of the toes and fingers were humanlike in appearance.

A Typical Almas

Adult Almases have been described as five feet or slightly taller, hairy, with noticeable eyebrow ridges, a receding chin, a jaw that juts out—and a shy manner. They eat small mammals and wild plants and use simple tools but have no language. According to British anthropologist Myra Shackley, their "very simple lifestyle and the nature of their

Some scientists believe Almases are surviving forms of prehistoric human beings, such as the Neanderthal man pictured here.

appearance suggests strongly that Almas[es] might represent the survival of a prehistoric way of life, and perhaps even of an earlier form of man. The best candidate is undoubtedly Neanderthal man." Neanderthals lived between 40,000 and 100,000 years ago. The classic Neanderthal had a large, thick skull with heavy brow ridges, a sloping forehead, and a chinless jaw. The link between Neanderthal man and human beings is unclear.

Chris Stringer is another British anthropologist open to the idea of the Almases' existence. Still, he finds many things in Almas reports that do not fit "accepted ideas about the Neanderthals." Among them are the creatures' physical features, like "bent knees, ... turned-in feet, ... long arms, forearms, hands and fingers, [and] small flat noses," as well as their "lack of language, culture, meat-eating and fire."

Sources:

Bord, Janet, and Colin Bord, *The Evidence for Bigfoot and Other Man-Beasts,* Wellingborough, Northamptonshire, England: The Aquarian Press, 1984.
Sanderson, Ivan T., *Abominable Snowmen: Legend Come to Life,* Philadelphia: Chilton Book Company, 1961.
Shackley, Myra, *Still Living?: Yeti, Sasquatch and the Neanderthal Enigma,* New York: Thames and London, 1983.
Stringer, Chris, "Wanted: One Wildman, Dead or Alive," *New Scientist,* August 11, 1983, p. 422.

YEREN

For centuries, in remote areas of central and southern China, residents and travelers have spoken of something called a "wild man," or *yeren.* In early writings, the creature was also referred to as a "hill ghost," "mountain monster," "man bear," or something "monkeylike, but not a monkey." One seventeenth-century account from the Hubei province offered this description: "In the remote mountains of Fangxian County, there are rock caves, in which live hairy men as tall as three meters [over nine feet]. They often come down to hunt dogs and chickens in the villages. They fight with whoever resists."

Although in the late 1950s some Chinese scientists took an active interest in the **yeti**—the "abominable snowman" of the Himalayas—they gave little notice to their own hairy giants, for they considered

Chinese poster: Have You Seen the Wild Man?

yeren merely popular folklore figures. Those who claimed contact with the creatures were mostly peasants or soldiers in the provinces (though two scientists also claimed to have seen the animal).

Sightings

Biologist Wang Tselin reported seeing a yeren killed in 1940 in the Gansu area. He described the creature as a female about six and a half feet tall and covered with grayish-brown hair, the human and ape features of her face reminding him of a type of prehistoric human being. In 1950 geologist Fan Jingquan said he twice observed two yeren, seemingly a mother and son, in a mountain forest.

The first official examination of the yeren question took place in 1961, after the reported killing of a female by road builders in a thick forest in the Xishuang Banna area. By the time members of the Chinese Academy of Sciences got to the site, though, the body was no longer there, and the scientists concluded that the animal was nothing more than a gibbon (a small tailless ape). This verdict halted government interest in the yeren for the next 15 years. Two decades later, Zhou Guoxing, an anthropologist with the Beijing Natural History Museum, interviewed a journalist who had been connected with the 1961 investigation. "He stated that the animal which had been killed was not a gibbon, but an unknown animal of human shape," Zhou related.

A 1976 incident involving a yeren and several witnesses renewed interest in the creature and brought it worldwide attention for the first time. Early on the morning of May 14, six local government officials driving home from a meeting spotted a "strange, tailless creature with reddish fur" on a country highway near Chunshuya, Hubei province. Switching the headlights to high, the driver followed the animal as it tried to escape up a slope along the roadside. But it slipped and landed right in front of the jeep. The five passengers jumped out and surrounded the beast, which was now on all fours and staring directly into the lights.

Afraid to get too close, the unarmed witnesses moved to within six feet of the creature. One of them tossed a rock at its rear end, causing it to stand briefly. This frightened the group, which retreated. The animal then lumbered away, this time making a successful climb up the slope.

Group members described the creature as more than six feet tall. Covered with thick brown-red and purple-red wavy hair, it had a fat belly and large buttocks. Its eyes looked almost human. Still it had the large ears of an ape and the jutting snout of a monkey.

Investigations Commence

The Chunshuya sighting caused a stir at the Chinese Academy of Sciences, which sent 110 investigators into the field the next year. They

> Switching the headlights to high, the driver followed the animal as it tried to escape up a slope along the roadside. But it slipped and landed right in front of the jeep.

focused their efforts on the forests of Fang County and the Sennongjia area of Hubei—a huge forest preserve of steep mountains and deep valleys where a wide variety of rare and exotic animals, including the giant panda (discovered only in 1869), lived. None of the investigators had a personal sighting, but they interviewed witnesses and collected footprints, hair, and feces that supposedly originated with yeren.

Zhou Guoxing, one of the expedition leaders, later noted that there seemed to be two types of yeren. There was "a larger one of about two meters in height [around six feet] and a smaller one, about one meter in height [three feet]." The two types also had a very different footprint, with the large yeren's appearing "remarkably similar to that of a man" and the smaller creature's being "more similar to the footprint of an ape or monkey, with the largest toe evidently pointing outwards."

The Smaller Yeren

To Zhou and others, the existence of the smaller type of yeren seemed almost certain. The anthropologist pointed out that both living and dead specimens of the creature might already be in scientists' hands. One was killed on May 23, 1957, near the village of Zhuanxian in Zhejiang province. A biology teacher there preserved its hands and feet. When Zhou learned of this in 1981, he went and collected the specimens. After a long study he concluded that they "belonged to a kind of large stump-tailed monkey unknown to science." He thought the creature was a stump-tailed macaque. Not long afterward just such an animal was captured in the Huang Mountain region and taken to the Hefei Zoo.

On the other hand, Ohio State University anthropologist Frank E. Poirier believed that yeren reports were probably sightings of a rare, endangered animal that lived in the region but was seldom seen: the golden monkey. But after a 1989 expedition, he changed his mind. Noting that local Chinese residents used the term "yeren" (which means wild man) to describe a number of animals—including bears, apes, and monkeys—he felt that an unknown yeren might exist after all. Poirier himself, in fact, was once mistaken for a yeren after villagers who had never seen a Caucasian man discovered him, half-clothed, napping by a river. Poirier and his colleague J. Richard Greenwell also thought that the smaller yeren might be "orangutans, ... either the known species, or more likely, a related species—perhaps even a fossil form—populations of which may [have survived] in rugged and isolated pockets of the country."

The Larger Yeren: Bigfoot's Cousin?

While the smaller yeren is of major interest to primate scientists, the other yeren seems to be a find of a different nature: a Chinese cousin of North America's **Bigfoot**. Walking on two legs, it stands between six and eight feet tall and has a strikingly humanlike face. One witness gave this description of a male yeren to Chinese Academy of Sciences researchers: "He was about seven feet tall, with shoulders wider than a man's, a sloping forehead, deep-set eyes and ... his jaw jutted out.... His hair was dark brown, more than a foot long and hung loosely over his shoulders. His whole face, except for the nose and ears, was covered with short hairs. His arms hung below his knees.... He didn't have a tail, and the hair on his body was short."

Investigators have collected dozens of hairs, supposedly from yeren, and examined them in laboratories. Studying samples from different areas of China, physicists at Fudan University found that they were indeed different—with the proportion of iron to zinc 50 times greater than that found in human hair and seven times greater than in the hair of known primates. According to Poirier and Greenwell, this seems to suggest that "some specific Wildman hairs derive from a higher primate not yet known to zoology." A second testing of the samples by others brought the same results.

Biologists at East China Normal University used a scanning electron microscope to examine yeren hairs, which they compared to those of humans and primates. They concluded that the yeren hairs were different from both the human and primate samples, but they most closely matched the human hair. This is not surprising given that eyewitness accounts of the creature describe it as more human than ape.

Zoologists receptive to the idea that a large yeren may exist have a favorite theory (shared by Bigfoot researchers). They suggest that such a creature is a surviving *Gigantopithecus,* a giant early primate that is thought to have walked upright, on two legs. Believed to have become extinct in China some 300,000 years ago, the animal had existed for about eight million years. "It takes only a little 'push' to propose its survival another half-million years to the present time," Poirier and Greenwell wrote, pointing out that the giant panda—which is just as old—shares the same native home.

Sources:

Bord, Janet, and Colin Bord, *The Evidence for Bigfoot and Other Man-Beasts,* Wellingborough, Northamptonshire, England: The Aquarian Press, 1984.

Coleman, Loren, *The Yeti and the Yeren,* Portland, Maine: The Author, 1992.

Greenwell, J. Richard, and Frank E. Poirier, "Further Investigations into the Reported *Yeren,*—The Wildman of China," *Cryptozoology* 8, 1989, pp. 47-57.

Poirier, Frank E., Hu Hongxing, and Chung-Min Chen, "The Evidence for Wildman in Hubei Province, People's Republic of China," *Cryptozoology* 2, winter 1983, pp. 25-39.

YOWIE

The yowie is Australia's version of **Bigfoot.** The existence of *this* ape-man-like creature would be more incredible than most others reported around the world, for Australia has been separated from the Asian continent for some 70 million years. This disconnection of land masses occurred far too long ago for anthropoid apes (those that are large, tailless, and semi-upright) to have crossed over and evolved into the kind of creature Australians have reported seeing for years.

The Yahoo

During the nineteenth century, European immigrants to Australia noted that the native aborigines were terrified of something called a *yahoo* or *devil-devil.* The writer of an article in an 1842 issue of *Australian and New Zealand Monthly Magazine* wondered if the creatures were merely imaginary, though some Australian naturalists believed that yahoos were real animals. Because of the creatures' "scarceness, slyness, and solitary habits," according to the article, "man has not succeeded in obtaining a specimen." It concluded that yowies were "most likely to be one of the monkey tribe." Two years later, in her *Notes and Sketches of New South Wales During Residence in the Colony from 1839 to 1844,* Mrs. Charles Meredith noted the aborigines' fear of the yahoo, and reported that the creature "lives in the tops of the steepest and rockiest mountains, which are totally inaccessible to all human beings."

YAHOO?

No one knows how the aborigines came to use the word "yahoo." In English it means a crude or stupid person. In the eighteenth and nineteenth century, English speakers sometimes used it to describe orangutans. Oddly enough, native inhabitants of the Bahamas also call their local apeman the "yahoo."

After awhile, Australian settlers began seeing the yahoo, too. An 1881 newspaper article reported that two or three local men saw a creature that looked like a "huge monkey or baboon ... somewhat larger than a man." On October 3, 1894, while riding in the

New South Wales bush in the middle of the afternoon, Johnnie McWilliams said he spotted a "wild man or gorilla" that stepped out from behind a tree, looked at him briefly, and dashed for a wooded hillside a mile away. Judging McWilliams a "truthful and manly fellow" when recording his story, the *Queanbeyan Observer* of November 30 also noted that "for many years there have been tales of trappers coming across enormous tracks of some unknown animals in the mountain wilds around Snowball."

Around the turn of the century, Joseph and William Webb were camped on a range in New South Wales. There they reportedly fired on a frightening-looking apelike creature that left "footprints, long, like a man's, but with longer, spreading toes"; its stride was also greater than a man's. According to John Gale in *An Alpine Excursion* (1903), the two found "no blood or other evidence of their shot having taken effect." And on August 7, 1903, the *Queanbeyan Observer* printed a letter from a man who claimed to have witnessed the killing of a yahoo by aborigines.

In the *Sydney Herald* of October 23, 1912, cattleman and poet Sydney Wheeler Jephcott wrote about the remarkable adventure of his neighbor, George Summerell. While riding his horse between Bombala and Bemboka around noon on October 12, Summerell came upon "a strange animal, which, on all fours, was drinking from the creek. As it was covered with gray hair, the first thought that rose to Summerell's mind was: 'What an immense kangaroo.' But hearing the horse's feet on the track, it rose to its full height, of about 7 ft., and looked quietly at the horseman. Then stooping down again, it finished its drink, and then, picking up a stick that lay by it, walked steadily away up a slope to the ... side of the road, and disappeared among the rocks and timber 150 yards away."

Jephcott added, "Summerell described the face as being like that of an ape or man, minus forehead and chin, with a great trunk all of one size from shoulder to hips, and with arms that nearly reached to its ankles."

After hearing his neighbor's report, Jephcott himself rode to the site. There he found several footprints that supported the story and found that "the handprints where the animal had stooped at the edge of the water" were "especially plain." Jephcott observed that the hands were humanlike, except that the little fingers were bent away "much like the thumbs." He found the feet "enormously long and ugly"—and with only four toes! These toes were long and flexible. "Even in the prints which had sunk deepest into the mud there was no trace of the 'thumb' of the characteristic ape's 'foot'," he noted.

Besides the fresh foot- and hand-prints, Jephcott could make out older ones; the animal had crossed that way before. Wanting to make casts of the tracks, the cattleman returned two days later with plaster. He gave his casts of two footprints and one handprint to a Professor David at the local university. While admitting that the copies were less than perfect, David thought that "any reasonable being will be satisfied by the inspection of these three casts that something quite unknown and unsuspected by science remains to be brought to light."

From Yahoo to Yowie

In more recent times in Australia, the word "yowie" has been used to describe huge, shaggy, man-like creatures. Like yahoo sightings, reports of yowies seem to occur almost always in the south and central coastal regions of New South Wales and Queensland's Gold Coast. The terms *yahoo* and *yowie* may well describe the same mysterious creature.

In any case, reports of yowies or yahoos span the entire twentieth century. In 1971 a team of Royal Australian Air Force surveyors landed in a helicopter on top of unclimbable Sentinel Mountain and were astonished to find huge manlike tracks (though too large for a man) in the mud. On April 13, 1976, in Grose Valley near Katoomba, New South Wales, five backpackers reported coming upon a bad-smelling, five-foot-tall yowie—a female, judging from its large breasts. And on March 5, 1978, a man cutting trees near Springbrook on the Gold Coast reported hearing what sounded like a grunting pig. He went into the forest looking for it but instead spotted "about 12 ft. in front of me, ... this big black hairy man-thing. It looked more like a gorilla than anything. It had huge hands, and one of them was wrapped around a sapling .... It had a flat black shiny face, with two big yellow eyes and a hole for a mouth. It just stared at me, and I stared back. I was so numb I couldn't even raise the axe I had in my hand."

"It had a flat black shiny face, with two big yellow eyes and a hole for a mouth. It just stared at me, and I stared back."

Rex Gilroy, who formed the Yowie Research Center in the late 1970s, claims to have collected over 3,000 reports.

Of course, none of this has changed the minds of Australian scientists. As one clearly put it, "The first and only primates to have lived in Australia were human beings." Graham Joyner, however, who has written much on the mystery, suggests that the "yahoo was an undiscovered marsupial [pouched mammal] of roughly bear-like conformation, which was referred to ... throughout most of the 19th and 20th centuries.... The Yowie, on the other hand, is a recent fiction."

Sources:

Bord, Janet, and Colin Bord, *Alien Animals,* Harrisburg, Pennsylvania: Stackpole Books, 1981.
Cryptozoology magazine, the following issues: 3, 1984, pp. 55-57; 4, 1985, pp. 106-112; 5, 1986, pp. 47-54; 6, 1987, pp. 124-129; 8, 1989, pp. 27-36; 9, 1990, pp. 41-51 and 116-119.

Extinction Reconsidered

- LIVING DINOSAURS
- MOKELE-MBEMBE
- PTEROSAUR SIGHTINGS
- THYLACINE
- THE MYSTERY OF THE SIRRUSH
- PALUXY FOOTPRINTS

Extinction Reconsidered

LIVING DINOSAURS

Do dinosaurs still exist? Does the question sound ridiculous? Indeed, most scientists believe—and we have all been taught— that these giant reptiles became extinct some 65 million years ago. Still, dinosaur sightings in remote regions of the world *are* reported from time to time! A handful of scientists, explorers, and nature writers have tried to make sense of these "unbelievable" accounts and, where possible, investigate them.

Much of the investigation has centered on a legendary creature generally referred to as **mokele-mbembe** and described as a sauropod-like animal. (Sauropods were huge plant-eating dinosaurs with long necks and tails, small heads, bulky bodies, and stumplike legs; *Diplodocus, Apatosaurus [Brontosaurus],* and *Brachiosaurus* were sauropods.) The first printed mention of the huge, plate-shaped footprints linked with the beasts appeared in a 1776 history of French missionaries in west-central Africa. In the next two centuries missionaries, colonial officials, hunters, explorers, and natives would give remarkably similar descriptions of the animals that supposedly made those tracks.

All sighting reports in recent years have come from the swampy, remote Likouala region of the Congo, an area in central Africa on both sides of the Congo river. In 1980 and 1981 University of Chicago biologist Roy P. Mackal led two expeditions there, the first in the company of herpetologist (reptile and amphibian scientist) James H. Powell, Jr., who had heard mokele-mbembe stories while doing crocodile research in west-central Africa. Neither expedition had a sighting, though Mackal and his companions did interview a number of native witness-

Engraving of an ichthyosaur and a plesiosaur, from Louis Figuier, *The World before the Deluge,* 1865.

es. The creatures, greatly feared, were said to live in the swamps and rivers. A band of Pygmies had supposedly killed one at Lake Tele around 1959.

Though Mackal's expeditions were not able to reach remote Lake Tele, a competing group headed by American engineer Herman Regusters successfully made the trip. Regusters and his wife, Kia Van Dusen, claimed that they saw huge, long-necked animals several times, both in the water and in the swampy areas around the lake. Congolese government biologist Marcellin Agnagna, who was a member of Mackal's second expedition, also arrived in the area in the spring of 1982 and reported a single sighting. Both the Regusters and Agnagna said that camera problems kept them from photographing the fantastic animals. Three more expeditions to the area, one English and two Japanese, brought no new sightings.

Other Dinosaurs in Africa

While Regusters was at Lake Tele he heard a strange story. The local people told him that a few months earlier, in February 1981, the bodies of three adult male elephants had been found floating in the water. The cause of death seemed to be two large puncture wounds in the stomach area of each. These were not bullet holes, and the elephants still had their tusks, suggesting that poachers had not killed them. The natives blamed the deaths on a mysterious horned creature that lived in the nearby forests.

They called the mysterious creature *emela ntouka,* "killer of elephants." Nearly every report described it as the size of an elephant— or larger—with heavy legs that supported the body from beneath (not from the side, as in a crocodile) and a long, thick tail. Its face was like that of a rhinoceros, with a single horn attached to the front of its head. Comfortable in water or on land, it was a plant-eater, but it nonetheless killed elephants and buffalos with its great horn. In his 1987 book *A Living Dinosaur?,* Mackal suggested that such an animal, if it existed, was likely to be a kind of prehistoric rhinoceros or a horned dinosaur, like the triceratops.

Mackal also collected a handful of hazy reports about *mbielu mbielu mbielu,* "the animal with planks growing out of its back"—said to look like a stegosaur. Sightings of *nguma monene,* a huge serpent-like reptile with a sawlike ridge along its back and four legs along its sides, proved to be more credible. Among the witnesses of this animal was American missionary Joseph Ellis, who, in November 1971, said he saw such a creature leave the Mataba River and disappear into the tall grass. While Ellis did not get a complete look at the animal—he did not see its head and neck—he guessed from the portions of the body he observed above the water that it was over 30 feet long!

Ellis knew the animals of the Congo well and was positive that the creature could not have been a crocodile. Reports from native witnesses, which did include descriptions of the head and a long tail, suggested to Mackal that "we are dealing with a living link between lizards and snakes," perhaps a "lizard type ... from a primitive, semi-aquatic group known as dolichosaurs."

In 1932 biologist Ivan T. Sanderson and animal collector W. M. (Gerald) Russell had a strange and frightening experience in the Mamfe Pool, part of the Mainyu River in western Cameroon. The two men, with native guides, were in separate boats passing clifflike river banks dotted with deep caves when they suddenly heard ear-shattering roars—as if huge animals were fighting in one of them.

Swirling currents sucked both boats near the thundering cave's opening. At that point, Sanderson would recall, there "came another gargantuan gurgling roar and something enormous rose out of the

Nearly every report described it as the size of an elephant— or larger—with heavy legs that supported the body from beneath (not from the side, as in a crocodile) and a long, thick tail.

water, turned it to sherry-colored foam and then, again roaring, plunged below. This 'thing' was shiny black and was the *head* of something, shaped like a seal but flattened.... It was about the size of a full-grown hippopotamus—the head, I mean."

Sanderson and Russell decided not to stick around to observe anything more. Upstream they found big tracks that could not have been left by a hippopotamus— because hippos did not live in the area; natives said that the awful creatures had killed them all. Still, the strange animals were not flesh-eaters but fed instead on the liana fruits that grew along the rivers. According to Sanderson, the natives called the creatures *m'kuoo m'bemboo*.

If the part of the animal the explorers saw really was its head, then the creature was probably not the sauropodlike mokele-mbembe (sauropods have small heads). Mackal found during his own expeditions 50 years later that some native peoples used the same words to describe any large, dangerous animal living in rivers, lakes, or swamps.

Dinosaurs in South America

In his 1912 novel *The Lost World,* Sir Arthur Conan Doyle wrote of a band of hardy English explorers who discovered an isolated area in South America's Amazon River basin where prehistoric monsters lived on millions of years past their time. Considering that the tale has been a favorite of readers the world over for decades, it is surprising that so few claims of dinosaur sightings have come from South America in real life.

But one account was published in the *New York Herald* of January 11, 1911. It was written by a German named Franz Herrmann Schmidt, who claimed that one day in October 1907, he and his companion Capt. Rudolph Pfleng and their Indian guides entered a valley of swamps and lakes in a remote region of Peru. There they discovered some strange, huge tracks made by unknown animals, along with crushed trees and plants. They also found the area odd because it lacked the usual alligators, iguanas, and water snakes.

Despite the guides' fear, the expedition camped in the valley that night. The next morning the explorers got back into their boat and continued their search for the mystery animals. Just before noon they found fresh tracks along the shore. Pfleng declared that he was going to follow them inland, regardless of the danger. Then they heard the screams of a group of monkeys that were gathering berries in some nearby trees.

According to Schmidt: "[A] large dark something half hidden among the branches shot up among [the monkeys] and there was a great commotion." The frightened guides quickly paddled the boat away from shore, and while Pfleng and Schmidt could see very little then, they were able to hear "a great moving of plants and a sound like heavy slaps of a great paddle, mingled with the cries of some of the monkeys moving rapidly away from the lake." Then there was silence.

After about ten minutes, the plants near the lake began to stir again and the expedition members finally saw "the frightful monster." Unbothered by their presence, it began to enter the water and came to within 150 feet of them. The creature was gigantic; Schmidt figured it was "35 feet long, with at least 12 of this devoted to head and neck." Its head was "about the size of a beer keg and was shaped like that of a tapir, as if the snout was used for pulling things or taking hold of them." Its neck was thick and snakelike, and instead of forelegs it had "great heavy clawed flippers." Schmidt observed that its "heavy blunt tail" was covered with "rough horny lumps"; in fact, the entire surface of the creature's body was "knotted like an alligator's side."

Pfleng and Schmidt began shooting at the creature with their rifles. The bullets seemed to annoy it, but they drew no blood—the one that hit the creature's head flew off as if it had met with solid rock. Seven shots were fired, each reaching its target. In order to escape them, the creature suddenly plunged underwater and nearly overturned the explorers' boat! The monster reappeared some distance away. Schmidt reported that "after a few seconds' gaze it began to swim toward us, and as our bullets seemed to have no effect we took flight in earnest. Losing sight of it behind an island, we did not pick it up again and were just as well pleased."

The creature was gigantic; Schmidt figured it "was 35 feet long, with at least 12 of this devoted to head and neck."

Giant Footprints

According to Schmidt's records, the rest of the expedition's experiences along the Solimes River were ordinary. But because Pfleng died a few months later of fever, the incredible account of the mystery beast could not be supported by a second witness. Still, Schmidt's report was not the only one describing a huge swamp-dwelling creature in remote South America. In the early twentieth century, Lieutenant Colonel Percy H. Fawcett, who surveyed the jungle for Britain's Royal Geographical Society, wrote that natives had told him about "the tracks of some gigantic animal" seen in the swamps along the part of the Acre River where Peru, Bolivia, and Brazil meet—a few hundred miles from the site of Schmidt and Pfleng's strange experience. But the natives admitted that they had never actually seen the creature that left the prints. Fawcett also noted that farther south, along the Peru-Bolivian border, huge tracks of an unknown animal had been found.

Even Stranger Dinosaur Sightings

While the notion of dinosaurs still living in deepest Africa and South America is, at least, somewhat plausible, the presence of such creatures in the United States or Europe is all but impossible. Still, such sightings have been reported!

In a letter published in the August 22, 1982, issue of *Empire Magazine,* Myrtle Snow of Pagosa Springs, Colorado, wrote that in May 1935, when she was three years old, she saw "five baby dinosaurs" near her hometown. A few months later a local farmer shot one after it took some of his sheep. "My grandfather took us to see it the next morning," she said. "It was about seven feet tall, was gray, had a head like a snake, short front legs with claws that resembled chicken feet, large stout back legs and a long tail."

And these were not her only sightings! There were two more. In 1937 Snow saw another dinosaur in a cave, but this time it appeared to be dark green. And on the evening of October 23, 1978, in a driving rain, she spotted one crossing a field not far from where she had had her 1937 sighting.

In another case, in 1934, a South Dakota farmer claimed that a giant, four-legged reptile had forced his tractor off the road before disappearing into nearby Campbell Lake. Investigators found huge tracks on the shore. In addition, even before the sighting was reported, sheep and other small animals had been mysteriously vanishing.

Finally, a man reported being attacked by a "15-foot reptile, like a dinosaur," at Forli, Italy, in December 1970. Fifty miles northwest of

A South Dakota farmer claimed that a giant, four-legged reptile had forced his tractor off the road before disappearing into nearby Campbell Lake.

Dinosaur attack scene in 1933 horror film classic *King Kong*.

there, in June 1975, a monster appeared in a tomato field near Goro and badly frightened a farmer named Maurizio Tombini, who news accounts said had "a reputation for seriousness." The monster, according to news reports, measured about 10 feet long, had legs, and its feet left remarkable tracks. Tombini compared it to a "gigantic lizard" and denied that it was a crocodile. According to police, several other people also reported sightings. These witnesses noted that the creature had a wolflike howl.

Sources:

Heuvelmans, Bernard, *On the Track of Unknown Animals,* New York: Hill and Wang, 1958.
Ley, Willy, *Exotic Zoology,* New York: Viking Press, 1959.
Mackal, Roy P., *A Living Dinosaur?: In Search of Mokele-Mbembe,* New York: E. J. Brill, 1987.
Mackal, Roy P., *Searching for Hidden Animals,* Garden City, New York: Doubleday and Company, 1980.
Sanderson, Ivan T., *More "Things",* New York: Pyramid Books, 1969.

MOKELE-MBEMBE

The fascinating story of mokele-mbembe—pronounced "mo-kay-lee mmmbem-bee," a Lingala word meaning "one who stops rivers"—began in print, at least, in 1776. A book written by Abbe Lievain Bonaventure Proyart about French priests trying to bring Catholicism to the people of west-central Africa also contained a great deal of careful information about the animals of the region. It told of a startling discovery in the forest, where priests noted tracks left by an animal "which was not seen but which must have been monstrous": each clawed print measured about three feet across.

SAUROPODS

Sauropods were huge plant-eating reptiles with long necks and tails, small heads, bulky bodies, and stumplike legs; *Diplodocus, Apatosaurus (Brontosaurus)*, and *Brachiosaurus* were sauropods.

In the twentieth century Bernard Heuvelmans, the founder of cryptozoology (the study of unknown or unexpected animals), would figure that an animal that made such tracks must have been about the size of a hippopotamus or elephant. What could such an animal have been? (Or still be?) Legend—backed up by a number of eyewitness sightings—points to a sauropod, a type of dinosaur thought to have become extinct some 65 million years ago!

In the early 1870s Alfred Aloysius Smith, a young Englishman who worked for a British trading firm, was sent to the French African settlement of Gabon. In the course of his work, he traveled up and down the Ogooue River. Years later South African novelist Ethelreda Lewis would help him record his adventures in what would become the much-read book *Trader Horn,* published in 1927. In it he referred to mysterious animals that lived in the African swamps and rivers. "I've seen the *Amali's* footprints," he recalled. "About the size of a good frying pan ... and three claws instead o' five." In 1909, while on a westward journey along the rivers of central Africa, Lieutenant Paul Gratz, too, wrote of a scaleless, clawed swamp creature that frightened natives living near Lake Bangweulu in northern Rhodesia (now Zambia).

"Half Elephant, Half Dragon"

Carl Hagenbeck, a world-famous animal collector, was the first to bring wide attention to the subject. In his 1909 autobiography, *Beasts and Men,* he recalled how he had come to learn of the creature. At separate times an employee on a collecting expedition, Hans Schomburgh, and an English big-game hunter had told him about a "huge,

A map of Africa: Many mokele-mbembe sightings took place in central African countries such as the People's Republic of the Congo, Cameroon, Central African Republic, and Gabon.

monster, half elephant, half dragon," said to live in central Africa. And before that, collector and naturalist Joseph Menges had informed him of similar reports from natives describing what sounded to Hagenbeck like "some kind of dinosaur, seemingly akin to the brontosaurs." So fascinated was Hagenbeck, in fact, that he sent an expedition to the huge, swampy region where the beast reportedly lived. Disease and hostile natives kept the investigators from reaching the location, though, and Hagenbeck had to abandon his search.

Schomburgh told Hagenbeck that at Lake Bangweulu in Northern Rhodesia (now Zambia) he had been surprised to find no hippopotamuses. His native guides explained that this was because a strange animal that lived in the lake had killed the hippos. Five hundred miles to the west, in the Dililo marshes, he heard descriptions of a similar creature.

These accounts caused quite a stir in Africa, Europe, and the Unites States. Newspapers repeated the stories, with opinions ranging from harsh doubt to breathless excitement. The sensation faded after a few months, though, and in 1911, in a geographical journal, Northern

Rhodesian colonial official Frank H. Melland made this statement: "I have never heard so much as a rumor of any animal that could be supposed to resemble a brontosaurus, or a dinosaur, which has been reputed to inhabit these swamps."

Then, in 1913, the German government sent Captain Freiherr von Stein zu Lausnitz to survey colonial Cameroon, which bordered the African Congo. In his official report, not published until some years later, he noted that in areas of the lower Ubangi, Sanga, and Ikelemba rivers in the Congo, many people—including experienced hunting guides who knew the local wildlife well—spoke of something called mokele-mbembe. Von Stein wrote: "The animal is said to be of a brownish-gray color with a smooth skin, its size approximately that of an elephant, at least that of a hippopotamus. It is said to have a long and very flexible neck.... A few spoke about a long muscular tail like that of an alligator. Canoes coming near it are said to be doomed; the animal is said to attack vessels at once and to kill the crews but without eating the bodies."

> "The animal is said to be of a brownish-gray color with a smooth skin, its size approximately that of an elephant, at least that of a hippopotamus."

Von Stein added that the creature reportedly lived in caves at sharp bends along the river. "It is said to climb the shore even at daytime in search of food; its diet is said to be entirely vegetable.... The preferred plant was shown to me; it is a kind of liana with large white blossoms, with a milky sap and applelike fruits. At the Ssombo river I was shown a path said to have been made by this animal in order to get at its food. The path was fresh and there were plants of the described type nearby." Because there were so many tracks of other animals on the path, however, Stein could not make out those of the creature.

During the next few decades, two brontosaur-hunting expeditions were launched, but without much success. In a 1938 exploration, German Leo von Boxberger collected many mokele-mbembe reports but lost them in an attack on him and his group by unfriendly natives.

Outside the regions where the creatures reportedly lived, mokele-mbembe would have been forgotten had it not been for the continued interest of cryptozoologists Willy Ley, Ivan T. Sanderson—who wrote about them in a 1948 *Saturday Evening Post* article—and Heuvelmans. Heuvelmans included an entire chapter on the beasts in his 1958 book *On the Track of Unknown Animals*.

Into the Heart of Darkness

In the 1960s a young herpetologist (reptile and amphibian scientist) named James H. Powell, Jr., became interested in Africa's mystery

A representation of what a mokele-mbembe might look like.

sauropod after reading about it in the writings of Ley, Sanderson, and Heuvelmans. While conducting field research on rain-forest crocodiles in west-central Africa in 1972, he tried to enter the People's Republic of the Congo to investigate the mokele-mbembe puzzle for himself. He was not allowed to enter the country; after four years of trying, Powell gave up and set off for Gabon and the remote regions where *Trader Horn* author Smith had seen tracks of strange animals so many decades before.

Natives Provide Strong Evidence

There Powell eventually found a witness who had seen the mystery beast. Without being asked, the witness mentioned the plant that, according to most reports, comprised the creature's diet. Shown pictures of different animals, the witness pointed to one of a diplodocus. Picture tests given to other native observers brought the same identification. In early 1979 Powell returned to the area to gather additional testimony from his first witness and from others.

A third expedition was launched in February 1980. This time Roy P. Mackal, a University of Chicago biologist with a keen interest in

Map of People's Republic of the Congo and surrounding areas.

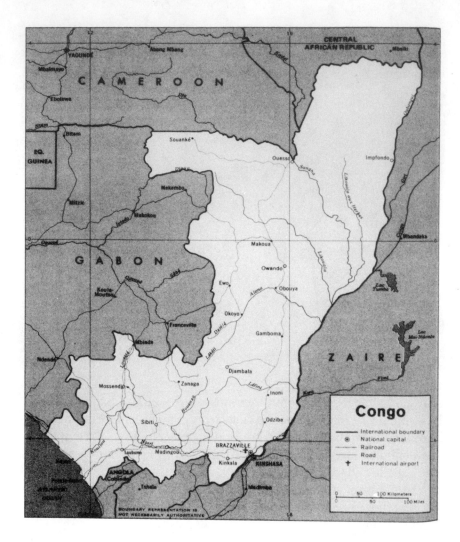

strange animal reports, went with Powell. The two focused their explorations on the northern Congo, between the Sanga and Ubangi rivers. Mackal thought that growing human traffic on the waterways might have pushed mokele-mbembe into the remote Likoula region—mostly swamp and rain forest and still largely unexplored.

The two scientists journeyed into the great swamp but observed nothing. They decided to use what little remained collecting the testimony of witnesses. American missionary Eugene Thomas, who had lived on the Ubangi River for many years and had often heard mokele-mbembe stories, was able to direct them to several native observers. The descriptions given were remarkably similar: animals 15 to 30 feet

Roy P. Mackal

(1925-)

Roy P. Mackal is a well-respected figure in cryptozoology. After serving in World War II, Mackal took his Ph.D. from the University of Chicago, where he spent his professional life until retirement in 1990.

Mackal taught and conducted research in the fields of biology and chemistry and made a number of major discoveries in viral research and genetic engineering. But Mackal has had many interests. An inventor and engineer with several patents to his credit, he is also the editor and publisher of a journal dedicated to the study of Liberian stamps and is writing a biography of Victorian actress Maude Adams.

He is best known, though, for his cryptozoological investigations and writings. Between 1965 and 1975 he was the scientific director of the Loch Ness Phenomena Investigation Bureau. His 1976 book *The Monsters of Loch Ness* is considered a cryptozoological classic.

In 1980 Mackal published a book intended for a popular audience, called *Searching for Hidden Animals*. After two expeditions to the Congo to pursue reports of mokele-mbembe, he wrote *A Living Dinosaur?* Since then he has participated in an expedition that investigated pterosaur sightings in southwest Africa. Mackal was also a cofounder of the International Society of Cryptozoology and has served as its vice president since 1982.

long, most with snakelike heads and necks and long, thin tails. Their bodies were bulbous, like that of a hippo. The largest specimens were "the size of a small elephant." Mackal and Powell were told that the beasts had "stubby legs, and that the hind feet [had] three claws." The creatures were described as hairless. Again, witnesses pointed to a sauropod when shown pictures of different animals for comparison.

The natives said that the animals, while they did not eat flesh, would overturn canoes that went into the rivers, lakes, and streams where they lived and that the local people would kill them. Mackal and Powell learned of a mokele-mbembe killing, sometime around 1959, after Pygmies trapped one in a channel going into Lake Tele. Later, it was reported, they ate its flesh—and all of them died.

In late 1981 Mackal returned to the area, this time with ecologist J. Richard Greenwell, Congolese government biologist Marcellin Agnagna, and others. They interviewed more native witnesses—though this was made difficult at times by the widespread belief that anyone who talked about mokele-mbembe would die soon afterward. Expedition members did not see any of the creatures themselves, although one time, as they were rounding a curve in the Likouala River, they heard a great "plop" sound. Then a large wake or track was seen on the surface of the water, suggesting that a large animal had gone—and remained—below. Hippopotamuses did not live in the area. Residents had told expedition members that mokele-mbembe were often seen at sharp bends in the rivers where the water was deepest.

The expedition members were also shown a trail of freshly broken branches through which an animal between five and seven feet high had passed on its way to a pool where a mokele-mbembe was said to live. There were 12-inch round tracks leading to the pool, but nowhere were there any tracks leading out of it!

Unable to break through the thick swamp growth, the expedition did not make it to the shores of Lake Tele. Two later expeditions claimed to do so, however, and in each case reported sightings of mokele-mbembe.

Sightings by Scientists

Around the time of the second Mackal expedition, American engineer Herman Regusters led a group—with much difficulty—to Tele. There members of the group camped for well over two weeks, during which they reported several sightings of the creature's head and neck poking out of the water. Once they heard a "low windy roar" on the lake, which "increased to a deep-throated trumpeting growl." Then Regusters and his wife, Kia Van Dusen, claimed that they saw a huge creature moving through the swamp along the lake's edge. Another time Regusters observed it or a similar animal through binoculars. It had a slender, eight-foot neck, a small head, and 15 feet of back;

It had a slender, eight-foot neck, a small head, and 15 feet of back; Regusters guessed that with its tail (which he did not see), the creature would measure "30 to 35 feet long."

Regusters guessed that with its tail (which he did not see), the creature would measure "30 to 35 feet long." However, intense humidity caused the expedition's cameras to fail, so there were no photographs of these remarkable sights.

In April 1983 Agnagna led an all-Congolese government expedition to Tele. On the morning of May 1, he and two local villagers set out to film animal and bird species in the forest surrounding the lake. One of Agnagna's companions fell into a muddy pool and went to the lake to wash himself. There he spotted something in the water and called for Agnagna, who waded far out until he, too, could see the large and remarkable animal about 1,000 feet away. The creature resembled a mokele-mbembe.

Agnagna carefully watched the animal for the next 20 minutes. He could make out a wide back, long, thin neck, and small head. This portion measured about 18 feet; with a tail (which the biologist guessed was under water), the animal would have been a good deal longer. The animal finally disappeared below the lake's surface. While he took photographs of the creature, Agnagna wrote that "the emotion and alarm at this sudden, unexpected event" must have caused him to set his camera incorrectly, a mistake he discovered only later, when the film was processed. He claimed that no photographs survived.

Yet at an International Society of Cryptozoology meeting in Paris in 1984, Agnagna gave a slightly different version of the sighting and his camera problems in a formal paper and interviews. And he produced snapshots of the lake creature taken with a still camera. These photographs showed only a small, distant, unidentifiable image—which is not surprising considering how far Agnagna was from it. The biologist never explained why he had changed his story.

Operation Congo

Other mokele-mbembe expeditions took place in the next few years in an exploration effort called Operation Congo. And in one of these, Agnagna's behavior was again called into question. Hired by four eager young Englishmen to lead them to Lake Tele in mid-1986, the biologist was accused of stealing the group's film and supplies (a matter which eventually ended up in court) and causing other disturbances. In addition, no sightings of mokele-mbembe were made.

Agnagna accompanied two Japanese expeditions in September 1987 and the spring of 1988. The second group made it to Tele, where they saw nothing out of the ordinary. Like other Operation Congo members before them, the Japanese interviewed a number of people who claimed to have seen the animals at some point in their lives.

A Not-So-Impossible Animal?

During his second expedition, Mackal collected more than 30 detailed reports of mokele-mbembe. He felt that they described "a small sauropod so well that I find it impossible not to accept the identification. Each of the reports was a firsthand, eyewitness account by informants from widely differing ethnic, cultural, religious, and geographical backgrounds."

With no body or bone or skin samples as evidence, those who have not seen mokele-mbembe for themselves must make their judgments from this sort of testimony. Although the existence of a modern-day sauropod is hard to believe, some think it is not altogether out of the question. While it is thought that dinosaurs became extinct—over a large span of time—some 65 million years ago, the Congo basin's geography and climate have remained the same for at least that long. Crocodiles, a close relative of dinosaurs, have survived all that time without much change. In other words, the survival of a small population of dinosaurs in a remote, stable, and suitable place is not totally crazy!

Sources:

Heuvelmans, Bernard, *On the Track of Unknown Animals,* New York: Hill and Wang, 1958.
Ley, Willy, *Exotic Zoology,* New York: Viking Press, 1959.
Mackal, Roy P., *A Living Dinosaur?: In Search of Mokele-Mbembe,* New York: E. J. Brill, 1987.
Mackal, Roy P., *Searching for Hidden Animals,* Garden City, New York: Doubleday and Company, 1980.
Sanderson, Ivan T., *More "Things",* New York: Pyramid Books, 1969.

PTEROSAUR SIGHTINGS

Pterosaurs, commonly and mistakenly referred to as pterodactyls, are extinct flying reptiles of the order Pterosauria, common in the Mesozoic era (from about 160 to 60 million years ago). They were not true flying reptiles, nor ancestors of birds; instead, they glided on winds and air currents—more like bats.

The wing of a pterosaur consisted of a thin layer of skin, stretched out along an *extremely* long fourth finger on the hand, then down to meet the lower leg. Early varieties of pterosaurs were generally small and had fully toothed jaws and long tails. Later forms were often large, had stumps for tails, and fewer teeth in jaws shaped like beaks. Since their legs were weak and their wings very heavy, pterosaurs were practically helpless on land. Eventually, the large reptiles were replaced by birds, which were better flyers.

Sightings

On January 11, 1976, two ranch hands near Poteet, Texas, just south of San Antonio, sighted a five-foot-tall birdlike creature standing in the water of a stock tank. "He started flying," witness Jessie Garcia reported, "but I never saw him flap his wings. He made no noise at all."

Around the same time, two sisters, Libby and Deany Ford, observed a "big black bird" near a pond northeast of Brownsville, near the Texas-Mexico border. "It was as big as me," Libby said, "and it had a face like a bat." Later, as the two girls looked through a book in an effort to identify the creature, they found out what it was.

> ### TYPES OF PTEROSAURS
>
> The pterodactylus was a small pterosaur with a 12-inch wingspan, a small number of teeth, and a stump of a tail. The last and greatest pterosaur, the pteranodon, had a wingspan of more than 20 feet; its beak had no teeth and there was a huge bony crest on the back of its head.

Driving to work on an isolated country lane southwest of San Antonio on the morning of February 24, three elementary school teachers saw a shadow cover the entire road. The object causing it, which was passing low overhead, looked like a huge bird with a 15- to 20-foot wingspan. "I could see the skeleton of this bird through the skin or feathers or whatever," witness Patricia Bryant said. According to observer David Rendon, "It just glided. It didn't fly. It was no higher than the telephone line. It had a huge breast. It had different legs, and it had huge wings, but the wings were very peculiar like. It had a bony structure, you know, like when you hold a bat by the wing tips, like it has bones at the top and in-between."

Having never seen anything like it, the three witnesses rushed to an encyclopedia as soon as they got to school. After some searching they found what they were looking for. They learned that the animal they had observed was not a mystery creature after all.

Pterosaurs in flight.

At 3:55 A.M. on September 14, 1982, ambulance technician James Thompson was driving along Highway 100, a few miles east of Los Fresnos, Texas, and midway between Harlingen and Brownsville. He suddenly spotted a "large birdlike object" pass low over the highway, 150 feet in front of him. Its tail was so strange-looking that it practically stopped him in his tracks. He hit the brakes, pulled his vehicle to the side of the road, and keenly stared at the strange object, which he at first had trouble believing was a living creature.

"I expected him to land like a model airplane," Thompson said. Then "he flapped his wings enough to get above the grass.... It had a black, or grayish, rough texture. It wasn't feathers. I'm quite sure it was a hide-type covering." Its thin body, which ended in a "fin," stretched over eight feet; its wingspan was five to six feet. The wings appeared to have "indentations." At the back of the head was a hump like a Brahma bull's. There was "almost no neck at all."

Later Thompson looked at books, trying to identify the "bird." Like the Ford sisters and the San Antonio teachers more than six years earlier, he had no real difficulty finding out what he had seen; the books indicated to him, as it had to the others, that he had seen an extinct pterosaur!

African "Breaker of Boats"

In the early twentieth century, a traveler and writer named Frank Melland worked for the British colonial service in Northern Rhodesia (now Zambia). While there he learned of a flying creature that lived along certain rivers. Called *kongamato*—"breaker of boats"—it was considered very dangerous. Natives said it was "like a lizard with membranous wings like a bat."

Melland wrote about the creature in his 1923 book *In Witchbound Africa*. From the natives he learned that its "wing-spread was from 4 to 7 feet across, [and] that the general color was red. It was believed to have no feathers but only skin on its body, and was believed to have teeth in its beak: these last two points no one could be sure of, as no one ever saw a kongamato close and lived to tell the tale." Amazingly, when Melland showed the local residents two books he had containing pictures of pterosaurs, "every native present immediately and unhesitatingly picked it out and identified it as a kongamato!"

The natives insisted that the flying reptile they described still existed. While unsure about this claim, Melland at least believed that the creature had lived sometime "within the memory of man." He concluded, "Whether it is scientifically possible that a reptile that existed in the mesozoic age could exist in the climatic conditions of to-day I have not the necessary knowledge to decide."

Looking back on his days as an African game warden, Colonel R. S. Pitman published his memoirs, *A Game Warden Takes Stock,* in 1942. In the book he recalled that when in Northern Rhodesia he had heard of a frightening mythical beast that brought death to those who looked at it. It was said to have lived (and possibly still lived) in the thick, swampy forest region near the Angola and Congo borders. What most fascinated Pitman about the mystery beast was that it was both batlike and birdlike—and gigantic—resembling the prehistoric creature known as the pterosaur.

Similarly, in his 1947 book *Witchcraft and Magic in Africa,* Frederick Kaigh referred to a spot on the "Rhodesian-Congo border near the north-eastern border of the Jiundu Swamp, a foetid [smelly], eerie place in which the pterodactyl is locally supposed to survive with spiritual powers of great evil."

According to Carl Pleijel of the Swedish Museum of Natural History, a sighting of such a pterosaur-like creature took place in Kenya in 1974. The witnesses were members of a British expedition, Pleijel told writer Jan-Ove Sundberg. Not long after this report, Sundberg also learned of a second sighting over a swamp in Namibia in late 1975 by an American expedition.

Namibia has been the source of other such reports. In the summer of 1988, cryptozoologist Roy P. Mackal traveled there with a small group of associates. He was particularly interested in an isolated private desert area where sightings of "flying snakes" continued to be reported. Mackal interviewed witnesses, who said that the animals indeed had wings—of 30 feet, no less—but no feathers. The creatures appeared to live in the caves and cracks in the many kopjes (grassland hills) that dotted the landscape. Expedition members found ostrich bones in almost unreachable spots atop kopjes, suggesting that kills had been carried there by flying creatures. One expedition member

> What most fascinated Pitman about the mystery beast was that it was both batlike and birdlike—and gigantic—resembling the prehistoric creature known as the pterosaur.

A pterosaur in a scene from the movie *The Animal World.*

who stayed on after Mackal returned to the United States reported seeing one of the creatures from a thousand feet away. It was, he said, black with white markings and had huge wings, which it used to glide through the air.

Sources:

Clark, Jerome, and Loren Coleman, *Creatures of the Outer Edge,* New York: Warner Books, 1978.

Coleman, Loren, *Curious Encounters: Phantom Trains, Spooky Spots, and Other Mysterious Wonders,* Boston: Faber and Faber, 1985.

Heuvelmans, Bernard, *On the Track of Unknown Animals,* New York: Hill and Wang, 1958.

Mackal, Roy P., *Searching for Hidden Animals,* Garden City, New York: Doubleday and Company, 1980.

THYLACINE

One of cryptozoology's most interesting puzzles involves the thylacine, an Australian animal that has been officially declared extinct—yet may not be. The case of the thylacine is actually a mystery that has two parts.

A "Tasmanian Tiger"

The thylacine, a flesh-eating marsupial (pouched mammal), evolved on the Australian mainland late in the age of mammals. Though it looked like a mixture of a fox, a wolf, a tiger, and a hyena, it was actually related to the opossum (zoologists believe they share a common ancestor).

The male thylacine measured over six feet long between head and tail. Its head looked like that of a fox or a dog, but beginning mid-back and going all the way to the tail, it had tigerlike stripes (from which it got its popular nickname, "Tasmanian tiger"). Its long, bunched rear resembled a hyena's and ended in a stiff, unwagging tail. Its fur was coarse and a sandy-brown color. Females were a little smaller, but with twice the number of stripes, which started just behind the neck. They also had a pouch—as all female marsupials do— but it faced the rear, perhaps to protect its young as it moved through the undergrowth.

> ## MARSUPIALS
>
> A marsupial is any mammal of the order Marsupialia, which includes kangaroos, opossums, bandicoots, and wombats. The female of most species lacks a placenta—the organ that, in most mammals, joins the unborn young to the mother so the fetus can get nourishment. Instead of the placenta a marsupial mammal has an abdominal pouch called a marsupium. Located outside the mother's body, the marsupium contains milk glands and shelters the young until they are fully developed.

History

About 12,000 years ago, thylacines were driven off the mainland of Australia, probably when Indonesian sailors brought dingoes (a reddish-brown wild dog) over, which proved to be excellent hunters. At least that is what zoologists think, because no fossil record of thylacines on the mainland can be found from that time on. It is believed that the animal retreated to Tasmania. While now an island state off Australia's southeast coast, Tasmania then was connected to the continent by a land bridge. The first mention of a thylacine in print was in an 1805 Tasmanian newspaper, which called the animal "destructive."

Convinced that thylacines were behind the mass killings of sheep on ranches, officials began a campaign to wipe out the "tigers"

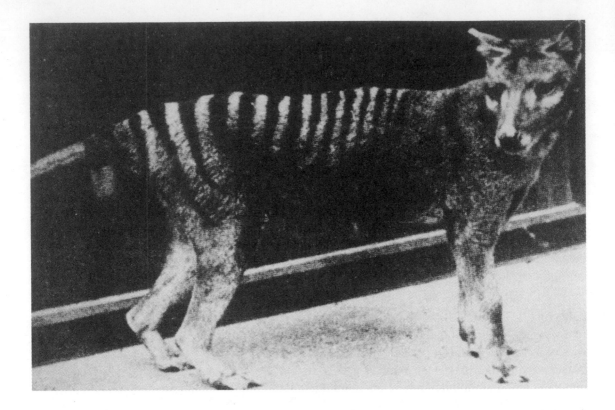

The last officially recognized thylacine, which died in captivity in 1936.

(although, according to modern experts, wild dogs and human rustlers were a far greater threat to livestock than the hated thylacines ever were). Both private companies and the government offered rewards for thylacine scalps—and the killings began. By the early twentieth century, the animals had become a rare sight. Bounty hunters were not their only enemies, though; a distemper virus destroyed many of them, and settlers were claiming more and more of their natural home. Still, armed human beings brought about the thylacine's ultimate extinction. "Farmers continued to see the creature as a menace," two historians of the thylacine wrote, "long after it was [incapable] of reproducing itself in any numbers."

According to the records, the last specimen for which a bounty was paid was killed in 1909. The last time a thylacine was shot was in 1930. And, captured in 1933, the last one on earth died on September 7, 1936, in Tasmania's Hobart Domain Zoo, just two months after the state passed a law declaring the thylacine a protected species. "Benjamin," as the one remaining thylacine was named, "was tame and could be patted," according to keeper Frank Darby, but "it was frequently morose and showed no affection."

The First Mystery

Only after the thylacine was gone for good did most Tasmanians begin to feel sorry for what they had done. In time, the Tasmanian coat of arms would proudly show two thylacines, and Australians would consider it their most beloved lost animal. Its disappearance would come to be viewed as a national tragedy.

Yet as little as a year after Benjamin's death and the thylacine's official extinction, Australia's Animals and Birds Protection Board sent two investigators into the mountains of northwestern Tasmania to see if, perhaps, a few thylacines remained. They returned with a handful of promising reports of sightings collected from residents of the area. While not hard proof, the accounts did encourage the board to set up further searches. And in 1938 an expedition found the first physical evidence: tracks with the thylacine's unusual five-toed front paws and four-toed hind paws.

World War II stopped further investigation, but in late 1945 a private expedition viewed a set of tracks and heard some sighting reports—though none of its members saw anything themselves. Then Australian wildlife experts did nothing about the thylacine question for a number of years. That is, until 1957, when zoologist Eric R. Guiler, chairman of the Animals and Birds Protection Board, went to Broadmarsh to check out a mysterious animal that was killing sheep. Guiler had no doubts that the tracks he saw were those of a thylacine. Convinced that the animal still lived, Guiler launched nine expeditions between 1957 and 1966, during which he gathered a great deal of evidence. Still, he could produce no body, nor did he have a personal sighting.

In 1968 other researchers created the Tiger Center, a place where witnesses could report sightings. Search parties continued to explore the bush (a wilderness region in Australia). And a late-1970s project sponsored by the World Wildlife Fund set up a number of automatic cameras at locations where witnesses said they had seen thylacines; bait was placed to lure the animals across an infra-red beam that would trigger a photograph. Nine different species of animals were caught on film, particularly the Tasmanian devil (an animal which had, from time to time, been mistaken for the thylacine). In his official report in 1980,

---

TASMANIAN DEVIL

The *Tasmanian devil* is a powerful, flesh-eating marsupial—or pouched mammal— found only on the island of Tasmania. (It was once found on mainland Australia as well.) It is the size of a large cat or badger, and its blackish fur is marked with white patches on the throat, sides, and rump. The animal has a huge appetite and often kills species larger than itself. It lives in burrows in rocky areas. Its evil-looking face and fierce snarl are believed to be the reasons behind its frightening name.

project leader Steven J. Smith of the National Parks and Wildlife Service (NPWS) concluded that thylacines were indeed extinct.

But by 1982, in a published survey of 104 sightings reported to the NPWS between 1970 and 1980, Smith had changed his mind. Along with coauthor D. E. Rounsevell, he felt that the best course of action in finding the few thylacines that might remain was to carefully study "the growing collection of reported sightings"—most clustered in the northern regions of the state, where most of the killings had taken place so many decades ago.

In the meantime, Guiler also conducted a hidden-camera operation, with the same poor results. Regardless, he remained convinced that thylacines still existed because of continued sightings and tracks.

Events in the thylacine puzzle took a new turn one rainy night in March 1982. An NPWS park ranger in a forested area of northwestern Tasmania awoke from a nap in the back seat of his car. He turned on his spotlight and shined it on an animal 20 feet away. He said it was a thylacine, "an adult male in excellent condition, with 12 black stripes on a sandy coat." However, the rain wiped out any tracks it might have made.

The NPWS did not make the sighting public until January 1984, hoping to keep away the curious, who might frighten the animal and whatever companions lived with it. Yet the NPWS announcement was not an official statement that the thylacine was no longer extinct. After all, agency personnel could not produce the animal. In addition, they were afraid of the problems an official statement might bring: what would happen to mining and timber companies the property of which was discovered to be the habitat of the thylacine? The endangered animals would have to be protected; would mineral and lumber rights— along with business profits and the tax money they provided the country—have to be relinquished?

Since then other expeditions have been launched, but Tasmania's thylacine has not been found. Doubters think that sighting reports are just wishful thinking or mistaken identifications of other animals, especially wild dogs. In any case, sightings continue. In 1991 as many as 13 accounts were reported; wildlife officials judged three of them "very good." Zoologist Bob Green remarked of thylacines: "They are extremely cunning animals. For every one that's seen, I believe they see a thousand humans. I have received samples of dung and footprints sent in by experienced bushmen who know what they have seen. I believe that the thylacine not only exists but is coming back strongly."

The Second Mystery

In 1981, following a number of sightings of an unusual animal in a southwestern area of Western Australia, the state hired native tracker Kevin Cameron to investigate. In due time Cameron would claim to have seen the animal himself, and he identified it as a thylacine.

Even those who seriously consider that thylacines may have survived in Tasmania have a hard time believing reports like this. Not only do fossils show that no thylacines lived on the mainland in the past 12,000 years, but there is also no proof that the animals were known to Australia's native inhabitants, the aborigines, or to the Europeans who settled the continent in the nineteenth century.

In 1951 a man from Dwellingup visited the Western Australian Museum in Perth, where he displayed photographs and casts of tracks of what he believed was a thylacine. But the staff zoologist there, Athol M. Douglas, rejected the man's eyewitness account and supporting evidence. Some years later other reports of a strange sheep-killing animal led Douglas into the bush, where he tracked and killed the culprit, a house dog gone wild. The experience only made him doubt thylacine reports further. Even so, over the years he was called in to examine the slaughtered bodies of kangaroos and sheep from time to time. And he was bothered that the animals appeared to have been slain in exactly the way that thylacines—and not dogs or dingoes—would kill their victims.

In February 1985 all of Douglas's doubts disappeared when tracker Cameron handed him five color photographs. They showed the side view of an animal burrowing at the base of a tree. Though its face was hidden in the brush, its striped back and long, stiff tail could only be that of a thylacine. The tracker could not tell Douglas where he had taken the pictures, but he did produce casts of the animal's prints. Douglas thought that Cameron's description of the creature's behavior matched similar accounts in scientific writings. Because Cameron could barely read, this information made the zoologist believe his witness even more.

Fake Photos

Still, Cameron was acting odd and secretive, and Douglas thought that something about the photographs might be fishy. With some difficulty, the zoologist got Cameron to give him permission to publish the pictures with an article he had written for the British magazine *New Scientist*. Only then did Cameron show him the original negatives of the film, which proved that the tracker had, indeed, been lying.

As Douglas later recalled in *Cryptozoology:* "The film had been cut, frames were missing.... There were no photographs of the animal bounding away. Furthermore, in one negative, there was a shadow of another person pointing what could be an over-under .12 shotgun. Cameron had told me he had been alone. It would have been practically impossible for an animal as alert as a thylacine to remain stationary for so long while human activity was going on in its vicinity." Also, the zoologist wondered why the animal's head was never shown.

New Scientist readers noticed inconsistencies with the photographs as well. For one thing, the animal did not move at all from one picture to the next. Furthermore, shadow patterns in the photographs showed that at least an hour, or even more, separated some shots from the rest. To critics this could only mean one thing—that, over time, Cameron had photographed a stuffed model of a thylacine.

But Douglas thought it more likely that one of the pictures, the first taken, showed a living thylacine about to be shot by the shadowy man pointing the gun. The zoologist suspected that the rest of the photographs were taken later, after the animal had been dead for some time and was stiff with rigor mortis. Douglas hoped that someone would find the animal's dead body, but nobody ever did. Perhaps that is because there is a $5,000 fine for anyone convicted of killing the (officially extinct) thylacine.

The Evidence Builds

In 1966 a Western Australia Museum team had found a thylacine's remains in a cave near Mundrabrilla Station. Carbon dating showed that the body was 4,500 years old (all other thylacine fossil remains found on mainland Australia had been there 12,000 years or longer!). And, according to zoologist Douglas, a possible mistake in dating (due to contamination from groundwater that soaked the thylacine body) could make the specimen much more recent than that! Compared to a dingo body that Douglas found in the cave in 1986 (which was hairless, dry, and odorless, and thought to be 20 years old at most), the thylacine remains were, according to the zoologist, "in a far superior state of preservation." To him, the condition of the thylacine's body suggested that it had died no more than a year earlier, probably less!

The state of Western Australia (which makes up about one-third of the Australian continent) is not the only part of the mainland to claim thylacine sightings. According to investigator Rex Gilroy, many reports of "large striped dog-like animals, possibly thylacines" have been recorded in other parts of the country. He added that "plaster casts have been made of tracks found on the mainland," and these "compare with others from Tasmania, leaving little doubt as to the animal's identity."

Thylacine sightings have also taken place in the mountain wilderness of the Namadgi-Kosciusco National Park, along the New South Wales-Victoria border. There ranger Peter Simon reported seeing such an animal in broad daylight for several seconds some 100 feet away. In

---

OFFICIALLY EXTINCT AND MISPLACED, TOO?

On April 7, 1974, at 3:30 A.M., Joan Gilbert spotted a "strange striped creature, half cat and half dog," as it passed in front of her car's headlights. "It was," she recalled, "the most peculiar animal I have ever seen. It had stripes, a long thin tail, and ... was as big as a medium-sized dog." When she looked through reference books at the library, she discovered that it was an animal she had never heard of before: a thylacine. Funny thing, though—the sighting did not take place in Tasmania. It did not take place in Western Australia, or Victoria, or New South Wales. It happened outside of Bournemouth, in England!

1990, when Graeme O'Neill wrote an article about the thylacine mystery for Melbourne's leading newspaper, *The Age,* he received many cards and letters from Victoria residents reporting their own quite believable—and remarkably similar—sightings of the animal.

To Australian writer Tony Healy, there is something downright spooky about mainland thylacines. He noted that the night before ranger Simon's sighting, his hunting dogs refused to get out of the truck after they and their master heard harsh, thylacine-like panting sounds in the bush. In 1982 a Western Australia farm couple who claimed to have lost livestock to thylacines told a Perth newspaper that a "prickly feeling" at the back of their necks was always their first warning that the animals were near.

Sources:

Douglas, Athol M., "The Thylacine: A Case for Current Existence on Mainland Australia," *Cryptozoology* 9, 1990, pp. 13-25.

Douglas, Athol M., "Tigers in Western Australia?," *New Scientist* 110,1505, April 24, 1986, pp. 44-47.

Guiler, Eric R., *Thylacine: The Tragedy of the Tasmanian Tiger,* Oxford, England: Oxford University Press, 1985.

Wilford, John Noble, "Automatic Cameras Stalk Tasmania's Rare Tiger," *New York Times,* May 27, 1980.

THE MYSTERY OF THE SIRRUSH

It has long been believed that the sirrush was an imaginary animal. Or was it?

Around 600 B.C., during King Nebuchadnezzar's reign in Babylonia, an ancient country in southwest Asia, an artist carved a series of images of three different animals in the huge archway of Babylon's grand Ishtar Gate and on the high walls surrounding the road that approached it. The three beasts depicted were the lion, the rimi (a now-extinct wild ox), and the sirrush, which looked like a dragon. It has long been believed that the sirrush was an imaginary animal. Or was it?

Fascinated by the "zoological puzzle" of the sirrush, writer Willy Ley described its appearance thus: "[It has] a slender body covered with scales, a long slender scaly tail, and a long slim scaly neck bearing a serpent's head. Although the mouth is closed, a long forked

A dragon. Mythological creature or surviving dinosaur?

tongue protrudes. There are flaps of skin attached to the back of the head, which is adorned (and armed) with a straight horn."

One of the books of the Bible related that Nebuchadnezzar's priests kept a "great dragon or serpent, which they of Babylon worshipped." And many years earlier, in the Old Testament's Book of Job, the sirrush may have been referred to by another name. The Bible described a "Behemoth" that ate grass and laid "under the shady trees, in the cover of the reed, and fens [low land covered with water or swamps]." The creature had mighty strength, its bones were "like bars of iron," and it had a "tail like a cedar."

The behemoth's identity has long puzzled Bible experts, who believe that Job was writing about a real animal. University of Chicago biologist Roy P. Mackal offered this idea: "The behemoth's tail is compared to a cedar, which suggests a sauropod. This identification is reinforced by other factors. Not only the behemoth's physical nature, but also its habits and food preferences are compatible with a sauropod's. Both live in swampy areas with trees, reeds and fens.

The modern discoverer of the Ishtar Gate, German archaeologist Robert Koldeway, seriously considered that the sirrush was a real animal. For he noted that unlike descriptions of other fantastic beasts in Babylonian art, images of the sirrush remained unchanged over centuries. Still, Koldeway felt that saurians did not live at the same time as human beings and that the Babylonians did not have the skills to reconstruct such animals from fossil remains.

Babylonian Dinosaur Sightings in the African Congo

But Babylonians were known to have reached the African Congo—the home of the **mokele-mbembe**—in their travels. Ley, Mackal, and noted zoologist Bernard Heuvelmans have all suggested that the Babylonians heard of such creatures while there, perhaps sighted them, or even took specimens home.

Some modern scholars, Adrienne Mayor for one, believe that ancient peoples did, in fact, know of, and had interest in, prehistoric animals. Mayor has attested, "Reliable ancient sources relate that, when fossils were discovered in antiquity, they were transported with great care, identified, preserved, and sometimes traded. Reconstructed models or the remains of 'unknown' species were displayed in Greece and Rome." If such was the case with the sirrush, however, the fossilized remains would have had to come from elsewhere, as dinosaur fossils have never been found in the Mesopotamian region.

Sources:

Heuvelmans, Bernard, *On the Track of Unknown Animals,* New York: Hill and Wang, 1958.
Ley, Willy, *Exotic Zoology,* New York: Viking Press, 1959.
Mackal Roy P., *A Living Dinosaur?: In Search of Mokele-Mbembe,* New York: E. J. Brill, 1987.
Mackal, Roy P., *Searching for Hidden Animals,* Garden City, New York: Doubleday and Company, 1980.

PALUXY FOOTPRINTS

In the late 1930s a field explorer for the American Museum of Natural History named Roland Bird made a discovery in the limestone bed of the Paluxy River near Glen Rose, Texas, that upset one of science's most basic concepts—how life began on earth. By this time most scientists believed in the theory of *evolution* formulated by Charles Darwin in the mid-nineteenth century, which states that complex types of life developed, over time, from lower, or more simple, forms. Scientists believed that dinosaurs and human beings did not exist on the earth at the same time, that man appeared 60 million years after dinosaurs became extinct. Yet Bird discovered fossil tracks of dinosaurs and—what looked like—humans together in the same Cretaceous rock, 100 million years old! It was true that the "human" prints were *very* large—15 to 20 inches in length and eight inches in width—but they did show believable insteps and heels.

Yet Bird discovered fossil tracks of dinosaurs and—what looked like—humans together in the same Cretaceous rock, 100 million years old!

Evolutionism versus Creationism

A second theory about how life began on earth is called *creationism*. Based word for word on the Bible's Book of Genesis, it states that all living things, as they now exist, were created by God all at once. The Paluxy tracks seemed to support the beliefs of the creationists because they showed that simple and complex life forms did exist together in the past; creationists also held that the tracks proved that the earth was not as old as most scientists believed, that dinosaurs died in the Great Flood (in 4000 B.C.) described in the Bible, and that—again, according to the Bible—giants had once walked the earth (also see entry: **The Search for Noah's Ark**). For more than four decades, evolutionists and creationists argued back and forth about the footprints, with evolution scientists feeling that the "human" tracks were carved in later or that they really belonged to dinosaurs, but time and wear had kept the reptiles' special toe marks from being preserved.

It was not until the 1980s that the puzzle was finally solved. Glen J. Kuban, a computer programmer from Ohio who had been studying the footprints on and off for four years, found faint colors in the Paluxy tracks limestone in the pattern of dinosaur toes. In other words, different rock materials from those making up the rest of the tracks had filled in the toe marks and later hardened. At first dinosaur experts didn't believe Kuban's findings because it was believed that bipedal (upright, two-legged) dinosaurs never pressed the full weight of the soles of their feet on the ground, walking, instead, on their toes. But after other paleontologists found the same color differences in similar tracks near Clayton, New Mexico, they accepted Kuban's explanation as fact. Kuban and a friend, Ronnie Hastings, invited leading creation scientists to the Paluxy site and persuaded them that these were dinosaur—and not human—footprints after all.

Sources:

Kitcher, Philip, *Abusing Science: The Case Against Creationism,* Cambridge, Massachusetts: The MIT Press, 1982.
Steiger, Brad, *Worlds Before Our Own,* New York: Berkley-Putnam, 1978.
Wilford, John Noble, "Fossils of 'Man Tracks' Shown to Be Dinosaurian," *New York Times,* June 17, 1986.

Other Fantastic Creatures

- REPTILE MEN

- MOTHMAN

- BLACK DOGS

- CRAWFORDSVILLE MONSTER

- ONZA

- RI

Other Fantastic Creatures

REPTILE MEN

The 1954 science-fiction film *The Creature from the Black Lagoon* featured a strange animal from the Amazon River that walked upright on two legs but had gills and scales. While reports of such "reptile men" are not common, they do pop up from time to time. As early as 1878 a creature measuring six feet five inches tall and covered with "fish scales" was described at a Louisville, Kentucky, theater sideshow as the "Wild Man of the Woods." While the creature was probably an actor in costume who was after the money of his foolish audience, residents in a nearby area did report seeing a bipedal (two-legged) "giant lizard" nearly a century later!

More puzzling was the November 1958 account of a Riverside, California, man. While driving near the Santa Ana River he was attacked by a creature with a head like a scarecrow, shiny eyes, and scales; it left long scratches on his windshield. As witness Charles Wetzel sped away, he hit the monster and drove over it. The following evening another driver in the area reported a similar experience.

Weirder still was the case of Mrs. Darwin Johnson of Evansville, Indiana. While swimming in the Ohio River on August 21, 1955, she was dragged under the water by a clawlike hand that gripped her knee. Every time she struggled to reach the surface the unknown assailant pulled her down again. The thumping sound she made while grasping a friend's inner tube finally scared the attacker away. While never actually seen, the creature left a green palm stain on Mrs. Johnson's knee and scratches severe enough to warrant a trip to the doctor.

The reptile man in the 1954 film *The Creature from the Black Lagoon.*

That same year, along the Miami River in Loveland, Ohio, a man driving home from work at 3:30 A.M. on May 25 came upon a strange scene. Parking his car, he watched three awful-looking creatures with lopsided chests, wide, lipless, froglike mouths, and wrinkles instead of hair on their heads; one held a device that emitted sparks, and an odd odor filled the air. The witness reported the incident to his local police chief.

Nearly 17 years later, at 1 A.M. on March 3, 1972, two Loveland police officers saw a similar creature: a four-foot-tall, frog-faced, two-legged beast with leathery skin. The monster jumped a roadside guard rail on its way down to the Little Miami River. About two weeks later one of the officers reported a similar sighting, with the creature lying by the side of the road before it crossed a guard rail. The policeman shot at it but missed. A local farmer also reported seeing the monster.

On August 19, 1972, at Thetis Lake in British Columbia, Canada, a silver creature emerged from the water to chase two young men from the beach. One of the witnesses received cuts on his hand from the six sharp points atop the monster's head. A few days later, another person got a look at the creature, also noting a sharp point on its head. In addition, the witness claimed it had a "scaly" human-shaped body, "monster face," and "great big ears."

The true identity of these reptile men have not been found to this day.

Sources:

Coleman, Loren, *Curious Encounters: Phantom Trains, Spooky Spots, and Other Mysterious Wonders,* Boston: Faber and Faber, 1985.

Keel, John A., *Strange Creatures from Time and Space,* Greenwich, Connecticut: Fawcett Books, 1970.

In March 1972 several badly frightened Loveland residents, including two police officers, reported encounters with a bizarre frog-faced biped.

MOTHMAN

Late on the evening of November 15, 1966, as they drove past an abandoned TNT factory near Point Pleasant, West Virginia, two young married couples spotted two large eyes, two inches wide and six inches apart, attached to something that was "shaped like a man, but bigger. Maybe six or seven feet tall. And it had big wings folded against its back." The eyes were "hypnotic," the witnesses agreed. When the creature started to move, the four panicked and sped away. But they saw the same or a similar monster on a hillside near the road! It spread its batlike wings, rose into the air, and followed the car—which by now was going 100 mph.

"That bird kept right up with us," Roger Scarberry, one of the group, said to investigator John A. Keel. "It wasn't even flapping its wings." The witnesses told local deputy sheriff Millard Halstead that it

A drawing of Mothman, based on eyewitness descriptions.

made a sound like a "record played at high speed or the squeak of a mouse." It followed them on Highway 62 right to the Point Pleasant city limits.

The two couples were not the only people to see the creature that night. Another group of four claimed to have seen it not once but three times! A third sighting took place that evening. At 10:30 P.M. Newell Partridge, a builder who lived outside Salem, West Virginia (about 90 miles from Point Pleasant), was watching television when suddenly the screen went blank. Then a "fine herringbone pattern appeared on the tube, and ... the set started a loud whining noise, winding up to a high pitch, peaking and breaking off.... It sounded like a generator winding up." Partridge's dog Bandit began to howl on the porch and continued even after the set was turned off.

Partridge stepped outside, where he saw Bandit facing toward the hay barn 150 yards away. "I shined the light in that direction," he told West Virginia writer Gray Barker, "and it picked up two red circles, or eyes, which looked like bicycle reflectors"—only much larger. Something about the sight deeply frightened him, for he was certain that they were not animal eyes.

The snarling Bandit, an experienced hunting dog, shot off toward the creature. Partridge called to him to stop, but the dog paid no attention. At this point the man went inside to get a gun but then decided not to go outside again. He slept that night with the weapon by his side. By the morning he realized that Bandit had not returned. And the dog had not shown up two days later when Partridge read a newspaper report of the Point Pleasant sightings.

One detail in the newspaper account particularly grabbed his attention: Roger Scarberry had stated that as they entered Point Pleasant's city limits, the two couples had seen the body of a big dog by the side of the road. And a few minutes later, on their way back out of town, the dog was gone. Partridge immediately thought of Bandit, who would never be seen again. All that remained of him were his prints in the mud. "Those tracks were going in a circle, as if that dog had been chasing his tail—though he never did that," his master recalled. "There were no other tracks of any kind."

And there seemed to be another connection between the two sightings. Deputy Halstead had experienced strange interference on his police radio when he approached the TNT factory. It was loud and sounded something like a record or tape played at high speed. He finally had to turn the radio off.

The next day, after a press meeting called by Sheriff George Johnson, the story was reported across the country. One newspaperman dubbed the creature "Mothman" after a villain on the *Batman* television series.

More Sightings

From that time to November 1967, a number of other sightings occurred. On the evening of November 16, 1966, for instance, three adults—one carrying an infant—were walking back to their car after visiting friends. Suddenly, something rose up slowly from the ground. One witness, Marcella Bennett, was so frightened that she dropped her baby. It was a "big gray thing, bigger than a man," and it had no head. But it did have two large glowing red circles at the top of its torso. As huge wings unfolded from behind it, Raymond Wamsley snatched up the child and guided the two women inside the house they had just left. It seemed that the creature followed them to the porch, because they could hear sounds there and, worse still, see its eyes peering through the window. By the time the police arrived, however, it was gone. Bennett was upset for weeks afterward and, like other Mothman witnesses, eventually sought medical attention.

John Keel, the main investigator of the Mothman sightings, wrote that at least 100 people had seen the creature. From their accounts he put together a description. According to reports, it stood between five and seven feet tall, was broader than a man, and walked in a clumsy, shuffling manner on humanlike legs. It made a squeaky sound. The eyes, which Keel said "seemed to have been more terrifying than the tremendous size of the creature," were set near the top of the shoulders. Its wings were batlike but did not flap when it flew. When it took off from the ground, it went "straight up, like a helicopter," according to one observer. Witnesses described its skin color as gray or brown. Two observers said that they heard a mechanical humming as it flew above them.

After 1967 Mothman sightings died away. (Only one later account, in October 1974 from Elma, New York, was reported.) Nonetheless, Keel did locate a woman who said that she had met such a creature on

> And it seemed that the creature followed them to the porch, because they could hear sounds there and, worse still, see its eyes peering through the window.

a highway one evening in 1961, on the West Virginia side of the Ohio River. She told Keel: "It was much larger than a man. A big gray figure. It stood in the middle of the road. Then a pair of wings unfolded from its back, and they practically filled the whole road. It almost looked like a small airplane. Then it took off straight up ... disappearing out of sight in seconds."

REEL LIFE

Mothra, 1962.

Classic Japanese monster movie about an enraged giant caterpillar that invades Tokyo while searching for the Alilenas, a set of very tiny, twin princesses who have been kidnapped by an evil nightclub owner in the pursuit of big profits. After tiring of crushing buildings and wreaking havoc, the enormous crawly thing zips up into a cocoon and emerges as Mothra, a moth distinguished by both its size and bad attitude. Mothra and the wee princesses make appearances in later Godzilla epics.

Big Bird?

Almost all who investigated the Mothman sightings believed that it was no hoax. The most popular "ordinary" explanation came from West Virginia University biologist Robert Smith, who suggested that the witnesses had seen sandhill cranes. Such cranes are not native to Ohio or West Virginia, but some *could* have migrated down from the plains of Canada.

On November 26, 1966, a small group of people near Lowell, Ohio (70 miles north of Point Pleasant), did report seeing a number of oversized birds in some trees. When approached, the birds flew away and settled on a nearby ridge. From the descriptions—four or five feet tall, with long necks, six-inch bills, and a "reddish cast" in the head area—they *were* probably sandhill cranes. Still, they did not seem to resemble the creature that Mothman witnesses described! In fact, all who saw the monster rejected the sandhill crane identification.

On the other hand, Keel suspected that in a small number of Mothman sightings, excitable observers—frightened by the stories that they had heard—might have mistaken owls seen briefly on dark country roads for something more extraordinary. Regardless, Mothman still resisted easy explanations, for unlike many other monsters, this one had a lot of evidence behind it: a great number of multiple-witness sightings by people that investigators and police officers considered very reliable.

Mothman Across the Sea

Mothman's one known appearance outside Ohio and West Virginia was in England, along a country road near Sandling Park, Hythe, Kent,

John Alva Keel is one of the most widely read, influential, and controversial writers on mysterious happenings. Like many anomalists, as a young man Keel was
influenced by Charles Fort, the often outrageous theo-
rist and collector of anomalies (also see entry: Falls
from the Sky).

Along with many other writings, Keel produced two
major books in the early 1970s, *UFOs: Operation Trojan
Horse* and *The Mothman Prophecies*. Though these works
deal with UFOs, Keel denies that he is a ufologist. His
ideas are, in fact, closer to occultism (the study of
supernatural powers) than science, and many consider
him a demonologist (one who studies evil spirits).

Keel theorizes that ultraterrestrial gods (gods from
another reality beyond our knowledge) once lived on,
and ruled, the earth. They left when an early form of
the human species began to populate the planet, but,
unhappy to have to leave, the gods warred against
early humans. Later, some of the gods tried to enlist
Neanderthals in their war, and interbreeding between
the ultraterrestrials and Neanderthals resulted in the
human race as we know it.

Keel believes that humanity's long history of inter-
action with the supernatural proves the existence of
the gods of old as well as the modern Judeo-Christian
God. To Keel men in black, monsters, UFOs, and even
Mothman are modern versions of the devils and demons
of past times.

on November 16, 1963. Four young people reportedly saw a "star"
cross the night sky and disappear behind trees not far from them.
Frightened, they started to run but stopped soon afterward to
watch a golden, oval-shaped light floating a few feet above a field
about 80 yards from them. Then the UFO moved into a wooded
area and was lost from view.

Suddenly, the observers saw a dark shape shuffling toward
them from across the field. It was black, human-sized, and head-

Sandhill cranes—although they fit the description, eyewitnesses saw no resemblance to Mothman.

less, and it had wings that looked like a bat's. At this point the four witnesses left running!

Other people sighted a similar UFO over the next few nights. On November 23, two men who had come to take a look at the area found a "vast expanse of bracken [large coarse ferns] that had been flattened." They also claimed to have seen three huge footprints, two feet long and nine inches wide, pressed an inch deep into the soil.

Sources:

Barker, Gray, *The Silver Bridge,* Clarksburg, West Virginia: Saucerian Books, 1970.
Keel, John A., *The Mothman Prophecies,* New York: E. P. Dutton and Company, 1975.
Keel, John A., *Strange Creatures from Time and Space,* Greenwich, Connecticut: Fawcett Gold Medal, 1970.

BLACK DOGS

A complex, worldwide folklore surrounds certain black dogs, supernatural canines that frequently appear at crossroads and are sometimes connected to the underworld. The lore is most fully documented in Britain, although the American South has its own colorful oral tradition among African Americans. In Mississippi in the early part of the twentieth century, black countryfolk told folklorist N. N. Puckett about huge black dogs with "big red eyes glowing like chunks of fire."

Most tales and reports of supernatural canines describe them as black, but white, gray, and yellow dogs also figure in some stories. Typically, a black dog meets a traveler on a dark road and either guides him to safety or threatens him. Or its appearance may be a sign of the witness's coming death. Black dogs may also attach themselves to families; this idea inspired Sir Arthur Conan Doyle to write the most famous of his Sherlock Holmes novels, *The Hound of the Baskervilles*. Black dogs are said to have glowing eyes, and they often vanish in an instant. Sometimes, especially in accounts from long ago, the black dog is a shape-shifter, at some point revealing his true identity as the devil.

Sometimes, especially in accounts from long ago, the black dog is a shape-shifter, at some point revealing his true identity as the devil.

Sightings

In his writings, Theo Brown, a leading expert on black-dog lore, has suggested that actual events may be behind a number of legendary tales; indeed, black-dog sightings by reliable witnesses are plentiful.

The first recorded black-dog sighting can be found in a French manuscript, *Annales Franorum Regnum,* dating from 856. The author reported that after a sudden darkness fell over a local church midway through a service, a large dog with fiercely glowing eyes appeared. It dashed about as if searching for something, then suddenly vanished. On August 4, 1577, in Bongay, England, a black dog entered a church during a violent storm, ran through the aisle, killed two worshippers, and injured another by burning him severely. That same day a similar attack occurred at a church in Blibery, seven miles away. These events were related by Abraham Fleming—who had been an eyewitness to the Bongay rampage—and published soon after in *A Straunge Wunder in Bongay.*

REEL LIFE

The Hound of the Baskervilles, 1939.

The curse of a demonic hound threatens descendants of an English noble family until Sherlock Holmes and his faithful assistant Dr. Watson solve the mystery.

Twentieth-century reports of black dogs tend to be less dramatic. Many seem simply to be a variety of ghost story. Typical of these is the account Theodore Ebert of Pottsville, Pennsylvania, gave folklorist George Korson in the 1950s:

One night when I was a boy walking with friends along Seven Stars Road, a big black dog appeared from nowhere and came between me and one of my pals. And I went to pet the dog, but it disappeared from right under me. Just like the snap of a finger it disappeared.

In fact there is no shortage of modern-day black-dog sightings, at least from the early decades of the twentieth century. Englishwoman Ethel H. Rudkin collected a number of reports from her native Lincolnshire and published them in 1938 in *Folklore*. She felt that having had a black-dog experience of her own helped her "get such good first-hand stories." She also wrote, "I have never yet had a Black Dog story from anyone who was weak in body or mind." Unlike ghostly canines elsewhere, those described by Rudkin seemed to have gentle natures.

More recently, what appeared to be a Great Dane reportedly stepped in front of a moving car on Exeter Road in Okehampton, England, on October 25, 1969. Before the driver could stop, the car passed through the animal, which then disappeared! In April 1972 a member of Britain's coast guard saw a "large, black hound-type dog on the beach" at Great Yarmouth. "It was about a quarter of a mile from me," he told the *London Evening News*. "What made me watch it was that it was running, then stopping, as if looking for someone. As I watched, it vanished before my eyes."

Witnesses often mention the creature's glowing eyes. Occasionally, they see little more than the eyes but guess for one reason or another that they belong to a ghostly dog. In the early 1920s young Delmer Clark of La Crosse, Wisconsin, saw "something that looked with shining eyes, with the face of a dog"; in the darkness he thought he could make out a "dark black body." When he saw the creature again a week later in the same location near his home, he kicked at it, only to find his foot inside its mouth! The creature seemed to be expecting it. When Clark screamed, the "dog" disappeared. "I can still see it clearly as I talk now," the man remarked, recalling the incident for his son, author Jerome Clark, in 1976.

In a small number of reports, black dogs are linked—directly or indirectly—to UFOs. One such case was reported in South Africa in 1963. Two men driving at night on the Potchefstroom/Vereeniging road observed a large, doglike animal crossing the highway in front of them. Moments later a UFO appeared and buzzed their vehicle several times, sending them on a frantic escape. Most likely there *was* a large dog in the vicinity, and only coincidence tied it to the UFO. In a case a decade later, though, several Georgia youths claimed that they saw "10 big, black hairy dogs" run from a landed UFO and through a cemetery in Savannah.

Sources:

Bord, Janet, and Colin Bord, *Alien Animals,* Harrisburg, Pennsylvania: Stackpole Books, 1981.

Clark, Jerome, and Loren Coleman, *Creatures of the Outer Edge,* New York: Warner Books, 1978.

BLUES SINGER'S PACT WITH A HELLHOUND

In the 1930s Mississippi native Robert Johnson, the great folk-blues singer/guitarist, did not deny rumors that he had gotten his talents in a midnight deal with a man in black (the devil) whom he met at a crossroads. Johnson even hinted at this event in his 1936 recording "Cross Road Blues." He further commented on this pact in another blues song the following year: "I've got to keep movin'.... There's a hellhound on my trail."

CRAWFORDSVILLE MONSTER

According to a story in the September 5, 1891, issue of the *Indianapolis Journal,* at 2 o'clock on the previous morning in Crawfordsville, Indiana, a "horrible apparition" appeared in the western sky, seen by two men hitching up a wagon. One hundred feet in the air, 20 feet long, and eight feet wide, the headless, oblong thing moved itself along with several pairs of fins and circled a nearby house. It disappeared to the east for a short time and then returned. As curious as the two men were about the strange creature, they decided to run in the opposite direction! They were not, however, the only witnesses. A Methodist pastor, G. W. Switzer, and his wife also observed the monster.

The creature returned the following evening, and this time hundreds of Crawfordsville citizens saw its wildly flapping fins and flaming red "eye." The monster "squirmed as if in agony" and made a

At one point it swooped over a band of onlookers, who swore they felt its "hot breath."

"wheezing, plaintive sound" as it hovered at 300 feet. At one point it swooped over a band of onlookers, who swore they felt its "hot breath."

Many years later anomalist (collector and cataloger of reports of strange physical events) Charles Fort came across the story in a September issue of the *Brooklyn Eagle*. He doubted the account and was "convinced that there had probably never been a Reverend G. W. Switzer of Crawfordsville." Still, he investigated and to his surprise found that the reverend did exist. He wrote to the man, who promised to send Fort a full description of his sighting as soon as he got back from some travels. Unfortunately, Fort reported, "I have been unable to get him to send that account.... The problem is: Did a 'headless monster' appear in Crawfordsville, in September, 1891?"

In time Vincent Gaddis, a Crawfordsville newspaper reporter and writer about unexplained events, would be able to find out more. He interviewed the town's older residents, who confirmed that the story was true and told him about the September 6 group sighting, which had not been reported in the press. Gaddis wrote that "all the reports refer to this object as a living thing"—in other words, it resembled one of the atmospheric life forms, or "space animals" (see box).

Sources:

Fort, Charles, *The Books of Charles Fort,* New York: Henry Holt and Company, 1941.

ONZA

The onza is Mexico's most famous mystery cat, reported for centuries in the remote Sierra Madre Occidental in the northwestern part of the country. Though its existence has not been *officially* recognized by zoologists, few doubt that the animal is, indeed, real.

Other Fantastic Creatures

A Wolflike Cat

To the Aztecs, the onza—or *cuitlamiztli,* as they called it—was a separate animal from the two other large cats, the puma and the jaguar, that lived in the region. After the Spanish conquerors arrived, they called on Aztec emperor Montezuma, who showed them his great zoo. Spaniard Bernal Diaz del Castillo noted that besides jaguars and pumas, he observed another type of big cat that "resembled the wolf."

The later Spanish settlers of northwestern Mexico noted the presence in the wild of a wolflike cat—with long ears, a long, narrow body, and long, thin legs. They gave it the name *onza,* referring to the cheetahs of Asia and Africa that it resembled. They also remarked on its fierceness. "It is not as timid as the [puma]," Father Ignaz Pfefferkorn, a Jesuit missionary stationed in Sonora, wrote in 1757, "and he who ventures to attack it must be well on his guard." According to Father Johann Jakob Baegert, who worked with the Guaricura Indians in Baja California in the mid-eighteenth century, "One onza dared to invade my neighbor's mission while I was visiting, and attacked a 14-year-old boy in broad daylight and practically in full view of all the people; and a few years ago another killed the strongest and most respected soldier" in the area.

Yet outside northwestern Mexico, the onza was practically unknown. The few mentions of it in print attracted no attention, and zoologists continued to believe that only pumas and jaguars lived in the area. No serious scientific expeditions into the rugged country—which in many places was even too wild to reach on horseback—were ever undertaken to try to answer the onza question.

Then, in the 1930s, two experienced hunting guides, Dale and Clell Lee, were working in the mountains of Sonora when

Front cover of Robert Marshall's book *The Onza.*

JAGUAR

A jaguar is a large cat (*Felis onca*) of tropical America that is bigger and stockier than the Asian/African leopard and is tan or beige with black spots.

Although there are similarities, the onza's features differ from those of the puma, pictured here.

they heard about the onza for the first time. Some time later, while taking Indiana banker Joseph H. Shirk to hunt jaguars on the wildlife-rich La Silla Mountain, they treed and killed a strange cat that they immediately realized was something they had never seen before. In fact, it looked exactly like the onzas that local residents said lived in the region. After measuring and photographing the animal, they butchered it. Shirk kept the skull and skin. Their present whereabouts are unknown.

Sure that they had found something important, the Lees described the animal to American zoologists. They were stunned when both the scientists and newspaper accounts laughed at their story. Not accustomed to having their honesty questioned, the upset brothers refused to discuss the experience ever again—that is, until the 1950s, when an Arizona man named Robert Marshall became friends with Dale Lee and thoughtfully recorded the man's testimony. Marshall even went down to Mexico to investigate further. He wrote about his trip in the 1961 book *The Onza*. Except for a single review in a scientific journal, the work attracted no attention at all.

A Modern Look at the Onza

In 1982, at a meeting at the Smithsonian Institution in Washington, D.C., the International Society of Cryptozoology (ISC) was formed. Now, for the first time, biological scientists interested in unknown, unrecognized, or doubted animals had a formal organization through which research could be done. Cryptozoologists, in fact, were among the very few people outside of northwestern Mexico who had heard about the onza.

Ecologist and ISC secretary J. Richard Greenwell lived in Tucson, Arizona. When he learned that Dale Lee and Robert Marshall also lived there, his interest in the onza grew. Marshall showed Greenwell an onza skull that he owned and gave him a cast of its row of upper teeth. Greenwell then took the cast to a West German mammal expert, Helmut Hemmer, who suspected that onzas were leftovers of a prehistoric species of North American cheetah, the *Acinonyx trumani*. While comparisons with fossil skulls eventually ruled out this identification, the case of the mysterious onza was finally beginning to stir scientific interest.

While searching without success for the long-missing onza skull given to Shirk back in the 1930s, Greenwell and Marshall joined forces with two mammalogists (scientists who study mammals) who were also interested in the subject: Troy Best of the University of New Mexico and E. Lendell Cockrum of the University of Arizona. Through Cockrum they met a Mexican rancher who had a perfect skull of an onza killed by another rancher, Jesus Vega. Meanwhile Best, an expert on pumas, had located another onza skull in the Academy of Natural Sciences in Philadelphia.

Then, at 10:30 on the evening of January 1, 1986, two deer hunters in Sinaloa, Mexico, shot and killed a large cat. It was clearly not a jaguar, and they had no idea what it was. Recalling that a few months earlier a rancher friend had talked with visiting scientists about an unusual animal, they alerted Manuel Vega, who recognized the crea-

> Recalling that a few months earlier a rancher friend had talked with visiting scientists about an unusual animal, they alerted Manuel Vega, who recognized the creature as an onza as soon as he saw it.

ture as an onza as soon as he saw it; indeed, it was Vega's father who had shot the onza whose skull had brought the scientists there in the first place.

Through the help of a wealthy local family, the body of the animal was placed in a freezer at a large fish company in Mazatlan, and Greenwell was called. Greenwell and Best arrived and, over time, photographed and dissected the creature at a regional government laboratory located in the city. Greenwell wrote: "Upon inspection, the cat, a female, appeared to be as described by the native people. It had a remarkably gracile [slim and graceful] body, with long, slender legs and a long tail. The ears also seemed very long for a puma ... and small horizontal stripes were found on the inside of the forelimbs, which as far as has been determined to date, are not found in puma." Greenwell added that the animal appeared to be about four years old and weighed below the range for adult female pumas. Its total length, however, was normal for a female puma—except for the unusually long tail.

Tissue samples and organs were taken to the United States for further study. But in the following years, Greenwell and Best were too busy with other projects to give much time to the matter. A quick comparison of the onza's tissue samples to those of pumas was done at Texas Tech University; it revealed many similarities and no major differences. Still, conclusions cannot be drawn from a single test of this sort, since animals of different species are often closely related genetically.

Consistent scientific indifference to the onza is puzzling. According to one account, in 1986 ranchers trapped an onza in northern Sonora, near the Arizona border, and kept it alive for a few days while they tried to get officials to take a look at it. Finally, after none expressed interest, its keepers killed the animal and disposed of its body in the dry bed of a stream.

Sources:

Marshall, Robert, *The Onza,* New York: Exposition Press, 1961.

RI

While conducting field studies in New Ireland, an island of Papua New Guinea, University of Virginia cultural anthropologist Roy Wagner heard stories of strange water creatures. Called "ri" (pronounced *ree*) by the local residents, the animals were believed to be air-breathing mammals; they appeared regularly off the island's central and southern coasts. Natives described them as quite human in appearance—except that their torsos had no legs and ended in a pair of side fins; they compared ri to the mermaids on tuna fish cans.

In November 1979, from the coastal village of Ramat, Wagner saw what a native told him was a ri several hundred yards out in Pamat Bay. Wagner recorded the sighting: "Something large [was] swimming at the surface in a broad arc toward the shore. We watched as it came closer, and the best view I got was of a long, dark body swimming at the surface horizontally. Suddenly, a sawfish jumped immediately in front of it, ... and the dark object submerged and did not reappear."

Wagner interviewed a number of islanders who said that they had eaten ri flesh. They did not consider the creatures to be intelligent beings like humans. The ri communicated by whistling and fed on fish. Wagner was certain that his informants were not confusing the animals with dugongs, the plant-eating water mammals also called "sea cows." He was also sure that the islanders were not confusing ri with dolphins.

Wagner's report, published in the first issue of *Cryptozoology* (the journal of the International Society of Cryptozoology or ISC), created quite a sensation. In the summer of 1983 Wagner, ISC secretary J. Richard Greenwell, and two other men traveled to New Ireland, interviewed witnesses, and saw a ri themselves. The sighting took place on the afternoon of July 5, from the village of Nokon on Elizabeth Bay. Every ten minutes the creature, who was plainly feeding, would surface for a few seconds. Because its appearances were brief, decent photographs of the animal proved impossible. It looked to be five to seven feet long, skinny, and had a mammal's tail. Attempts to capture a specimen using a net met with difficulty and had to be given up. The expedition members had other, though briefer, sightings of what appeared to be the same animal.

Ri vs. the Dugong

The researchers returned to the United States convinced that the ri was some kind of unusual animal, not a known animal to which the

> Natives described them as quite human in appearance—except that their torsos had no legs and ended in a pair of side fins; they compared ri to the mermaids on tuna fish cans.

A dugong.

local people had attached fantastic features or abilities. Still, they noted that villagers farther north did regard the dugong and the ri as the same creature. Other islanders, however, insisted that they were different—and the investigators tended to agree. The ri stayed underwater as long as ten minutes, while all written information about the dugong had it coming up for air every one or two minutes. Marine biologist Paul Anderson, a specialist in dugongs, sent Greenwell a film of these animals surfacing. Greenwell thought that the shape and actions of the dugongs did not resemble those of the creatures he and his expedition partners had seen.

Mystery Solved

A second expedition in February 1985 solved the mystery. A well-equipped group sponsored by the Ecosophical Research Association saw a ri in Nokon Bay from the deck of the diving ship *Reef Explorer*. When the animal dived, Captain Kerry Piesch (and ship) followed it underwater and took three photographs. Slightly over five feet long, the animal was greenish-gray in color, with a neckless head and short, paddle-like limbs. It was indeed a dugong!

Expedition member Tom Williams later wondered how stories of the ri—another chapter in the age-old myth of merfolk (mermaids and mermen)—could have started and continued "in the face of the obvious reality of the dugong." He recognized, however, that something in human nature and imagination leaps beyond the clear facts and reasonable explanations that our senses and science provide. After this second expedition, Greenwell concluded, "Although we have not found a new species, we have uncovered new data on dugong behavior in deeper water."

Sources:

Wagner, Roy, J. Richard Greenwell, Gale J. Raymond, and Kurt Von Nieda, "Further Investigations into the Biological and Cultural Affinities of the Ri," *Cryptozoology* 2, winter 1983, pp. 113-125.

Williams, Thomas R., "Identification of the Ri Through Further Fieldwork in New Ireland, Papua New Guinea," *Cryptozoology* 4, 1985, pp. 61-68.

Monsters of the Deep

- UNIDENTIFIED SUBMARINE OBJECTS

- GIANT OCTOPUS

- GIANT SQUID

- SEA SERPENTS

Monsters of the Deep

UNIDENTIFIED SUBMARINE OBJECTS

While sailing in the Atlantic Ocean near the equator in the early morning hours of October 28, 1902, the *Fort Salisbury* came upon an incredible sight. In the ship's log, Second Officer A. H. Raymer noted a "dark object, with long, luminous trailing wake" in a "phosphorescent sea." On the object were what appeared to be two bright "masthead" or "steamer's lights." Still, Raymer thought the dark mass was some kind of bioluminescent whale, for it sank below the surface of the water as they drew nearer to it.

Approaching the watery trail it left behind, Raymer again came upon the object, or rather, its scaly back as it slowly lowered itself in the water. It was still too early in the morning for a clear look, but the scales appeared to be a foot across and "dotted in places with barnacle growth." The thing was some 30 feet across at its widest point, tapering "at the extreme end." It was "about 500 ft. to 600 ft." in length.

Raymer noted that "the monster's progress could be distinctly heard." He also reported that "the wet shiny back of the monster was dotted with twinkling phosphorescent lights, and was encircled with a band of white phosphorescent sea." A helmsman and a lookout also witnessed the sight.

This account was reported in the *London Daily Mail* of November 9, 1902. When interviewed, the ship's captain—who was not himself a witness—remarked of his second officer, "I can only

BIOLUMINESCENT ORGANISMS

Bioluminescent organisms are plants and animals that make their own light. They do this by changing chemical energy into light energy. Different plants and animals produce different bioluminescent chemicals. Bioluminescent organisms are especially common in places where no light penetrates, like the depths of the ocean.

say that he is very earnest on the subject and has, together with the lookout and the helmsman, seen something in the water, of a huge nature, as specified."

Demon of the Deep

An even more fantastic story was published in a Washington newspaper, the *Tacoma Daily Ledger,* on July 3, 1893. The witnesses were members of a fishing party that left Tacoma on the afternoon of July 1 and were camping that evening on Henderson Island, not far from a large group of surveyors. One of the fishermen related that he was startled awake some time after midnight (though he could not be certain because his watch and all others belonging to the group had mysteriously stopped) by "a most horrible noise [that] rang out in the clear morning air, and instantly the whole air was filled with a strong current of electricity that caused every nerve in the body to sting with pain." A bright light also flashed constantly; "at first I thought it was a thunderstorm," the witness said, "but as no rain accompanied it, and as both light and sound came off the bay, I turned my head in that direction." What he saw was "a most horrible–looking monster."

By now, according to the witness, every man in the fishing camp, as well as the nearby surveyors, had "gathered on the bank of the stream.... The monster slowly drew in toward the shore, and as it approached, from its head poured out a stream of water that looked like blue fire. All the while the air seemed to be filled with electricity, and the sensation experienced was as if each man had on a suit of clothes formed of the fine points of needles."

One of the surveyors foolishly took a few steps forward and some of the water being shot from the monster's head reached him; "he instantly fell to the ground and lay as though dead." A second man tried to pull the fellow's body to safety, but he was also struck by the water and met the same fate. That was enough for the rest of the group! They rushed into the woods in a panic.

But even in the woods, the "demon of the deep," as the witness called it, "sent out flashes of light that illuminated the surrounding country for miles, and his roar—which sounded like the roar of thunder—became terrific." But the monster then changed direction, "and in an instant ... disappeared beneath the waters of the bay," though those present "for some time ... were able to trace its course by a bright luminous light that was on the surface of the water." Afterward, left in total darkness, the men struggled to find their way back to the bay.

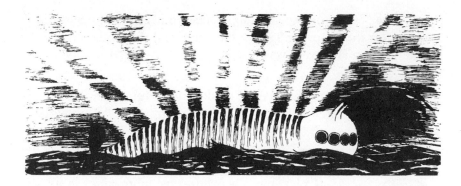

Fortunately their fallen companions were unconscious, not dead. As all
awaited daybreak, the two revived.

As the witness described the "monster fish," it was "150 feet long"
and 30 feet around "at its thickest part." It had a head shaped like that
of a walrus, with six dull eyes the size of dinner plates. "At intervals of
about every eight feet from its head to its tail a substance that had the
appearance of a copper band encircled its body, and it was from these
many bands that the powerful electric current appeared to come," the
witness said. "Near the center of its head were two hornlike sub-
stances, ... it was through them that the electrically charged water was
thrown." Stranger still, "its tail ... was shaped like a propeller and
seemed to revolve."

Other USOs

But not all reports of unidentified submarine objects (USOs) are
quite so fantastic. Even in the nineteenth century, some surprisingly
believable accounts were reported. One such example occurred on
June 18, 1845, in the eastern Mediterranean Sea. The crew of the brig
Victoria saw three bright, glowing objects emerge from the water and
shoot into the sky, where they were visible for ten minutes.

Professor Baden–Powell collected testimony from the crew and
other witnesses and published it in an 1861 issue of *Report of the
British Association*. One man who observed the sight from land said
the objects were larger than the moon and had things like sails or
streamers trailing from them. He and other witnesses, who had
watched the objects for 20 minutes to an hour, said they appeared to be
joined together.

On November 12, 1887, a "large ball of fire" ("enormous" by one
account) rose from the sea near Cape Race, Newfoundland, Canada.

When it was 50 feet in the air it approached a nearby ship, the British steamer *Siberian,* moving against the wind as it did. It then retreated and flew away. The event was discussed in *Nature, L'Astronomie,* and *Meteorological Journal.*

There have been a number of modern USO reports as well; most have been associated with UFOs. But some of these "otherworldly" sightings may have been of earthly submarines in unexpected places. During the 1960s and 1970s, for example, Scandinavia was beset by submarines in its surrounding waters, and some writers claimed that the vessels were of mysterious origin. They were, in fact, Soviet craft on spy missions.

Below are some of the more puzzling modern USO reports:

Off the Alaska coast, summer 1945

Around sunset, a large round object, some 200 feet across, emerged from the sea about a mile from the U.S. Army transport Delarof. After rising in the air a short distance, it approached the ship, circling it silently two or three times before it flew off and disappeared into the southwest.

North Atlantic, late summer 1954

The crew of the Dutch ship Groote Beer observed a flat, moon-shaped object rise out of the ocean. Watching it through binoculars, Captain Jan P. Boshoff noted that it was gray and ringed by bright lights. It flew off with amazing speed.

That same night it or another unknown object was seen by the Honduran freighter Aliki P., which was sailing in the same general area. It radioed the Long Island Coast Guard: "Observed ball of fire moving in and out of water without being extinguished. Trailing white smoke. Moving in erratic course, finally disappeared."

REEL LIFE

The Beast from 20,000 Fathoms, 1953.

Atomic testing defrosts a giant dinosaur in the Arctic; the hungry monster proceeds onward to its former breeding grounds, now New York City. The saurian-on-the-loose formula is fun, and good special effects bring it to life.

Octaman, 1971.

Comical thriller featuring non-threatening octopus-man discovered by scientists in Mexico. By the director of *The Creature of the Black Lagoon.*

20,000 Leagues Under the Sea, 1954.

From a futuristic submarine, Captain Nemo wages war on the surface world. A shipwrecked scientist and sailor do their best to thwart Nemo's dastardly schemes. Buoyant Disney version of French writer Jules Verne's 1870 novel.

Westchester County, New York, September 17, 1955

Around 1:30 A.M.., a couple named Bordes was rowing out onto a lake on Titicus Reservoir to fish when they saw an object come out of the water a few feet from their boat. Rose-colored and glowing, it was the size and shape of a basketball. After rising a foot in the air, it fell back into the water with a loud splash and disappeared. Frightened, the Bordeses headed for shore. On the way, they saw two wavy parallel lights, 30 feet long, on or just below the surface of the water at the center of the lake. A round, yellowish-white light hung above them. This light acted like a rotating spotlight; it appeared to be attached to what looked like a dim gray form in the water. The couple watched the object for a time and even tried to approach it; when they left it was still there. The couple were certain that they had not seen another boat.

Shag Harbor, Nova Scotia, October 4, 1967

Just before midnight, two men driving in a car saw a row of bright reddish-orange lights. They "came off and on one at a time," according to Nova Scotia's Yarmouth Light Herald (October 12). Five other people in a car stopped and watched the lights fly off to the water, where they changed into a single bright white light that bobbed on the waves. Many others, including a Royal Canadian Mounted Police officer, also saw the light, and a number of boats set out to find it. "Within an hour," the paper related, "the boats had arrived in the area where the object had disappeared, and reported finding a very large patch of bubbling water and foam. One fisherman described the froth as 80 feet wide and yellowish in color and said that he had never seen anything like it before in the area."

"Within an hour," the paper related, "the boats had arrived in the area where the object had disappeared, and reported finding a very large patch of bubbling water and foam."

Underwater civilization?

Taking reports like these and combining them with **Bermuda Triangle** disappearance stories, biologist Ivan T. Sanderson wrote a book, *Invisible Residents* (1970), about an advanced underwater civilization of OINTS (Other Intelligences) that were sometimes forced to seize planes and ships to keep their presence secret. "If a superior technological type of intelligent civilization(s) developed on this planet under water," he wrote, "they would very likely have gotten much farther ahead than we have, having had several millions, and possibly up to a billion years' headstart on us, life as we know it having started in the sea."

While Sanderson had no real evidence for his extraordinary ideas, it has been suggested from time to time that space beings maintain bases in oceans and lakes, and that their craft are exploring these watery regions as they allegedly explore the earth's land areas.

Sources:

Coleman, Loren, *Curious Encounters: Phantom Trains, Spooky Spots, and Other Mysterious Wonders,* Boston: Faber and Faber, 1985.

Heuvelmans, Bernard, *In the Wake of the Sea-Serpents,* New York: Hill and Wang, 1968.

Sanderson, Ivan T., *Invisible Residents: A Disquisition upon Certain Matters Maritime, and the Possibility of Intelligent Life Under the Waters of This Earth,* New York: World Publishing Company, 1970.

GIANT OCTOPUS

Bicycling on Anastasia Island, Florida, on the evening of November 30, 1896, Saint Augustine residents Herbert Coles and Dunham Coretter found the immense remains of a water animal on the beach. Because of its great weight, the huge carcass had sunk far into the sand when Coles and Coretter spotted it. They did not take measurements, but they knew right away that it was bigger than anything they had ever heard of.

The next day DeWitt Webb, a physician and founder of the St. Augustine Historical Society and Institute of Science, went to the site with several associates. The group concluded that the creature, which appeared to have been beached just days before, weighed nearly five tons. The parts that were visible measured 23 feet in length, four feet high, and 18 feet across the widest part of the back. The skin was a faint pink that seemed almost white and had a silvery cast to it. It was not a whale, Webb decided. It could only be some kind of octopus—of a size never before imagined.

Webb and his assistants returned to the beach as time and weather allowed over the next few days and took photographs—since lost—of the decayed, mutilated remains. One assistant, alone on one trip, reportedly found large pieces of arms while digging near the carcass. According to an account in the April 1897 issue of *American Naturalist,* "One arm was lying west of the body, 23 feet long; one stump of arm, west of body, about four feet; three arms lying south of body and from appear-

A common
octopus.

ance attached ... longest one measured over 32 feet, the other arms were three to five feet shorter." It appeared that the animal had been attacked and partially torn apart before its body had washed ashore.

Soon afterward a strong storm arose, and the carcass floated out to sea. It washed back to shore two miles south of the original site.

A Case of Mistaken Identity

Webb began writing letters to scientists he thought would be interested in the find. One, dated December 8, 1896, made its way to A. E. Verrill, a Yale University zoologist known for his pioneering work on the once legendary—but now recognized—giant squid or Kraken. Verrill disagreed with Webb's suggestion that the carcass was of an octopus, for the largest known specimen of its kind measured 25 feet. He thought that the beached creature was a giant squid and said so briefly in the January 1897 issue of the *American Journal of Science*. But with further information, he accepted the giant octopus identification.

> **MOLLUSKS**
>
> Mollusks make up the second-largest group of invertebrate animals (those without a backbone). They are soft-bodied, and most have a distinct shell. Mollusks usually live in water and include scallops, clams, oysters, mussels, snails, squids, and octopuses.

From comparing the arm pieces of the beached animal to those of known octopus specimens, he reached a fantastic conclusion: its full arm length must have been at least 75 feet! Truly monstrous in size, it would have measured 200 feet from tentacle tip to tentacle tip. Though Webb had been most instrumental in bringing the find to the attention of the scientific community, Verrill named the new animal after himself: *Octopus giganteus Verrill*.

Meanwhile, stormy weather conditions had moved the carcass once again. By the time it settled in its third location, even more of the body was missing. Regardless, what remained was still too heavy to move. Finally, in a January 17, 1897, letter to W. H. Dall, curator of mollusks at the National Museum in Washington, D. C., Webb related how he had had some luck rolling the creature out of its pit along some heavy planking with the help of four horses and six men. Now resting on planks 40 feet higher on the beach, the specimen was safe from washing away once more.

In the letter to Dall, Webb elaborated on the specimen:

A good part of the mantle or head remains attached near to the more slender part of the body.... The body was then opened for the entire length of 21 feet.... The slender part of the body was

entirely empty of internal organs. And the organs of the remainder were not large and did not look as if the animal had been long dead.... The muscular coat which seems to be all there is of the invertebrate is from two and three to six inches in thickness.

He noted no tailfin or other fins, "no beak or head or eyes remaining," and "no pen to be found nor any evidence of any bony structure whatever." (The "pen" Webb referred to is quill-pen-shaped cartilage found in all squids.)

Though Webb urged Dall and Verrill to visit the site and inspect the carcass personally, they did not. Instead, they told Webb to continue his efforts and keep sending them information. However, they ignored the information he sent them. Dall, for instance, kept calling the creature a "cuttlefish" (a cephalopod mollusk related to squids and octopuses, but with ten arms and a hard internal shell).

Webb sent Verrill samples of the creature's remains on February 23. That very day the zoologist declared in letters to both *Science* and the *New York Herald* that the carcass was probably from the "upper part of the head and nose of a sperm whale." Professor Frederic Augustus Lucas of the National Museum examined other samples and decided that they were whale "blubber, nothing more nor less." He also criticized Webb's "imaginative eye" and lack of training. Other cephalopod experts seemed to accept Lucas's explanation. While Webb strongly protested in print, his letters went unanswered. Eventually, the remains of *Octopus giganteus Verrill* rotted away, and the event was forgotten for the next six decades.

Return of the Monster

In 1957 Forrest G. Wood, Jr., curator of the research laboratories of Marineland, Florida, came upon a yellowed newspaper clipping about the Anastasia Island creature. Though an expert on octopuses, Wood had never heard of it.

Fascinated, he launched an investigation that eventually revealed that the Smithsonian Institution still had samples of the animal. They were examined by University of Florida octopus expert Joseph F. Gennaro, Jr., who concluded: "The evidence appears unmistakable that the St. Augustine sea monster was in fact an octopus."

But when Wood and Gennaro published their findings in three articles in the March 1971 issue of *Natural History,* the cause of marine biology was hardly advanced. The editors of the magazine included so many odd and silly comments along with the articles that some readers thought the whole thing a hoax. Wood and Gennaro found out that this was done on purpose—and Wood angrily wrote a letter of complaint to *Natural History,* which it refused to publish. To make matters worse, the *Ocean Citation Journal Index,* which prints briefs of journal articles, stated that the men had concluded that the animal was a *giant squid.* Wood and Gennaro later found out that this misstatement, too, was no accident.

In the mid-1980s, Roy P. Mackal, a University of Chicago biologist, conducted another study of the samples. He found that they were connective tissue and "not blubber." He stated, "I interpret these results as consistent with, and supportive of, Webb and Verrill's identification of the carcass as that of a gigantic cephalopod, probably an octopus, not referable to any known species."

Mystery of the Globsters

A carcass discovered in August 1960 on a northwestern beach on the Australian island of Tasmania may have been an animal like the one found in Florida. But here again the investigation was handled badly.

Word of the find, made by a rancher and two cowboys working for him, did not reach Hobart, the capital of Tasmania, until months later. First an air search was needed to locate the carcass. Then a four-man scientific team led by zoologist Bruce Mollison of the Commonwealth Scientific and Industrial Research Organization (CSIRO) traveled to the barren site in early March 1962. After Mollison examined the carcass he reported, "One is always seeking some explanation, and you try to add up everything, but this does not add up yet."

The carcass was very odd. Without eyes, head, or bones, it had skin that looked "creamy" and felt "rubbery." It was also "hairy."

Over the next week and a half, the Tasmanian "globster" (a descriptive word created by zoologist Ivan T. Sanderson) appeared in headlines all over the world, and the Australian government was flooded with questions. Under heavy pressure for answers, the government flew a team of zoologists from Hobart to the site for what was supposed to be a complete investigation. But the group returned the next day.

The official report stated that because of the length of time that had passed between the beaching of the animal and its examination, "it is not possible to specifically identify it from our investigations so far." Still, the scientists felt that the remains were "a decomposing portion of a large marine animal" and did not resemble whale blubber. But oddly, the same day he received this report, Senator John Gorton, minister for the Commonwealth of Australia, told the press that "your monster is a large lump of decomposing blubber, probably torn off a whale."

This conclusion disturbed Mollison, who stated that the samples he had taken "could not be identified." And University of Tasmania zoologist A. M. Clark declared that "it was clearly not a whale" (suspecting, instead, a giant ray). Also angered by Gorton's comment was cowboy Jack Boote, one of the animal's discoverers. He suspected the government was trying to cover up the fact that it had acted too slowly on the matter. "They had to say it was nothing new to cover up the fact they hadn't done anything about it before," Boote insisted. "The thing I saw was not a whale or any part of a whale."

None of the laboratory reports, either supporting or denying the whale identification, were ever published. The affair ended in confusion and neglect.

More Globsters

Perhaps these issues could have been settled in 1970 when another globster washed up onto a beach in the same area of northwestern Tasmania. It was found—believe it or not—by the same ranch owner who had come upon the first one: Ben Fenton. Remembering the trouble he had gone through ten years earlier, Fenton was not pleased with his discovery. He told a reporter for the local newspaper, "Be careful you don't quote me as saying it is a monster. I don't know what it is, and I'm making no guesses—not after the last lot." But this time not a single scientist came to investigate.

In March 1965 a globster had appeared on Muriwai Beach on the eastern shore of New Zealand's North Island. It was 30 feet long, eight feet high, and "hairy," according to press accounts. Auckland University zoologist J. E. Morton was quoted as saying, "I can't think of anything it resembles." Another globster washed up on a Mangrove Bay beach in Bermuda in May 1988. Samples were taken of the creature, but results from laboratory tests have yet to be published.

Looking over the cases, J. Richard Greenwell of the International Society of Cryptozoology noted that the "descriptions—and photos—are similar in all cases. All the carcasses were described as tough and hard to cut, usually odorless, and very 'stringy,' which is often called 'hairy.' And, curiously, all seem to be more or less unidentifiable by experts."

Until more is known, it is not certain that the globsters and the St. Augustine creature were the same kind of animal. Nor is it certain that either animal was a giant octopus. Still, this identification remains a possibility.

> "At its thickest the tentacle was as big as a muscular man's upper arm.... It had bumps along it, and one of these hooked on to the edge of the boat."

Sightings

If giant octopuses are real, they would not often be seen, simply because octopuses are bottom-dwelling animals. Still, sightings do occur from time to time. Bahamian fishermen speak of seeing "giant scuttles," and cephalopod expert Forrest Wood, for one, finds their testimony believable.

In late December 1989, press accounts described a frightening Christmas Eve occurrence off Manticao in the southern Philippines. A group of people in a boat carrying an infant's body that was to be buried on a nearby island were startled to see an octopus tentacle flop over the side of the craft. "At its thickest it was as big as a muscular man's upper arm," boat owner Eleuterio Sarino said. "It had bumps along it, and one of these hooked on to the edge of the boat." Another passenger, Jerry Alvarez, said, "I saw other huge tentacles under the water and, though the light was poor even when I used my torch [flashlight], I'm convinced I saw a head down there with big eyes." The tentacles, he claimed, were eight feet long.

The boat began to rock from side to side and then overturned. The passengers waded safely to shore 200 yards away.

In recent years, marine biologists have turned their attention to the extraordinary and sometimes unknown animals that live deep in the world's oceans. Perhaps now more information about this extraordinary creature, if it truly exists, will surface.

Sources:

Gennaro, Joseph F., Jr., "The Creature Revealed," *Natural History* 80,3, March 1971, pp. 24, 84.

Mackal, Roy P., *Searching for Hidden Animals,* Garden City, New York: Doubleday and Company, 1980.

Wood, F. G., "In Which Bahamian Fishermen Recount Their Adventures with the Beast," *Natural History* 80,3, March 1971, pp. 84, 86-87.

Wood, F. G., "Stupefying Colossus of the Deep," *Natural History* 80,3, March 1971, pp. 14, 16, 18, 20-24.

Yoon, Carol Kaesuk, "In Dark Seas, Biologists Sight a Riot of Life," *New York Times,* June 2, 1992.

GIANT SQUID

On November 30, 1861, as they sailed in the Canary Islands, the crew of the French gunboat *Alecton* came upon a giant sea monster. When the sailors tried to capture it, the creature swam off. Bullets and cannonfire failed to stop it. After a long chase the ship got close enough so that a harpoon could be hurled into the creature's flesh. Then a noose was put around its body, but the rope slipped until it reached the back fins. As the crew tried to lift it into the ship, the monster's body broke free. All but a small part of the tail slipped back into the water.

On landing at the island city of Tenerife, the *Alecton*'s commander contacted the French consul there and showed him the tail specimen. He also wrote up an official report, which was read at the December 30 meeting of the French Academy of Sciences. It was not well received; speaking for academy members, Arthur Mangin stated that no "wise" person—"especially the man of science"—would report such an extraordinary creature, whose very existence went against the laws of nature.

In other words, the ship's crew had to be lying or imagining the incident. In the *Alecton* case, though, witnesses had the unhappy experience of coming upon a strange but real animal a few years before its existence would be officially recognized. The crew had seen a giant squid—and a fairly small example of one. It was about 24 feet long from the tip of its tail to the end of its arms. Much larger squids are known to exist, and ones of *gigantic* size are suspected.

In 1861 the crew of the French steamer *Alecton* tried unsuccessfully to capture a giant squid.

Early Descriptions

In the eighteenth century, Bishop Erik Pontoppidan wrote about the Kraken, a legendary monster of the north seas, in his important zoological book *The Natural History of Norway* (1752–53). Though Pontoppidan did some exaggerating (he said the creature measured "about an English mile and a half" across and its arms could pull the "largest man-of-war [warship] ... down to the bottom"), he described the giant squid fairly accurately.

Other early descriptions of the giant squid were usually treated as mere imagination and folklore. Thus a very early account of a stranding and killing of a giant squid in Ireland's Dingle Bay in October 1673 attracted little attention when it was published. But now, the fantastic details with the giant squid in mind makes a great deal of sense. The report spoke of a beast with "two heads and Ten horns, and upon ... the said Horns about 800 Buttons, ... and in each of them a set of Teeth." The creature was 19 feet long, with a body "bigger than a Horse, ... and two very large Eyes." Squids, of course, have only one head, but the "little head" is the siphon through which water is pumped to propel the animal. The "horns" are the arms or tentacles, and the "buttons" are the toothed suckers on them.

The first scientist to undertake a complete study of the Kraken was nineteenth-century Danish zoologist Johan Japetus Steenstrup. He uncovered records of what sounded like giant squid strandings as early as 1639 (on Iceland's coast). He also collected pieces of specimens and gave a lecture on the subject to the Society of Scandinavian Naturalists in 1847. But his talk stirred little interest. Six years later Steenstrup obtained the pharynx and beak of a specimen from fishermen who cut up the rest, as they usually did, for bait (to them the Kraken had always been both real and useful). The zoologist published a description of the animal and gave it its scientific name, *Architeuthis,* in 1857.

Steenstrup's work continued to be ignored. The collective testimony of the *Alecton* crew did not help his case in the least. Zoology textbooks paid no attention to Steenstrup's new animal—until the 1870s, when a series of strandings on Canada's Newfoundland and Labrador shores brought some open-minded scientists, including *American Naturalist* editor A. S. Packard, to investigate.

In October 1873, a fisherman named Theophile Piccot and his son chopped off a tentacle of a giant squid they had come upon in the waters off Great Bell Island near Saint John's, Newfoundland. Piccot told Geological Commission of Canada investigator Alexander Murray that 10 feet of the tentacle had been left on the body; their piece measured 25 feet. Piccot claimed the animal was immense: roughly 60 feet long and from five to ten feet across.

Giant and Beyond

In the decades since, with the mystery of the giant squid effectively solved, other questions have emerged. For instance, what do the creatures eat, how do they live, and how do they reproduce? No live specimen has ever been captured for lengthy scientific observation. But the most pressing question of all is: how giant can a giant squid get?

The fact that the giant squid's primary enemy is the sperm whale might offer a clue. (The male sperm whale can reach 70 feet in length.) A rare witnessed battle between these two giants of the ocean was said to occur late on an evening in 1875 at the entrance to the Straits of Malacca (connecting the Indian Ocean with the South China Sea). Frank T. Bullen's *The Cruise of the Cachalot* (1924) described the event from an eyewitness's point of view:

> There was a violent commotion in the sea.... Getting the night-glasses out of the cabin scuttle, ... [I saw a] very large sperm whale was locked in deadly conflict with a cuttle-fish, or

squid, almost as large as himself, whose interminable tentacles seemed to enlace the whole of his great body. The head of the whale especially seemed a perfect network of writhing arms—naturally, I suppose, for it appeared as if the whale had the tail part of the mollusc in his jaws, and, in a business-like, methodical way, was sawing through it. By the side of the black columnar head of the whale appeared the head of the great squid, as awful an object as one could well imagine even in a fevered dream.... The eyes were very remarkable from their size and blackness.... They were, at least, a foot in diameter, and, seen under such conditions, looked decidedly eerie and hobgoblinlike.

Even without such remarkable eyewitness testimony, we know that squid–whale battles take place for two reasons: squid remains found in whale stomachs and vomit and sucker scars on whales. Both of these can help us guess how large squids may become.

The largest squid specimen documented by science was found on a New Zealand beach in 1880 and measured about 65 feet. Two scientists who investigated reported that much of the length (30 to 36 feet) "consisted of the tentacles." But the scientists also noted that "dead squid are notably elastic and easily stretched," and that fact kept their measurements from being entirely reliable. Still, the animal was huge. Other eyewitness accounts have reported 80- to 90-foot specimens.

Though direct sightings of giant squids are rare and poorly documented, many whalers have reported seeing amazing materials vomited up by sperm whales as they are dying. Bullen saw a "massive fragment of cuttle-fish—tentacle or arm—as thick as a stout man's body, and six or seven sucking-discs or *acetabula* on it. These were about as large as a saucer, and on their inner edge were thickly set with hooks or claws all around the rim, sharp as needles, and almost the shape and size of a tiger's."

Sucker Scars

Before scientists recognized that the Kraken was real, the strange round marks that they found on sperm whales puzzled them. Eventually they learned that they were sucker scars, made by giant squids locked in brave but losing battles with whales determined to eat them. Scars have been found to measure as much as 18 inches across.

Some teuthologists (zoologists who study cephalopods: squids, cuttlefish, and octopuses) argue that sucker scars are unreliable for judging the size of squids; in the words of Clyde F. E. Roper and Kenneth J. Boss, "a scar grows as a whale grows." But other zoological writers disagree. Bernard Heuvelmans, the founder of cryptozoology, noted that "scars are rare on female whales" and that "a baby whale would be kept well away from such huge brutes, and, if attacked, would hardly survive." In other words, giant squids are most likely to leave their marks on fully grown adult male sperm whales.

At any rate, there is no shortage of testimony concerning extraordinary squid remains in whale bellies. One ship captain noted an arm or tentacle 45 feet long and two and one-half feet thick, and others have reported those in the 25- to 35-foot range.

Giant squids, which are rarely seen, spend most of their lives in moderately deep to very deep waters. (The strandings seem to occur when a sick squid dies and rises to the surface, washing to shore.) A complete scientific survey of the ocean depths has only now just begun, and it is thought that merely one-tenth of one percent of it has been studied so far. Some of the scientists involved in this research hope especially to see a giant squid and even larger and stranger creatures.

> One ship captain noted an arm or tentacle 45 feet long and 2 1/2 feet thick, and others have reported those in the 25- to 35-foot range.

Sources:

Heuvelmans, Bernard, *In the Wake of the Sea-Serpents,* New York: Hill and Wang, 1968.

Ley, Willy, *Exotic Zoology,* New York: The Viking Press, 1959.

Yoon, Carol Kaesuk, "In Dark Seas, Biologists Sight a Riot of Life," *New York Times,* June 2, 1992.

SEA SERPENTS

The American ship *Silas Richards* was sailing off St. George's Bank south of Nova Scotia, Canada, at 6:30 P.M. on June 16, 1826, when its captain, Henry Holdredge, and a passenger, Englishman William Warburton, saw the oddest sight: a huge, many-humped snakelike creature moving slowly toward the boat. Warburton raced below deck to tell the other passengers, but only a handful of them were interested. "The remainder refused to come up," Warburton recalled, "saying there had been too many hoaxes of that kind already."

Over several centuries, the mystery of the sea serpent has been the subject of heated debate. Despite credible accounts from reliable witnesses going back hundreds of years, "the great unknown," as the creature was once called, has often been blamed on mistakes, lies, or wild imaginings. By the time of the *Silas Richards* sighting, the sea serpent had become—in the words of cryptozoology pioneer Bernard Heuvelmans—the "very symbol of a hoax."

Early History

Though sea serpents have long appeared in myths and legends, the first description of one as a real animal appeared in a 1555 work by Olaus Magnus, a Catholic archbishop of Uppsala, Sweden. He wrote that sailors off the coast of Norway had often seen a "serpent ... of vast magnitude, namely 200 feet long, and moreover 20 feet thick." A dangerous beast, it lived in caves along the shore and fed on both land and ocean creatures, including—from time to time—the unlucky seaman!

Historians who followed Magnus also noted that "serpents" were seen regularly in the North Sea (the part of the Atlantic Ocean between Europe and Great Britain), though not everyone considered them dangerous. In 1666 Adam Olschlager wrote of a sighting of a "large serpent, which seen from afar, had the thickness of a wine barrel, and 25 windings. These serpents are said to appear on the surface of the water only in calm weather and at certain times."

In 1734 a Protestant priest, Hans Egede, saw a "monster" about 100 feet long rise from the water off the coast of Greenland. He recorded the experience in a book published in 1741. A little more than a decade later, Bishop Erik Pontoppidan wrote *The Natural History of Norway* (1752-53), an important book that addressed sea serpents, **merfolk** (mermaids and mermen), and the Kraken (**giant squid**).

Some serpents were reported to have large foreheads, some had pointed snouts, and some had flat snouts "like that of a cow or horse, with large nostrils, and several stiff hairs standing out on each side like whiskers."

A sea serpent in the "Sea of Darkness" to the south and west of Europe. Woodcut from Olaus Manus's *Historia de Gentibus Spetentrionalibus,* 1555.

Because of the testimonies of reliable people, Pontoppidan believed that all of these doubted creatures were real. He also felt that sea serpents involved more than one type of animal, for descriptions of them included different details. Some serpents were reported to have large foreheads, some had pointed snouts, and some had flat snouts "like that of a cow or horse, with large nostrils, and several stiff hairs standing out on each side like whiskers." Over the next two centuries Pontoppidan's writings on sea serpents would be referenced again and again in discussions of the subject.

In the Americas

In *An Account of Two Voyages to New England* (1674), John Josselyn recalled a 1639 conversation with members of the Massachusetts colony. "They told me of a sea-serpent or snake, that lay coiled upon a rock at Cape Ann," he wrote. This is the first known printed account of an American sea serpent. In the next century and a half, thousands of residents of New England and Canada's coastal provinces would observe similar creatures.

One such account was from Captain George Little of the frigate *Boston.* In May 1780, while in Broad Bay off the Maine coast at sunrise, he "discovered a huge Serpent, or monster, coming down the Bay, on the surface of the water." Deciding to chase the creature, Little and several crew members boarded an armed cutter, and when it got to within 100 feet of the beast, he gave the order to fire. But at the same time the serpent dove below the surface of the water. "He was not less than from 45 to 50 feet in length," Little related. "The largest diameter of his

Sea serpent seen frequently off Gloucester, Massachusetts, in the early nineteenth century.

body, I should judge, was 15 inches; his head nearly the size of that of a man, which he carried four or five feet above the water. He wore every appearance of a common black snake."

A year earlier the crew of the American gunship *Protector* had also had an extraordinary experience off the Maine coast, in Penobscot Bay. One of the witnesses was 18-year-old ensign Edward Preble, who would go on to become a notable figure in U.S. naval history. When *Last of the Mohicans* author James Fenimore Cooper wrote Preble's biography, he included an account of the strange event:

> The day was clear and calm, when a large serpent was discovered outside the ship. The animal was lying on the water quite motionless. After inspecting it with the glasses [binoculars] for some time, Capt. Williams ordered Preble to man and arm a large boat, and endeavor to destroy the creature; or at least to go as near to it as he could.

> Preble shoved off, and pulled directly toward the monster. As the boat neared it, the serpent raised its head about ten feet above the surface of the water, looking about it. It then began to move slowly away from the boat. Preble pushed on, his men pulling [their oars] with all their force, and the animal being at no great distance, the swivel was discharged loaded with bullets. The discharge produced no other effect than to quicken the speed of the monster, which soon ran the boat out of sight.

There would be other sightings in the following decades. But New England's sea serpent would not become a matter of worldwide interest until the second decade of the nineteenth century. Over a period of several years, from Boston up to Cape Ann at the northeastern tip of Massachusetts, many witnesses on both ship and shore would see the animal.

Witness Solomon Allen III, for instance, saw the creature on August 12, 13, and 14, 1817, in Gloucester harbor. Judging the sea serpent "to be between eighty and ninety feet in length," Allen thought its head looked snakelike, but it was "nearly as large as the head of a horse." He also noted that when the creature "moved on the surface of the water, his motion was slow, at times playing about in circles, and sometimes moving nearly straight forward. When he disappeared, he sunk apparently down."

On June 6, 1819, Hawkins Wheeler also got a clear view of the sea serpent. "The creature was entirely black; the head, which perfectly resembled a snake's, was elevated from four to seven feet above the surface of the water, and his back appeared to be composed of bunches or humps, ... I think I saw as many as ten or twelve." Wheeler thought the humps were caused by the wavy motion of the animal; he guessed its length at 50 feet. Also that year, on August 14, Samuel Cabot noticed the serpent's "eight or ten regular bunches" or humps as well. Guessing the creature's length at 80 feet, Cabot similarly noted that it carried its "serpent shaped" head above the water.

A Sea Serpent Investigation

As the result of these sightings, the Linnean Society of New England met in Boston on August 19, 1817, to lay out a plan of investigation. The group selected three men—a judge, a physician, and a naturalist—to interview witnesses and get sworn statements from them. In the meantime, sea serpent sightings continued. The testimony that the men collected, and further accounts from later witnesses led to this general description of the creature: It was huge, snakelike, dark on the top and lighter on its underside, moving with vertical waves or undulations.

The animal, however, could not have been a serpent. Snakes and other reptiles move from side to side, not up and down. Regardless, the society investigators concluded that the animal was a huge reptile that was remaining close to shore because it had laid its eggs there. Repeated searches revealed no such eggs. But when a farmer killed a three-foot black snake in a field just off Cape Ann, he noticed it had a series of bumps along its back—just as the sea serpent was reported to have.

It was huge, snakelike, dark on the top and lighter on its underside, moving with vertical waves or undulations.

The Linnean Society foolishly agreed with the farmer's suggestion that this was a recently hatched baby sea serpent. Afterward, another scientist, Alexandre Lesuerur, demonstrated that the specimen was no more than a deformed specimen of the common black snake. Though Lesuerur did not intend to make the entire sea serpent investigation seem senseless, his discovery was hailed by nonbelievers and doubting journalists, and the entire affair ended in disaster for hopeful investigators.

The Great Unknown

No amount of laughter, however, could stop the sightings, which kept coming in from all over the world. But fear of ridicule did stop some people from reporting them. When the great American statesman Daniel Webster saw a sea serpent while on a fishing trip off the Massachusetts coast, he pleaded with his companion, "For God's sake never say a word about this to anyone, for if it should be known that I have seen the sea serpent, I should never hear the last of it."

Despite all attempts to explain away sightings of sea serpents, there were still some scientists who supported their existence. While most sea serpent accounts were reported in newspapers, a few made their way into scientific journals. But for every scientist who felt that his "evidence" demonstrated that sea serpents were real, there were ten times as many who had "proof" that the creatures were not. Finally, in 1847 *Zoologist* editor Edward Newman made a bold move by opening the pages of his journal to a fair-minded discussion of the subject. In addition, he scolded nonbelievers for ignoring "fact and observation" simply because the sea serpent "ought not to be."

Not Just a Fish Story

Perhaps the most famous sea serpent report of all time took place a year later. It occurred late in the afternoon of August 6, 1848, and the witnesses were the captain and crew of the frigate *Daedalus,* on their way back to England from Africa's Cape of Good Hope. Soon after the ship's arrival at Plymouth on October 4, several newspapers reported rumors that the captain and crew had experienced a spectacular 20-minute sea serpent encounter. Navy officials asked Captain Peter M'Quhae to either deny or describe the event.

On October 11 M'Quhae told Admiral Sir W. H. Gage about the incident in a letter, which was reprinted in the *London Times.* He, along

Illustrated London News 1848 depiction of a sea serpent seen by Captain M'Quhae from the *Daedalus*.

THE 'DÆDALUS' SEA-SERPENT

with other officers and crew members, had spotted "an enormous serpent, with head and shoulders kept about four feet ... above the surface of the sea.... There was at the very least 60 feet of the animal." The witnesses were unable to tell how the creature moved itself through the water, even though it came so close to their boat that, in M'Quhae's words, "had it been a man of my acquaintance, I should easily have recognized his features with the naked eye." Moving at a speed of about 12 to 15 miles per hour, "it was never," according to the captain, "during the 20 minutes that it continued in sight of our glasses, once below the surface of the water." Fifteen or 16 inches around, the serpent had the head of a snake. "It had no fins, but something like the mane of a horse, or rather a bunch of seaweed, washed about its back."

Soon afterward the *Zoologist* published the private notes of another witness, Lieutenant Edgar Drummond. His account matched M'Quhae's except for one detail: he thought the "mane" along the creature's back looked more like a fin. Ten years later another officer recalled the event in a letter to the *Times*. To him the animal appeared more like a lizard than a snake, "as its movement was steady and uniform, as if propelled by fins, not by any undulatory power."

These accounts caused an uproar. Sea serpent disbelievers were especially alarmed that respectable, experienced British officers would report such a sight. They scrambled to provide other explanations. One doubter felt that M'Quhae and his crew had mistaken a patch of seaweed for a creature. Another, the great anatomy scientist Sir Richard Owens, suggested that the sailors had come upon a giant seal and that their excitement and imaginations had supplied the "unseal-like" details.

Writing in the *Times,* M'Quhae boldly defended himself and his crew against the famous professor Owens, who happened to be the navy's consultant on sea serpents (and who said that they were less likely to exist than ghosts). The captain stood by every detail of his story and—in the opinion of many—won the argument. Still, scientific support for the sea serpent seemed to dwindle, despite the great many reports from reliable men and women.

The point was also raised that if sea serpents existed, why did they never get stranded on beaches, their dead bodies settling the mystery once and for all? This was a good question but one full of problems. For when unusual remains *were found,* scientists sometimes refused to examine them, so strong were their negative feelings about sea serpents. On the other hand, when examinations were carried out, the bodies usually ended up being those of known sea animals. This further weakened the case for the sea serpent's existence.

In 1892 A. C. Oudemans revived the fading mystery with the publication of his important book *The Great Sea Serpent,* the most careful and complete study of the subject yet to appear. In 591 pages the respected Dutch zoologist examined 187 cases, concluding that all sea serpent sightings were of a single species of animal, a gigantic long-necked seal.

In 1933 reports of strange animals in a Scottish lake caused a sensation; in fact, the **Loch Ness monster** would capture worldwide attention. For a period of time, the Ness story reminded scientists and others of the still-unsolved mystery of the sea serpent. Oudemans, for one, believed that one of the Ness animals would soon be caught or killed, and this would finally reveal the identity of the sea serpent as well.

Cadborosaurus

There was also a flurry of reports of a sea serpent off the coast of British Columbia in 1933. Sightings had occurred there in the past, going back to at least 1897, but the Loch Ness uproar made water monsters popular again. Soon the Canadian animal was given the name Cadborosaurus, which combined its home, Cadboro Bay, with the Greek word for lizard, *sauros*. Cadborosaurus soon became "Caddy."

The first widely reported sighting of Caddy took place on October 8, 1933, and involved a very reliable witness: Major W. H. Langley, a legal counselor and member of the British Columbia government. Sailing his sloop past Chatham Island early in the afternoon, he spotted a greenish-brown serpent with a sawlike body "every bit as big as a whale." He guessed it was 80 feet long.

In 1937, according to an account related to investigators years later, whalers killed a sperm wale off the Queen Charlotte Islands in northern British Columbia. When they cut open its stomach, they found the half-digested remains of a 10-foot-long snakey creature with a horselike head and humped back. They threw the remarkable specimen back into the ocean.

Reports like these captured the interest of two scientists, University of British Columbia oceanographer Paul LeBlond and Royal British Columbia Museum marine biologist Edward Bousfield, who over the years investigated a great many of them. By 1992 they had become so convinced that sea serpents were real that they said so in a formal lecture at a meeting of the American Society of Zoologists.

Chessie

Another well-known sea serpent was Chessie, the Chesapeake Bay monster in Maryland. It got its name in 1982, following a number of sightings in the spring and summer. One of these was made by Robert and Karen Frew on May 31, 1982. At 7 P.M., while entertaining guests outside their home overlooking the bay at Love Point on the northern tip of Kent Island, they saw a strange creature 200 feet from shore in calm water only five feet deep.

Robert Frew watched the animal through binoculars for a few minutes before getting his video camera. Then he focused on the creature, which disappeared below the surface of the water several times during the sighting. The closest it came to shore was around 100 feet, though it did come to within 50 feet of some boys who were playing on a pile of underwater rocks. Though the Frews and their friends shouted to alert the boys (their efforts captured on the videotape), the children never heard them—or saw the animal.

The witnesses guessed that the creature was 30 to 35 feet long and about a foot around. While much of it remained under water, each time it reappeared above the surface they could make out a little bit more. They could see humps on the back. The head was shaped like a football, only "a little more round." It was the odd shape of the head, in fact, that made Robert Frew think that the creature was something other than a snake. Familiar with a wide variety of sea life, the Frews were sure they had not mistaken a known animal for a mysterious sea creature.

On August 20 seven scientists from the Smithsonian Institution in Washington, D. C., along with members of the National Aquarium and Maryland's Department of Natural Resources, met to view and discuss the Frew videotape. The Smithsonian's George Zug reported the group's conclusion: "All viewers of the tape came away with a strong impression of an animate [living] object.... We could not identify the object.... These sightings are not isolated phenomena, for they have been reported regularly for the past several years."

Other Types of Sea Serpents

And reports of sea serpents in the world's oceans continue. Since the 1982 founding of the International Society of Cryptozoology (ISC), the membership of which includes a number of notable biologists, serious research into the subject has been made both possible and even somewhat respectable. ISC president Bernard Heuvelmans, in fact, published the most complete volume ever written about the mystery, the enormous *In the Wake of the Sea-Serpents,* in 1968.

In his book Heuvelmans described and examined every known sea serpent account, believable or otherwise, through 1966. There were 587 of them! Of those, he judged 358 to be real observations of unknown animals. Unlike most investigators of sea serpent mysteries, he decided that the sightings did not describe a single species of animal. The differences in details could not just be explained away as mistakes or imagination—they were important. But even though details varied, enough were repeated to create patterns. This led Heuvelmans to believe that several separate, unknown water animals were being describe, among them the following:

Long-necked (48 sightings)

Description: A long neck angled toward the head; hump or humps on the back; no tail; two horns, sometimes described as ears.
Classification: Almost certainly a pinniped. (A pinniped is a flesh-

Sea monster photographed by Robert Le Serrec, at Stonehaven Bay, Hook Island, Australia, in 1964.

eating water mammal with four flippers for limbs, like a seal or a walrus.) **Range:** Widespread.

Merhorse (37 sightings)

Description: Floating mane; medium to long neck; big eyes; hair or whiskers on face. **Classification**: Probably a pinniped. **Range**: Widespread.

Many-humped (33 sightings)

Description: String of humps on back; slender neck of medium length; small but striking eyes; dark stripes on top of the body, white on underside, white stripes on neck. **Classification:** Cetacean. (A cetacean is a water mammal with a large head, fishlike—nearly hairless—body, and paddle-shaped front limbs, like a whale, dolphin, or porpoise.) **Range:** North Atlantic.

Many-finned (20 sightings)

Description: Triangular fins that look like large peaks; short, slender neck. **Classification**: Cetacean. **Range**: Tropical waters.

Super-Otter (13 sightings)

Description: Slender, medium-length neck and long, tapering tail; several vertical bends in the body. **Classification:** Uncertain, but possibly a surviving form of primitive cetacean. **Range:** North Atlantic (possibly extinct; last known sighting in 1848).

Super-Eel (12 sightings)

Description: Serpent's body; long tapering tail. **Classification**: Fish. **Range**: Widespread.

While Heuvelmans knew he had not solved the problem of the sea serpent with his book, he felt that he had shed a great deal of light on the subject. "To solve the whole complex problem, without being able to examine the remains of the animals in question, we need many more detailed and exact reports," he noted. When conducting his study, he had been forced to leave out many accounts because of lack of detail. Heuvelmans also counted 49 hoaxes and 52 mistaken identifications among the reports he collected.

Like every other twentieth-century investigator, Heuvelmans did not think that sea serpents were actual serpents or reptiles. Mammals were the most frequent candidates for the many cases that he studied. But he agreed that an unknown reptile might have been sighted on rare occasions. His book contained just four reports of what he called a "marine saurian," a huge lizard- or crocodile-shaped creature spotted in tropical waters.

According to Heuvelmans, if such a creature existed, it might be "a surviving thalattosucian, ... a true crocodile of an ancient group, a specifically and exclusively oceanic one, which flourished from the Jurassic to the Cretaceous periods. But it could also be a surviving monosaur, a sea cousin of the monitors [a dragonlike, mostly tropical, lizard] of today. It would not be surprising if it had survived for so long at sea, since it is well designed to dive deep and remain unseen."

And what answer did Heuvelmans have for the frequently asked question of why sea serpents don't get stranded on beaches? The beasts responsible for such sightings, he wrote, "all belong by nature to the category of animals least likely to be stranded, and quite capable of getting off the shore again, if by misfortune they are." So it appears that such creatures probably die far out to sea.

As time goes on, scientists are learning more and more about the mysterious plants and animals that live deep and unobserved in the world's oceans. The sea serpent's time may be here at last.

Sources:

Costello, Peter, *In Search of Lake Monsters,* New York: Coward, McCann and Geoghegan, 1974.
Gould, Rupert T., *The Case for the Sea Serpent,* London: Philip Allan, 1930.
Heuvelmans, Bernard, *In the Wake of the Sea-Serpents,* New York: Hill and Wang, 1968.
Yoon, Carol Kaesuk, "In Dark Seas, Biologists Sight a Riot of Life," *New York Times,* June 2, 1992.

Freshwater Monsters

- LAKE MONSTERS

- LOCH NESS MONSTERS

- CHAMP

- MORAG

- OGOPOGO

- WHITE RIVER MONSTER

Freshwater Monsters

LAKE MONSTERS

At 7 P.M. on February 22, 1968, farmer Stephen Coyne arrived at the dry bog near Lough Nahooin, Ireland, one of a series of small lakes linked by streams that run through Connemara. With him were his eight-year-old son and the family dog. In the water he noticed a black object, and thinking it was his dog, he whistled for it. But the dog came bounding up from somewhere else. The moment it saw the object in the water, it stopped and stared.

The object proved to be a strange animal with a narrow, polelike head (without visible eyes) and a neck nearly a foot around. It was swimming in many directions, thrusting its head and neck underwater from time to time. Whenever this happened, two humps on its back and—sometimes—a flat tail would come into view. Once the tail was seen near the head, showing that the animal was both long and flexible. Its skin was black, slick, and hairless. The creature appeared to be at least 12 feet long.

One time, bothered by the dog's barking, it swam toward the group, its mouth open. Coyne stepped forward to protect the dog and the creature retreated, continuing its casual, directionless movement through the water. Soon father and son were joined by the five other members of the Coyne family. The animal remained clearly in view, sometimes as close as five or six yards. It was still there when darkness fell and the Coynes decided to go home.

The Coyne family's experience is one of the most credible in a long history of lake monster sightings. These have ranged from the clearly phony to the seemingly real. In the Coyne's case, a team of experienced cryptozoological investigators, including University of Chicago biologist Roy P. Mackal, interviewed the adult and child witnesses soon after the sighting. They found their testimonies solid.

A few months later, as the investigators were trying to snare the creature by dragging the tiny lake, they met Thomas Connely, a local man who had seen the same or a similar creature in September as it plunged into the water from the bank. They also heard reports from other lakes in this remote area of western Ireland.

In a case like this, mistaken identification or runaway imagination seems as unlikely as the creature the Coynes claimed to have seen. Sightings of lake monsters are frequent in the modern world. Some of the reports (often well detailed and with accompanying photographs) are known or suspected to be fake. Some of the reports can be reasonably explained. And some reports are just plain mysteries.

Water Horses

Some contemporary writers on lake monsters have linked modern reports—especially those from the monster-haunted lochs and loughs (Gaelic words for lakes) of Scotland and Ireland—to folklore about "water horses." They argue that in these legendary tales lies hidden evidence that unusual lake creatures really do exist. The link is a shaky one, though. The only two things that lake monster reports and water horse legends have in common are their freshwater homes and that many lake monsters are reported to have heads that look like that of a horse. Beyond this connection, the water horse (known as the "kelpie" in the Scottish Highlands) is a separate creature altogether.

The water horse is believed by many to be a dangerous shape-changer that can appear either as a shaggy man who leaps out of the dark onto the back of a lone traveler and frightens or crushes him to death or as a young horse, which after tricking an unknowing soul onto its back plunges to the bottom of the nearest lake, killing its rider.

Though water horses are discussed at length in folklore writings, it is almost impossible to find "sightings" of them; rumors and folktales supply the details about the creatures' appearance and habits. Yet one rare "sighting" was reported by Mary Falconer of Achlyness, West Sutherland, Scotland, one afternoon in the summer of 1938. Walking with a companion near Loch Garget Beag, she noticed a herd of 13 ponies grazing near the water. Because she was carrying a heavy sack of venison, Falconer thought she would borrow one of the horses for the rest of her trip to Rhiconich. The idea came to her because she spotted among the animals a white horse that looked exactly like her neighbor's.

But as she approached the animal, she found that it was too big to be her friend's horse. When she saw that it had water weeds tangled in its mane, she knew at once that it was a water horse. At that moment, it and the rest of the herd raced for the lake and disappeared below the surface! According to folklorist R. Macdonald Robertson, Falconer's companion supported every detail of her story.

PLESIOSAURS

Plesiosaurs were a suborder of prehistoric reptiles that dominated the seas during the Cretaceous period (136 to 65 million years ago). Their bodies were short, broad, and flat. They had short, pointed tails. Their small heads were supported by long, slender necks, ideal for darting into the water to catch fish. Plesiosaurs swam with a rowing movement, using their four powerful, diamond-shaped flippers like paddles. They were often quite large, measuring up to 40 feet in length.

Appearance

The twentieth-century image of a lake monster is that of a long-necked, plesiosaurlike animal. But before our modern age, with its scientific instruments and photographic evidence, freshwater monsters were usually described as great serpents. These serpents did not always remain in the water and were often dangerous.

In 1636, for example, Norwegian churchman Nicolas Gramius reported that a great serpent that had lived in the Mjos and Branz rivers made its way to the sea during a flood. "From the shores of the ... river, he crossed fields," Gramius related. "People saw him moving like a long ship's mast, overturning all that he met on his path, even trees and huts."

In more recent times (as in sightings reported in central Wisconsin in the 1890s), the lake monster has been described as 10 to 20 feet long, snake-shaped, and moving with an undulating or wavy motion. Snakes and other reptiles move from side to side, not up and down, but this wavy movement has nonetheless been described in many reports. Such accounts, while sketchy, survive in local newspapers. Mackal and

many other trained cryptozoologists feel that this description of a lake monster is consistent with descriptions of the *zeuglodon,* a primitive, snakelike whale believed to no longer exist.

The Freshwater Dragon

The freshwater "dragon," on the other hand, surfaced as recently as October 18, 1946, in the Clearwater River near Rocky Mountain House in Alberta, Canada. Farmer Robert Forbes claimed to have seen a huge, horned, scaly-skinned monster with fiery eyes and long, flashing teeth dart its head out of the water long enough to swallow–whole–a calf that happened to be grazing on the bank.

Creature-Haunted Lakes

Lake monsters are reported worldwide, but are poorly documented. A list of the earth's "creature-haunted" lakes–about 300 of them–appeared in the spring 1979 issue of *Pursuit* magazine. Because many of these lakes got their reputations from questionable nineteenth-century newspaper stories and frontier tall tales, the number is not a dependable one.

Outside North America and the British Isles, most serious investigation has focused on Scandinavian lakes, especially in Norway. While these efforts have brought no solid results, some of the eyewitness reports there have been believable and impressive. Most evidence based on instrument findings has come from Loch Ness, where investigations began in the 1930s and continue today. Films, photographs, and sonar (sound wave) trackings have drawn a great deal of attention to "Nessie" (the **Loch Ness monster**) and strongly suggest that *something* unusual is going on in Scotland's most famous lake.

> ### MIGRATING MONSTERS
>
> Norwegians once believed that monsters grew in lakes until they were too big to live there any longer; then they migrated to the sea. It is not entirely impossible that these monsters were large eels, which have been known to migrate as much as 20 miles overland.

Sources:

Bord, Janet, and Colin Bord, *Alien Animals,* Harrisburg, Pennsylvania: Stackpole Books, 1981.

Coleman, Loren, *Mysterious America,* Boston: Faber and Faber, 1983.

Heuvelmans, Bernard, *In the Wake of the Sea-Serpents,* New York: Hill and Wang, 1968.

Holiday, F. W., *The Dragon and the Disc: An Investigation into the Totally Fantastic,* New York: W. W. Norton and Company, 1973.

LOCH NESS MONSTERS

The first report of Scotland's lake monster "Nessie" is traced by believers back to A.D. 565. A man swimming in the river Ness, at the north end of the loch (lake), was reportedly killed by the beast. St.

Columba, so the story goes, came upon some men carrying the body and was told about the unusual death. He sent a companion into the river, which attracted the attention of the creature; it rose up and moved threateningly toward the swimmer. As the others looked on in terror, Columba formed the sign of the cross and commanded the monster to depart in the name of God. According to a Latin text compiled by St. Adamnan a century later, the "beast, on hearing this voice of the saint, was terrified and fled backwards more rapidly than he came."

The account did not describe what the "beast" looked like, nor was its fierce behavior typical of the loch's modern monster. Still, those devoted to the Ness mystery considered the story important. Other unclear references to large animals in the loch appeared in documents over the centuries, with equally weak links to contemporary Nessie reports. Some writers on lake monsters, for instance, tried to connect widespread European folktales about "water horses"—known in Scotland as "kelpies"—with modern Ness sightings (also see **Lake Monsters**). The only feature that the supernatural kelpies and some modern Ness monsters share is their horselike heads.

Thousands of Sightings

The Loch Ness monster became a worldwide sensation in the 1930s, but there had been many sightings before that time. During the 1930s, residents of the loch area and others hearing the reports came forward with their own sightings from earlier in the century or before. In 1934, for instance, D. Mackenzie wrote to Rupert T. Gould, author of *The Loch Ness Monster and Others* (1934), the first book on the Ness mystery. In the letter Mackenzie recalled a sighting in 1871 or 1872 when, on a sunny October day, he saw what looked "rather like an upturned boat ... wriggling and churning up the water." On October 20, 1933, *The Scotsman* published a letter from the duke of Portland, who remembered that in 1895, while involved with salmon fishing in the area, he had heard many mentions of "a horrible great beastie ... which appeared in Loch Ness." And two groups of witnesses recalled seeing a large elephant-gray animal with a small head at the end of a long neck as it "waddled" from land into the water back in 1879 and 1880.

Such descriptive terms as upturned boat, elephant-gray color, small head, and long neck would commonly appear in later Nessie

Though largely forgotten today, Rupert Thomas Gould was a pioneering writer on mysterious phenomena and a popular public figure in England. He wrote the first book on the Loch Ness monster and would go on to write two books about sea serpents and two best-selling books, *Oddities* (1928) and *Enigmas* (1929), which covered a wide range of anomalies.

Born in England and educated at Dartmouth College, Gould worked for the Royal Navy for many years. In the 1930s he hosted a BBC radio program for children called *The Stargazer*. His show, on which he discussed the many mysteries of science and history that so fascinated him, was immensely successful.

Though Gould's life and career overlapped with American anomalist Charles Fort's, the two men could hardly have been more different in approach (also see entry: Falls from the Sky). Fort used his data on a vast range of anomalies to create a sometimes outrageous worldview that mocked the pretensions of scientists and scholars. Gould, on the other hand, chose his subjects carefully, learned everything he could about them, and proceeded scientifically and logically. While Fort came up with revolutionary ideas, Gould was the more reliable and accurate anomalist.

reports. Sightings would eventually number in the thousands. Biologist Roy P. Mackal, known for his keen interest in lake monsters, noted in the mid-1970s that "over the years there have been at least 10,000 known *reported* sightings at Loch Ness but less than a third of these *recorded*."

The "Classic" Monster

In July 1930, three local men had a strange experience while fishing from a boat in Loch Ness; one of the witnesses recalled the event in the *Northern Chronicle* (August 27). Noticing "a commotion about 600 yards up the loch," the man saw "a spray being thrown up into the air at a considerable height." So strong was the rush of water, he reported, that it "caused our boat to rock violently." The source of the ruckus seemed to be something large, "traveling at fifteen knots [nautical miles]." Nearly "twenty feet" of it was visible, "standing three feet or so out of the water." The witness said it was "without doubt a living creature" and not "anything normal."

Though this newspaper account brought letters from other readers relating their own or other people's experiences with mysterious animals in the loch, the matter attracted only local attention.

That would change with an incident that took place on the afternoon of April 14, 1933, near Abriachan, a village on the northwest side of Loch Ness. A couple in a passing car spotted a mass of churning water and stopped. Over the next few minutes, they watched an "enormous animal rolling and plunging" out on the loch. The May 2 issue of the *Inverness Courier* ran the story, written by Alex Campbell, who would later claim his own sightings. *Courier* editor Evan Barron called the animal a "monster," and the report attracted some attention around Scotland. Then, as other sightings came in (it seems that the expansion of an old road along the northern shore of the loch had cleared away many natural viewing obstructions), the world eventually took notice. By October, with over 20 reports recorded since the April 14 sighting, the "Loch Ness monster" was born.

Over the years, a clear picture of the monster has emerged. The classic "Nessie" has a long, vertical neck with a small head. Near the end of the neck, some witnesses have reported seeing what looks like a mane of hair, and the head may be horselike in appearance. The long, tapering body may have one, two, or three humps and a long, thick tail. Those who have claimed to see Nessie on land usually report fins, which allow for clumsy forward movement on land but rapid movement in the water. Its color ranges from dark gray to dark brown to black. It surfaces and descends quickly and vertically. It almost always appears when the lake is calm.

A Number of Nessies

Several Nessie experts argue that if the loch is the home of an unusual animal, more than one specimen must exist. Early writers like Gould thought that the lake was home to a single creature, but many feel that the monster must be part of a breeding group. In fact, sightings of more than one creature, though rare, have been made from time to time. The *Scottish Daily Press* of July 14, 1937, for example, told of eight people who observed "three Monsters about 300 yards out in the loch. In the center were two black shiny humps, 5 ft. long and protruding 2 ft. out of the water and on either side was a smaller Monster."

Also, the sizes of the creatures described suggest that there is more than one Nessie. Lengths range from as little as three feet (in rare reports of "baby monsters") to as much as 65 feet! Still, most sightings report creatures between 15 and 30 feet long.

Blurry image, said to be the Loch Ness monster, taken by a tourist at Fort Augustus, Scotland, in 1934.

Land Sightings

Among the thousands of sightings of Nessie, there are a group of reports that teeter on the edge of incredibility—land sightings. Henry H. Bauer, a scientist interested in the Ness mystery, commented:

> A considerable but unavoidable embarrassment to the most hardheaded hunters is the existence of a small number of reports of Nessies having been seen on land. In Nessiedom these events have a place that is not unlike that of the 'close encounters of the third kind' in ufology. One is brought squarely up against ... apparently responsible and plausible individuals who insist on ... experiences of the most extremely improbable sort.

Bauer added that such land sightings have been a part of the mystery from the beginning and that they have made belief in Nessies far more difficult.

The most famous of the land sightings took place on the afternoon of July 22, 1933. As they drove down the east side of the loch between Dores and Foyers, Mr. and Mrs. F. T. G. Spicer said they saw a strange animal 200 yards ahead of them. "It did not move in the usual reptilian fashion," Mr. Spicer said, "but with these arches. The body shot across the road in jerks, but because of the slope we could not see its lower parts and saw no limbs." Twenty-five to 30 feet long, it had an elephant-gray color, a bulky body, and a long neck. "We saw no tail," he recalled, "nor did I notice any mouth on what I took to be the head of the creature." The Spicers called the animal, which disappeared into the coarse ferns along the loch, a "loathsome sight."

At around 1 A.M. on January 5, 1934, veterinary student W. Arthur Grant was riding his motorcycle just north of Abriachan when he nearly collided with a strange creature. It lurched across the road, crashed through some nearby plants, and splashed into the loch, disappearing at once. Grant later related: "It had a head rather like a snake or an eel, flat at the top, with a large oval eye, longish neck and somewhat larger tail. The body was much thicker towards the tail than was the front portion. In color it was black or brown and had a skin rather like that of a whale."

The last known land sighting, said to have taken place on February 28, 1960, was of a similarly classic specimen. In mid-afternoon, Torquil MacLeod observed a long-necked animal with flippers through his binoculars. The upper half of the creature was on the shore, with the lower half tapering off into the loch. He watched for nine minutes before it turned and "flopped into the water and apparently went straight down."

Other Oddities

There are plenty of land sightings that do not describe the classic Nessie. Some of them are quite bizarre and give scientifically trained Ness investigators headaches trying to understand them.

In June 1990 *Scots Magazine,* for instance, published Colonel L. Fordyce's account of a land sighting that he and his wife had experienced in April 1932. Driving through the woods one morning along the south side of the loch, they saw "an enormous animal" cross the road 150 yards ahead on its way to the water. "It had the gait of an elephant," he recalled, "but looked like a cross between a very large horse and a camel, with a hump on its back and a small head on a long neck.... From the rear it looked grey and shaggy." It had long, thin legs and a thin, hairy tail. Because it was a year before the Loch Ness monster was publicly recognized, the couple had no clue as to what they were seeing. They thought it was a freak animal escaped from a zoo.

Strange as it may seem, other unlikely beasts have been reported. According to a letter written in 1933 to *The Scotsman* by Patrick Rose, a lake monster "which was a cross between a horse and a camel" had been reported by one of Rose's ancestors way back in 1771. In 1912, from a distance of no more than a few yards, a group of children at Inchnacardoch Bay saw something resembling a long-necked camel enter the loch. A pale, sandy color, it had four legs.

But that was not the end of reports of outlandish beasts in or near the loch. Driving along its northern shore early one April morning in 1923, Alfred Cruickshank reportedly spotted a creature with "a large humped body standing about six feet high with its belly trailing on the ground." Around "twelve feet long," it had a tail of equal length. Its four legs were as thick as an elephant's, and it had large webbed feet. The head was "big and pug-nosed and was set right on the body," and Cruickshank thought the animal looked like an "enormous hippo." Before disappearing into the water, the beast gave a "sharp bark." And in December 1933, a Mrs. Reid claimed to have seen what looked to her like a dark, hairy hippopotamus as it rested on the loch shore.

Land sightings all but stopped after the mid-1930s. But beasts other than the classic monster were still seen in the water. A correspondent writing in the June 7, 1933, issue of the Scottish newspaper *Argus,* for example, claimed that when flying over the loch the week before, he and his companions had seen "in the depths a shape resembling a large alligator, the size of which would be about 25 feet long by four feet wide." Just one year earlier, a woman had spotted a six- to eight-foot animal swimming up the river Ness that she described as a "crocodile." What's more, according to some early nineteenth-century reports, a critter akin to a "great salamander" also appeared in the loch from time to time.

Photographs

Despite these troubling descriptions, the majority of Nessie reports are of a long-necked creature that resembles nothing so much as a plesiosaur, a plant-eating water reptile thought to have become extinct some 65 million years ago. In most Nessie sightings, descriptions vary only in the reported size of the beast.

Hugh Gray, who lived at Foyers on the loch's southeast shore, took the first picture of Nessie on November 13, 1933 (see page 420). He was 200 yards away and about 40 feet above the water. The photograph shows an unclear large object that appears to be moving vigorously. Something extends from its left side, possibly a neck or fin; Gray thought it was the neck, with the head under water. While generally considered genuine, the picture is too fuzzy to settle anything. As J. R. Norman of the British Museum of Natural History said at the time, "I am afraid that the photo does not bring the mystery any nearer to a solution."

The following April, Robert Kenneth Wilson claimed to take what would become the most famous of all Nessie still pictures, the "surgeon's photograph," though Wilson was, in fact, a gynecologist. The widely reproduced picture (actually the first, and better, of two) shows the head and long, curving neck of what appears to be a plesiosaur. Predictably, Wilson's photograph stirred a flurry of argu-

The first photo of Nessie, taken by Hugh Grant in 1933, was deemed authentic, but, like many later photos, it was too blurred to prove anything.

ments for and against its authenticity. Even the date on which it was taken was questioned. And the lesser-known second photograph, showing just the head and a small part of the neck, led some scientists to argue that the animal was small–perhaps a diving bird or an otter.

These arguments appeared minor (and foolish!) when Ness researchers Alastair Boyd and David Martin came forward 60 years later with a bombshell: the "surgeon's photograph" was a fake! A 90-year-old man had confessed this to the two just before his death in November 1993.

It seemed that back in 1933, the *Daily Mail* had hired colorful film-maker Marmaduke "Duke" Wetherell to find Nessie. He hatched a scheme and carried it out with the help of his son, Ian, and Spurling, his stepson. Spurling made a Nessie model–one foot tall and 18 inches long--from molded plastic, wood, and a toy submarine from Woolworth's weighted down with strips of lead. Duke and Ian photographed it in the shallows of a quiet bay in the loch and quickly sank it when they heard someone approach. Wilson was the respectable "middleman" they chose to get the pictures developed. Going along with the hoax to be a good sport, he never imagined that it would be so successful and said little about the photos throughout his lifetime.

There would be more photographs of the monster. On August 24, 1934, F. C. Adams took an important shot of what looked like a fin attached to an unseen large animal thrashing around in the water near the surface of the loch. Other photographs showed unusual tracks in the water, different from those left by passing boats or other normal lake traffic. Dramatic close-ups of the monster, from pictures taken by Frank Searle (in the early to mid-1970s) and Anthony "Doc" Shiels (1977), have appeared in many magazines and books, but serious researchers consider them hoaxes.

Underwater photographs taken in 1972 and 1975 looked like more evidence in Nessie's favor. On the night of August 7, 1972, investigators of the Massachusetts-based Academy of Applied Sciences and the Loch Ness Investigation Bureau were patrolling the waters near Urquhart Bay. One boat contained a sonar (sound wave) device; another held strobe and camera equipment. (A strobe is an instrument that employs a flashtube for high-speed lighting that is sometimes used in photography.) At 1 A.M. sonar picked up an unidentified target about 120 feet away, within range of an underwater strobe camera but apparently above or below its beam, as nothing was captured on film. Forty minutes later, two large objects, 20 to 30 feet long and about 12 feet apart, were tracked, as were some salmon fleeing before them. The traces stopped after a few minutes.

Academy investigators took the film from the underwater camera to the Unites States to have it developed at the head office of photographic-equipment company Eastman Kodak. Two frames showed what looked like a big flipper attached to a body of rough texture. A third showed blurry images of two objects (just where the sonar echoes had placed them). The clearer of these objects suggested a classic Nessie: long neck, bulky body, and fins.

To improve the flipper photographs, which were murky because of the loch's peat-sogged water, the researchers took them to the Jet Propulsion Laboratory (JPL), where state-of-the-art photo studies were regularly performed for official, military, and scientific agencies. There, through a standard computer-enhancement technique, much of the graininess of the original photographs was removed. These clearer pictures would appear in *Nature* magazine and elsewhere. "This technique has proven to be a real tool," academy investigators wrote. "It has been used to clarify images from space probes, in forensics to help identify fingerprints, and in medical research to classify human chromosomes." And "it cannot create patterns where there are none."

The flipper in the pictures appeared to be four to six feet long. Those who studied the sonar records agreed that the objects detected by the sound waves were also the subjects of the photographs. To British television newsman Nicholas Witchell (author of a popular book on the monster), this "coincidence of the sonar and the photography ... presented indisputable proof of the animal's presence. The one cross-checked ... the other. Here was the breakthrough." Scientists and journalists did take notice. Even *Time* magazine, which has historically avoided covering strange claims of any kind, stated, "Now the skeptics may have to re-examine their doubts."

In June 1975 the academy team produced even more amazing evidence. This time it was two dramatic pictures, taken about seven hours apart on the morning of June 20. The first showed, according to *Technology Review,* the "upper torso, neck and head of a living creature." Again Ness's murky water made this identification less than certain; still, little imagination was needed to detect the features. Even more startling was the second photograph. It appeared to be the monster's head, just five feet from the camera! It was horselike and even had the small horns that some observers had reported. According to the investigators, "Measurements indicate the 'neck' to be about one-and-one-half feet thick, the 'mouth' nine inches long and five inches wide, and the horn on the central ridge six inches

Freshwater Monsters

long." The photograph quickly became known as the "gargoyle head" picture.

At first, scientific response to this newest piece of Nessie evidence made believers hopeful. Because of the pictures, zoologists from Washington D.C.'s Smithsonian Institution, the Royal Ontario Museum, Harvard University, the New England Aquarium, and other important institutions either outright supported Nessie's existence or declared that it was now a real possibility. But scientists from London's Natural History Museum expressed doubt, which would spread. Because a portion of the neck near the head in the first 1975 photograph was not visible (lost in the shadows, according to believers), they did not feel that the photo indicated the creature existed. "This probably should be interpreted as two objects," they wrote; "conceivably various floating objects could assume this form."

Certainty about the academy photographs began to erode. In 1984 the popular-science magazine *Discover* objected to the computer enhancements performed on the 1972 flipper photographs, claiming that secret retouching had turned "grainy and indistinct" images into false evidence of an unknown animal. But the academy had not tried to hide anything, clearly admitting to computer assistance with the photographs. And Allan Gillespie, who worked on the pictures at JPL, knew that the academy was not trying to make something out of nothing. "The outline of the flipper is visible in the original," he stated.

Then Adrian Shine of the Loch Ness and Morar Project insisted that the 1975 "gargoyle head" was really a rotting tree stump. Shine brought the stump to the loch's surface and photographed it and displayed the resulting print next to the head picture, remarking on the similarities. Most observers could find no resemblance. And Tim Dinsdale, one of the most famous of Nessie's hunters, suggested a different explanation for the object in the photo: turning its angle would reveal a car or truck's engine block with exhaust pipe. Such things were often tossed into Urquhart Bay to anchor boats.

So what first seemed clear evidence of Nessie's existence only brought more questions in the end. Still, in its favor, the academy photographs look to most observers more like animal parts than anything else.

IS LOCH NESS A SUITABLE HOME FOR NESSIE?

More evidence challenging the existence of Nessie surfaced in late 1993. A team of scientists studying the ecology of Loch Ness revealed that the lake has such a small fish population that it could not possibly support a family of monster-sized predators.

Former Royal Air Force pilot Tim Dinsdale displays a model he made of the Loch Ness Monster.

Film Clips

Malcolm Irvine of Scottish Film Productions took the first motion-picture film of Nessie on December 12, 1933, in Urquhart Bay. Two minutes long, it showed a long, dark object that barely protruded above the water's surface 100 yards away. Like most Nessie films that would come later, it was intriguing but would provide no answers.

The whereabouts of one film that might have held some answers is unknown–if it ever existed at all. Said to have been taken sometime in the 1930s by a London physician named McRae, it supposedly showed several minutes' footage of a three-humped creature with a cone-shaped head, two horns, a stiff mane down a long neck, and—at one point, when the animal rolled over—a flipper. According to McRae's close friend, artist Alastair Dallas, the doctor feared ridicule and decided not to release the film. Nessie investigator F. W. Holiday learned about it from Dallas in the early 1960s.

The coming decades would bring many more Nessie films. In 1977 biologist Mackal reviewed 22 of them. He dismissed nearly half because of poor quality. Six involved mistaken identifications of known objects. And five contained "positive evidence." Among the most important of these was one taken by Dinsdale.

On April 23, 1960, on the last day of a six-day watch of the loch, Dinsdale was sitting in his car on a hill near Foyers on the eastern shore. Suddenly he spotted an unusual-looking, motionless object two-thirds of a mile across the water. With his binoculars he saw a "long oval shape" that "had fullness and girth and stood well above the water." "It began to move," he related. "I saw ripples break away from the further end, and I knew at once I was looking at the extraordinary humped back of some huge living creature!" He filmed it with a 16-mm camera for four minutes as it swam away, partially underwater. Running out of film, he stopped the camera in the hope that the creature would show its head and neck. It did not.

Wisely, Dinsdale later filmed an associate sailing a boat in the same direction that the creature had taken. In 1966, when Britain's Joint Air Reconnaissance Intelligence Center (JARIC) studied the first film, it used the second reel for comparison. Center members were able to closely guess the boat's size and speed. Then, turning to the first film, they determined that the object was definitely not a boat (a favored explanation), but "probably ... an animate object." They also figured that the hump was between 12 and 16 feet long and about three feet above the water. The object was moving around 10 mph. The Dinsdale film is considered a major piece of evidence of Nessie's existence, and in the years since no one has seriously challenged the JARIC study.

Sonar

Sonar has tracked Nessie-like targets many times. The first tracings were recorded in 1954, when a commercial vessel noted a large moving object passing 480 feet below it. And between 1968 and 1970, using sonar devices from shore and on boats, D. G. Tucker of the University of Birmingham and his associates tracked 20-foot living things that swam and dived near the bottom and sides of the loch. Sometimes they were tracked in groups; one time the group counted from five to eight members. Their behavior, speed, and size convinced Tucker that they were not fish.

Investigators have continued to make sonar trackings of creatures in the loch. The Loch Ness and Morar Project and technology and electronics companies have been behind many of them. In 1987 the most involved and well known of these, Operation Deepscan, brought more than 20 vessels to the loch surface for a three-day sonar sweep, between October 8 and 10. Though they covered only the lake's southern half, ten contacts were recorded.

Explanations

The idea that the loch's monsters are large eels is one unusual but believable explanation. Elephant seals or sea cows (plant-eating water mammals like the dugong, or manatee) have also been named as unusual but believable candidates. The only problem is that none of these look much like what witnesses report or what the photographs and films seem to show.

Of the extraordinary explanations the most popular is that the animals are surviving plesiosaurs that have adapted to Ness's cold temperatures. But a few investigators, like Mackal, favor the zeuglodon theory, named for a primitive, snakelike whale also thought to have become extinct long ago. No single theory satisfies all the data, and investigators of the Loch Ness mystery disagree even on what "the data" is. Meanwhile, the search continues.

Sources:

Bauer, Henry H., *The Enigma of Loch Ness: Making Sense of a Mystery,* Urbana, Illinois: University of Illinois Press, 1986.
Binns, Ronald, *The Loch Ness Mystery Solved,* Buffalo, New York: Prometheus Books, 1984.
Dinsdale, Tim, *Loch Ness Monster,* fourth edition, Boston: Routledge and Kegan Paul, 1982.
Ellis, William S., "Loch Ness: The Lake and the Legend," *National Geographic* 151,6, June 1977, pp. 759-779.
Holiday, F. W., *The Dragon and the Disc: An Investigation into the Totally Fantastic,* New York: W. W. Norton and Company, 1973.
Holiday, F. W., *The Great Orm of Loch Ness: A Practical Inquiry into the Nature and Habits of Water-Monsters,* New York: W. W. Norton and Company, 1969.
Mackal, Roy P., *The Monsters of Loch Ness,* Chicago: The Swallow Press, 1976.
Witchell, Nicholas, *The Loch Ness Story,* Baltimore: Penguin Books, 1975.

CHAMP

Champ is, at least according to some, Lake Champlain's version of the Loch Ness monster: a large, long-necked animal that looks like a plesiosaur, a water reptile that became extinct some 65 million years ago (also see entry: **Lake Monsters**). But in reality, eyewitness accounts describe many different creatures. There have been more than 300 recorded sightings of Champ, according to Joseph Zarzynski, who has investigated and written about the monster.

The popular belief is that Samuel de Champlain, the French explorer after whom the lake was named, was the first white man to see the monster. He was supposed to have mentioned it in a 1609 account of his travels on the Saint Lawrence and other rivers. But he only refers to large fish in his report. His description suggests garfish, which can still be found in Champlain today.

Early Sightings

The story of Champ really begins, more or less, in 1873 when the first known newspaper story about a monster in Lake Champlain appeared in the *Whitehall Times* on July 9. In this and other early accounts, the monster was described as a different animal from our modern version—a giant serpent and not a plesiosaur.

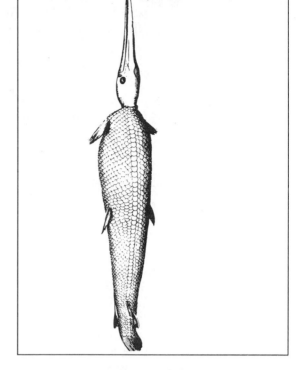

The "monster" reported by Samuel de Champlain; from *Historia Canadensis* (Paris, 1664) by Father François De Colux.

According to the *Times,* a railroad work crew laying tracks on the lakeshore near Dresden, New York, "saw a head of an enormous serpent sticking out of the water and approaching them from the opposite shore." So terrified were the men that they stood paralyzed for a while before scattering. The monster turned toward the open water and then:

> As he rapidly swam away, portions of his body, which seemed to be covered with bright silver-like scales, glistened in the sun like burnished [polished] metal.... From his nostrils he would occasionally spurt [streams] of water above his head.... The appearance of his head was round and flat, with a hood spreading out from the lower part.... His eyes were small and piercing, his mouth broad and provided with two rows of teeth, which he displayed to his beholders.

> As he moved off ... portions of his body appeared above the surface of the water, while his tail, which resembled that of a fish, was thrown out of the water quite often.... A quarter-mile into the lake, the creature sank suddenly out of sight.

Within a few days of the Dresden event, farmers were complaining of missing livestock. Tracks and other marks on the ground suggested that something had dragged the animals into the lake. In caves along the waterside, local residents claimed that "bright and hideous looking eyes" could sometimes be seen in the darkness. A few days later a young farmer saw the serpent in a lakeside marsh, with something that looked like a turtle in its mouth. He fired on it, and the creature disappeared into the water.

LAKE CHAMPLAIN

Formed about 10,000 years ago out of melting glaciers, Champlain is a deep, cold-water, 109-mile lake. It runs along the New York/Vermont border and into Quebec, where it drains into the Saint Lawrence River and finally the North Atlantic Ocean. The largest North American body of water outside the Great Lakes, it is the home to some 80 different species of fish.

Other sightings and livestock kills followed, and search parties prowled the shoreline and surrounding farms. In early August the small steamship *W. B. Eddy* struck the serpent and nearly overturned. On August 9 the crew of the *Molyneaux* believed it had the monster trapped in the thick weeds of Axehelve Bay. Though no one could actually see it, guns were fired into the thickets. The *Whitehall Times* of August 13 printed one witness's account of the results:

Our ears were greeted by a most unearthly noise.... The order was given (by Captain Belden) to steam away as the head of the mammoth snake appeared through the tangled vines and brushwood. The greyish hood upon his head flopped backwards and forwards.... Great ridges of silver appeared above the surface of the water, undulating and scintillating in the bright sun like the highly polished surface of a warrior's silver helmet.... His eyes resembled two burning coals, fairly snapping fire, as its rage increased, while the rows of long and formidable teeth, pearly white and wicked looking, sent an indescribable thrill through us, which we shall never forget. The body seemed to be about 18 to 20 inches thick in the middle, and 36 to 40 feet long.

As the *Molyneaux* retreated, more shots were fired at "the great moving, waving mass of silver." As the creature "lashed the water with his fishlike tail and gave great spasmodic, powerful lurches with his broad flat head," the crew knew that their gunfire was taking its toll. Finally, two well-placed shots from just 25 feet away hit their mark, and "streams of red blood spurted from its head." After one last "spasmodic twist," the monster "disappeared beneath the red sea of blood."

Attempts to raise the body proved unsuccessful. Searchers hoped to collect the $50,000 reward offered by entertainer P. T. Barnum, who

List of Champ sightings, beginning with Samuel de Champlain.

wanted the "hide of the great Champlain serpent to add to my mammoth World's Fair Show."

All these events reportedly took place in the Dresden area at the southwestern edge of the lake. When the monster (or a relative) returned a few years later, it had moved to Champlain's northwestern side, near Plattsburgh.

On July 31, 1883, the *Plattsburgh Morning Telegram* reported that Clinton County Sheriff Nathan H. Mooney had seen an "enormous snake or water serpent ... 25 to 35 feet in length." Three years later, beginning in the summer of 1886, sightings were recorded almost daily from practically every part of the lake. One man fishing near Plattsburgh claimed to have hooked what he first thought was a huge fish. But when he and three other witnesses finally saw its head they realized it was a "horrible creature." The line snapped, and the terrifying catch fortunately disappeared underwater!

Sightings continued into the next year. At two o'clock one morning in May 1887, for instance, a farm boy heard strange noises and went to the lakeshore. A mile out in the water he spotted a big serpent "making noises like a steamboat." In several other cases witnesses claimed that the creature had threatened them, swimming fiercely at them and forcing their quick retreat. In one gripping account reported in early July, picnickers from Charlotte, Vermont, noticed the beast from their spot near the lake. Seventy-five feet long and as big around as a barrel, it bore down on the group until several women screamed. It then turned around and swam off.

Shortly afterward, this incredible report was published in the *Plattsburgh Morning Telegram:*

> The sea serpent ... has left the lake and is making his way overland in the direction of Lake George [New York]. He was seen last night about five o'clock by a farmer driving to his barn with a load of hay. Chancing to look behind him ... he saw ... gliding along like a snake with its head raised about four feet from the ground ... an immense monster anywhere from 25 to 75 feet in length, ... covered with scales.

A few sightings of the monster, though, revealed unserpentlike details. In September 1889 a group of fishermen chased the creature; it had, they reported, "many large fins" (*Essex County Republic,* September 26). In the summer of 1899, a witness reported seeing a 35-foot-long serpent with a broad, flat tail raised a few feet above the water (*Plattsburgh Republican,* August 5). This feature—if truly observed—makes the animal a mammal, not a reptile. Perhaps, as some have suggested, it was a zeuglodon, a snakelike whale thought to have become extinct some 20 million years ago.

The Twentieth-Century Monster

If anything, the confusion about Champ's identity has grown in the twentieth century. Indeed, the plesiosaurlike Champ would become the "classic" monster only in the 1970s. Elderly residents of the Champlain area would claim to recall seeing plesiosaurlike creatures—with long necks and bulky reptile bodies—earlier in the century. But investigators would suspect that their memories had been influenced by the monster's more recent image.

In fact, twentieth-century accounts before 1970 seemed to describe a variety of creatures. Huge snakes often were reported, as in the century before. Some mentioned scales, which snakes do not have. Others seemed to describe large fish, perhaps sturgeons. And in a few cases, sightings suggested (nonprehistoric) whales and eels.

In the summer of 1899, a witness reported seeing a 35-foot-long serpent with a broad, flat tail raised a few feet above the water.

In one of the very rare twentieth-century land sightings–this one made from a passing car in the spring of 1961—Thomas E. Morse reported what "appeared to be a monstrous eel with white teeth that raked rearward in the mouth." It was resting on the shore of Champlain's North West Bay.

A Champ sighting that took place in the summer of 1970 is particularly interesting. It involved separate witnesses and shows just how differently people can view the same thing. The *Plattsburgh Valley News* of August 9, 1978, published two accounts written by the witnesses, who had not spoken in the eight years since their shared sighting. Richard Spear recalled seeing the creature with his 13-year-old daughter as the two of them sat atop a ferry heading toward the Essex, New York, shore. Another ferry witness was Happy Marsh.

In her account, Marsh (who also claimed to have seen an identical animal in 1965 or 1966) described "a large snakelike creature, swimming with her head above water, held as snakes do, with coils behind." She guessed that it was "between 18 and 20 feet long.... It was black, and swimming slowly. Her head was three feet long, wrinkled like a raisin, with a small ridge down the back."

Spear, on the other hand, described an animal that looked more like a plesiosaur. It was barrel-shaped and had "two 'bumps' ... each rising to about three feet above the surface and four feet in length." When his daughter used binoculars, she saw its head, which she said looked like a horse's. The creature was "dark brownish-olive" in color.

Champ vs. the Loch Ness Monster

Reviewing Joseph W. Zarzynski's 1984 book *Champ: Beyond the Legend,* Henry H. Bauer, a leading expert on the **Loch Ness monster,** complained that the author's effort to link the two animals made little sense. He stated: "The listed sightings [of Champ] include a goodly number of descriptions as 'snakelike,' which has never been said of Nessie; smooth skin is reported whereas Nessie's is rough, warty; eyes are featured several times, and fins and manes, which are almost totally lacking in reports from Loch Ness."

Still, some clear reports of a Ness-like animal in Lake Champlain do exist. The "prehistoric monster" that Orville Wells saw in Champlain's Treadwell Bay in 1976 (and later sketched) resembled the creatures of Loch Ness. Several other witnesses have specifically said that what they saw looked like a "dinosaur." And the Mansi photograph–the most

Joseph Zarzynski, director of Lake Champlain Phenomena Investigation, readying a sonar tripod for use in his search for Champ.

important piece of evidence that Champ is real—clearly shows a plesiosaurlike animal.

The Mansi Photograph

In early July 1977, a Connecticut couple, Anthony and Sandra Mansi, were vacationing in Vermont. Just past Saint Alban's Bay and somewhere near the Canadian border, they stopped so that their two small children could play in Champlain's water. They parked their car and walked 100 to 200 feet across a field, then went down a six-foot bank to the waterline. As the children waded near the shore, Mansi went back to the car for his sunglasses and a camera.

Some moments later Mrs. Mansi noticed bubbles in the water about 150 feet away. Soon a huge animal with a small head, long neck, and humped back rose to the surface. Mrs. Mansi thought it looked prehistoric.

By this time her husband had returned, and he, too, watched the thing with growing alarm. He and Sandra called the children (who were unaware of what was happening in the water behind them and never saw the creature). Anthony tossed the camera to Sandra, telling her to take a picture. She took one photograph before the animal sank——it did not dive—under the water. The sighting lasted between two and four minutes.

Afraid that they would be ridiculed, the Mansis kept their experience a secret. They placed the photograph, which turned out quite well, in a family album! In time they lost the negative. Eventually Mrs. Mansi showed the picture to friends, and by 1980 rumors of it had reached Zarzynski, a social studies teacher in Wilton, New York. He won the couple's trust and began an investigation.

He showed the photograph to a number of experts, including George Zug at the Smithsonian Institution's Museum of Natural History. Zug said it resembled no known animal in the lake or elsewhere. Roy Mackal, biologist and vice president of the International Society of Cryptozoology, also examined it. Soon afterward B. Roy Freiden of the University of Arizona's Optical Sciences Center made a careful study of the photograph.

Freiden determined that the photograph had not been tampered with—no one had imposed Champ's image over a picture of the lake. The wave patterns around the animal also suggested that what Mrs. Mansi had observed was true: the "object" had come up from under the surface instead of moving along the water (as would be the case if it were, say, an artificial device being pulled by a rope).

Freiden could not make out the object's exact size because the photograph provided no other features for comparison. It did not, for example, show the shoreline, which would have helped investigators determine the size of the object and its distance from observers. But University of British Columbia oceanographer Paul LeBlond found another method for at least guessing at the size: by measuring the length of the waves around the object. Using wind speed and the distance of open water over which it blew, LeBlond figured that the waves in the photograph were between 16 and 39 feet long. Then that part of the "unknown object" above water was compared with the waves. It was determined that its length ranged from 24 to 78 feet!

If the enormous "object" in the photograph was artificial, what an extraordinary—and expensive—hoax! And if it was a trick, why did Mrs. Mansi wait for more than three years before allowing it to become public? And what is more, why would she take only *one* photograph? In all the time since the sighting, no evidence has emerged suggesting a hoax. The Mansi photograph remains a mystery. And it also supports the often-questioned link between Champ and Nessie.

The Continuing Investigation

In the 1970s Zarzynski formed the Lake Champlain Phenomena Investigation (LCPI). The LCPI interviews witnesses and searches for historical references to Champ. It also keeps a close eye on the lake—visually and electronically (so far with little results).

Nonetheless, the creature's existence may be based on hoaxes or mistaken identifications. Certainly the many different descriptions of the beast suggest that Champ is wholly imaginary or a catchall name for a variety of animals—some known but out of place, some unknown. Because Champlain is linked to the ocean, it is possible that oversized sea animals wandering in and out are behind the Champ legend. Better evidence is needed to get to the bottom of the mystery at Lake Champlain.

Sources:

Coleman, Loren, *Mysterious America,* Boston: Faber and Faber, 1983.
Zarzynski, Joseph W., *Champ: Beyond the Legend,* Port Henry, New York: Bannister Publications, 1984.

MORAG

On April 3, 1971, Ewen Gillies, a lifelong resident of a house overlooking Loch Morar, saw the creature for the first time. His 12-year-old son John had noticed it a few minutes before, while walking down a road near the shore. He told his father, who stepped outside on the clear, sunny morning and looked out at the lake. Not quite half a mile away, a huge animal lay in the water, its three- or four-foot neck pointed straight up and curving slightly at the top. It was hard to tell where the neck ended and the head began. Two or three humps moving up and down slightly ran along its back. The skin was black and shiny. The creature was around 30 feet long.

Gillies went into the house to get a camera. He took two pictures from an upstairs window just before the creature lowered its head, straightened its body, and sank below the surface. The pictures did not turn out, but no one accused Gillies of concocting the story, for Loch Morar's monster—Morag—had been seen before.

Loch Morar, Inverness, Scotland, haunt of Morag.

Early History

Morag comes from the Gaelic word *Mhorag,* the name of a monster that was once believed to be the spirit of the loch. A shape-changing mermaid, it was thought to mean death if glimpsed by a member of the Gillies clan, who had lived in the area for centuries. As time passed and people migrated from this wild, remote region of Scotland, the old folklore faded away. Morag was then considered a strange—but not super-natural—creature seen by some but rarely discussed.

Because of Morag's rich folkloric past, researchers have had difficulty tracing individual sightings back before the late nineteenth century. Interviews with elderly residents, however—like those by investigator Elizabeth Montgomery Campbell in the 1970s—have revealed that locals remember seeing the beast when they were young.

> ### LOCH MORAR
>
> Loch Morar is 70 miles southwest of Scotland's much more famous Loch Ness. Eleven miles long and a mile and a half across at its widest point, it is separated from the sea by only a quarter of a mile and is one of Scotland's deepest lakes. According to reports that go back decades (and perhaps even centuries), it is the home of monsters very much like those reported at Loch Ness and other Scottish and Irish lakes.

Witnesses

Lady Brinckman was one such witness; she lived on an estate near the loch around the turn of the century. She recalled an incident in the summer of 1895 in an unpublished memoir written decades later. She related that "one evening, it was getting towards dinner time and I was sitting looking back, when suddenly, I saw a great shape rise up out of the loch, a good way off." Asking her two male companions if it were a boat, one replied, "It'll just be the monster." He said such sightings of the monster were not uncommon.

Folklorist R. Macdonald Robertson recorded a story from Alexander Macdonnell describing an event that took place early in the century. "Some years ago, we were proceeding one morning down the loch in the estate motor launch from Meoble to Morar pier with some school-children and other persons on board," recalled the witness. "As we were passing Bracarina Point, on the north side, some of the children [excitedly] shouted out: 'Oh look! What is that big thing on the bank over there?' The beast would be about the size of a full-grown Indian elephant, and it plunged off the rocks into the water with a terrific splash." Robertson noted that a number of other reliable witnesses had seen Loch Morar's monster. One observer described the typical sighting, "a huge, shapeless, dark mass rising out of the water like a small island."

In September 1931 young Sir John Hope (Lord Glendevon) had an odd experience in the loch. While it involved no direct sighting, it clearly suggested the presence of some huge unknown animal. He, his brother, a friend, and a local guide had gone out on a boat to fish in a deep part of Morar. Hope, who was holding a long trout rod, felt something grab his line, dragging it "directly downwards at such a pace that it would have been madness to try and stop it with my fingers. In a very few seconds the whole line, including the backing, had gone and the end of the rod broke." Hope said that whatever took the bait was "something ... heavier than I have experienced before or since."

What could the creature have been? A salmon—if one that size even existed—would have traveled parallel to the surface of the water instead of making a steep vertical descent. A seal might swim downward, but no seals were known to live anywhere near Loch Morar. But such descents are described in a great many lake monster sightings. Glendevon recalled that when he and his companions asked their guide what the animal could have been, the man "mumbled something and said he thought we had better go home." Glendevon suspected that the guide knew more than he was telling.

The Loch Morar Survey

After 1933, the year the first photograph of the Loch Ness monster appeared, Morag also received some attention. A few witnesses came forward and described sightings of large, fast-moving humps in the

> "The beast would be about the size of a full-grown Indian elephant, and it plunged off the rocks into the water with a terrific splash."

Whatever took the bait was something heavier than Sir John Hope had ever experienced.

water or of long-necked creatures, usually about 30 feet long, in Loch Morar. In February 1970 several members of the Loch Ness Investigation Bureau formed the Loch Morar Survey. Over the next few years they launched investigations as their limited time and funds permitted. On July 14, 1970, one of them, marine biologist Neil Bass, spotted a "hump-shaped black object" in the lake. He called to his associates, but the hump disappeared before they had a chance to see it.

Bass reported that "within half a minute," though, "a disturbance was witnessed by all of us ... followed by radiating water rings which traveled to form a circle, at maximum 50 yards in diameter." It was made by something very large. Bass believed that the unknown "object" was a large living creature unfamiliar to him.

Perhaps the most dramatic Morag event recorded took place on August 16, 1969. It was also the only sighting ever to be reported in newspapers across the world. It occurred as two local men, Duncan McDonell and William Simpson, were on their way back from a fishing trip at the north end of the loch. It was just after 9 P.M. and the sun had gone down, but there was still plenty of light.

McDonell, who was at the wheel, turned around after hearing a splash behind them. To his amazement, a creature was coming directly toward them, at about 20 to 30 mph! Within seconds it struck the side of the boat, then slowed down or stopped. Though McDonell felt the collision was an accident, he was still afraid that the huge animal would overturn them. He grabbed an oar and tried to push it away. Meanwhile Simpson had rushed into the cabin to turn off the motor. He returned with a rifle and fired a single shot at the beast, seemingly with no effect. It moved away and sank out of sight. The incident lasted five minutes.

When interviewed by members of the Loch Ness Investigation Bureau, the two agreed that the creature had been some 25 to 30 feet long, with rough, dirty brown skin. Three humps, about 18 inches high, stood out of the water, and at one point McDonell had spotted the animal's snakelike head just above the surface.

Theories

Loch Morar lies in a deep valley carved out by glaciers on Scotland's west-central coast. Twelve thousand years ago, as the ice retreated, ocean water is believed to have entered the lake, bringing with it a wealth of sea life. Even after the saltwater retreated, for a few thousand years the sea animals in the loch might have found it fairly easy to return to their ocean home. For back then, sea level at high tide would have been within a few feet of loch level.

There is no doubt that Loch Morar has enough food—fish, plankton, and other living matter—to feed a population of large animals. It is one of nine Highland lakes with "monster" histories and reports. (Besides Ness, the others are Oich, Canisp, Assynt, Arkaig, Shiel, Lochy, and Quoich.) Most sightings at Morar and elsewhere describe creatures that resemble the supposedly long-extinct plesiosaur. If such animals survive, however (and there is no evidence to support this in fossil records), they would have had to adapt to far colder water temperatures than their ancestors were used to. Roy P. Mackal, a biologist with a keen interest in lake monsters, argues that Morag, Nessie, and their relatives are zeuglodons: primitive, snakelike whales generally thought to have become extinct some 20 million years ago.

Is the idea of surviving giant prehistoric reptiles and mammals too fantastic? The lake creatures that people report seeing often look like plesiosaurs and zeuglodons. It seems equally fantastic to explain away these sightings as something more acceptable—like sharks, seals, or seaweed, which these "monsters" simply do not resemble. In the meantime, the mystery at Loch Morar continues.

Sources:

Campbell, Elizabeth Montgomery, and David Solomon, *The Search for Morag,* New York: Walker and Company, 1973.

Holiday, F. W., *The Dragon and the Disc: An Investigation into the Totally Fantastic,* New York: W. W. Norton and Company, 1973.

Mackal, Roy P., *The Monsters of Loch Ness,* Chicago: The Swallow Press, 1976.

OGOPOGO

Around eight o'clock on a pleasant morning in mid-July 1974, a teenage girl was swimming just offshore in Lake Okanagan, located in the southern interior of British Columbia, Canada. She was heading for a raft a quarter of a mile from the beach and was only three feet from it when a huge, heavy something bumped against her legs. Surprised and frightened, she grabbed for the raft and climbed aboard.

From there she looked into the clear water and saw a strange animal 15 or 20 feet away. "I could see a hump or coil which was eight feet long and four feet above the water," she told J. Richard Greenwell of the International Society of Cryptozoology more than a decade later. "It was traveling ... away from me ... and it swam very slowly.... Five to 10 feet behind the hump, about five to eight feet below the surface, I could see its tail. The tail was forked and horizontal like a whale's, and it was four to six feet wide. As the hump submerged, the tail came to the surface until its tip poked above the water about a foot." Soon the girl lost sight of the creature. The whole experience had lasted just four or five minutes.

Another witness, Mrs. B. Clark, told Greenwell that the animal was a "very dull dark gray" color and moved in an undulating or wavy manner. She had the "impression that the head joined the body without a neck—like a fish or snake....This thing looked more like a whale than a fish, but I have never seen a whale that skinny and snaky-looking before."

The Zeuglodon

But in fact, such a whale existed, at least at one time. Evidence of the animal has been found in fossils, but these are 20 million years old or more. Known to zoologists and paleontologists, the creature is the *Basilosaurus,* or zeuglodon. For decades, something very much like it has been reported in Lake Okanagan. Since 1926 the animal has been called Ogopogo (the word taken from a song).

Despite its silly name, Ogopogo is one of the most credible of the world's lake monsters. Reports of it are strikingly similar. And they do not include the giant serpents found in folklore or the plesiosaurlike creatures made famous at Loch Ness. What is more, zeuglodons are known to only a few people, mainly paleontologists and cryptozoologists.

American Indians living on or around Lake Okanagan were familiar with Ogopogo long before the white settlers came to the area. *Naitaka,* the serpentlike creature, figured in many of their supernatural legends. Around 1860, when the first white settlers arrived in the Lake Okanagan area, they too began to suspect that strange animals lived in the water. One early sighting by settlers took place in the mid-1870s, when two witnesses on opposite sides of the lake watched a long, snakelike creature swim against the wind and current. At first both observers had mistaken the object for a log. Over the years many other witnesses would describe "logs that came alive."

By the 1920s hunting parties from Canada and the United States scoured Okanagan, hoping to kill a specimen. Sightings continued on and off over the decades. One of the more impressive accounts took place on July 2, 1949, in the early evening, when a party aboard an offshore boat saw a strange animal 100 feet away. It had a "forked" horizontal tail like a whale and moved its snakelike body in an undulating manner (reptiles move from side to side, not up and down). About 30 feet of a smooth, dark back was visible. The head was under water, perhaps feeding. Another witness saw the creature from land.

More Sightings

A 1967 sighting by nearly 20 people at Okanagan's southern tip made the whale identification even stronger: "It had a head like a bucket and was spouting water," one witness said. On July 30, 1989, when Ogopogo appeared 1,000 feet away from an investigative team of the British Columbia Cryptozoology Club, John Kirk got a clear view through a telescope. "The animal's skin was whale-like," he reported.

Looking at more than 200 Ogopogo reports collected by Mary Moon, University of Chicago biologist Roy P. Mackal put together this general description: "The animals look most like a log, elongated, serpentine, no thickened body centrally, about 12 meters [40 feet long], although a range of smaller sizes has been reported and a few larger, up to say 20 meters [70 feet]." He noted that the skin was generally smooth and dark green, brown, or black in color, although a few plates or scales had been reported by close observers. "Most of the back is smooth," he added, "although a portion is saw-toothed, ragged-edged, or serrated. Sparse hair or hair-bristle structures are reported around the head, and

Ogopogo, monster of British Columbia's Lake Okanagan and star of "Ogopogo Days."

in a few cases a mane or comblike structure has been observed at the back of the neck."

To Mackal, these features "fit one and only one known creature"—the zeuglodon. He noted that identical animals had been reported off the coast of British Columbia and in other Canadian lakes. Mackal suggested that Ogopogos were freshwater-adapted versions of the prehistoric zeuglodon, which lived in the oceans.

Since there are no convincing photographs of Ogopogo and no sonar (sound wave) traces or other evidence from instruments, the case for Ogopogo rests entirely on eyewitness testimony.

Sources:

Conklin, Ellis E., "Ogopogo Brouhaha," *Seattle Post-Intelligencer,* March 7, 1991.

Greenwell, J. Richard, "Interview: The Lady of the Lake Talks about Ogopogo," *The ISC Newsletter* 5,6, summer 1986, pp. 1-3.

Mackal, Roy P., *Searching for Hidden Animals,* Garden City, New York: Doubleday and Company, 1980.

WHITE RIVER MONSTER

From about 1915 through the early 1970s, residents of Newport, in northeastern Arkansas, reported seeing a "monster" in the White River, which flows through the town. Sightings were not continuous but tended to occur in bunches. In July 1937, for example, a number of local people saw either strange disturbances in the water or caught glimpses of the creature.

One witness was Bramblett Bateman, who gave sworn testimony that he had seen, on or around July 1, "something appear on the surface of the water." Because he was 375 feet away from the creature, he could not make out its full length or size but guessed that it was around "12 feet long and four or five feet wide." Nor could he make out its head or tail. The animal remained in its position for about five minutes. In later sightings, Bateman saw the creature "move up and down the river."

Jackson County Deputy Sheriff Z. B. Reid was with Bateman when the creature appeared later that July day. They saw "a lot of foam and bubbles coming up in a circle about 30 feet in diameter some 300 feet" from them. Then, many feet farther up the river, the creature surfaced. To Reid, it looked like a "large sturgeon or cat fish. It went down in about two minutes."

The next widely reported series of sightings occurred in June and July 1971. One witness reported seeing a "creature the size of a boxcar thrashing." He added that "it looked as if the thing was peeling all over, but it was a smooth type of skin or flesh." Another witness took a blurry photograph of a large surfacing form on June 28. The witness also described the monster's roar, a combination of a cow's lowing and a horse's whinny. Other observers also reported the roar. And on those rare occasions when the animal's face was briefly seen, it was said to have a jutting "bone" on its forehead.

A Frightening Experience

Ollie Ritcherson and Joey Dupree's brush with the White River monster was the most frightening. They were cruising near Towhead Island looking for the creature when their boat collided with something. Their vessel rose in the air on the back of some huge animal that they were not clearly able to see. The pair had come to the site because two weeks earlier huge tracks leading to and from the river had been found on the island. Each of the three-toed tracks was 14 inches long

> They were cruising near Towhead Island looking for the creature when their boat collided with something. Their vessel rose in the air on the back of some huge animal that they were not clearly able to see.

Could an elephant seal, like the one shown here, have wandered away from its normal habitat and adopted the White River as its home?

and eight inches wide, with a large pad and another toe with a spur extending at an angle. There was evidence, in the form of bent trees and crushed plants, that a large animal had walked on the island and even laid down there.

To biologist Roy P. Mackal, the case of the White River monster seemed "a clear-cut instance of a known aquatic animal outside its normal habitat or range and therefore unidentified by the observers unfamiliar with the type. The animal in question clearly was a large male

THE ELEPHANT SEAL

The elephant seal, or sea elephant, is the largest of the fin-footed mammals or pinnipeds (the groups of meat-eating water mammals, like seals and walruses, whose four limbs are flippers); it is even larger than the walrus. Males commonly reach 18 feet in length and can weigh up to 5,000 pounds. The male has a flabby snout of about 18 inches that inflates with air when the animal is excited or angry; release of the air produces a deep roar.

elephant seal." He suggested that the creature wandered up through the mouth of the Mississippi River to the White River, which branches off in east-central Arkansas.

Sources:

Mackal, Roy P., *Searching for Hidden Animals: An Inquiry into Zoological Mysteries,* Garden City, New York: Doubleday and Company, 1980.

Folklore in the Flesh

- **FLYING DRAGONS AND OTHER SKY SERPENTS**

- **FAIRIES**

- **COTTINGLEY FAIRY PHOTOGRAPHS**

- **MERFOLK**

- **WEREWOLVES**

- **THUNDERBIRDS**

- **THE SEARCH FOR NOAH'S ARK**

Folklore in the Flesh

Woodcut from c. 1500 of an armored knight being chased by a flying dragon.

FLYING DRAGONS AND OTHER SKY SERPENTS

From ancient times through the twentieth century, sightings of flying dragons and snakes have been recorded. Such stories first appeared in medieval writings. Henry, Archdeacon of Huntington in medieval England, noted in *Historia Anglorum* that in A.D. 774, "red signs appeared in the sky after sunset, and horrid serpents were seen in Sudsexe, with great amazement." Nineteen years later a similar sight was recorded and construed as a sign of worse things to come: "Terrible portents appeared.... These were exceptional flashes of lightning, and fiery dragons were seen flying in the air, and soon followed a great famine."

According to the publication *Knighton's Continuator,* in April 1388 a "flying dragon was seen ... in many places." On December 5, 1762, a "twisting serpent" lit up the sky as it slowly lowered itself over Bideford, Devonshire, England, then disappeared. It had been visible for six minutes.

Though we expect to read of unbelievable magical events in early writings, like those of the Middle Ages, it can be disturbing to find them recorded in fairly recent times. In the mid-1800s, for example, Nebraska settlers claimed to have witnessed equally strange sights. Western historian Mari Sandoz noted that "back in the hard times of 1857-58 there were stories of a flying serpent that hovered over a Missouri River steamboat slowing for a landing. In the late dusk it was like a great undulating [wavy] serpent, in and out of the lowering clouds, breathing fire, it seemed, with lighted streaks along the sides." A frontier folksong from the period refers to a "flyin' engine/ Without no wing or wheel/ It came a-roarin' in the sky/ With lights along the side/ And scales like a serpent's hide."

The song's mention of a "flyin' engine" may suggest that the object was some sort of unearthly machine (UFO?) rather than a living creature—but other tales seem to demonstrate otherwise. In June 1873 farmers near Bonham, Texas, saw an "enormous serpent" in a cloud and were "seriously frightened." The *Bonham Enterprise* reported: "It seemed to be as large and as long as a telegraph pole, was of a yellow striped color, and seemed to float along without effort. They could see it coil itself up, turn over, and thrust forward its huge head as if striking at something, displaying the maneuvers of a genuine snake."

When the *New York Times* heard of the account a few days later, it called it "the very worst case of delirium tremens on record." The *Times* had nothing to say about another incident, however, that was recorded in a Kansas newspaper, the *Fort Scott Monitor,* a few days earlier. Its June 27 issue reported that at sunrise on the previous morning, "when the disc of the sun was about halfway above the horizon, the form of a huge serpent, apparently perfect in form, was plainly seen encircling it and was visible for some moments."

Since frontier newspapers were full of practical jokes and tall tales, it is hard to take many of these accounts of flying serpents seriously. Consider this story of a man who signed himself "R. B." in a letter to the editor of the *Frederick News,* a Maryland paper, on November 29, 1883. He reported that at 6:30 one morning, while he was standing on

A dragon.

a hilltop, a "monstrous dragon with glaring eye-balls, and mouth wide open displaying a tongue, which hung like a flame of fire from its jaws, reared and plunged" in the sky over Catoctin Mountain.

More Flying Snakes and Other Terrors

In the late 1930s, J. L. B. Smith, a South African chemist with a keen interest in ichthyology (the study of fish), and an associate, Marjorie Courtenay-Latimer, made zoological history when they discovered the coelacanth, a large fish that—to that point—had only been known through fossil records and was thought to have been extinct for some 60 million years.

Smith was also fascinated by reports of other animals generally thought to no longer exist. For a time he exchanged letters with members of a German missionary family; they told him that while living near Mount Kilimanjaro (in northeast Tanzania near the Kenya border), one of them had had a close sighting of a "flying dragon." But the creature was known even before this incident, from the many accounts that native witnesses had reported.

Flying snake.

For her part, Courtenay-Latimer once investigated reports of similar creatures in southern Namibia (then South-West Africa). In one case, native shepherds had walked off their jobs after complaining that their employer, the white owner of a large ranch, did not take their reports of a large flying snake that lived in the nearby mountains seriously. With no one left to watch the livestock, the farmer sent his 16-year-old son to the site. When the boy failed to return that evening, a search party set out to the mountains to look for him. He was found unconscious.

Even after regaining consciousness, the young man could not speak for three days because—his doctor said—he was in shock. Finally, the son related that he had been relaxing beneath a tree when a sudden roaring noise, like a powerful wind current, startled him. As he looked up, he saw a huge "snake" flying down from a ridge. The closer it got, the louder the roaring became. All around the sheep were scattering. The creature landed in a cloud of dust. The boy noticed a strong odor, like burned brass, and at this point passed out.

Courtenay-Latimer arrived on the scene soon afterward. She interviewed witnesses, including other farmers and local police officers, and examined some marks that the creature had reportedly left on the ground. She was told that police had seen the creature disappear into a crack in the mountain; sticks of dynamite were thrown into the opening, which, on combustion, brought a low moaning sound from within—and then silence. The creature was never seen again.

Roy P. Mackal, a scientist who investigates and writes about mysterious animals, contacted Courtenay-Latimer about the account some years later. He wrote, "A snake, even a very large one, hurtling or falling over a ledge or mountain precipice hardly would disturb the air as described. In fact, it is hard to attribute such a disturbance even to a large gliding creature, suggesting instead that some kind of wing action must have been involved." And he wondered, "Could some species of pterodactyl with elongated body and tail still survive?"

In another instance, the *New York Times* reported that on May 27, 1888, in Darlington County, South Carolina, three women strolling through the woods "were suddenly startled by the appearance of a huge serpent moving through the air above them. The serpent was ... sailing through the air with a speed equal to that of a hawk or buzzard but without any visible means of propulsion." According to the account, the frightening creature was around 15 feet long and "was also seen by a number of people in other parts of the county early in the afternoon of the same day." These observers noted that the animal made "a hissing noise which could be distinctly heard."

Sources:

Evans, Jonathan D., "The Dragon," *Mythical and Fabulous Creatures: A Source Book and Research Guide,* edited by Malcolm South, New York: Greenwood Press, 1987.
Sandoz, Mari, *Love Songs to the Plains,* Lincoln, Nebraska: University of Nebraska Press, 1966.

FAIRIES

As he walked down a country road near Barron, Wisconsin, one summer night in 1919, 13-year-old Harry Anderson saw a very strange sight. The bright moonlight revealed 20 little men, walking in single file in his direction! But when they passed, they paid no attention to him. Young Anderson noticed that the men were dressed in leather knee pants held up by suspenders. They wore no shirts, were bald, and their skin was pale white. Though all were making "mumbling" sounds, they did not seem to be communicating with one another. Terrified, Anderson continued on his way and did not look back. The bizarre event remained vivid in his memory for the rest of his life.

To most people in the modern world, fairies are no more than imaginary creatures. They are usually seen in children's entertainment and are almost always portrayed as tiny, winged, and good-hearted. This widespread version of the fairy comes from romantic literature. It does not reflect worldwide fairy folklore, where the beings are described very differently.

Tradition and Its Mysteries

A century or two ago, Anderson would have had little doubt about the identity of the strange figures he had come upon. This would be especially true if he had lived in a Celtic country (Brittany, Ireland, Scotland, Wales), where, according to popular belief, the roads, rocks, caves, fields, rivers, lakes, and forests abounded with creatures of highly unpredictable natures.

Contrary to popular modern images, the fairies of folklore never had wings and were not necessarily kind-hearted.

Only the unwise and unwary called these creatures "fairies," because they did not like to hear their proper name spoken. Because a fairy could be listening at any time, Celtic countryfolk used various flattering names—such as the "good people," the "Gentry," the "honest folk," or the "fair tribe," to describe them.

There was a wide variety of fairy folk. Still, they were more or less human in form, though sometimes taller or shorter (and never bore wings, despite popular modern portrayals). And their behavior was recognizably human. They had governments, societies, occupations, art and music, and conflicts. They married, had children, waged war, and died. At the same time they possessed supernatural powers—which made them bewildering and sometimes dangerous. Few human beings wanted the company of fairies, and most went out of their way to avoid them!

How fairy beliefs began is, according to Stewart Sanderson, "one of the most difficult problems in the study of folklore." Folklorists and anthropologists have theorized that the original fairies were perhaps human members of conquered races who took to the hills to escape their captors and whose descendants were sighted at rare times and mistaken for supernatural beings. It has also been suggested that fairies were the old gods and spirits that man believed in before modern religions took hold. And sometimes, in Christian countries, fairies have been associated with fallen angels. Regardless of origin, belief in fairies has existed in practically every traditional culture. Indeed, the notion that hidden races share the earth with us has been around for most of human history.

An Early Study

Folklorists have learned about fairies through myths, legends, and tales told by countryfolk or found in old printed sources. One of the great early studies on the subject was Robert Kirk's *The Secret Common-Wealth* (1691). Kirk was a Presbyterian clergyman of the Scottish Highlands who had a keen interest in the supernatural lore of the area. He was convinced that fairies were real, for how could such a widespread belief, he asked, "spring of nothing?" For Kirk, fairies were of a "middle nature between man and angel," with bodies "somewhat of the nature of a condensed cloud," and dressed and spoke "like the people and country under which they [lived]." They were usually invisible to the human eye but could sometimes be heard. They often traveled through the air and could steal anything they liked, from food to human babies! People with "second sight" (psychics) were sometimes more able to see them.

Few modern scholars have admitted to believing in fairies. The major exception was W. Y. Evans-Wentz, author of the well-regarded *The Fairy-Faith in Celtic Countries,* first published in 1911. Evans-Wentz, an anthropologist of religion with a Ph.D. from Oxford University, traveled throughout the British Isles and Brittany, on France's northwest coast, and reported the results in a thick book that remains a classic of folklore studies. Evans-Wentz also believed in genies, demons, and other extraordinary beings.

Bad Luck Follows Capture

Years ago, when belief in fairies was still strong, folklorists were able to collect firsthand accounts from fairy witnesses. One such tale was told by an old, blind Irish farmer. The farmer claimed that some years earlier he had captured a fairy, a dark-skinned, two-foot-high figure wearing a red cap, green clothes, and boots.

"I gripped him close in my arms and took him home," the farmer related. "I called to the woman [the farmer's wife] to look at what I had got. 'What doll is it you have there?' she cried. 'A living one,' I said, and put it on the dresser. We feared to lose it; we kept the door locked. It talked and muttered to itself queer words.... It might have been near a fortnight since we had the fairy, when I said to the woman, 'Sure, if we show it in the great city we will be made up [rich].' So we put it in a cage. At night we would leave the cage door open, and we would hear it stirring through the house."

Soon, however, the fairy escaped. Not long afterward the man lost his sight. Other bad luck befell the couple—which the man viewed as the fairy's punishment for its imprisonment.

Midwife to a Troll

Another, earlier fairy episode had a happier ending. It was related in a sworn statement given by Swedish clergyman P. Rahm on April 12, 1671. It seems that late one evening 11 years earlier as he and his wife were sitting and talking in their farmhouse, a little man came to their door. Apparently the fellow's wife was in childbirth, and he begged Mrs. Rahm to go with him and help her. The couple did not know what to do, for they knew that the little man—"of a dark complexion, and dressed in old gray clothes" was a troll. They feared letting Mrs. Rahm go with him, but they also feared the evil that trolls were known to bring upon humans who did not treat them respectfully. After the little man repeated his request several times, Mr. Rahm "read some prayers over [my] wife to bless her, and bid her in God's name go with him."

Mrs. Rahm reported that she seemed to travel on the wind to the little man's dwelling, where his wife lay, in much pain, in a small, dark room. With Mrs. Rahm's help, however, the troll's wife delivered a healthy child. The little man thanked Mrs. Rahm, and she was carried home on the wind as before. The next day, she found pieces of silver on a shelf in the farmhouse sitting room.

Grateful Fairies

Mari Sion of Llanddeusant, Anglesey, Wales, told a folklorist of her own early twentieth-century experience with a fairy family. She recalled that one moonlit night, as she, her husband, and their chil-

With Mrs. Rahm's help, the troll's wife delivered a healthy child. The little man thanked Mrs. Rahm, and she was carried home on the wind.

dren were sitting by the fire, there was a knock on their door. The callers were a man, woman, and baby. The largest of them, the man, was only two feet tall. "I should be thankful for the loan of a bowl with water and a coal of fire," the woman said. "I should like to wash this little child. I do not want them at once. We shall come again after you have gone to bed."

Mrs. Sion put out the requested items before she and her family went to bed. During the night they could hear the comings and goings of the little people. In the morning, the Sions found everything in order, except for the bowl, which lay upside down. Underneath it were four shillings.

Other Sightings

Edward Williams, a respected British clergyman, wrote about a fairy experience he had had in 1757, when he was seven years old. Playing in a field in Wales with some friends, Williams and his companions saw seven or eight tiny couples dressed in red—each figure carrying a white kerchief—some 100 yards away. One of the little men chased the children and nearly caught one, who, according to Williams, got a "full and clear view of his ancient, swarthy, grim complexion" before escaping. During the chase one of the other figures shouted at the pursuer in an unknown language. The incident puzzled Dr. Williams all of his life.

The Rev. Sabine Baring-Gould, a nineteenth-century historian and folklorist, also wrote about his fairy experience as a child. When he was four years old and traveling in a carriage with his parents, "I saw legions of dwarfs of about two feet high running along beside the horses; some sat laughing on the pole, some were scrambling up the harness to get on the backs of the horses." His parents saw nothing. Baring-Gould's wife and son also experienced fairy sightings.

One moonlit night in 1842, a Stowmarket, England, man came upon strange fairy activity. He related the incident to a local historian. While passing through a meadow he spotted a dozen fairies, "the biggest about three feet high, and small ones like dolls. Their dresses sparkled as if with spangles.... They were moving round hand in hand in a ring, no noise came from them. They seemed light and shadowy, not like solid bodies." He could not see their faces because he was some distance away. Fearful that the fairies would discover him, he sped home. When the man brought three companions back to the site to observe the fairies, they were gone.

> While passing through a meadow, he spotted a dozen fairies, "the biggest about three feet high, and small ones like dolls. Their dresses sparkled as if with spangles."

Over a century later, on April 30, 1973, an educated London woman named Mary Treadgold was traveling by bus through the Highlands of Scotland. When the vehicle pulled over to the side of a narrow road near the town of Mull to let an oncoming car pass by, Treadgold reflexively glanced out the window. There, in a peat field, she saw a "small figure, about 18 inches high, a young man with his foot on a spade ... arrested in the act of digging." She noted that "he had a thin, keen face" and brightly colored clothing. A tiny sack "stood at his side. He was ... not a dwarf, nor a child, nor ... a plastic garden gnome. He was a perfectly formed living being like any of us, only in miniature." When the bus resumed its course, the figure was lost from view. Later, when Treadgold asked a Highland acquaintance about the sighting, the woman related that "friends of hers had seen similar small people on Mull, and that Mull was known for this."

Fairy Music

Many people claimed to have heard fairy music. Isle of Man fiddler William Cain swore he heard music coming from a brightly lit glass palace that he spotted one night in a mountain glen. He stopped and listened, then went home and learned the tune, which he later performed widely. In the summer of 1922, while sitting on the bank of England's Teign River, composer Thomas Wood heard a strange voice calling him by his first name. Though he searched with binoculars, he could not find the speaker. Then he heard, "overhead, faint as a breath," then ever louder, "music in the air. It lasted 20 minutes," he told writer Harold T. Wilkins. "Portable wireless sets [radios] were unknown in 1922.... This music ... sounded like the weaving together of tenuous fairy sounds." Listening with great care, he wrote down the notes.

In 1972, while strolling along the shore of a peninsula in Scotland's Western Highlands, American folksinger Artie Traum heard "thousands of voices" chanting in a strange harmony to the sound of fiddles and pipes.

Today, belief in fairies is all but extinct. That is, except in Iceland, where a recent university survey showed that as much as 55 percent of the population thought the existence of elves (*huldufolk* or "hidden people") certain, probable, or possible. Only 10 percent rejected the idea altogether. Belief is so strong there that construction and road projects are sometimes delayed so that psychics can negotiate with the invisible folk who dwell in Icelandic fields, forests, rocks, and harbors. A 1990 *Wall Street Journal* article noted that "humans and huldufolk usu-

Jacques F. Vallee

(1910-1986)

Jacques Francis Vallee was born in France. After receiving a master's degree in astrophysics, he moved to the United States. While attending Northwestern University, he met J. Allen Hynek, chief scientific consultant on UFOs to the Air Force (also see entry: Unidentified Flying Objects), who headed the astronomy department. Hynek, a one-time UFO doubter, was becoming convinced that there was much to be learned from open-minded UFO research. After Vallee and Hynek began meeting to discuss their views in 1963, Hynek completely broke with the Air Force's anti-UFO line.

Vallee obtained his Ph.D. and ran a computer business, but continued writing and investigating UFOs. In his 1969 book *Passport to Magonia*, he surprised his readers by suggesting that UFO phenomena were beyond science's ability to describe and categorize. To understand UFOs, he said, one would need to immerse oneself in traditional supernatural beliefs in fairies and other fabulous beings.

Vallee believed that most unexplained sightings had their origins in another reality beyond our knowledge. Therefore UFOs and other oddities appear to us in the ways our culture conditions us to expect. Thus, a nineteenth-century Irish peasant saw elves, while his or her modern counterpart might see extraterrestrial humanoids. Vallee wrote many books arguing that UFOs are neither space visitors nor hallucinatory "psychosocial" phenomena; he believed that UFOs are supernatural occurrences.

ally get on well. Midwives have told [folklorist Hallfredur] Eiriksson about delivering elf babies. Farmers say they have milked elf cows. Sometimes, the two peoples fall in love, though affairs of the heart often end badly."

Fairies or Aliens?

It is likely that most fairy sightings would be reported differently today; in this age of UFOs, an encounter with "little people" would no doubt be treated as a meeting with space visitors. In fact, UFO literature contains a handful of incidents that feature elements one might find in traditional fairy lore.

Some writers, in fact, have suggested that UFO sightings and fairy experiences are one and the same. In his *Passport to Magonia* (1969), Jacques Vallee wrote that supernatural shape-shifting beings exist, and that they can appear—depending on the observer's beliefs—as fairies or extraterrestrials. More recent theorists, like Hilary Evans, writing in *Gods, Spirits, Cosmic Guardians* (1987), argue that all encounters with extraordinary beings occur in altered states of consciousness and are hallucinations. Though this psychosocial explanation seems to make some sense, it is actually as weak as the far-fetched ideas of Vallee. Both theories lack physical evidence to support them.

Sources:

Briggs, Katherine, *An Encyclopedia of Fairies: Hobgoblins, Brownies, Bogies, and Other Supernatural Creatures,* New York: Pantheon Books, 1976.

Doyle, Arthur Conan, *The Coming of the Fairies,* New York: George H. Doran Company, 1922.

Evans, Hilary, *Gods, Spirits, Cosmic Guardians: A Comparative Study of the Encounter Experience,* Wellingborough, Northamptonshire, England: The Aquarian Press, 1987.

Vallee, Jacques, *Passport to Magonia: From Folklore to Flying Saucers,* Chicago: Henry Regnery Company, 1969.

COTTINGLEY FAIRY PHOTOGRAPHS

In 1917 two young English girls, Frances Griffiths, 10, and her 13-year-old cousin Elsie Wright, were living in Cottingley, near Bradford, Yorkshire. Frances's father was a soldier fighting in World War I; she and her mother were staying at the Wright house until he returned home. One day Frances entered the house soaking wet and claimed that she had fallen into the brook while playing with the

Frances Griffiths and the Cottingley fairies.

fairies the girls had befriended in a nearby glen. Her mother did not believe her, and Frances was punished.

Feeling sorry for her cousin and best friend, Elsie hit upon an idea: they would borrow her father's camera and photograph the fairies.

Elsie told her father that she was going to take a picture of her cousin, and he gave her his camera and a single glass plate (which was used in photography before the advent of film). An hour later the girls returned and said that they now had proof that the fairies were real. When Elsie's doubting father developed the picture he saw an image of Frances facing the camera as four miniature winged women dressed in filmy clothing danced in front of her!

The girls refused to admit that they had photographed paper cutouts, even though their parents were certain that they had. Still, one month later, Mr. Wright gave the girls the camera and another plate. They returned with a second picture, this time showing a sitting Elsie signaling an elflike figure to jump up on her lap! Convinced that the joke was getting out of hand, Wright barred the girls from using the camera again.

Before the war Frances had lived in South Africa. When she wrote a friend there she enclosed copies of the two fairy photographs. On the back of one she noted, "Elsie and I are very freindly [sic] with the beck [brook] fairies. It is funny I did not see them in Africa. It must be to [sic] hot for them there." When rediscovered and published (in the *Cape Town Argus,* November 25, 1922), Frances's words would be taken as evidence of the girls' sincerity and the photographs' authenticity.

When Elsie's doubting father developed the picture he saw an image of Frances facing the camera as four miniature winged women dressed in filmy clothing danced in front of her!

The Case

The photographs would become the subject of one the strangest and most hotly debated cases in the history of photography. When Polly Wright, Elsie's mother, attended a lecture on folklore in 1920, she mentioned the photographs to the speaker. He requested the prints, which were shown to H. Snelling, an expert on photography. Snelling's pronouncement that the pictures were genuine would be quoted for decades afterward. (It would not be known until 1983 that he had retouched the first photograph—badly over-exposed—transforming it into the clear version that was widely seen.)

A well-known London figure, Edward L. Gardner, befriended the Wrights. At the urging of Sherlock Holmes author Sir Arthur Conan Doyle, Gardner took the photos to the Kodak laboratory in London. There, Doyle reported, "two experts were unable to find any flaw, but refused to testify to the genuineness of them, in view of some possible trap." When Gardner gave Elsie a modern camera, she and Frances provided three more fairy photographs!

In December 1920 *The Strand* magazine published Doyle's article on the first two pictures, and the next March a follow-up piece included the later three. The story received worldwide publicity. Much of it was unfavorable, though, focusing on how the illustrious author could have fallen for such an obvious hoax.

Cottingley photograph of Elsie Wright and fairy.

Yet attempts to discredit the photographs were not successful. Models for the Cottingley fairy figures could not be found. Furthermore, when spiritualist Geoffrey Hodson visited the beck in the girls' company, he reported seeing many such beings.

There would be no more Cottingley fairy photographs after that. Still, the mystery lived on. Doyle wrote an entire book on the case, *The Coming of the Fairies,* in 1922. In 1945 Gardner published a book-length account of the episode, and the photographs were reprinted in newspapers and magazines from time to time. Elsie and Frances seemed to stand by the pictures, but gave vague answers when asked about them. Then, in 1972, Elsie sent two cameras, along with other materials related to the case, to Sotheby's (an auction house) for sale; with them she included a letter confessing for the first time that the photographs were fakes. Sotheby's returned the letter, failing to recognize what it had in its possession.

In the early 1980s the *British Journal of Photography* began a reinvestigation of the case, based on research by editor Geoffrey Crawley. Frances and Elsie gave him their signed, formal confessions in early 1983. The two had agreed that the truth—that the pictures were a "practical joke" that "fell flat on its face"—would be withheld until the deaths of the photographs' major supporters, Doyle, Gardner, and Gardner's son Leslie.

A gifted young artist, Elsie had created the figures using fairies pictured in a popular children's book, *Princess Mary's Gift Book,* as her models. But to the end, the two women would not reveal the photographic techniques they used, promising to reveal them in books they were writing. Both died, however, before finishing the works. Nonetheless, Frances would always insist that while the photographs were fake, she *had* seen real fairies in the beck!

Sources:

Doyle, Arthur Conan, *The Coming of the Fairies,* New York: George H. Doran Company, 1922.
Gardner, Edward L., *Fairies: The Cottingley Photographs and Their Sequel,* London: Theosophical Publishing House, 1945.
Vallee, Jacques, *Passport to Magonia: From Folklore to Flying Saucers,* Chicago: Henry Regnery Company, 1969.

MERFOLK

Belief in merfolk—mermaids and mermen—has been around since ancient times. The Babylonian god Oannes, who rose from the Erythraean Sea to grant knowledge and culture to the human race, was said to be human to the waist and fish-shaped from the waist down. Merfolk-like gods and goddesses were also worshiped in Syria, India, China, Greece, and Rome. In later centuries a worldwide folklore would develop around these creatures and actual sightings would be claimed.

One of the earliest people to write about the creatures was first-century Roman naturalist Pliny the Elder. He had no doubt that Merfolk existed because of the many sightings reported by coastal residents. He even noted, "Many of these Nereides or Mermaids were seen cast upon the sands, and lying dead."

In northern Europe the merfolk legend took on a different twist; seal-folk or selkies were seals when they lived in the water. But when they wished to pass themselves off as people on land, they simply removed their seal skins! In many folktales merfolk do the same. They shed their fishy forms, marry land-bound mortals, and

> **THE GREY SELKIE OF SULE SKERRIE, A CLASSIC FOLK BALLAD**
>
> I am a man upon the land
> I am a selkie [seal]
> in the sea.

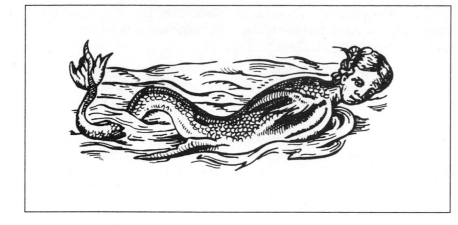

For a sailor, seeing a mermaid was often a sign of coming death at sea.

even have children. Then an overwhelming homesickness for the sea overtakes them, and they are gone in a splash.

Sailors usually interpreted the sighting of a mermaid as a sign of coming death, often in the fierce storm that would frequently follow such a visitation. In the traditional ballad "The Mermaid," a ship's crew spots one of the creatures sitting on a rock with a comb and a glass in its hand. The captain states: "This fishy mermaid has warned me of our doom/ And we shall sink to the bottom of the sea ..../ And three times around spun our gallant ship .../ And she went to the bottom of the sea."

Merfolk of Scotland

But mermaids were more than legendary creatures. Actual sightings by reliable witnesses were reported throughout the Middle Ages. And such sightings continued into modern times.

On January 12, 1809, two women standing on a beach at Sandside, Caithness, in remote northeastern Scotland, saw what looked like the face of a young woman—"round and plump and of a bright pink hue"— in the sea. The creature then disappeared into the water, reappearing a short time later. When the women were able to observe more of its body, they could see that it had well-formed human breasts. From time to time it lifted a long, thin white arm above the waves and tossed back its long green hair.

After one of the witnesses published her account of the sighting, William Munro wrote a letter to the *London Times* (September 8, 1809) recalling his own mermaid experience. Twelve years earlier, while walking along the shore of Sandside Bay, he spotted what looked like "an unclothed female, sitting upon a rock extending into the sea, and apparently in the action of combing its hair, which flowed around its shoulders, and was of a light brown color."

Munro reported that the creature's "forehead was round, the face plump, the cheeks ruddy, the eyes blue, the mouth and lips of a natural form," and that "the breasts and the abdomen, the arms and fingers [were] of the size of a full-grown body of the human species." The creature did not seem to notice him as he watched, and it continued to comb its hair, "which was long and thick, and of which it appeared to be proud." Then, after a few minutes, the mermaid slipped back into the sea.

It seemed that such creatures were particularly active off the coast of Scotland during this period. In a long survey of mermaid and merman sightings, the *London Mirror* of November 16, 1822, listed a similar account officially sworn to by young John McIsaac. On the afternoon of October 13, 1811, the fellow saw a strange creature "on a black rock on the seacoast." He stated that "the upper half of it was white, and of the shape of a human body" (though its arms were unusually short), while its bottom half was scaly, shiny, and ranged from reddish-grey to reddish-green in color. "The animal was between four and five feet long" and had a tail that it spread "like a fan."

As with Munro's mermaid, the creature McIsaac observed had long hair that it liked to stroke. After two hours of lying on the rock, McIsaac's creature "tumbled clumsily into the sea," allowing him to see "every feature of its face, having all the appearance of a human being." Because the creature was now half covered with water and was "constantly, with both hands stroking and washing its breasts," McIsaac could not tell if it was a female. The animal eventually disappeared.

Five days later another eyewitness gave sworn testimony before the same local sheriff as had McIsaac. Katherine Loynachan stated that on the afternoon of October 13, the same time day on which McIsaac had spotted his mermaid, as she was herding cattle near the seashore, she saw a creature slide off one of the rocks and drop into the water, surfacing six yards out. It had long, dark hair, white skin on its upper body, and dark brown skin on its lower half, which was fishlike. When it reapproached the shore she saw its face clearly and it looked small and white—like a child's. And, as noted in other sightings, it was "constantly rubbing or washing its breast." After a time it swam away.

SEAWEED GREEN

Unlike the golden-haired mermaids of legend and Disney movies, those in eyewitness accounts usually have darker hair, from green to black. Many witnesses of mermaids noted their long, thick hair, of which—green or not—they seemed proud.

At first Katherine did not trust what she saw; she told herself that a boy had fallen out of a boat and was seeking rescue. As her father later recalled, she came running home to tell him about a strange boy who was swimming along the shore. She and her father and mother then went looking for the lad but found nothing.

A series of sightings took place off Scotland's west coast in the summer of 1814. One incident involved a group of children, who saw what they at first thought was a drowning woman. But, according to a letter published in the *York Chronicle* (September 1), closer examination revealed what appeared to be a mermaid: the upper half resembled a fair, long-haired, rosy- cheeked woman (except that its lower arms and hands were as small as a child's), and the bottom half looked like "an immense large cuddy fish ... in color and shape." Some of the children brought nearby farmers to the scene, and one of them prepared to shoot the creature with his rifle. But the others kept him from doing so. Instead he whistled at the mermaid, which glanced at him. It "remained in sight for two hours, at times making a hissing noise like a goose," the *Chronicle* reported. The creature was seen two more times, "always early in the morning and when the sea was calm."

On August 15 of that year, two fishermen were a quarter-mile from shore at Port Gordon when they spotted a merman. According to an account in the *Caledonian Mercury,* it had a dark face, small eyes, flat nose, large mouth, and very long arms. Soon afterward it was joined by what the men guessed was its mate, for this second creature had long hair, fair skin, and breasts. Frightened by the strange sight, the fishermen raced to shore, with the creatures gazing at them all the while!

Around 1830 people working along the shore of Benbecula island, off Scotland's northwest coast, spotted a small creature, half woman and half fish, turning somersaults in the water. Some men tried to capture it, but they had no success. Finally, a boy hit it on the back with some stones, and it disappeared. A few days later the body washed up on shore two miles away.

District Sheriff Duncan Shaw examined the body carefully. He reported that "the upper part of the creature was about the size of a well-fed child of three or four years of age, with an abnormally developed breast. The hair was long, dark, and glossy, while the skin was white, soft and tender. The lower part of the body was like a salmon, but without scales." The creature was buried in the presence of a number of island residents at a graveyard in Nunton. "The grave is pointed out to this day," folklorist R. MacDonald Robertson stated in 1961. "I have seen it myself."

DUGONGS AND MANATEES

Dugongs and manatees are large aquatic plant-eating mammals from the sirenian, or sea cow, family. They have thick, heavy bodies with weak front flippers, no hind legs, and tails ending in flattened fins. Their gray skin is hairless, except for whiskers on the face. The female has a pair of mammary glands (breasts) on her chest and holds her pup in her flippers while nursing. It has been suggested that the manatee, which surfaces to nurse, is the source of mermaid sightings. While both animals are most often found in warm, shallow, protected waters, the dugong may be sighted farther out to sea.

Merfolk in the Americas

Christopher Columbus is easily the most famous observer of mermaids. On his voyage of discovery in the West Indies, he saw three of them "leaping a good distance out of the sea" and found them "not so fair as they are painted." From the behavior he described, it is more likely that he had spotted a trio of sea mammals known as dugongs.

Other sightings in the Americas followed. While explorer John Smith was sailing through the West Indies in 1614, he spotted a young woman in the water. So attractive was she that Smith began to "feel the first pains of love." That is, until he discovered that "from below the waist the woman gave way to the fish!" Four years earlier, while sailing a small boat into a harbor at St. John's, Newfoundland, Canada, a Captain Whitbourne saw a strange creature that resembled a woman swimming in his direction. Alarmed, he quickly backed away. The creature then turned around and tried to board another boat, this one belonging to William Hawkridge. He banged it on the head! It disappeared under the water.

That mermaid was lucky compared to a merman sighted during the seventeenth century in Casco Bay, off the southern coast of Maine. When it tried to enter the boat of a Mr. Mitter, the boat owner reportedly slashed off one of its arms. The creature sank, "dying the waters purple with its blood," according to one writer. Not long after that, in the waters off Nova Scotia, Canada, crews of three French vessels sighted another merman. They chased it and tried to capture it with ropes but without success. "He brushed

his mossy hair out of his eyes which seemed to cover his body as well," the captain of one of the ships recorded.

Another sighting was recorded by a very reliable witness, New World explorer Henry Hudson, for whom the Hudson River is named. On the evening of June 15, 1610, two members of his crew observed a mermaid. She had white skin, long black hair, and "her back and breasts were like a woman's"; she also had "the tail of a porpoise." The men got a good look at her because she came "close to the ship's side, looking earnestly on the men." Commenting on the sighting, nineteenth-century naturalist Philip Gosse remarked: "Seals and walruses must have been as familiar to those polar mariners as cows to a milkmaid. Unless the whole story was a concocted lie between the two men, reasonless and objectless, and the worthy old navigator doubtless knew the character of his men, they must have seen some form of being as yet unrecognized."

In 1797 a Dr. Chisholm visited the tiny island of Berbice in the Caribbean. There Governor Van Battenburgh and others told him of repeated sightings in the island's rivers of strange creatures that the Indians call *mene mamma* (mother of waters). In his 1801 book *Malignant Fever in the West Indies,* Chisholm wrote: "The upper portion resembles the human figure.... The lower portion resembles the tail

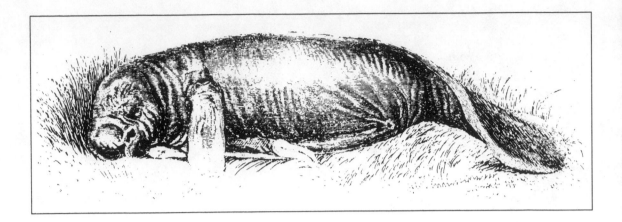

A sea cow.

portion of a fish ... not unlike that of the dolphin.... They have been generally observed in a sitting posture in the water, none of the lower extremity being discovered until they are disturbed.... They have been always seen ... smoothing their hair, or stroking their faces and breasts with their hands, or something resembling hands.... They have been frequently taken for Indian women bathing.

Theories

One proposed explanation for mermaid sightings is that they are sea cows—manatees and dugongs—which, in the words of scientist Richard Carrington, "became 'transformed' into a mermaid by the expectant attention of the superstitious mariners. However, a survey conducted by Gwen Benwell and Arthur Waugh, authors of *Sea Enchantress* (1965), shows that nearly three-quarters of such sightings occurred far from areas where dugongs and manatees are known to exist. Secondly, and more importantly, the animals hardly resemble the creatures described in the sightings.

But the sea cow explanation should not be dismissed in all cases. The people of New Ireland, an island province of Papua New Guinea, for instance, frequently reported seeing what sounded like merfolk: creatures that looked human down to their waists and had legless lower trunks ending in two side fins. They called the creatures **ri**, and when anthropologist Roy Wagner visited the island in the late 1970s, they told him the animals resembled the mermaids on tuna-fish cans. Understandably, he was intrigued. After experiencing a sighting himself, Wagner was positive that the creatures were not dugongs.

But a February 1985 expedition by American scientists produced underwater photographs of a ri—and it was without a doubt a dugong. One part of the mystery was solved. But expedition member Thomas R. Williams still wondered "how myths of merfolk can arise and persist in the face of the obvious reality of the dugong."

Two *Nature* writers proposed a second explanation for merfolk sightings. Studying Norse merman reports, they concluded that atmospheric changes or inversions could create strange optical effects, resulting in distortions on the ocean surface. Thus killer whales, walruses, and even jutting rocks could be perceived by sailors as merfolk. These atmospheric inversions were also responsible for the storms that so often followed merfolk sightings. After reviewing the study, behavioral scientist David J. Hufford felt that the explanation had some merit.

Michel Meurger, a French folklorist and expert on the lore of fabulous water beasts, feels that biological explanations of merfolk sightings are useless. He considers sightings as "visionary experiences," or vivid hallucinations that take their shape from popular superstitions.

Another theory purports that merfolk are simply an undiscovered species. Bernard Heuvelmans, the founder of cryptozoology (the science of unknown animals), stated in a 1986 paper, "Only a still-unrecorded species of recent Sirenia [sea cows], or possibly—though much less likely—an unknown form of primate adapted to sea-life, could explain the abundance and persistence of merfolk reports in certain seas up to modern times." Benwell and Waugh came to the same conclusion. Many dismiss this explanation, however, because no remains of the creatures—often spotted close to shore—have ever been studied scientifically.

Sources:

Beck, Horace, *Folklore and the Sea,* Middletown, Connecticut: The Marine Historical Association/Wesleyan University Press, 1973.

Benwell, Gwen, and Arthur Waugh, *Sea Enchantress: The Tale of the Mermaid and Her Kin,* New York: The Citadel Press, 1965.

Berman, Ruth, "Mermaids," *Mythical and Fabulous Creatures: A Source Book and Research Guide,* edited by Malcolm South, Connecticut: Greenwood Press, 1987.

Costello, Peter, *The Magic Zoo: The Natural History of Fabulous Animals,* New York: St. Martin's Press, 1979.

WEREWOLVES

Human beings have believed in *lycanthropy,* the transformation of a man or woman into a wolf or wolflike human, since ancient times. One of the earliest tales of such a transformation is in Greek mythology: Zeus punished Lykaon for serving him and other gods human flesh by turning him into a wolf. Inspired by this myth, a cult in long-ago Arcadia (Greece) required that each new member sacrifice a human being, which made the sacrificer a "wolf" for nine years. Several references in ancient writings indicate this early fascination with man-wolves.

The word "werewolf" first saw print in the eleventh century. The first half of the name comes from the Teutonic *wer,* meaning "man"; thus a werewolf is a man-wolf. Though known to most of us simply as a subject of horror movies and novels, the werewolf was once feared as a real-life terror.

History has demonstrated that belief in human-animal transformations featured not only wolves, but also bears, big cats, hyenas, and other fierce creatures. But of all of these the werewolf is best known, no doubt because the wolf was the predator most feared by Europeans. Medieval and later accounts tell of attacks by wolves on human beings (also see entry: **Beast of Gevaudan**), usually during wars and hard winters.

Though zoologists today assure us that wolves are generally harmless to people (the harm, in fact, is more frequently done *by* people *to* wolves), "it is difficult," in the words of folklorists W. M. S. Russell and Clair Russell, "to believe that all the past accounts [of wolf attack] are legendary." For "modern wolves have had many generations' experience of fire-arms, and are likely to be more cautious than their ancestors." In fifteenth- to eighteenth-century books on hunting, in fact, "werewolf" was the name given to a wolf that had developed a taste for human flesh.

In northern Europe, wolfmen or "berserkers" were warriors dressed in clothing made of wolf skin. They were well-known murderers and deeply feared. At the same time, however, in Germany it was believed that after death, honored ancestors had become wolves. In the Baltic and Slavic regions of Europe, people worshipped a temperamental wolf god: it could protect, but it could also turn on its faithful without warning. As Christianity rose to power, priests condemned such pagan beliefs as satanic.

At times in the past, werewolves have been considered the devil's agents (also see entry: **Black Dogs**). Religious writers debated

A red wolf.

whether Satan really turned humans into wolves, or whether they were simply perceived as such by those whom the devil had under his spell. Many eventually concluded that only God—whose powers were greater than Satan's—could actually effect such physical transformations.

And some people believed that they themselves were werewolves. Several of these reported that they rubbed themselves with a salve to bring on the transformation. The salve contained hallucination-producing plants like henbane and deadly nightshade. The potion was called "witches' salve," and was also supposedly used by witches to cover themselves before flying off to sabbats—midnight ceremonies of devil worship. By the time of the Renaissance witch trials, many writers felt that both sabbats and human-wolf transformations occurred only in the drugged imagination.

Others writers thought that mental illness was behind a person's belief that he or she could turn into a wolf or had seen others do so. And it was thought that sometimes the devil further confused these already disturbed individuals. In Germany in 1589, for example, Stubbe Peeter was tried for 25 years of hideous crimes, including murder of adults and children (including his own son), cannibalism, incest, and attacks on animals. Peeter claimed to have made a pact with Satan, who provided him with a belt that turned him into a wolf. Nine years later French officials arrested beggar Jacques Roulet after they found him crouching in a bush and covered with blood from the badly mutilated body of a 15-year-old boy discovered nearby. In his confession, Roulet said he had slain the youth while a werewolf, the transformation occurring after he had rubbed himself with a salve.

Several people reported that they rubbed themselves with a salve in order to become a werewolf.

BIG FOOT MIX

ESSENCE OF THUNDER BIRD

WERE WOLF JUICE

EU DE MOTH MAN

YETI NECTAR

Modern psychiatry views lycanthropy as a serious mental illness. According to psychiatrists Frida G. Surawicz and Richard Banta, it can be triggered by drug abuse, brain damage, or other causes. Psychoanalyst Nandor Fodor felt the belief in wolf-man transformations "cannot be traced to a point in historic time or to particular civilizations"; rather, it springs from deep within the human mind. Similarly, psychologist Robert Eisler theorized that the wolf, representing nature at its animal fiercest, lies deep in the human subconscious, a kind of memory from a time when early human beings were hunter-killers. In rare cases this buried information may rise up to overwhelm a person's consciousness, forcing him or her to actually identify with the wolf.

Sightings

Werewolves are found not only in mythology, folklore, and popular culture, but in modern sighting reports as well, though these are few and most are poorly documented.

In a 1960 issue of the magazine *Fate,* Mrs. Delburt Gregg of Greggton, Texas, told of an experience with a shape-changing creature. Such reports are very rare in modern times. The other sightings discussed below are simply of creatures that resembled man-wolves; nobody on record claims to have seen one becoming another. Gregg did not make such a claim either, but she came close in a tale that sounds more like the beginning of a werewolf novel than a real-life experience.

One night in July of 1958, while her husband was away on business, Mrs. Gregg moved her bed close to a screened window hoping to catch a cool breeze from an approaching thunderstorm. She dozed off for a short time before she heard a scratching sound on the screen. In a flash of lightning she saw a "huge, shaggy, wolflike creature ... clawing at the screen and glaring at me with baleful, glowing, slitted eyes. I could see its bared white fangs."

She leaped from bed and grabbed a flashlight as the creature fled through the yard and into a clump of bushes. "I watched for the animal to come out of the bushes," she wrote, "but, after a short time, instead of a great shaggy wolf running out, the figure of an extremely tall man suddenly parted the thick foliage and walked hurriedly down the road, disappearing into the darkness."

More common modern American werewolf tales take the form of those told by a number of Ohio residents between July and October 1972. They reported seeing a six- to eight-foot-tall creature, which one witness described as "human, with an oversized, wolflike head, and an elongated nose." Another said it had "huge, hairy feet, fangs, and it ran from side to side, like a caveman in the movies." It also had glowing red eyes. One early morning it reportedly sneaked up behind a trainman working along the tracks in downtown Defiance and whacked him with a piece of lumber.

One day in January 1970, four youths from Gallup, New Mexico, reportedly encountered what they called a "werewolf" along the side

In 1972 some Ohio residents reported seeing a six- to eight–foot–tall creature, which one witness described as "human, with an oversized, wolflike head, and an elongated nose."

of a road near Whitewater. It managed to keep up with their car, which was going around 45 miles per hour! One witness related: "It was about five feet seven, and I was surprised it could go so fast. At first I thought my friends were playing a joke on me, but when I found out they weren't, I was scared! We rolled up the windows real fast and locked the doors of the car. I started driving faster, about 60, but it was hard because that highway has a lot of sharp turns. Someone finally got a gun out and shot it. I know it got hit and it fell down, but there was no blood. I know it couldn't be a person because people cannot move that fast." (This creature, in fact, fits the description of a "skin-walker" —what Navajos of the Southwest call their version of a werewolf—which travels incredibly fast.)

In the fall of 1973, western Pennsylvania experienced a flurry of sightings of strange creatures, some linked to UFO reports. Investigator Stan Gordon noted that one type of being observed "was said to be between five and six feet tall. It was described as looking just like an extremely muscular man with a covering of thick dark hair.... This creature appeared to have superior agility.... From footprints discovered, the stride of the creatures varies between 52 and 57 inches." Two sketches published in *Flying Saucer Review* (July 1974) indicated that the beast strongly resembled traditional werewolves, a fact of which—incredibly—neither witnesses nor investigators took note, however.

REEL LIFE

I Was a Teenage Werewolf, 1957.

A troubled young man—played by a very young Michael Landon in his first feature film appearance—suffers from teen angst and goes to a psychiatrist. The good doctor turns out to be a bad hypnotist, and Landon's regression therapy takes him beyond childhood into his primal past, where he sprouts facial and knuckle hair.

Werewolf of London, 1935.

A scientist searching for a rare Tibetan flower is attacked by a werewolf. He scoffs at the legend, but once he's back in London, he goes on a murderous rampage every time the moon is full. Dated but worth watching as the first werewolf movie made.

The Wolf Man, 1941.

Fun, absorbing classic horror with Lon Chaney, Jr., as a man bitten by werewolf Bela Lugosi. His dad thinks he's gone nuts, and his screaming girlfriend just doesn't understand. Chilling and thrilling!

A Few Explanations

If these werewolf stories are not outright hoaxes, they would seem to point to the presence of extraordinary, otherworldly creatures. Still, more conventional explanations for what witnesses have observed do

Lon Chaney, Jr., as the Wolf Man in the 1941 film classic.

exist. For example, in Kansas during July 1974, several people reported coming upon what one newspaper described as a "young child about 10 or 12 years old, with bloody, matted hair, dressed in tattered clothing, running through vines and brush in a wooded area in the northwest edge of Delphos." She was dubbed the "wolf girl." Though local officials never located her, she may well have been a runaway or abandoned child.

Some in the medical community have suggested that sightings of werewolves have really been of individuals with a rare genetic disease called porphyria. Porphyria sufferers are plagued by tissue destruction in the face and fingers, open sores, and extreme sensitivity to light. Their facial skin may take on a brownish cast, and they may also suffer from mental illness. The inability to tolerate light, plus shame stemming from physical deformities, may lead the afflicted to venture out only at night. "These features," British neurologist L. Illis wrote in a 1964 issue of *Proceedings of the Royal Society of Medicine,* "fit well with the description, in older literature, of werewolves."

Sources:

Cheilik, Michael, "The Werewolf," *Mythical and Fabulous Creatures: A Source Book and Research Guide,* edited by Malcolm South, Connecticut: Greenwood Press, 1987.

Clark, Jerome, and Loren Coleman, *Creatures of the Outer Edge,* New York: Warner Books, 1978.

Fodor, Nancy, *The Haunted Mind: A Psychoanalyst Looks at the Supernatural,* New York: Garrett Publications, 1959.

THUNDERBIRDS

Many Native North American tribes once believed in "thunderbirds," giant supernatural flying creatures that caused thunder by flapping their wings and lightning by closing their eyes. Thunderbirds were said to war with other supernatural creatures, and they sometimes granted favors to human beings. The mythological beasts can often be seen on totem poles, pillars carved and painted with symbols and mythical or historical incidents.

Thunderbirds in Pennsylvania

In modern times, those who study accounts of strange animals sometimes use the term *thunderbirds* to describe the unlikely giant birds that are seen and reported from time to time. The heavy forests of north-central Pennsylvania have long seemed a favorite spot of the huge creatures; in 1973 Pennsylvania writer Robert R. Lyman declared that "their present home is in the southern edge of the Black Forest.... All reports for the past 20 years have come from that area." He insisted, "Thunderbirds are not a thing of the past. They are with us today, but few will believe it except those who see them."

Lyman himself claimed to have seen one of the birds in the early 1940s. When first observed, it was sitting on a road near Coudersport. It then rose a few feet into the air and spread its wings, which measured at least 20 feet! It flew into the dense woods that lined the high-

"Its wingspread appeared to be as wide as the streambed, which I would say was about 75 feet."

way. Like most other witnesses, Lyman thought that the bird looked like a "very large vulture," brown, with a short neck and "very narrow" wings. (Vultures are large birds of prey, related to the hawks, eagles, and falcons, but with weaker claws and a bald head. Their diet is usually made up of flesh from animals they find that are already dead.)

Lyman felt that the specimen he saw was just a young bird. In 1969 the wife of Clinton County sheriff John Boyle saw a huge gray bird land in the middle of Little Pine Creek while she was sitting in front of the couple's wilderness cabin. A few moments later it rose to fly away and "its wingspread," she said, "appeared to be as wide as the streambed, which I would say was about 75 feet." Also that summer three men claimed to have seen a thunderbird snatch up a 15-pound fawn near Kettle Creek.

Just east of Clinton County, over in Jersey Shore, Pennsylvania, many accounts of thunderbirds have been reported over the years. On

October 28, 1970, for instance, several people driving west of town saw a startling sight. One of the eyewitnesses, Judith Dingler, described it as a "gigantic winged creature soaring towards Jersey Shore. It was dark colored, and its wingspread was almost like [that of] an airplane."

Pennsylvania's thunderbird stories have been traced well back into the nineteenth century. Records of the sightings, however, have been spotty. If in print at all, they usually appear as short reports in local newspapers.

Still, sightings of thunderbirds, especially those describing giant vultures or eagles, can be found all across the country. And the reports are so similar that Mark A. Hall, the leading expert on the subject, has pieced together a general description of the birds, based on eyewitness accounts. He notes that what makes them most remarkable are their size and lifting strength—far greater than "those of any known bird living today anywhere in the world." While the dimensions of wingspans, of course, can only be guessed, sometimes measurable objects close by have offered reliable comparisons. Wingspreads seem to range from 15 to 20 feet; the birds themselves appear to be from four to eight feet tall. They are generally dark in color: brown, gray, or black.

CONDORS

Condors are large vultures found in the high peaks of the Andes Mountains of South America and the Coast Range of southern California. They are the largest living birds. They are constant eaters and prefer the remains of already dead animals because they have weak talons and lack the strength of other birds that hunt for their food. They will attack live animals when they must but look for those that are most helpless. Condors have keen sight and are skillful soarers, riding the updrafts around their mountain homes. They are usually seen alone. The Andean condor has black feathers with white wing patches and a white ring of downy feathers around a bare neck; the gray head is also bare. The rare California condor is all black with white wing bands.

Attack of the Giant Vultures

In July 1925, two visitors to the Canadian Rocky Mountains of Alberta spotted what they thought was an eagle high in the sky. As it approached a 7,500-foot mountain peak, they noticed that it was huge and brown and—even more surprisingly—carrying a large animal in its talons (claws). Shouts from the observers caused it to drop the animal, which turned out to be a 15-pound mule-deer fawn.

Bird experts insist that such a report—and there are many more like it—describes the impossible. The largest predatory birds, such as the eagle, attack only "small mammals, reptiles, fish, and perhaps, some other birds," maintains wildlife expert Roger A. Caras, for example. The largest American bird, the rare and endangered California condor, has a wingspan of slightly over ten feet (though one specimen captured early in the century did measure 11' 4"). Even so, its weak talons do not permit it to carry prey; instead, it usually feeds on the remains of animals that are already dead.

Following are some sightings of the vulture variety of thunderbirds:

Kentucky, 1870

A "monster bird, something like [a] condor," landed on a barn owned by James Pepples of Stanford. Pepples fired at the creature, wounding and capturing it. A press account at the time reported that the bird measured "seven feet from tip to tip" and "was of a black color." It is not known what became of the animal.

Illinois-Missouri border, 1948

A number of people reported seeing a huge bird that resembled a condor. And they also claimed that it was about the size of a Piper Cub airplane!

California condor.

Puerto Rico, 1975

During a flurry of unexplained night killings of farm animals and pets, livestock owners sometimes reported being awakened by a "loud screech" and the sound of giant wings flapping. Several witnesses claimed daylight sightings of what one called a "whitish-colored gigantic condor or vulture."

Northern California, October 1975

Residents of a Walnut Creek neighborhood saw a huge bird, over five feet tall, with a "head like a vulture" and gray wings. Five minutes later it flew away, revealing a 15-foot wingspan. Around the same time, a number of people observed the same or a similar bird sitting on a rooftop in nearby East Bay.

Birds Attacking Humans

A remarkable series of events that took place in 1977 attracted wide public attention. They began on the evening of July 25 in Lawndale in central Illinois. Three boys, one of them ten-year-old Marlon Lowe, were playing outside when they saw two large birds in the sky. The animals swooped down towards one of the boys, who jumped into a swimming pool to escape.

They then turned to Marlon, grabbing him by the straps of his sleeveless shirt and lifting him two feet above the ground. As Marlon screamed, his parents, Jake and Ruth Lowe, and two friends, Jim and Betty Daniels, heard him and witnessed the awful sight of the boy held in the talons of a flying bird. Marlon was beating at the creature with his fists, and finally, after carrying him for about 40 feet, it dropped him. By this time Mrs. Lowe was following close behind. With her son safe on the ground at last, she noted that "the birds just cleared the top of the camper, went beneath some telephone wires and flapped their wings—very gracefully—one more time," before they flew off toward some tall trees edging a nearby creek.

According to witnesses, the birds were black, with white rings on their long necks. They had curved beaks and eight- to ten-foot wing-spreads. After checking in books at the library, the Lowes decided that the birds looked like condors.

Bird experts and other officials wasted no time in judging the event impossible—and declaring everyone involved in it liars. The Lowes found themselves the focus of many cruel comments. Marlon himself suffered from nightmares for weeks afterward, though he received no physical injuries in the ordeal. The Lowes and their friends were not the only people, however, who reported seeing strange birds in the area. Other people reported sighting unusually large birds for two weeks thereafter.

Monster Eagles

In his 1975 book *Dangerous to Man,* Roger Caras wrote that while totally untrue, "the stories about eagles carrying off human babies, and even small children, are absolutely endless." Some who have investigated such reports, however, might disagree with Caras, though the ability of a normal-sized eagle—which never weighs much over seven pounds—to carry anything but the smallest animals has never been proven. Yet at least one such kidnapping, however "impossible," has been well documented.

On June 5, 1932, Svanhild Hansen, a 42-pound, five-year-old girl, was taken from her parents' farm in Leka, Norway, by a huge eagle. The bird carried her more than a mile before it dropped her on a high ledge,

> Marlon was beating at the creature with his fists, and finally, after carrying him for about 40 feet, it dropped him.

continuing to circle overhead. When rescuers reached the ledge the child was asleep. Except for a few small scratches, she was unharmed. Zoologist Hartvig Huit-feldt-Kaas spent a month investigating the story and found it "completely reliable." The eagle—if that is what it was—was seen several more times.

There have been many other cases of kidnappings by eagles, though most are considerably less well documented. All of them do not have happy endings. Felix A. Pouchet's 1868 nature encyclopedia, *The Universe*, tells a horrifying story from the French Alps that reportedly took place in 1838:

> A little girl, five years old, called Marie Delex, was playing with one of her companions on a mossy slope of the mountain, when all at once an eagle swooped down upon her and carried her away in spite of the cries and presence of her young friend. Some peasants, hearing the screams, hastened to the spot but sought in vain for the child, for they found nothing but one of her shoes on the edge of a precipice. The child was not carried to the eagle's nest, where only two eaglets were seen surrounded by heaps of goat and sheep bones. It was not until two months later that a shepherd discovered the corpse of Marie Delex, frightfully mutilated, and lying upon a rock half a league from where she had been borne off.

A Tippah County, Mississippi, schoolteacher recorded a similar case in the fall of 1868. Noting that the eagles in the area had been very troublesome for some time, carrying off pigs, lambs, and other animals, she wrote that "no one thought that they would attempt to prey upon children." But "at recess, the little boys were out some distance from the [school]house, playing marbles, when their sport was interrupted by a large eagle sweeping down and picking up little Jemmie Kenney, a boy of eight years." When the teacher ran outside, "the eagle was so high" that rescue was impossible. The child died after the eagle eventually dropped him.

A tale that ended less tragically goes back to July 12, 1763, and the mountains of Germany. There a peasant couple left their three-year-old

THUNDERBIRD PHOTOGRAPH

In 1963 Jack Pearl wrote an article about a large bird-like creature in the men's action magazine *Saga*. Pearl insisted that in 1886 the *Tombstone Epitaph* had "published a photograph of a huge bird nailed to a wall. The newspaper said it had been shot by two prospectors and hauled into town by wagon. Lined up in front of the bird were six grown men with their arms outstretched, fingertip to fingertip. The creature measured about 36 feet from wingtip to wingtip." Unfortunately no one could produce the photo.

After receiving many letters and inquiries on the subject, the *Epitaph* conducted a complete search of its back issues but could find no such photograph. A far-reaching survey of other Arizona and California papers of the period brought the same empty results.

Janet Bord

(1945-)
and
Colin Bord

(1931-)

Janet Gregory met Colin Bord at a UFO study group in London in 1969. They were both interested in "earth mysteries: the study of prehistoric sites, folklore, [and] 'earth energies,'" according to Janet. Colin, a photographer, and Janet, an editor, were married in 1971. Together, the Bords developed the Fortean Picture Library for the *Fortean Times*. They have also written many books on a wide range of anomalies, from cryptozoology to UFOs to ancient British "earth mysteries" and folklore—like the history of the legendary Thunderbird.

About their approach to anomalies, Janet wrote: "We aim to be totally open-minded, though not gullible.... We know that mankind does not have all the answers and that there certainly are many mysteries which are little understood. Yet we try to maintain a commonsense approach to all mysteries, and we acknowledge that hoaxers are ever-present.... We have seen that some people become so immersed in the study of their chosen phenomenon that they cannot be objective.

"But above all, after 20 years of intense interest in mysteries and strange phenomena, we retain our youthful curiosity about all the anomalous happenings which are reported, we retain our sense of humor when an intriguing mystery is shown to have a prosaic [everyday] explanation, and we retain our intense interest in the human psyche, which after all is responsible for at least 50 percent of all mysteries."

In 1985 the Bords moved into an old stone house in a remote area of North Wales, where they continue to write about anomalies. One recent book, *Life Beyond Planet Earth?* (1991), examines the spectrum of evidence and folklore from astronomers' search for extraterrestrial life to the stories of flying-saucer contactees.

daughter lying asleep by a stream as they cut grass a short distance away. When they went to check on her, they were horrified to find her missing. A frantic search turned up nothing until a man passing by on the other side of the hill heard a child crying. As he went to investigate, he was startled at the sight of a huge eagle flying above him. And on the ground he found the little girl, her arm torn and bruised. When the child was returned to her parents, they and her rescuer figured that the bird had carried her well over 1,400 feet!

To twentieth-century zoologist C. H. Keeling, this eagle-kidnapping story is one of the most believable of the many on record. Still, he noted that *all* such stories seem to ignore the "simple and unalterable fact ... that no eagle on earth can carry off more than its own weight."

The Problem of Explanation

Most ornithologists (bird scientists) don't concern themselves with thunderbird reports, other than to reject them as foolishness. Illinois State University bird expert Angelo P. Capparella tried to explain why. "The lack of interest of most ornithologists in Thunderbirds is probably due to two factors," he wrote. "First, there is the lack of sightings from the legions of competent amateur birdwatchers.... [The] number of good birdwatchers scanning the skies of the U.S. and Canada is impressive. Every year, surprising observations of birds far from their normal range are documented, often photographically. How have Thunderbirds escaped their roving eyes?" A second reason, Capparella pointed out, is that such creatures have been reported in areas that lack the kind of constant food supply that the birds' huge appetites would require.

In addition, mistaken identifications have figured in thunderbird sightings. In some cases, witnesses have confused cranes, blue herons, and turkey buzzards with more extraordinary and mysterious birds.

Sources:

Bord, Janet, and Colin Bord, *Alien Animals,* Harrisburg, Pennsylvania: Stackpole Books, 1981.

Caras, Roger A., *Dangerous to Man: The Definitive Story of Wildlife's Reputed Dangers,* revised edition, South Hackensack, New Jersey: Stoeger Publishing Company, 1975.

Clark, Jerome, and Loren Coleman, *Creatures of the Outer Edge,* New York: Warner Books, 1978.

Coleman, Loren, *Curious Encounters: Phantom Trains, Spooky Spots, and Other Mysterious Wonders,* Boston: Faber and Faber, 1985.

Hall, Mark A., *Thunderbirds!: The Living Legend of Giant Birds,* Bloomington, Minnesota: Mark A. Hall Publications and Research, 1988.

THE SEARCH FOR NOAH'S ARK

Mount Ararat on Turkey's eastern border has been the site of many expeditions in the search for Noah's ark.

The Old Testament's Book of Genesis relates the story of Noah and his family, who, along with representatives of various animal species, escaped the Great Flood in a tremendous ark. After 40 days and 40 nights, the ark came to rest "upon the mountains of Ararat." Those who read the Bible as history (literalists and Christian fundamentalists, for example) place this event in the year 2345 B.C., though the Genesis account was recorded some 1,300 years later. Because of a lack of scientific evidence, however, most geologists and archaeologists doubt that any such worldwide flood ever took place.

In the view of many scholars, the story should be read as one of the many creation myths from all over the world about huge floods and chosen survivors. These narratives do not prove that a global flood occurred; rather, they are most likely tales of local floods, which, to victims, seemed to destroy all the world they knew.

To fundamentalists, however, such a view is not acceptable. So for a long time hopeful seekers have looked for the remains of Noah's ark on Mount Ararat. For if the Genesis story of Noah could be substantiated, this first book of the Bible's chronicle of other matters—particularly the Creation itself—could arguably also be trusted. There is in fact a Mount Ararat, or more specifically, two: Great Ararat (16,900 ft.) and Little Ararat (12,900 ft.). The peaks are connected by a rocky ridge between 7,000 and 8,000 feet high; they lie along Turkey's eastern border.

Because the name Ararat was not given to these mountains until roughly the eleventh century, many sources have placed the final resting place of the ark elsewhere. Most of the favored sites are in Turkey, but others include Greece, Armenia, and Iran.

Sightings and Searches

Despite shaky historical claims for an ark on Ararat, Jews and Christians have nonetheless continued to target this location. Around 1670 a Dutchman named Jan Struys, captured and enslaved by bandits in Armenia, reportedly met a hermit on Ararat. He treated the old man's illness, and in gratitude the hermit rewarded him with a "piece of hard wood of dark color" and a sparkling stone, both of which "he told me he had taken from under the Ark," according to Struys.

In the nineteenth century a number of searchers climbed the mountain but failed to find any sign of the ark. That is, until 1876, when James Bryce of England's Oxford University discovered a four-foot-long stick near the peak of Great Ararat. He declared it a piece of the ark.

On August 10, 1883, the *Chicago Tribune* published this report, which is clearly fascinating but almost certainly false:

> A paper at Constantinople announces the discovery of Noah's Ark. It appears that some Turkish commissioners appointed to investigate the avalanches on Mt. Ararat suddenly came on a gigantic structure of very dark wood, protruding from the glacier.... The Ark was in a good state of preservation.... They recognized it at once.

> There was an English-speaking man among them, who had presumably read his Bible, and he saw it was made of gopher wood, the ancient timber of the scripture, which, as everyone knows, grows only on the plains of the Euphrates. Effecting an entrance into the structure, which was painted brown, they found that ... the interior was divided into partitions 15 feet high.

> Into only three of these could they get, the others being full of ice, and how far the Ark extended into the glacier they could not tell. If, however, on being uncovered, it turns out to be 300 cubits long [the measurements cited in Genesis], it will go hard with disbelievers.

In 1892 Archdeacon John Joseph Nouri of the Chaldean Church reported that he had found the ark and even entered it. He also measured the structure, finding that it was indeed 300 cubits long.

During the following decades a number of ark expeditions were launched. Most ended in disappointment, though a few claimed sightings. A 1952 mission led by wealthy French industrialist Fernand Navarra produced samples of wood that, when first tested, dated back 5,000 years. But a later, more reliable test brought other findings: the wood was from A.D. 800 and was probably the remains of a monks' shrine built on the mountainside. When *Life* magazine published a photograph of a ship-shaped indentation in the mountain in 1960, an expe-

"It appears that some Turkish commissioners appointed to investigate the avalanches on Mt. Ararat suddenly came on a gigantic structure of very dark wood, protruding from the glacier."

dition raced there for an on-site look. The hollow turned out to be a natural formation created by a recent landslide.

Since then there have been other expeditions and claims, none especially notable. Most of the funding and personnel for these missions have come from fundamentalist groups. For them, the foundation of their religious beliefs is at stake: if the flood did not actually occur, and thus Noah and his ark did not exist, then other biblical pronouncements might also be questioned. Still, the findings of "arkeologists"—as ark investigators are called—have proven largely untrustworthy.

Critics have had no trouble finding flaws in arkeological thinking. Scientists Charles J. Cazeau and Stuart D. Scott, Jr., for example, remarked that "if the ark had come to rest near the summit of Ararat 5,000 years ago, it likely would have shifted by glacial movement to lower elevations long ago. To at least some extent, the ark would have broken up, the wood strewn about on the lower slopes of the mountain, easily accessible even to those who are not mountain climbers." Charles Fort, one of the first to compile accounts of strange and unexplained happenings, had this to say about the search: "I accept that anybody who is convinced that there are relics upon Mt. Ararat, has only to climb up Mt. Ararat, and he must find something that can be said to be part of Noah's Ark."

Sources:

Balsiger, Dave, and Charles Sellier, Jr., *In Search of Noah's Ark,* Los Angeles: Sunn Classic Books, 1976.

Cazeau, Charles J., and Stuart D. Scott, Jr., *Exploring the Unknown: Great Mysteries Reexamined,* New York: Plenum Press, 1979.

Fasold, David, *The Discovery of Noah's Ark,* London: Sidgwick and Jackson, 1990.

Other Strange Events

- SPONTANEOUS HUMAN COMBUSTION

- CATTLE MUTILATIONS

- CROP CIRCLES

- MAD GASSERS

Other Strange Events

SPONTANEOUS HUMAN COMBUSTION

Spontaneous human combustion (SHC) allegedly occurs when the heat inside a person's body becomes so great that he or she suddenly bursts into flames. The fire consumes both flesh and bones, leaving little more than ashes. Science has no explanation for the phenomenon.

One of the best-documented cases of SHC took place in 1951 in St. Petersburg, Florida, when a 67-year-old woman named Mary Reeser died under strange circumstances. Her body was discovered at 8 A.M. on July 2 when Reeser's landlady tried to enter her small apartment to deliver a message. The door handle was too hot to turn, so the landlady alerted two painters across the street, who broke down the door. Amid a great deal of smoke, they found Reeser's charred remains, reduced to ash except for one foot and what some accounts later claimed was a "shrunken skull" (the latter bit of information did not appear in the official report; a skull would ordinarily explode, not contract, in great heat). Ashes and a few coiled springs were all that remained of the overstuffed chair in which Mrs. Reeser had been sitting.

The incident attracted national attention and has been discussed often since in writings on SHC. But debate about such deaths goes back at least several centuries, and SHC was the subject of heated argument among eighteenth- and nineteenth-century medical practitioners. In a paper presented to the French Academy of Sciences in 1833, J. de Fontanelle reviewed a number of SHC cases and noted that victims tended to be old women fond of liquor. He also reported that fire damage did not extend to other flammable materials on or near the bodies. Reeser's nightgown, however, was incinerated, as was her chair.

Amid a great deal of smoke, they found Mrs. Reeser's charred remains, reduced to ash except for one foot and what some accounts later claimed was a "shrunken skull."

The most famous literary victim of SHC was Mr. Krook in Charles Dickens's *Bleak House*; illustration by Phiz.

In fact, for all the extraordinary claims surrounding Mary Reeser's death, some interpreted the evidence as pointing to a rather ordinary tragedy. When her son, a physician, saw her the evening before, Reeser told him that she had taken two sleeping pills. The official conclusion, that she fell asleep while smoking and burned up along with her flammable nightgown, is not unreasonable. Apparently, her own body fat—Reeser was overweight—further fed the flames.

One popular pre-twentieth-century theory about SHC was that those prone to alcohol abuse were particularly at risk—because the liquor in their systems made them more burnable. (The most famous literary victim of SHC was Mr. Krook in nineteenth-century British novelist Charles Dickens's *Bleak House*. Krook was intoxicated at the time of his extraordinary combustion.) There is no scientific basis for this connection, though there is a relationship between drunkenness and fire deaths. "Drunken persons," Joe Nickell and John F. Fischer wrote, are "more careless with fire and less able to properly respond to an accident."

In several articles questioning SHC claims, Nickell and Fischer noted that suspicious items were often found at the sites: "a broken oil lamp on the floor, a victim's pipe, a candlestick lying near the remains. But in addition there was often a large quantity of combustible material under the body to aid in its destruction: bedding, for example, or a chair's stuffing—even wooden flooring possibly impregnated with oils or waxes. Interestingly enough, there was evidence that melted human fat had increased the destruction in a number of instances."

"Protestations of the debunkers notwithstanding, the case *for* SHC is actually very good," wrote Larry E. Arnold, director of ParaScience International in Harrisburg, Pennsylvania. Arnold has investigated this hotly debated subject for 20 years.

Fires kill thousands of people each year, Arnold pointed out, yet rarely do firemen find victims reduced to ashes amid largely unsinged surroundings. "Why not?," he asked. "If dropping a cigarette or pipe on one's lap could transform a hapless human to ash within minutes, this would happen thousands of times annually. It doesn't. Something *else*— some thing(s) far less obvious—must cause a person to become a human fireball."

Firemen have told Arnold that classic SHC is unforgettable because its characteristics are so unusual. First: incineration of the victim can be more thorough than in a crematorium. Second: accelerants (like gasoline or kerosene, even alcohol) needed to fuel such an intense blaze are absent. Third: fire damage is incredibly localized—often nearby newspapers are unscorched, plastics unmelted. Fourth: rather than the terrible odor of burned flesh, a sweet "perfume" smell is sometimes detected.

> In a crematorium, a skeleton becomes wholly burned to dust only in heat above 3,000 degrees Fahrenheit for 12 hours—much hotter and longer than the worst house fire.

Dr. John Bentley's baffling burning in 1966 featured each of these mysterious traits. Overnight, the 92-year-old physician defied common sense and science when he burned through a highly flammable linoleum floor, leaving behind but half a leg, a mound of ashes, and a sweet smell. Yet paint on his bathtub only inches away did not blister, and rubber tips on his aluminum walker (with a melting point of only 1,200 degrees Fahrenheit) did not melt! No wonder a Pennsylvania State Police officer murmured that Dr. Bentley had died by "spontaneous human combustion."

The remains of Dr. John Bentley—a victim of SHC?

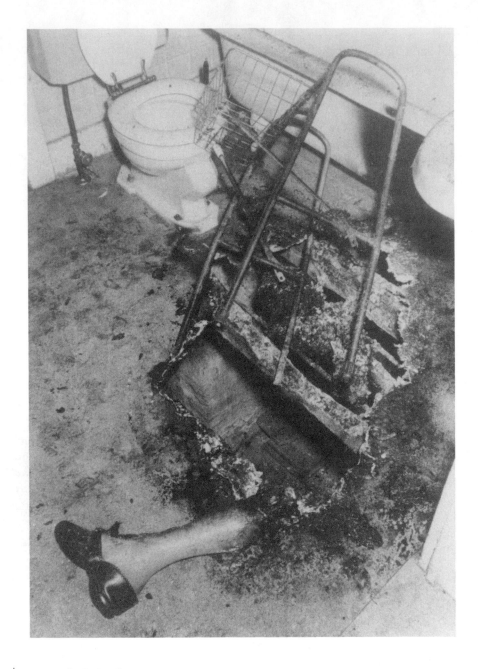

Partial SHC

More astounding, SHC is not always fatal! In 1974 Jack Angel, a traveling salesman, parked his motor home at a Georgia motel and went to sleep. He awoke to a real-life nightmare: his right hand and forearm were burned black. Amazingly, nothing around him was singed, not his pajamas, not even the sheets on which he slept! Puzzled physicians diagnosed his burns as "internal in origin"—that is, he burned from the inside out. They likened his injuries to a high-energy electricity burn, but no one could detect the source of the electricity, unless it came, suggested Arnold, from the electrical potential that Angel—and everyone—has naturally inside his or her own body.

SHC has even been witnessed. In 1980 Peter Jones of California *twice* watched smoke wisp out of his body—once from his forearm while driving his car and, later, from his feet as he was about to slip on his slippers one morning. His wife saw the second incident herself. "What was that? Were you smoking?" she cried out. He was, but not with cigarettes! Jones, like Angel, lived to tell an incredible story of surviving his own inflaming.

"That some strange fiery fate has befallen selected individuals throughout history is undeniable, *if* the evidence is examined," stated Arnold. "Inquiring minds will one day find the explanation to this phenomenon."

Sources:

Arnold, Larry E., "The Flaming Fate of Dr. Bentley," *Fate* 30,4, April 1977, pp. 66-72.
Arnold, Larry E., "The Man Who Survived Spontaneous Combustion," *Fate* 35,9, September 1982, pp. 60-65.
Harrison, Michael, *Fire from Heaven: A Study of Spontaneous Combustion in Human Beings,* London: Sidgwick and Jackson, 1976.
Nickell, Joe, and John H. Fischer, *Secrets of the Supernatural: Investigating the World's Occult Mysteries,* Buffalo, New York: Prometheus Books, 1988.

CATTLE MUTILATIONS

In the fall of 1973, farmers in Minnesota and Kansas reported that their cattle were dying mysteriously. It appeared that unknown forces had killed the animals, but without knives or bullets. Worse still, various body parts—usually eyes, ears, lips, sex organs, rectums, and tails—had been removed with surgical skill. Farmers also frequently claimed that the animals' blood had been drained. And strangest of all was the fact that the killers did all of these things without leaving footprints or any other signs of their presence behind.

Farmer looks at cow—one of many alleged cattle mutilations across Middle America and Canada.

Law officers were mystified. According to Deputy Gary Dir of Ottawa County, Kansas, "The large majority of these mutilations occurred near occupied houses. In no instances were the animals found less than a quarter-mile from the roadside and none ... more than a quarter-mile from an all-weather, well-traveled road." One carcass in Cloud County was discovered in a mud hole. Even so, there were no footprints!

In December a dozen Kansas sheriffs met to discuss the problem. Though they had little to go on, most agreed that members of a satanic cult were probably responsible for the killings. In southwestern Minnesota, however, officials disagreed. Lincoln County Sheriff Albert Thompson, who had investigated several of the mutilations, was certain that the animals had died of ordinary cattle diseases and that the so-called cuts were left by small animals that had chewed on the soft parts of the bodies. Regardless, many country people remained convinced that a group of Satan worshippers rumored to operate in the area, had killed the animals in bizarre sacrificial ceremonies.

When Kansas authorities brought the carcasses to the Kansas State University Veterinary Laboratory, pathologists found that the cause of death was blackleg, a bacterial disease often fatal to cattle. State brand commissioner Doyle Heft assured all that nothing out of the ordinary was afoot. Still, this did not put an end to wild theories about such "cattle mutilations."

Whether real or imagined, cases of cattle mutilation were being reported in other states in the Midwest and West and even into Canada's western provinces by 1974. And by the end of the decade, newspapers claimed that several thousand unexplained cattle deaths had taken place, with the killers' identities still unknown. Fear and imagination began to run rampant. Four predominant theories explaining the mutilations emerged. The first blamed cultists; a second alleged a government conspiracy in which agents were conducting secret chemical/biological-warfare experiments; a third pointed to UFOs and space beings; and the fourth blamed mass panic for what were, in fact, commonplace deaths.

The Satanist Theory

Police agencies in Idaho, Montana, and Alberta, Canada, did uncover a few cases in which satanist groups could be linked to cattle mutilations. Laboratory studies indicated that a small number of animals had been killed after being drugged. In Idaho a police informant infiltrated a group that claimed to mutilate cattle, though he did not personally witness such an act. Some reliable sightings of black-hooded figures were recorded, but without proof of their connection to animal deaths. And police officers, farmers, and ranchers sometimes stumbled on what they believed were signs of cult activity, such as stone altars and bodies of small animals.

Still, in 1975 Donald Flickinger, a Minneapolis-based agent of the U.S. Treasury Department's Alcohol, Tobacco and Firearms division, was assigned to investigate reports of a nationwide satanic network involved in animal and human mutilation. He found no supporting evidence.

Government Conspiracies

Theories about secret government involvement in cattle mutilations were not surprising during the 1970s, the era of the Vietnam War and the Watergate break-in, events that shattered the faith many Americans had in their government. Nonetheless, such notions were rarely based on proof. The only physical evidence to support this idea came to light in Lincoln County, Colorado, in 1975. A rancher found a blue

A rancher found a blue government bag near his mailbox. Inside he discovered plastic gloves, a bloody scalpel, a cow's ear, and part of a tongue.

government bag near his mailbox. Inside he discovered plastic gloves, a bloody scalpel, a cow's ear, and part of a tongue. The Colorado Bureau of Investigation could find no fingerprints on the items, nor could local law officers connect the animal parts with any cattle-mutilation reports known to them.

Reports of "mystery helicopters" also inspired government conspiracy hypotheses regarding cattle mutilations. Examining a number of sightings, "mutologists" Tom Adams and Gary Massey remarked that such aircraft "are almost entirely without identifying markings, or markings may appear to have been painted over or covered with something. The craft are frequently reported flying at abnormal, unsafe, or illegal altitudes. The mystery choppers may shy away if witnesses or law officers try to approach. On the other hand, there are several accounts of aggressive behavior on the part of the helicopter occupants, with witnesses chased, 'buzzed,' hovered-over or even fired upon." No direct link between these reports and cattle mutilations has ever been made, however.

Evil Aliens

To a number of mutologists, farmers, ranchers, and country police officers, the extraordinary way in which the cattle were killed—with supposedly precise incisions and with no footprints left behind—suggested mutilators from an extraordinary place: outer space. *Strange Harvest,* a documentary written and produced by Denver filmmaker Linda Moulton Howe in 1980, explored this idea. It attracted a great deal of attention and shaped popular beliefs about UFO-connected cattle mutilations.

Belief in cattle-killing space beings spread quickly, even without credible evidence. Of course, few UFO reports suggested a definitive connection to cattle deaths. One that did was related under hypnosis: a woman told University of Wyoming psychologist and ufologist R. Leo Sprinkle that she had seen a cow drawn up into a UFO "in a pale, yellow beam of light." She and her daughter were also taken inside the vessel, where they saw aliens cutting up the animal. Shortly afterwards, Sprinkle hypnotized a second woman who told a somewhat similar story.

These accounts, among others equally improbable, inspired a complex conspiracy theory that drew quite a following in the early 1990s. It was based on the belief that evil UFO beings had entered into an agreement with America's "secret government," which permitted the aliens to abduct and mutilate cattle and even to abduct human beings

A woman told University of Wyoming psychologist and ufologist R. Leo Sprinkle that she had seen a cow drawn up into a UFO "in a pale, yellow beam of light."

in exchange for extraterrestrial technology. In some versions, the government even allowed the mutilation of people. These wild stories, completely unsupported by evidence, have been spread through books, lectures, and videos by conspiracy theorists Milton William Cooper, William English, and others. All claim to have learned these terrible truths from unnamed government informants and secret documents.

Ordinary Causes

In 1979 the First Judicial District of New Mexico received a federal grant to investigate mutilations in that state. Former FBI agent Kenneth Rommel headed the study, and at its conclusion in April 1980, the report found no evidence of cattle mutilations. Rommel had worked on 24 cases in New Mexico and had kept in close contact with law officers while addressing reports in other states. He felt that all of the mutilations he investigated were ordinary, "what one would expect to find from normal predation [large animals hunting for food], scavenger activity [smaller creatures feeding on remains], and decomposition [decay] of a dead animal."

Rommel blamed faulty investigation, guesswork, unchecked imagination, and blatant stupidity for creating a mystery where there was none. His conclusions matched those of investigators in many other states but received more attention because he published them into a detailed official report. Social scientists who studied the cattle-mutilation panic viewed it as a case of mass hysteria born of exotic theories and unproven statements that were spread—without question—by the press.

In 1984 New York writers Daniel Kagan and Ian Summers wrote *Mute Evidence,* a careful, well-researched book on the subject. Examining the origins and development of the panic, Kagan and Summers found that a small group of "mutology" buffs, most of them also UFO enthusiasts, were to blame. According to the authors, none of these people:

> had access to any experts in veterinary medicine, livestock, or any other fields that bore on the cattle mutilation question, and it was obvious there was not one seriously qualified investigator in their underground. They were all amateurs, all poorly trained to deal with the subject, and all seemingly uniquely ignorant of research procedures and methods of constructing proven cases.... They had nothing going for them, yet they controlled the opinions of literally hundreds of thousands, perhaps millions of people, regarding cattle mutilations.

By the early 1980s press accounts claimed that as many as 10,000 mutilations had taken place, but Kagan and Summers knew better; they had checked official cattle mortality reports and found that cattle had died at a statistically average rate throughout the most intense years of the mutilation scare. The 10,000 figure was revealed as the invention of a mutologist who admitted that he had pulled the number out of thin air!

In 1991 an Arkansas newspaper reported on a "mutilated" heifer calf that a veterinarian determined had died of blackleg, the corpse of which had been disturbed by buzzards. Also included in the article was a quote from two "UFO investigators" who said that a whopping 700,000 mutilations had occurred and that alien beings had used "lasers" to do the cutting, evidence that even in light of the facts, tall tales of cattle-mutilation endure.

Sources:

Bayles, Fred, "Scoffers, Believers Abound in Mutilated-Cattle Mystery," *Washington Post,* January 1, 1986.

Howe, Linda Moulton, *An Alien Harvest: Further Evidence Linking Animal Mutilations and Human Abductions to Alien Life Forms,* Littleton, Colorado: Linda Moulton Howe Productions, 1989.

Kagan, Daniel, and Ian Summers, *Mute Evidence,* New York: Bantam Books, 1984.

CROP CIRCLES

Crop circles first attracted public attention in the early 1980s, when circular patterns were found in crops of growing grain in the countryside of southern England. Since then they have increased in both number and complexity, and the term now refers to a variety of patterns: from simple single circles to quintuplets (a central circle ringed by four smaller ones), to dumbbell shapes and combinations of these involving lines, bars, ladder-like rungs, and more. These intricate patterns are called "pictograms" because they resemble primitive rock paintings.

"Cereology," the study of crop circles, arose after the *Wiltshire Times* (August 15, 1980) published an article and photographs featuring circles found flattened in a field of oats in Bratton, Wiltshire, England. Each was about 60 feet across and swirled flat in a clockwise direction. The Bratton circles stirred the interest of both meteorologist George

Terence Meaden, of the Tornado and Storm Research Organization (TORO), and ufologist Ian Mrzyglod. Mrzyglod made two important discoveries: the circles showed no clear signs of radiation, and they were not really circles at all; the formations were slightly elliptical, an unexpected finding that seemed to argue against a hoax.

A year later, on August 19, 1981, three more circles were found in neighboring Hampshire County, alongside a main highway. Where the Bratton circles appeared random, these at Cheesefoot Head looked as if they had been laid out along a straight line. On either side of the main circle—again 60 feet across—were smaller circles of 25 feet. All were swirled clockwise.

The crop circles seemed to follow a pattern; they appeared mostly during the spring and summer growing season in the rolling grain fields west and southwest of London. This "enchanted" landscape was already home to other archaeological mysteries, including the monoliths of Stonehenge and Avebury, the pyramid-like peak of Silbury Hill, and carvings cut in the chalk hills.

While there is no public database recording the number and types of crop circles that appear yearly, the best available information suggests that during the years 1980 to 1987, between 100 and 120 circles were formed. During that time they also displayed several "mutations." Some circles were swirled counterclockwise; sometimes rings appeared around them. And crop circles varied in size, becoming a great deal larger or smaller.

In 1988 at least 112 circles were recorded, matching the combined total of the eight previous years. In 1989 the number almost tripled, to 305; it tripled again in the summer of 1990 to about 1,000. In 1991 there were 200 to 300 recorded circles, many of them the more complex pictogram type.

By the early 1990s, what had begun with a few simple circles a decade before had mushroomed into a mystery of worldwide scope, with well over 2,000 circles recorded around the globe. Similar circles—though rarely as numerous or complex as those found in England—were now noted in the Soviet Union, the United States, Canada, Australia, Japan, and other countries.

Characteristics

Generally, a crop circle occurs overnight, probably in the hour or two before dawn. It apparently happens in a matter of seconds, usually

> Generally, a crop circle occurs overnight, probably in the hour or two before dawn. It apparently happens in a matter of seconds, usually 60 or less.

A typical "simple" crop circle near Milk Hill, Wiltshire, England.

60 or less. The line between the affected and non-affected crop is almost always abrupt and dramatic. The flattened area is laid down in a spiral manner from the center outward. In addition, the crop is frequently flattened in layers lying in opposite or differing directions. Once in a while the plant stalks even appear to be braided or intertwined with one another. If a crop circle forms early in the growing season, the affected plants continue to grow and will "bounce back" to nearly normal height. Flattened later in the year, however, the stalks remain on the ground.

The stalks involved are laid down without breaking and show no signs of damage. This is true of even delicate plants, like rape, the source of canola oil. The plant stalks seem to go limp, almost as if they had been steamed or made more elastic. An encircling ring may

Meteorologist George Terence Meaden (kneeling) shows how the floors of some crop circles are laid down in layers. This particular formation appeared near Bishops Cannings, Wiltshire, in June 1990.

run counterclockwise to the central circle or vice versa, or both may be laid in the same direction. The smallest crop circle on record measured just eight inches across. And at Alton Barnes in 1990, a pictogram of complex crop circles stretched for nearly an eighth of a mile!

Witnessing the formation of a crop circle is rare. There are roughly three dozen such reports, most collected by Dr. Meaden and his associates at the Circles Effect Research Group (CERES), which is part of TORO. Typical is the account given by Gary and Vivienne Tomlinson published in the *Mail on Sunday* on August 25, 1991, a year after the event took place. The Tomlinsons were walking alongside a field of grain near the village of Hambledon when the plants to their right suddenly started rustling.

"There was a mist hovering above, and we heard a high-pitched sound," said Mrs. Tomlinson. "Then we felt a wind pushing us from the side and above. It was forcing down on our heads so that we could hardly stay upright; yet my husband's hair was standing on end. It was incredible. Then the whirling air seemed to branch into two and zig-zagged off into the distance. We could still see it like a light mist or fog, shimmering as it moved."

"Then we felt a wind pushing us from the side and above. It was forcing down on our heads so that we could hardly stay upright; yet my husband's hair was standing on end."

Meaden was particularly interested in the Tomlinson account because it seemed to support his own ideas about crop circles. He felt that the simple ones, at least, were formed by the breakdown of a standing, electrically charged whirlwind or plasma-vortex. Unlike regular whirlwinds such as dust devils and waterspouts, which suck in surrounding air, dust, or water at the base of a tunnel of rising air, Meaden's plasma-vortex falls apart, or collapses, in a descending burst of violent wind. It is this collapsing wind-form, surrounded at times by a ring of electrically charged air, that quickly cuts out crop circles. The meteorologist also felt strongly that the low-lying hills of southern England provided the perfect physical conditions for formation of these unusual whirlwinds.

Have crop circles occurred throughout history? This is an important consideration in any attempt to explain them. If crop circles can be established as a regular feature of the natural environment, then a weather-based theory like Meaden's makes sense. On the other hand, the theory is weakened if crop circles are shown to be a uniquely modern occurrence. How crop circles might have been reported in the past, then, is an issue worth investigating.

Fairy Rings

Unexpected circular shapes in crops or grasses have long been associated with so-called fairy rings. The typical fairy ring is caused by a mushroom fungus, *Marasmius oreades,* and has two stages. In the first, the fungus decomposes, or breaks down, living material, which spurs the growth of plants in the affected area; in the second, these plants become so abundant that all growth is choked out, resulting in the bare appearance of a ring worn down by the patter of many little feet—ostensibly those belonging to fairies.

But fairy rings are not as clear-cut and complex as crop circles. And they demonstrate either the presence or absence of growing plants, whereas the affected stalks of a true crop circle have simply "fallen over" in place. Still, it is useful in understanding crop circles to examine historical accounts of fairy and other rings from a modern viewpoint, weeding out old-time beliefs and superstitions.

John Aubrey's *Natural History of Wiltshire* relates an intriguing seventeenth-century account of fairy mischief that reportedly befell a clergyman named Mr. Hart employed by the Latin School at Yatton Keynal. He told a student that one evening he was particularly annoyed with the elves and fairies that frequently came down from the hills at dusk to sing and dance. As Hart approached one of "the green circles made by those spirits on the grass [called 'fairy dances' by the local people], he all at once saw innumerable small people dancing round and round, singing, and making all manner of small odd noises." Hart, "very greatly amazed," found that he could not "run away from them," feeling he was "kept there in a kind of enchantment." As soon as the fairies noticed him, they "[surrounded] him on all sides, and ... he fell down scarcely knowing what he did; and thereupon these little creatures pinched him all over, and made a sort of quick humming noise all the time; but at length they left him, and when the sun rose he found himself exactly in the midst of one of these fairy dances."

Compare this account with the Tomlinsons', reported three and a half centuries later, in the same general location. The fairy incident occurred in August, as did the Tomlinsons'. The humming sound Hart heard (minus the "pygmies" of course!) could be likened to the high-pitched sound noted by the couple. Could Hart's feeling of being "pinched ... all over" be the prickling sensation caused by static electricity or some other electromagnetic effect? Could his inability to run away and later, to remain standing, be the result of a strong wind?

Saucer Nests

Crop circles also recall the saucer nests mentioned in UFO writings: circular indentations that one could imagine to be left by hovering or grounded spacecraft. Two of the most notable saucer-nest cases took place at Tully, Queensland, Australia, in January 1966, and near Langenburg, Saskatchewan, Canada, on September 1, 1974. Both involved daytime UFO sightings. The Langenburg event is worth noting for several reasons: not only did it occur before the crop-circle craze, but it involved a reliable witness, photographs, and investigations by both the Royal Canadian Mounted Police and Ted Phillips, a Center for UFO Studies researcher then specializing in physical-trace cases.

At about 11 A.M. that September Sunday, 36-year-old Edwin Fuhr was cutting his family's rape crop with a mechanical harvester. The day was overcast and cool, with a falling mist and light showers in the area. Nearing the end of the field, Fuhr noticed what appeared to be a metallic dome some 50 feet away. He left his machine idling and approached the object on foot, coming to within 15 feet. It now looked like an upside-down stainless steel bowl, 11 feet across and about five feet high, and was spinning rapidly. It appeared to be hovering 12 to 18 inches above the ground.

Fuhr returned to his harvester. Now he could see four similar objects nesting nearby, arranged in a semicircle, all rapidly rotating. Because his machine was still running, he could not tell whether the spinning domes were emitting a sound or not. Then all five objects suddenly rose in the air to a height of about 200 feet, where they hovered in stair-step formation, no longer spinning. Eventually, each gave off a puff of gray vapor or smoke and vanished into the low clouds. Fuhr told Phillips that their departure created a "pressure that flattened the rape that was standing, and I thought, 'Oh, hell, here goes my crop,' and there was just a downward wind, no twirling wind. I had to hold onto my hat."

Though confused, Fuhr felt the episode lasted about "15 to 20 minutes." He also reported moments of paralysis during the experience—he simply could not move.

After the objects left, Fuhr found five circular areas spiraled flat in a clockwise direction. "I checked for burns," he said, "but I couldn't find any. *The grass wasn't broken off, it was flat, pressed down.* It didn't seem different from the other grass."

Other strange effects frequently mentioned in UFO close-encounter writings were also noted in the area. At about the same time as Fuhr's experience, the cattle in a neighboring field broke through their fencing in four places. The night before, Fuhr's own farm dogs had barked wildly. On Monday night they acted up again, and the following morning a sixth circle was found in the field. On the night of September 14, his dogs did the same, and a seventh circle was found on the Fuhr farm the next morning.

Still, the connection that fairy rings and saucer nests have to today's crop circles is shaky at best. But there have been reports of nocturnal (night) lights appearing at locations where crop circle formations have later been discovered. And at least two daytime videos of small lights sailing near or diving into existing circles have been recorded. These unknown lights further complicate the mystery.

Physical Effects

It has been reported that people standing close to crop circles have felt a number of physical effects. While such personal sensations are difficult to analyze, the Center for Crop Circle Studies has put together a record of these accounts. The most commonly cited aftereffect of visiting a crop circle is nausea, followed by headache and extreme fatigue. These symptoms last only briefly. On the other hand, some circle visitors tell of pleasant feelings.

The failure of electronic equipment in the presence of crop circles has been detected a number of times. This is especially true of still and video cameras, but also includes audio tape recorders. Once, circle investigators Colin Andrews and Pat Delgado recorded high-pitched warbling sounds while in the company of a British Broadcasting Company video crew.

Close scientific study of plant stalks from crop circles has opened up another area of investigation. American bio-physicist W. C. Levengood found that the nodes or knuckles of affected stalks appeared larger—slightly swollen—compared with normal samples. Examination of the stalks' microscopic cell-wall holes, through which nutrients pass, revealed stretched or larger pits—a sign of rapid microwave heating. In addition, seeds from affected stalks seemed to sprout more quickly than regular seeds. More testing in these areas is needed.

Hoaxes

Some crop circles are believed to be hoaxes. The question remains: how many and which ones? While some cereologists accept pictograms and other complex patterns and formations as genuine, those who believe in a meteorological explanation for the circles feel that anything beyond the simplest shapes are suspicious. Researchers have tried to reach an agreement on guidelines and methods for determining which crop circles are genuine. (Energy "dowsing"—using a divining rod—has been a frequently employed method, for example, but it is highly questionable.)

In most cases, "authentification" still depends on a ground-level, visual inspection of the formation and the experience of the investigator. Sometimes flying over a crop formation is helpful because hoaxes often appear crude or ragged from above.

Probably the biggest crop-circle hoaxers to have come forward are Doug Bower and David Chorley, two elderly Englishmen who claimed to have created some 250 complex formations. On September 9, 1991, the British tabloid *Today* published their detailed confessions. According to the pair, they began their deception in the summer of 1978 with a simple circle near Cheesefoot Head, Wiltshire, that was easily seen

How many—and
which—crop circles
are hoaxes?

from the road. Bower, who had lived in Australia from 1958 to 1966, said he got the idea from the saucer nests that had appeared during that time in Queensland. "We had a good giggle about the first one," Chorley recalled. "It was nice being out on a summer night, so we decided to do some more. But for three rotten years [the papers] never noticed what we were doing."

Bower and Chorley said that once the press and public did take note, they improved their methods and created more complex formations. Frequently they would include their initials—in the form of a double-D—in their handiwork. The two claimed that they finally came forward because others (like Andrews and Delgado, coauthors of two best-selling books on the subject and founders of Circles Phenomenon Research) were profiting from their secret efforts. With *Today's* help, they created a complex crop formation and invited Delgado to inspect it. Hoaxers Bower and Chorley at last became famous when the investigator declared their formation genuine.

Cereologists were embarrassed by Delgado's mistake. But they challenged Bower and Chorley again. The two made a second daytime circle before the media using the simple tools—string, rope, four-foot-long wooden planks, and a crude sighting device—that they claimed to have used in their early creations. The result was ragged and poorly constructed. (Perhaps more importantly, Bower and Chorley have yet to demonstrate their ability to create a complex crop-circle formation at night, when most appear.) Other groups, including the local Wessex Skeptics, have also created crop circles that have fooled experts.

Yet questions remain about human involvement. Some formations—such as the immense pictogram that appeared at Alton Barnes—are constructed on an enormous scale. Assuming that this and similar formations are hoaxes, why has no huge crop circle ever been discovered interrupted or abandoned—for whatever reason—halfway through completion?

In at least one well-documented case in the summer of 1991, Meaden and a team of visiting Japanese scientists were watching a field with electronic equipment that included radar (sound waves), magnetometers (which measure magnetic force), night-vision video cameras, and motion sensors. Blanketed by mist, a small dumbbell formation appeared; yet none of the sensing equipment noted intruders! In the years since crop circles first appeared, farmers and landowners in the affected areas have watched their property more closely than ever. But the number of hoaxers caught has remained quite small.

Competing Theories

UFOs, secret military experiments (that produce microwave or laser radiation), and psychokinesis (the movement of objects with the mind alone) have also been named as causes of crop circles. Doubters, of course, blame human activity—in other words, all crop-circle formations are hoaxes.

DOWSING AND CROP CIRCLES

Meaden's concept of a plasma-vortex, a hypothetical collapsing wind-form that could cut crop circles in a descending burst of violent wind, remains the only "mainstream" weather-based theory to offer an explanation for the formation of crop circles. Yet many cereologists feel that it simply does not account for all of the reported "behaviors" of the phenomenon. Some think that an unknown natural force or intelligence within the earth may be behind them. Richard Andrews, a dowser with the Center for Crop Circle Studies, has claimed that crop-circle patterns, or their energy fields, can be *dowsed* a year or more before the actual circle appears.

Dowsing is a folk method of finding underground water or minerals with a divining rod. The divining rod is usually a forked twig; the "diviner" holds the forked ends close to his body, and the stem supposedly points downward when he or she walks over the hidden water or desired mineral. Many believe that luck is behind most dowsing successes.

Whatever their origins, there is no doubt that English crop circles have captured the imagination of a curious public. For "unlike ghosts, poltergeists, or even UFOs," explained author Hilary Evans, "the circles are absolutely there for anyone to examine at will." Organizations, newsletters, books, videos, tours, and more have sprung up around them. With so much attention focused on crop circles from both inside and outside the scientific community, can a breakthrough be very far behind?

Sources:

Delgado, Pat, and Colin Andrews, *Circular Evidence,* London: Bloomsbury, 1989.

Delgado, Pat, and Colin Andrews, *Crop Circles: The Latest Evidence,* London: Bloomsbury, 1990.

Meaden, George Terence, "Circles in the Corn," *New Scientist,* June 23, 1990, pp. 47-49.

Meaden, George Terence, ed., *Circles from the Sky,* London: Souvenir Press, 1991.

Noyes, Ralph, ed., *The Crop Circle Enigma,* Bath, England: Gateway Books, 1990.

Randles, Jenny, and Paul Fuller, *Crop Circles: A Mystery Solved,* London: Robert Hale, 1990.

MAD GASSERS

In late summer of 1944, a mysterious assailant terrorized the small east-central Illinois town of Mattoon (population: 15,827). For two weeks townspeople reported frightening episodes of gassings in their homes. Their attacker would eventually be declared imaginary by local law officials, who considered the case one of mass hysteria. Historians and psychologists who later reviewed the case concurred with this conclusion. Still, unanswered questions about the Mattoon episode remain.

Mattoon's phantom-like menace first made his or her presence known on August 31 when a resident woke up feeling ill. He managed to get to the bathroom before throwing up. Returning to the bedroom, he asked his wife if she had left the gas on. She said she hadn't. But when trying to get up to check, she found she couldn't move. Elsewhere in town a young mother who heard her daughter coughing in another room also tried to leave her bed, but she too experienced this paralysis.

At 11 P.M. on September 1, a "sickening sweet odor in the bedroom" awoke another young mother, Mrs. Bert Kearney, from sleep. As the odor quickly grew stronger, she explained, "I began to feel a paral-

An artist's imaginative drawing of Mattoon's "mad gasser" depicts him as a not-quite-human, possibly extraterrestrial, being.

ysis of my legs and lower body. I got frightened and screamed." An hour and a half later, when her husband came home from work, he saw a strange man standing at the bedroom window. Kearney described him as "tall, dressed in dark clothing and wearing a tight-fitting cap." Kearney chased the prowler, but the man escaped.

These events took place before anyone had heard of a "mad gasser"; thus mass hysteria could not have been a factor. But the *Mat-*

toon Journal-Gazette soon picked up the story, covering it in a sensational way that frightened more than it informed. The newspaper also hinted that more incidents would follow; when further attacks did occur, they were illustrated in the same dramatic (and one could say irresponsible) manner.

Several other residents complained to police that the sudden flow of a "sickly sweet odor" into their homes had paralyzed them for as long as 90 minutes. No one else had seen the gasser, but late on the evening of September 5 as one couple was returning home, the wife noticed a white cloth by the front door. When she picked it up, she happened to sniff it. "I had sensations similar to coming in contact with an electric current," she recalled. "The feeling raced down my body to my feet and then seemed to settle in my knees. It was a feeling of paralysis." Soon her lips and face were burning and swelling, her mouth was bleeding, and she was vomiting.

These dramatic symptoms had passed by the time police arrived, but once at the scene, officers did discover what seemed to be the first physical evidence in the case: an empty lipstick tube and a skeleton key (a kind of filed-off master key that can open numerous locks) near where the noxious white cloth had lain. Even as officers were interviewing the couple, however, a woman elsewhere in town was hearing a prowler outside her bedroom window. Before she could sit up, a gas seeped into the room, and she was unable to move for several minutes.

Near midnight a woman called police to report that a man had tried to force his way through her door. Her screams frightened him off. Press accounts of the incident described the man as the "mad gasser." Despite the uncertainty of the identification, this was just the kind of story to fuel a growing panic. Two nights later, a woman and her 11-year-old daughter said they heard someone attempting to break open a window. They tried to get outside, but mysterious fumes overcame the mother and made her sick.

In a September 8 article on the gassings, the Decatur *Herald* noted: "Victims report that the first symptom is an electric shock which passes completely through the body. Later nausea develops, followed by partial paralysis. They also suffer burned mouths and throats and their faces become swollen."

No End in Sight

As the days passed and the attacks continued, Mattoon residents were outraged that local police had not been able to catch the gasser.

Several other residents complained to police that the sudden flow of a "sickly sweet odor" into their homes had paralyzed them for as long as 90 minutes.

A protest rally was planned. Armed citizens prowled the streets at night, ignoring the police commissioner's plea that they behave rationally. He admitted that a "gas maniac exists," but added that "many of the attacks are nothing more than hysteria. Fear of the gas man is entirely out of proportion to the menace of the relatively harmless gas he is spraying." Rumor had it that the gasser was a lunatic or an eccentric inventor.

The scare peaked on September 10, with two attacks striking five people. But by the next morning police were skeptical, pointing to a lack of solid evidence; they decided that all further "victims" would undergo physical and psychological testing. A chemical study of the cloth found five days earlier revealed little. The next evening, when the police received more calls from people reporting attacks, they dismissed them as false alarms (though in one case a physician who went to a victim's house smelled the gas himself).

At a press conference on the morning of September 12, the police chief told reporters: "Local police, in cooperation with state officers, have checked and rechecked all reported cases, and we find absolutely no evidence to support stories that have been told. Hysteria must be blamed for such seemingly accurate accounts of supposed victims." Beyond that, he theorized, the odor of carbon tetrachloride from a nearby chemical plant may have been carried on the wind. He did not explain why this had never been a problem for Mattoon residents in the past.

Even in the face of this official denial, the gasser made one last house call. On the evening of the 13th, a witness saw a "woman dressed in man's clothing" spray gas through a window into Bertha Burch's bedroom. The next morning Mrs. Burch and her adult son found footprints of high-heeled shoes under the window.

The Botetourt Gasser

In 1945, writing in the *Journal of Abnormal and Social Psychology,* Donald M. Johnson reviewed the Mattoon scare and concluded that the local newspaper's alarming coverage was responsible for the phenomenon from start to finish. Johnson's study would influence future investigations of mass panics.

But unknown to Johnson and most other examiners of the Mattoon episode, a strikingly similar series of events took place in Botetourt County, Virginia, in December 1933 and January 1934. The scare earned only local coverage, and it is unlikely that Mattoon residents were aware of it.

The first recorded Botetourt attack occurred at a farmhouse near Haymakertown late on the evening of December 22 when three separate gassings sickened eight members of a family and a visitor. Some of the victims thought they saw a man fleeing in the darkness. The gas caused nausea, headaches, facial swelling, and tightening of the mouth and throat muscles. One victim, a 19-year-old woman, suffered convulsions for weeks afterwards. A police officer who investigated found only one clue: the print of a woman's heel under the window where the gas was believed to have entered.

Over the next two weeks other people reported similar night attacks. In one case witnesses saw a 1933 Chevrolet with a man and a woman inside driving back and forth in front of a house around the time its occupants experienced a gassing. In another instance a young mother attending to her baby said she heard a rattling window shade and mumbling voices outside. Suddenly the room filled with gas, and her body felt numb. While on his way to call police after a gassing at his farm, F. B. Duval saw a man run toward a car parked on a country road and quickly drive away. Duval and an officer examined the site soon afterwards and found prints of a woman's shoes.

Amid growing panic, residents of the county armed themselves and prowled back roads in search of suspicious strangers. One even fired at a fleeing figure, who nonetheless eluded the shot. Another time, moments after a gas attack, one of its victims dashed outside in time to glimpse four men running away. By the time the witness returned with a gun, he could no longer see them, but he could still hear their voices. Of course, there were those who doubted that such attackers existed. But physicians who treated victims were certain that the gassings were real. The county sheriff was also convinced.

One of the last of the Virginia gassings was reported in nearby Roanoke County. Afterward, the victim found discolored snow with a sweet-smelling, oily substance in it. When studied, it turned out to be a mixture of sulfur, arsenic, and mineral oil—insecticide ingredients. A trail of footprints led from the house to the barn, but none were found leaving the barn. They were, according to press accounts, a "woman's tracks."

Michael T. Shoemaker, who investigated the episode in the 1980s, noted its many similarities to the later scare at Mattoon. "In both Mattoon and Botetourt," he observed, "the principal effects were the same: a sickeningly sweet odor, nausea, paralysis, facial swelling and unconsciousness. These effects were confirmed by doctors and, moreover, in both cases doctors smelled the gas. Both gassers made repeat attacks on one family, multiple attacks in one night and assaults on unoccupied houses. The pattern of explanation was also similar, progressing from pranksters to lunatics to hysteria. Tantalizing but useless clues were found," including *"a woman's print beneath a window."*

Gas attacks are still reported from time to time, typically in one building, such as a school, a factory, or a theater. For example, in March 1972 workers in a midwestern data-processing center complained of a mysterious odor that made them sick. Air, blood, and urine samples failed to detect anything out of the ordinary. When scientists who investigated the case eventually gave workers a false explanation—that an "atmospheric inversion" was responsible—the attacks of illness stopped!

Sources:

Coleman, Loren, *Mysterious America,* Boston: Faber and Faber, 1983.

Johnson, Donald M., "The 'Phantom Anesthetist' of Mattoon: A Field Study of Mass Hysteria," *Journal of Abnormal and Social Psychology* 40, 1945, pp. 175-186.

Shoemaker, Michael T., "The Mad Gasser of Botetourt," *Fate* 38,6, June, 1985, pp. 62-68.

INDEX

B

M

Mackal, Roy P. 271-274, 281-284, 286, 289-290, 299-300, 336, 362, 363-364, 467, 376, 478, 385, 390, 392-393, 395, 403
Mad Gassers 460-465
Manatees 418, 420
Mansi photograph 384-385
Mantell, Thomas F., Jr. 4
Marfa lights 116-117
Mariner 49 91-92
Marshall, Robert 319
Marsupials 268, 291, 293
Martians 20
Martin, Dorothy 13
Martyr, Deborah 256-257
Mattoon, Illinois 460
McClarin, Jim 220
Meaden, George Terence 451, 453-454
Meat: falls from the sky 136
Melland, Frank 288-289
Menger, Howard 63
Men in black 48-50, 311
Mental illness 423-424, 427
Menzel, Donald H. 13
Mercury 67
Merfolk 31, 322, 414
 and Christopher Columbus 418
 and Henry Hudson 419
"The Mermaid" 415
Mermaids 321, 387
Meteorites 142, 145, 162
Meteoroids 162
Meteorology 139-140
Meteors 111-112, 143
Meteors and meteorites 143-145
Mexico 316
Minnesota iceman 233-237
Missing Time 15
Mokelembembe 172, 174, 271, 278-286, 300
Mollusks 334
Momo 225-257
Money: falls from the sky 125
Mongolia 257-258
Mono Grande 249-254
Monroe County monster 211
Montezuma 317
Moodus noises 160-161
Moon hoax 61-62
Moon oddities 59-66
Moore, William L. 14, 66, 74, 81
Morag 386-391

The Morning of the Magicians 25
Morrocco, John D. 84
Moseley, James W. 30
Mothman 307-312
The Mothman Prophecies 311
Mothra 310
Mountain gorilla 171
Mount Ararat 436, 437
Mount Everest 241, 246
M'Quhae, Peter 350-352
Mussels: falls from the sky 131
Mute Evidence 449

N

Naitaka 392
Namibia 289
Napier, John 208, 217, 219, 231, 234-235, 244
The Narrative of Arthur Gordon Pym 55
National Aeronautics and Space Administration (NASA) 64-66
National Investigations Committee on Aerial Phenomena 65
Natural History magazine 336
The Natural History of Norway 342, 346
Nazca lines 25, 27-30
Nazis 57
Neanderthals 259-260, 311
Nebuchadnezzar 298-299
Nepal 241, 244, 246
"Nessie" 365-378
Nevada Test Site 84
New Age 45, 83
New Mexico 73-80, 111-113
Newton, Silas 75
New World Explorers Society 247
Noah's Ark 436
No Earthly Explanation 96
Nommos 31
North American Apes (NAPES) 202-203

O

Occultism 311
Octaman 330
Octopus 332-340
Office of Naval Research (ONR) 81, 83
Ogopogo 391-393
OINTS. *See* "Other Intelligences" (OINTS)
Okapi 171
One Hundred Thousand Years of Man's Unknown History 25

U

V

W